VISIBILITY ALGORITHMS IN THE PLANE

A human observer can effortlessly identify visible portions of geometric objects present in the environment. However, computations of visible portions of objects from a viewpoint involving thousands of objects is a time-consuming task even for high-speed computers. To solve such visibility problems, efficient algorithms have been designed. This book presents some of these visibility algorithms in two dimensions. Specifically, basic algorithms for point visibility, weak visibility, shortest paths, visibility graphs, link paths, and visibility queries are all discussed. Several geometric properties are also established through lemmas and theorems.

With over 300 figures and hundreds of exercises, this book is ideal for graduate students and researchers in the field of computational geometry. It will also be useful as a reference for researchers working in algorithms, robotics, computer graphics, and geometric graph theory, and some algorithms from the book can be used in a first course in computational geometry.

SUBIR KUMAR GHOSH is a professor of computer science at the Tata Institute of Fundamental Research, Mumbai, India and is a fellow of the Indian Academy of Sciences. He is the author of around 40 papers in the fields of computational geometry and graph theory and has worked as a visiting scientist in many reputed universities and research institutes around the world.

T0331714

VISIBILITY ALGORITHMS
IN THE PLANE

SUBIR KUMAR GHOSH

*School of Computer Science, Tata Institute of Fundamental Research,
Mumbai 400005, India*

Shaftesbury Road, Cambridge CB2 8EA, United Kingdom

One Liberty Plaza, 20th Floor, New York, NY 10006, USA

477 Williamstown Road, Port Melbourne, VIC 3207, Australia

314–321, 3rd Floor, Plot 3, Splendor Forum, Jasola District Centre, New Delhi – 110025, India

103 Penang Road, #05–06/07, Visioncrest Commercial, Singapore 238467

Cambridge University Press is part of Cambridge University Press & Assessment,
a department of the University of Cambridge.

We share the University's mission to contribute to society through the pursuit of
education, learning and research at the highest international levels of excellence.

www.cambridge.org
Information on this title: www.cambridge.org/9780521875745

First published 2007

A catalogue record for this publication is available from the British Library

ISBN   978-0-521-87574-5   Hardback

Dedicated to my loving parents

Contents

Preface

Education is the manifestation of the perfection already in man.

Swami Vivekananda (1863–1902)

This book is entirely devoted to the area of visibility algorithms in computational geometry and covers basic algorithms for visibility problems in two dimensions. It is intended primarily for graduate students and researchers in the field of computational geometry. It will also be useful as a reference/text for researchers working in algorithms, robotics, graphics and geometric graph theory.

The area of visibility algorithms started as a sub-area of computational geometry in the late 1970s. Many researchers have contributed significantly to this area in the last three decades and helped this area to mature considerably. The time has come to document the important algorithms in this area in a text book. Although some of the existing books in computational geometry have covered a few visibility algorithms, this book provides detailed algorithms for several important visibility problems. Hence, this book should not be viewed as another book on computational geometry but complementary to the existing books.

In some published papers, visibility algorithms are presented first and then the correctness arguments are given, based on geometric properties. While presenting an algorithm in this book, the geometric properties are first established through lemmas and theorems, and then the algorithm is derived from them. My experience indicates that this style of presentation generally helps a reader in getting a better grasp of the fundamentals of the algorithms. Moreover, this style has also helped in refining several visibility algorithms, which is a significant contribution of this book. In keeping with the distinctive approach of this book, all the algorithms herein have been explained using this approach.

Structure of the book

The book consists of eight chapters. The first chapter provides the background material for visibility, polygons and algorithms. Each chapter from 2 to 8 deals with a specific theme of visibility. In the first section (i.e., Problems and Results) of these chapters, results on visibility problems under the theme of the chapter are reviewed. In each intermediate section of a chapter, one or two algorithms are presented in detail or some properties of visibility are proved. Sometimes, two algorithms for the same problem are presented to show the improvement in time complexity or that the different approaches lead to the same time complexity. Two algorithms for two different types of polygons are also presented for the same problem. In the last section (i.e., Notes and Comments) of every chapter from 2 to 8, results on parallel or on-line algorithms for the problems considered in the chapter are mentioned. In the same section, some visibility issues connected to the theme of the chapter are discussed.

Exercises in the book are placed at suitable positions within a section to allow a reader to solve them while reading that section. This process of solving exercises will help in gaining a better understanding of the current topic of discussion.

Prerequisites

Some time back, I offered a graduate course in the Tata Institute of Fundamental Research entitled 'Algorithmic Visibility in the Plane' using a preliminary version of this manuscript. After every lecture, an appropriate section was given to each student for reading. In the next lecture, I asked them to explain the algorithms contained in that section. It was very satisfying to see that these students, who did not have any background in computational geometry prior to my course, had comprehensively followed the algorithms. However, the students had prior knowledge of algorithms and data structures. Courses on algorithms and data structures are essential prerequisites for understanding this book.

As stated earlier, this book is not meant as a first course in computational geometry. However, some algorithms herein can certainly be included in such a course in computational geometry. Moreover, this book can be used for assigning research projects to students. In addition, this book can be a natural choice for graduate-level seminar courses.

Acknowledgments

Over the last 5 years, many people have helped me in various ways in preparing this book. Partha Pratim Goswami and Sudebkumar Prasant Pal read the entire manuscript and have suggested several corrections and revisions. Amitava Bhattacharya and Tilikepalli Kavitha made suggestions for improving the presentation of the book. Discussions on the contents of the book with Binay Bhattacharya, Anil Maheshwari and Thomas Shermer in the initial phase helped me to organize the book in a better way. Discussions with Arnab Basu helped me to structure many sentences in a more meaningful way. My students helped me by identifying some typographical errors. I sincerely thank all of them. I would also like to thank John Barretto, Vivek Borkar, Raymond D'Mello, Daya Gaur, Nitin Gawandi, Ramesh Krishnamurti, Saswata Shannigrahi, Subhas Nandy, Paritosh Pandya, Sugata Sanyal, Sudeep Sarkar and Aniruddha Sen for their help during different phases in preparing the book. I take this opportunity to sincerely thank David Tranah of Cambridge University Press for his constant positive initiative for the publication of this manuscript. Finally, I gratefully acknowledge the constant support that my wife Sumana and son Rajarshi provided me with during the entire period of 5 years.

Subir Kumar Ghosh

Mumbai, India

1

Background

1.1 Notion of Visibility

Visibility is a natural phenomenon in everyday life. We see objects around us and then decide our movement accordingly. Seeing an object means identifying the portions of the object visible from the current position of an observer. The entire object may not be visible as some of its parts may be hidden from the observer. The observer also determines shapes and sizes of visible portions of an object. Visible portions of an object change as the observer moves from one position to another. Moreover, the observer may see several objects in different directions from its current position; the visible portions of these objects form the scene around the observer. Constructing such a scene continuously is very natural for a human observer as the human visual system can execute such tasks effortlessly.

Suppose a robot wants to move from a starting position to a target position without colliding with any object or obstacle around it. The robot constructs the scene around itself from its current position and then guides its motion in the free space lying between itself and the visible portion of the objects around it. The positions of the robot and the objects can be represented in the computer of the robot by their x, y and z co-ordinates and therefore, the scene consisting of visible portions of these objects can be computed for the current position of the robot. The problem of computing visible portions of given objects from a viewpoint has been studied extensively in computer graphics [115]. Since the scene is constructed from thousands of objects of different shapes and sizes lying in different positions, it becomes a complex task from a computational point of view. Even computing visible portions of one object in the presence of several other objects is a non-trivial task. Moreover, computing such a scene for every position on the path of the robot is a time-consuming task even for high-speed computers. Designing efficient algorithms for executing such movements of a robot in the presence of obstacles in a reasonable period of time is one of the objectives in the field of robot path planning [226].

The above problem of robot path planning can be reduced to the corresponding problem in two dimensions. If a mobile robot that maintains contact with the floor is projected on the floor, the two-dimensional footprint of the robot can be modeled as a polygon. Similar projections on the floor can now also be produced for all obstacles. This process yields a map consisting of polygons in two dimensions. The polygon corresponding to the robot can be navigated using this map by avoiding collisions with polygonal obstacles. Thus a collision-free path of the robot can be computed from its starting position to the target position. While navigating, the visible portions of polygonal obstacles are computed to construct the scene around the current position of the robot. Although such a representation in two dimensions has reduced the complexity of the robot path planning problem, designing efficient algorithms for such computations remains a challenging task.

The notion of visibility has also been used extensively in the context of the art gallery problem in computational geometry [271, 310, 333]. The art gallery problem is to determine the number of guards that are sufficient to see every point in the interior of an art gallery room. This means that every interior point of the room must be visible to one of the guards so that all paintings in the gallery remain guarded. There are many theorems and algorithms for the minimization of the number of guards and their placement in the art gallery room.

The study of visibility started way back in 1913 when Brunn [67] proved a theorem regarding the *kernel* of a set. Today visibility is used in many fields of computer science including robotics [66, 226, 249, 283], computer vision [139, 168] and computer graphics [93, 113, 115].

1.2 Polygon

A *polygon* P is defined as a closed region R in the plane bounded by a finite set of line segments (called *edges* of P) such that there exists a path between any two points of R which does not intersect any edge of P. Any endpoint of an edge of P is called a *vertex* of P, which is a point in the plane. Since P is a closed and bounded region, the boundary of P consists of cycles of edges of P, where two consecutive edges in a cycle share a vertex. If the boundary of P consists of two or more cycles, then P is called a *polygon with holes* (see Figure 1.1(a)). Otherwise, P is called a *simple polygon* or a *polygon without holes* (see Figure 1.1(b)). The region R is called the *internal region* or *interior* of P. Similarly, the regions of the plane excluding all points of R are called the *external regions* or *exterior* of P. A vertex of P is called *convex* if the interior angle at the vertex formed by two edges of that vertex is at most π; otherwise it is called *reflex*. Note that the interior angle at a vertex always faces the interior of P.

As defined above, a simple polygon P is a region of the plane bounded by a cycle of edges such that any pair of non-consecutive edges do not intersect. In this book,

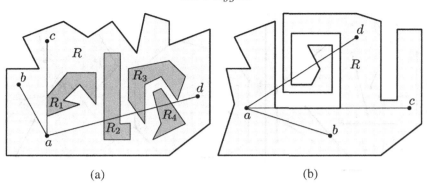

Figure 1.1 (a) In this polygon with holes, b and c are visible from a but not d. (b) In this simple polygon (or a polygon without holes), b and c are visible from a, but not d.

we assume that P is given as a doubly linked list of vertices. Each vertex has two fields containing x and y co-ordinates of the vertex and it has two pointers pointing to the next clockwise and counterclockwise vertices of P. It can be seen that if edges of P are traversed in counterclockwise (or clockwise) order, then the interior of P always lies to the left (respectively, right) of the edges of P.

Let c_0, c_1, c_2, ..., c_h be the cycles on the boundary of a polygon P with h holes, where c_0 represents the outer boundary of P. Let R_j denote the region of the plane enclosed by c_j for all $j \leq h$ (see Figure 1.1(a)). Since P is a closed and bounded region, $R_j \subset R_0$ for all $j > 0$. Moreover, $R_j \cap R_k = \emptyset$ where $k \neq j$ and $k > 0$. Therefore, $R = R_0 - (R_1 \cup R_2 \cup \ldots \cup R_h)$. Observe that if P is a simple polygon, then $R = R_0$ as the boundary of P consists of only one cycle c_0 (see Figure 1.1(b)). In this book, we assume that a polygon P with h holes is given in the form of h cycles, where vertices of each cycle are stored in a doubly linked list as stated above and there is an additional pointer to one vertex of each cycle of P to access that cycle.

Two points p and q in P are said to be *visible* if the line segment joining p and q contains no point on the exterior of P. This means that the segment pq lies totally inside P. This definition allows the segment pq to pass through a reflex vertex or graze along a polygonal edge. We also say that p *sees* q if p and q are visible in P. It is obvious that if p sees q, q also sees p. So, we sometime say that p and q are mutually visible. In Figure 1.1, the point a sees two points b and c, but not the point d.

Exercise 1.2.1 *Given two points p and q inside a polygon P, design a method to determine whether p and q are visible in P.*

Suppose a set of line segments in the plane is given such that they do not form a polygon. Let A denote the arrangement of these line segments in the plane (see

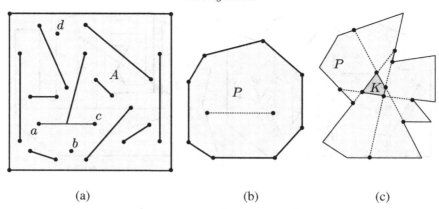

(a)   (b)   (c)

Figure 1.2 (a) In this arrangement of line segments A, points b and c are visible from a but not d. (b) A convex polygon P where any two points are mutually visible. (c) A star-shaped polygon P where the entire polygon is visible from any point of the kernel K.

Figure 1.2(a)). Two points p and q in the plane are said to be *visible* in the presence of A if the line segment joining p and q does not cross any line segment in A. This definition permits the segment pq to touch a line segment of A. In Figure 1.2, a point a sees two points b and c, but not the point d.

Using the definition of visibility in a polygon, we define two special classes of simple polygons called convex and star-shaped polygons. A simple polygon P is called *convex* if every pair of points in P is mutually visible [176] (see Figure 1.2(b)). It can be seen that the internal angle at every vertex of a convex polygon is at most π [327]. A convex polygon can also be defined as intersections of closed half-planes which is bounded. A simple polygon P is said to be *star-shaped* if there exists a point z inside P such that all points of P are visible from z (see Figure 1.2(c)). The set of all such points z of P is called the *kernel* of P. The kernel of P is always convex [67]. If P is a star-shaped polygon with respect to a point z, it can be seen that the order of vertices on the boundary of P is same as the angular order of vertices around z. We refer to this property by saying that the vertices of P are in *sorted angular order* around z. It follows from the theorem of Krasnosel'skii [223] that a simple polygon P is star-shaped if and only if every triple of convex vertices is visible from some point of P [334]. Note that a convex polygon is also a star-shaped polygon and all points of the convex polygon belong to the kernel.

Exercise 1.2.2 *Prove that a polygon P is star-shaped if and only if every triple of convex vertices is visible from some point of P [223].*

Exercise 1.2.3 *Prove that the kernel of a star-shaped polygon is convex.*

> **Exercise 1.2.4** *Draw two star-shaped polygons A and B such that each edge of A intersects every edge of B [291].*

1.3 Asymptotic Complexity

The time and space complexity of the sequential algorithms presented in this book are measured using the standard notation $O(f(n))$, where n is the size of the input to the algorithm. The notation $O(f(n))$ denotes the set of all functions $g(n)$ such that there exist positive constants c and n_0 with $|g(n)| \leq c|f(n)|$ for all $n \geq n_0$. We say that an algorithm runs in polynomial time if the running time of the algorithm is $O(n^k)$ for some constant k. The notation $\Omega(f(n))$ denotes the set of all functions $g(n)$ such that there exist positive constants c and n_0 with $g(n) \geq cf(n)$ for all $n \geq n_0$.

The idea of evaluating asymptotic efficiency of an algorithm is to know how the running time (or space) of the algorithm increases with the size of the input. The running time expressed using O notation gives a simple characterization of the efficiency of the algorithm, which in turn allows us to compare the efficiency of one algorithm with another. For more discussion on asymptotic efficiency of algorithms, see the book by Cormen *et al.* [96].

The *real* RAM (*Random Access Machine*) has become the standard model of computation for sequential algorithms in computational geometry. As stated in [291], the real RAM is a random access machine with infinite precision and real number arithmetic. The real RAM can be used to perform addition, subtraction, multiplication, division and comparisons on real numbers in unit time. In addition, various other operations such as indirect addressing of memory (integer address only), computing the intersection of two lines, computing the distance between two points, testing whether a vertex is convex are also available. These operations are assumed to take constant time for execution. For more details of these operations, see O'Rourke [272].

> **Exercise 1.3.1** *Is $O(2^n) = O(2^{O(n)})$?*

> **Exercise 1.3.2** *Given a point z and a polygon P, design an $O(n)$ time algorithm to test whether z lies in the interior of P [291].*

All parallel algorithms mentioned in this book (at the end of chapters) are designed for the *Parallel Random Access Machine* (PRAM) model of computations [35, 172, 211]. This can be viewed as the parallel analog of the sequential RAM. A PRAM consists of several independent sequential processors, each with its own private memory, communicating with one another through a global memory. In one unit of time, each processor can read one global or local memory location. PRAMs can be classified according to restrictions on global memory access. An *Exclusive-Read Exclusive-Write* (or EREW) PRAM is a PRAM for which simultaneous access to any memory location by different processors is forbidden for both reading and writing. In *Concurrent-Read Exclusive-Write* (or CREW) PRAM, simultaneous reads are allowed but not simultaneous writes. A *Concurrent-Read Concurrent-Write* (or CRCW) PRAM allows simultaneous reads and writes. PRAM models of computation allow for infinite precision real arithmetic, with all simple unary and binary operations being computable in $O(1)$ time by a single processor.

We say that a parallel algorithm in the PRAM model of computations runs in *polylogarithmic* time if it runs in $O(\log^k n)$ time using $O(n^m)$ processors, where k and m are constants and n is the size of the input to the algorithm. A problem is said to be in the class *NC* if it can be solved in polylogarithmic time using a polynomial number of processors. A parallel algorithm is called *optimal* if the product of the running time of a parallel algorithm and the number of processors used by the parallel algorithm is within a constant factor of the best sequential algorithm for the same problem.

1.4 Triangulation

In this section, we provide a brief overview of the results on triangulation of a polygon as there are visibility algorithms that depend on a first stage of computing a triangulation of the input polygon. A *triangulation* of a polygon P is a partition of P into triangles by diagonals (see Figure 1.3), where a line segment joining any two mutually visible vertices of P is called a *diagonal* of P [242]. Note that if a line segment joining two vertices u and v of P passes through another vertex w of P and the segment uv lies inside P, then uw and vw are diagonals and not uv.

Exercise 1.4.1 *Prove that every simple polygon admits triangulation [272].*

Exercise 1.4.2 *Using the proof of Exercise 1.4.1, design an $O(n^2)$ time algorithm for triangulating a simple polygon of n vertices [272].*

It can be seen that a triangulation of P is not unique as many subsets of diagonals give triangulations of the same polygon. The dual of a triangulation of P is a graph where every triangle is represented as a node of the graph and two nodes are connected by an arc in the graph if and only if their corresponding triangles share a diagonal (see Figure 1.3). Since there are three sides of a triangle, the degree of every node in the dual graph is at most three. A graph with no cycle is called a *tree*. In the following lemmas, we state some of the properties of triangulations of P.

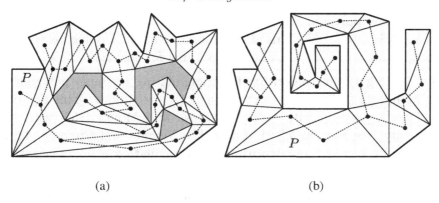

Figure 1.3 (a) A triangulation of a polygon with holes and its dual graph. (b) A triangulation of a simple polygon and its dual tree.

Lemma 1.4.1 *Every triangulation of a simple polygon of n vertices uses $n - 3$ diagonals and has $n - 2$ triangles.*

Corollary 1.4.2 *The sum of the internal angles of a simple polygon of n vertices is $(n - 2)\pi$.*

Lemma 1.4.3 *Every triangulation of a polygon with h holes with a total of n vertices uses $n + 3h - 3$ diagonals and has $n + 2h - 2$ triangles.*

Lemma 1.4.4 *The dual graph of a triangulation of a simple polygon is a tree.*

Lemma 1.4.5 *The dual graph of a triangulation of a polygon with holes must have a cycle.*

Exercise 1.4.3 *Prove that there is no cycle in the dual graph of a triangulation of a simple polygon.*

Exercise 1.4.4 *Let a graph G of m vertices denote the dual of a triangulation of a polygon with holes. Design an $O(m)$ time algorithm to locate a cycle in G.*

The first $O(n \log n)$ time algorithm for triangulating a simple polygon P was given by Garey *et al.* [148]. The first step of their algorithm is to partition P into *y-monotone* polygons. A simple polygon is called *y-monotone* if its boundary can be divided into two chains of vertices such that each chain has vertices with increasing y-coordinates. The partition of P into y-monotone polygons can be done in $O(n \log n)$ time by the algorithm of Lee and Preparata [233] for locating a point in a given set of regions. It has been shown by Garey *et al.* that each y-monotone polygon can be triangulated in a time that is proportional to the number of vertices of the y-monotone polygon. So, the overall time complexity of the algorithm for triangulating P is $O(n \log n)$. This algorithm also works for polygons with holes, as pointed out by Asano *et al.* [29], and it is optimal for this class of polygons.

Another $O(n \log n)$ time algorithm for triangulating a simple polygon was presented by Mehlhorn [257] and uses the *plane sweep* technique. This algorithm was generalized for a polygon with holes by Ghosh and Mount [165] with the same time complexity (see Section 5.3.2). Later, Bar-Yehuda and Chazelle [43] gave an $O(n + h \log^{1+\epsilon} h)$, $\epsilon > 0$ time algorithm for triangulating a polygon with h holes with a total of n vertices.

Many researchers worked for more than a decade on the problem of triangulating a simple polygon P in less than $O(n \log n)$ time. One approach was to consider special classes of simple polygons that could be triangulated in $O(n)$ time [48, 131, 142, 162, 183, 239, 280, 331, 342]. Another approach was to find algorithms whose running time was based on structural properties of simple polygons [78, 193]. Tarjan and Van Wyk [326] were the first to establish an improvement by proposing an $O(n \log \log n)$ time algorithm for this problem. Later, a simpler $O(n \log \log n)$ time algorithm was presented by Kirkpatrick *et al.* [217]. Finally, an $O(n)$ time optimal algorithm for this problem was presented by Chazelle [71] settling this long-standing open problem. We have the following theorem.

Theorem 1.4.6 *A simple polygon P of n vertices can be triangulated in $O(n)$ time.*

The algorithm of Chazelle [71] uses involved tools and notions such as a *planar separator theorem, polygon cutting theorem* and *conformality*. Although this algorithm does not use any complex data structure, it is conceptually difficult and too complex to be considered practical. Moreover, although it has been used as a preprocessing step for many of the visibility algorithms presented in this book, the development of a simple $O(n)$ time algorithm for triangulating a simple polygon remains an open problem.

1.5 The Art Gallery Problem

As stated in Section 1.1, the art gallery problem is to determine the number of guards that are sufficient to see every point in the interior of an art gallery room. The art gallery can be viewed as a polygon P of n vertices and the guards are stationary points in P. A point $z \in P$ is visible from a guard g if the line segment zg lies inside P. If guards are placed at vertices of P, they are called *vertex guards*. If guards are placed at any point of P, they are called *point guards*. Since guards placed at points or vertices are stationary, they are referred as *stationary guards*. If guards are mobile along a segment inside P, they are referred as *mobile guards*. If mobile guards move along edges of P, they are referred as *edge guards*.

Exercise 1.5.1 *Draw a simple polygon of 3k vertices for k > 1 showing that k stationary guards are necessary to see the entire polygon [91].*

In a conference in 1976, V. Klee first posed the art gallery problem (see [198]). Chavátal [91] showed that for a simple polygon P, $\lfloor n/3 \rfloor$ stationary guards are always sufficient and occasionally necessary to see or guard the entire P. Later, Fisk [141] gave a simple proof for this bound. Using this proof, Avis and Toussaint [41] designed an $O(n \log n)$ time algorithm for positioning guards at vertices of P. For mobile guards, O'Rourke [270] showed that $\lfloor n/4 \rfloor$ mobile guards are always sufficient and occasionally necessary. For edge guards, $\lfloor n/4 \rfloor$ edge guards appear to be sufficient, except for some types of polygons (see [333]).

Exercise 1.5.2 *Let P be a triangulated simple polygon of n vertices. Design an O(n) time algorithm for positioning at most $\lfloor n/3 \rfloor$ stationary guards at vertices of P such the entire P is visible for these guards [41, 141].*

A polygon is said to be *rectilinear* if its edges are aligned with a pair of orthogonal coordinate axes. For a simple rectilinear polygon P where edges of P are horizontal or vertical, Kahn *et al.* [207] showed that $\lfloor n/4 \rfloor$ stationary guards are always sufficient and occasionally necessary to guard P. An alternative proof for this bound was given later by O'Rourke [269]. These proofs first partition P into convex quadrilaterals and then $\lfloor n/4 \rfloor$ guards are placed in P. A convex quadrilaterization of P can be obtained by using the algorithms of Edelsbrunner *et al.* [121], Lubiw [250], Sack [299] and Sack and Toussaint [301]. For mobile guards in rectilinear polygons P, Aggarwal [11] proved that $\lfloor (3n + 4)/16 \rfloor$ mobile guards are always sufficient and occasionally necessary to guard P. Bjorling-Sachs [55] showed later that this bound also holds for edge guards in rectilinear polygons.

Exercise 1.5.3 *Let P be a triangulated simple polygon of n vertices. Design an O(n) time algorithm for partitioning P into convex quadrilaterals [250, 301].*

For a polygon P with h holes, O'Rourke [271] showed that P can always be guarded by at most $\lfloor (n + 2h)/3 \rfloor$ vertex guards. For point guards, Hoffmann *et al.* [194] and Bjorling-Sachs and Souvaine [56] proved independently that $\lceil (n+h)/3 \rceil$ point guards are always sufficient and occasionally necessary to guard P. Bjorling-Sachs and Souvaine also presented an $O(n^2)$ time algorithm for positioning guards in P. No tight bound is known on the number of mobile guards sufficient for guarding P. However, since $\lceil(n + h)/3\rceil$ point guards are sufficient for guarding P, the bound obviously holds for mobile guards. For an rectilinear polygon P with h holes, Györi et al. [182] showed that $\lfloor(3n + 4h + 4)/16\rfloor$ mobile guards are always sufficient and occasionally necessary for guarding P. For more details on art gallery theorems and algorithms, see O'Rourke [271], Shermer [310] and Urrutia [333]. We do not cover this subfield of visibility in this book.

The minimum guard problem is to locate the minimum number of guards for guarding a polygon with or without holes. O'Rourke and Supowit [276] proved that the minimum point, vertex and edge guard problems are NP-hard in polygons with holes. Even for simple polygons, these problems are NP-hard as shown by Lee and Lin [231].

There are approximation algorithms for these NP-hard problems. Ghosh [152] presented approximation algorithms for minimum vertex and edge guard problems for polygons P with or without holes. The approximation algorithms run in $O(n^5 \log n)$ time and yield solutions that can be at most $O(\log n)$ times the optimal solution. This means that the approximation ratio of these algorithms is $O(\log n)$. These algorithms partition the polygonal region into convex pieces and construct sets consisting of these convex pieces. Then the algorithms use an approximation algorithm for the minimum set-covering problem on these constructed sets to compute the solution for the minimum vertex and edge guard problems in P. Recently, Ghosh [158] has improved the running time of these approximation algorithms by improving the upper bound on the number of convex pieces in P. After improvement, the approximation algorithms run in $O(n^4)$ time for simple polygons and $O(n^5)$ time for polygons with holes.

Efrat and Har-Peled [122] also gave approximation algorithms for the minimum vertex guard problem in polygons with or without holes. Let c_{opt} denote the number of vertices in the optimal solution. Their approximation algorithm for simple polygons runs in $O(nc_{opt}^2 \log^4 n)$ time and the approximation ratio is $O(\log c_{opt})$. Their other approximation algorithm is for polygons with holes, which runs in $O(nhc_{opt}^3 polylog\ n)$ time, where h is the number of holes in the polygon. The approximation ratio is $O(\log n \log(c_{opt} \log n))$. For the minimum point guard problem in simple polygons, they gave an exact algorithm which runs in $O((nc_{opt})^{3(c_{opt}+1)})$ time.

Observe that in the worst case, c_{opt} can be a fraction of n. So, the approximation ratio of approximation algorithms of Ghosh [152, 158] and Efrat and Har-Peled [122] is $O(\log n)$ in the worst case. On the other hand, Eidenbenz [123, 124] showed that the problems of minimum vertex, point and edge guards in simple polygons are APX-hard. This implies that there exists a constant $\epsilon > 0$ such that no polynomial time approximation algorithm for these problems can guarantee an approximation ratio of $1 + \epsilon$ unless $P = NP$.

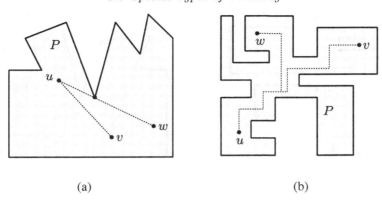

(a)   (b)

Figure 1.4 (a) The points u and v are clearly visible in P but u and w are not. (b) Points u and v are staircase visible in P. The point w is not staircase visible in P from u or v.

1.6 Special Types of Visibility

In this section, we mention some variations of visibility studied by researchers in the field of visibility. Breen [62, 63] introduced clear visibility, which is perhaps the smallest variation of standard visibility possible. Two points u and v in a polygon P are called *clearly visible* if the open line segment joining u and v lies in the interior of P. Note that clear visibility does not permit the line of sight to touch the boundary of P (see Figure 1.4(a)).

Let us consider staircase visibility between points in rectilinear polygons. This type of visibility has been studied by Culberson and Reckhow [99], Motwani *et al.* [263, 264], Reckhow and Culberson [296], Schiuerer and Wood [305] and Wood and Yamamoto [343]. If a path inside a rectilinear polygon P is monotone with respect to both axes, the path is called *staircase path* in P. Two points u and v in P are called *staircase visible* if there is a staircase path between u and v in P (see Figure 1.4(b)). Note that if two points u and v of P are visible under the standard definition of visibility, u and v are also staircase visible.

Staircase visibility has been generalized to $\mathcal{O}$-visibility, where $\mathcal{O}$ represents a set of two or more orientations between $0°$ and $180°$. If a path inside a rectilinear polygon P is monotone with respect to every direction in $\mathcal{O}$, the path is called $\mathcal{O}$-*staircase path* in P. Two points u and v in P are called $\mathcal{O}$-*visible* if there is an $\mathcal{O}$-staircase path between u and v in P. This type of visibility has been studied by Bremner [64], Bremner and Shermer [65], Rawlins [294], Rawlins and Wood [295], Schuierer *et al.* [304] and Schiuerer and Wood [305]. Fink and Wood [140] have studied $\mathcal{O}$-visibility in connection with convexity.

Like staircase visibility, rectangular visibility is generally used for points inside rectilinear polygons. If the sides of a rectangle are parallel to the axes, the rectangle is called *aligned*. For any two points u and v in a rectilinear polygon P, if the

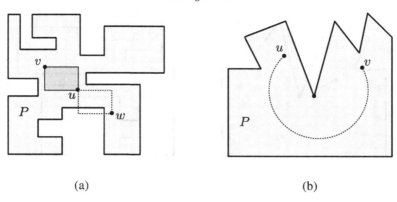

(a)   (b)

Figure 1.5 (a) The points u and v are rectangularly visible in P but u and w are not. (b) The points u and v are circularly visible in P.

aligned rectangle with u and v as opposite corners lies totally inside P, then u and v are called *rectangularly visible* (see Figure 1.5(a)). Rectangular visibility has been studied by Gewali [149], Gewali *et al.* [150], Keil [214], Munro *et al.* [265] and Overmars and Wood [279].

Circular visibility, another variation of visibility, has been studied by Agarwal and Sharir [8, 9], Chou and Woo [90] and Garcia-Lopez and Ramos-Alonso [147]. If two points u and v in a polygon P can be connected by a circular arc such that the circular arc lies totally inside P, then u and v are called *circularly visible* (see Figure 1.5(b)). Dean *et al.* [110] have studied X-ray visibility, which is another variation of visibility. Two points u and v are *X-ray visible* in a polygon P if the segment uv does intersect more than a fixed number of edges of P.

2
Point Visibility

2.1 Problems and Results

Determining the visible region of a geometric object from a given source under various constraints is a well-studied problem in computational geometry [30]. The *visibility polygon* $V(q)$ of a point q in a simple polygon P is the set of all points of P that are visible from q. In other words, $V(q) = \{p \in P \mid q \text{ sees } p\}$. A similar definition holds in a polygon with holes or an arrangement of segments. The problem of computing the visibility polygon $V(q)$ of a point q is related to *hidden line elimination problem* and it is a part of the rendering process in computer graphics [115]. Figure 2.1 shows $V(q)$ in a simple polygon, a polygon with holes, and a line segment arrangement. By definition, any $V(q)$ is a star-shaped polygon and q belongs to the kernel of P. The visibility polygon of a point in a line segment arrangement may not be always bounded.

Let ab be an edge on the boundary of $V(q)$ such that (i) no point of ab, except the points a and b, belong to the boundary of P, (ii) three points q, a and b are

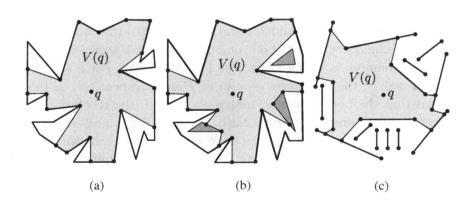

(a)   (b)   (c)

Figure 2.1 The visibility polygons of q (a) in a simple polygon, (b) in a polygon with holes, and (c) in a line segment arrangement.

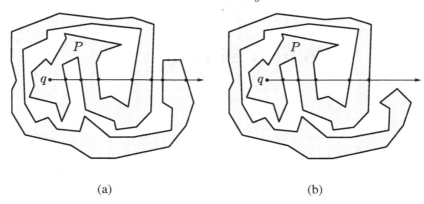

Figure 2.2 The revolution number of P with respect to q in (a) is two and in (b) is one.

collinear, and (iii) a or b is a vertex of P. Such an edge ab is called a *constructed edge* of $V(q)$. It can be seen that once constructed edges of $V(q)$ are known, the boundary of $V(q)$ can be constructed by adding the boundary of P between two consecutive constructed edges. Since each constructed edge can be computed in $O(n)$ time (see Exercise 2.1.1), a naive algorithm for computing $V(q)$ takes $O(n^2)$ time.

Exercise 2.1.1 *For each vertex v_i of a given polygon P (with or without holes), determine whether v_i is visible from q in $O(n)$ time and if v_i is visible from q, compute the constructed edge at v_i (if it exists) in $O(n)$ time.*

This problem for a simple polygon was first considered in a theoretical framework by Davis and Benedikt [107], who presented an $O(n^2)$ time algorithm. Then, El-Gindy and Avis [128] and Lee [230] presented $O(n)$ time algorithms for this problem. In Section 2.2.1, we present Lee's algorithm.

It has been shown in Joe [204] and Joe and Simpson [205] that both algorithms of ElGindy and Avis, and Lee may fail on some polygons with sufficient winding, i.e., if the revolution number is at least two (see Figure 2.2(a)). For a simple polygon P and a point $z \in P$, the *revolution number* of P with respect to z is the number of revolutions that the boundary of P makes about z. If the revolution number of P with respect to z is one (see Figure 2.2(b)), P is called a *non-winding polygon*. Joe and Simpson [205] suggested an $O(n)$ time algorithm for computing $V(q)$ which correctly handles winding in the polygon by keeping the count of the number of revolutions around q.

Exercise 2.1.2 *Given a point z inside or outside a simple polygon P of n vertices, design an $O(n)$ algorithm for computing the revolution number of P with respect to z.*

Observe that the portion of the boundary of the given simple polygon P, that makes the revolution number of P with respect to q more than one, is not visible from q. So, it is better to prune P before using the algorithm of ElGindy and Avis or Lee so that (i) the revolution number of the pruned polygon of P with respect to q is one, and (ii) the pruned polygon of P contains q and $V(q)$. In Section 2.2.2, we present the algorithm of Bhattacharya *et al.* [49] for pruning P that runs in linear time. This algorithm removes winding by locating a subset of *Jordon sequence* that is in the proper order and uses only one stack like the algorithm of Lee [230]. So, the algorithm of Bhattacharya *et al.* [49] can be viewed as a preprocessing step before $V(q)$ is computed by Lee's algorithm.

For a polygon with h holes with a total of n vertices, Asano [27] presented $O(n \log h)$ algorithms for computing $V(q)$ (see Figure 2.1(b)). Around the same time, Suri and O'Rourke [321] and Asano *et al.* [28] proposed $O(n \log n)$ time algorithms for this problem. Later, Heffernan and Mitchell [185] proposed an $O(n + h \log h)$ time algorithm for this problem. We present the algorithm of Asano [27] in Section 2.3.

Consider a simple polygon P such that the visibility polygon $V(q)$ of P from some point $q \in P$ is same as P, i.e., $P = V(q)$. Then P is a star-shaped polygon and q belongs to the kernel of P. For definitions of a star-shaped polygon and its kernel, see Section 1.2. So, the problem of recognizing the point visibility polygon is to locate a point $q \in P$ such that $P = V(q)$. In other words, a point $q \in P$ is to be located such that $V(q)$ does not have any constructed edge. Lee and Preparata [234] solved the recognition problem by presenting an $O(n)$ time algorithm for computing the kernel of P. If the kernel of P is non-empty, then P is the visibility polygon of P from any point of the kernel. We present the algorithm of Lee and Preparata in Section 2.4.

Exercise 2.1.3 *Let uv be an edge of a star-shaped polygon P, where v is a reflex vertex. Extend uv from v till it meets a point u' on the boundary of P. Prove that all points of the kernel of P lies on the same side of vu'.*

Exercise 2.1.4 *Let ab and cd be two constructed edges of the visibility polygon $V(q)$ of a point q inside a simple polygon P such that (i) a and d are reflex vertices of P, (ii) b and c are some points on the edges of P and (iii) the counterclockwise boundary from a to d passes through b and c. Prove that if there exists another such pair of constructed edges in $V(q)$, then P is not a star-shaped polygon.*

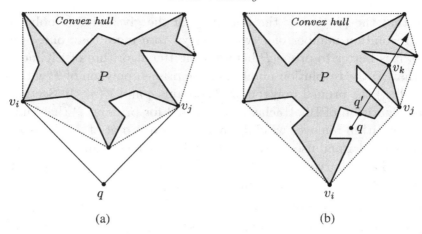

(a)   (b)

Figure 2.3 (a) The point q lies outside the convex hull of P. (b) The point q lies outside P but inside the convex hull of P.

2.2 Computing Visibility of a Point in Simple Polygons

2.2.1 Non-Winding Polygon: $O(n)$ Algorithm

In this section, we present the algorithm of Lee [230] for computing the visibility polygon $V(q)$ of a simple polygon P of n vertices from a point q in $O(n)$ time. The first step of the algorithm is to determine whether q lies inside or outside P. If q lies outside P, a simple polygon P' is constructed from P such that $q \in P'$ and $V(q) \subseteq P'$. Then, the procedure for computing the visibility polygon from an internal point can be used to compute $V(q)$ in P' as $q \in P'$.

Let us explain the procedure for constructing P' from P when q lies outside P. There are two situations depending on whether q lies inside the convex hull of P (see Figure 2.3). The *convex hull* of P is the smallest convex polygon containing P and it can be computed in $O(n)$ time by the algorithm of Graham and Yao [175]. If q lies outside the convex hull of P (see Figure 2.3(a)), draw two tangents (say, qv_i and qv_j) from q to the convex hull of P. Let $bd(P)$ denote the boundary of P. Observe that all points of $bd(P)$ visible from q lie between v_i and v_j *facing* q. So, $bd(P')$ consists of this part of $bd(P)$ between v_i and v_j and two tangents qv_i and qv_j. Now, q is an internal point of P'. Consider the other situation when q lies outside P but inside the convex hull of P (see Figure 2.3(b)). Draw a line from q passing through any vertex v_k of P (denoted as $\overrightarrow{qv_k}$). Let q' be the closest point of q among all points of intersections of $\overrightarrow{qv_k}$ with $bd(P)$. Starting from q', traverse $bd(P)$ in clockwise (and in counterclockwise) order till a convex hull vertex v_i (respectively, v_j) is reached. Note that v_i and v_j are consecutive vertices on the convex hull of P. So, $bd(P')$ consists of $bd(P)$ between v_i and v_j containing q', and the convex hull edge v_iv_j. Now, q is an internal point of P'.

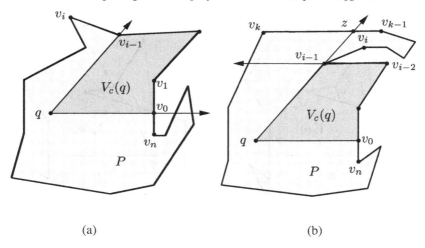

(a)   (b)

Figure 2.4 (a) The vertex v_i is pushed on the stack. (b) The vertices of $bd(v_i, v_{k-1})$ are not visible from q.

From now on, we consider that the given point q is an internal point of P. If the boundary of the given polygon P winds around q, the winding is removed from P by the algorithm in Section 2.2.2. Henceforth, we assume that $bd(P)$ does not wind around q. The problem is to compute $V(q)$ of P from q.

Exercise 2.2.1 *Let $p_i = (x_i, y_i)$, $p_j = (x_j, y_j)$, and $p_k = (x_k, y_k)$ be three points in the plane. Let $S = x_k(y_i - y_j) + y_k(x_j - x_i) + y_j x_i - y_i x_j$. Show that (i) if $S > 0$ then p_k lies to the left of $\overrightarrow{p_i p_j}$, (ii) if $S = 0$ then p_i, p_j and p_k are collinear, and (iii) if $S < 0$ then p_k lies to the right of $\overrightarrow{p_i p_j}$.*

We know that $V(q)$ is a star-shaped polygon, where q is a point in the kernel of $V(q)$. Let v_0 denote the closest point of q among the intersection points of $bd(P)$ with the horizontal line drawn from q to the right of q (see Figure 2.4(a)). We assume that the vertices of P are labeled $v_1, v_2, \ldots, v_n$ in counterclockwise order with v_1 as the next counterclockwise vertex after v_0. So, v_1 and v_n lie to the left and right of $\overrightarrow{qv_0}$, respectively.

Assume that the procedure for computing $V(q)$ has scanned $bd(P)$ in counterclockwise order from v_1 to v_{i-1} and v_i is the current vertex under consideration. The star-shaped polygon formed by the vertices and points on the stack at any stage along with q is referred to as the current visibility region $V_c(q)$. Let $bd(v_j, v_k)$ denote the counterclockwise boundary of P from v_j to v_k. We also assume that vertices (and the endpoints of constructed edges) on $bd(v_0, v_{i-1})$, which are found to be visible from q by the procedure, are pushed on a stack in the order they are encountered, where v_0 and v_{i-1} are at the bottom and top of the stack, respectively. So, the vertices and points in the stack are in sorted angular order around q. The

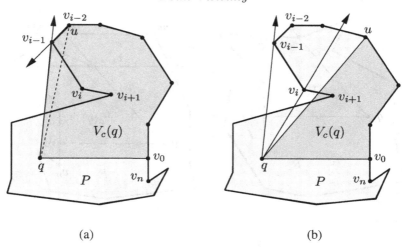

(a)   (b)

Figure 2.5 (a) The edge $v_{i-1}v_i$ intersects uq. (b) The edge $v_{i-1}v_i$ does not intersect uq.

procedure always ensures that the content of the stack satisfies this property at any stage of the execution. We have the following cases.

Case 1. The vertex v_i lies to the left of $\overrightarrow{qv_{i-1}}$ (Figure 2.4(a)).
Case 2. The vertex v_i lies to the right of $\overrightarrow{qv_{i-1}}$ (Figure 2.4(b) and Figure 2.5(a)).

   Case 2a. The vertex v_i lies to the right of $\overrightarrow{v_{i-2}v_{i-1}}$ (Figure 2.4(b)).
   Case 2b. The vertex v_i lies to the left of $\overrightarrow{v_{i-2}v_{i-1}}$ (Figure 2.5(a)).

Consider Case 1. Since v_i and the vertices and points in the stack are in sorted angular order with respect to q (see Figure 2.4(a)), v_i is pushed on the stack.

Consider Case 2. It can be seen that v_{i-1} and v_i cannot both be visible from q (see Figure 2.4(b) and Figure 2.5(a)), as either qv_i is intersected by $bd(v_0, v_{i-1})$ (Case 2a) or qv_{i-1} is intersected by $bd(v_{i+1}, v_n)$ (Case 2b).

Consider Case 2a. The vertex v_i and some of the subsequent vertices of v_i (yet to be scanned) are not visible from q (see Figure 2.4(b)). Let $v_{k-1}v_k$ be the first edge from v_{i+1} on $bd(v_{i+1}, v_n)$ in counterclockwise order such that $v_{k-1}v_k$ intersects $\overrightarrow{qv_{i-1}}$. Let z be the point of intersection. Note that v_k lies to the left of $\overrightarrow{qv_{i-1}}$ as $bd(P)$ does not wind around q. So, no vertices of $bd(v_i, v_{k-1})$ are visible from q and therefore, z is the next point of v_{i-1} on $bd(v_{i-1}v_n)$ visible from q. So, $v_i z$ is a constructed edge of $V(q)$, where q, v_{i-1} and z are collinear points. Push z and v_k on the stack, and v_{k+1} becomes the new v_i.

Consider Case 2b. The vertex v_{i-1} and some of the preceding vertices of v_i (currently on the stack) are not visible from q (see Figure 2.5(a)). Pop the stack to remove v_i. Let u denote the vertex on the top of the stack. The edge $v_{i-1}v_i$ is called a *forward edge*. While $v_{i-1}v_i$ intersects uq and u is a vertex of P, pop the stack.

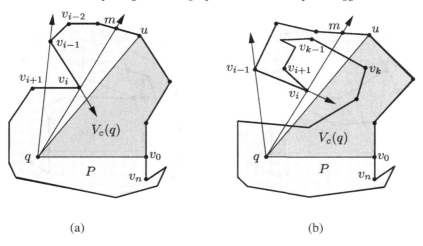

(a)   (b)

Figure 2.6 (a) Backtracking ends by pushing m and v_i on the stack. (b) Backtracking continues with $v_{k-1}v_k$ as the current forward edge.

Note that popped vertices are not visible from q as their visibility from q is blocked by $v_{i-1}v_i$. After the execution of this step of backtracking, there are two situations that can arise: (i) $v_{i-1}v_i$ does not intersect uq (see Figure 2.5(b)), and (ii) $v_{i-1}v_i$ intersects uq (see Figure 2.7).

In the first situation, the procedure decides whether further backtracking is required (see Figure 2.5(b) and Figure 2.6). If v_{i+1} lies to the right of $\overrightarrow{qv_i}$ (see Figure 2.5(b)), backtracking continues with v_iv_{i+1} as the current forward edge. Otherwise, v_{i+1} lies to the left of $\overrightarrow{qv_i}$ (see Figure 2.6). Let m be the intersection point of $\overrightarrow{qv_i}$ with the polygonal edge containing u. If v_{i+1} lies to the right of $\overrightarrow{v_{i-1}v_i}$, then the backtracking ends (see Figure 2.6(a)). Push m and v_i on the stack and v_{i+1} becomes the new v_i. If v_{i+1} lies to the left of $\overrightarrow{v_{i-1}v_i}$ (see Figure 2.6(b)), scan $bd(v_{i+1}, v_n)$ from v_{i+1} until a vertex v_k is found such that the edge $v_{k-1}v_k$ intersects mv_i. Backtracking continues with $v_{k-1}v_k$ as the current forward edge.

In the second situation, u is not a vertex of P (see Figure 2.7). Let w be the vertex immediately below u on the stack. So, uw is a constructed edge computed earlier by the procedure in Case 2a. Let p be the point of intersection of uq and $v_{i-1}v_i$. If $p \in qw$ (see Figure 2.7(a)), the visibility of both u and w from q is blocked by $v_{i-1}v_i$. Pop the stack. Backtracking continues and $v_{i-1}v_i$ remains the current forward edge. Otherwise, $v_{i-1}v_i$ has intersected uw as p belongs to uw (see Figure 2.7(b)). Scan $bd(v_{i+1}, v_n)$ from v_{i+1} until a vertex v_k is found such that the edge $v_{k-1}v_k$ has intersected wp at some point (say, z). So, the entire $bd(w, z)$ (excluding w and z) is not visible from q. Pop the stack. Push z and v_k on the stack. So, v_{k+1} becomes the new v_i. Note that we have assumed uw is a constructed edge computed earlier in Case 2a. It may so happen that the constructed edge ending at u (say, uu') has been computed in Case 2b at the end of an earlier backtracking

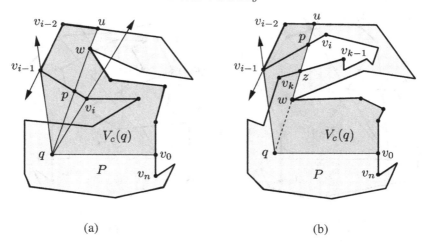

(a)   (b)

Figure 2.7 (a) The edge $v_{i-1}v_i$ does not intersect the constructed edge uw. (b) The edge $v_{i-1}v_i$ intersects uw at p, and the edge $v_{k-1}v_k$ intersects pw at z.

phase. It means that the vertex u' is the last vertex popped of the stack in the current backtracking phase. Therefore, q, w and u are not collinear. Hence, pop the stack and it becomes the first situation of the current backtracking.

In the following steps, we formally present the algorithm for computing $V(q)$. As before, we assume that v_0 is the closest point of $bd(P)$ to the right of q, and the vertex v_1 is the next counterclockwise vertex of v_0. Push v_0 on the stack and initialize i by 1.

Step 1. Push v_i on the stack *and* $i := i + 1$. *If* $i = n + 1$ *goto* Step 8.

Step 2. *If* v_i lies to the left of $\overrightarrow{qv_{i-1}}$ (Figure 2.4(a)) *then goto* Step 1 (Case 1).

Step 3. *If* v_i lies to the right of both $\overrightarrow{qv_{i-1}}$ *and* $\overrightarrow{v_{i-2}v_{i-1}}$ *then* (Case 2a)

Step 3a. Scan from v_{i+1} in counterclockwise order until a vertex v_k is found such that $v_{k-1}v_k$ intersects $\overrightarrow{qv_{i-1}}$ (Figure 2.4(b)). Let z be the point of intersection.

Step 3b. Push z on the stack, $i := k$ and *goto* Step 1.

Step 4. *If* v_i lies to the right of $\overrightarrow{qv_{i-1}}$ *and* to the left of $\overrightarrow{v_{i-2}v_{i-1}}$ (Figure 2.5(a)) *then* (Case 2b)

Step 4a. Let u denote the element on the top of the stack. Pop the stack.

Step 4b. *While* u is a vertex *and* $v_{i-1}v_i$ intersects uq, pop the stack (Figure 2.5(a)).

Step 5. *If* $v_{i-1}v_i$ does not intersect uq (Figure 2.5(b)) *then*

Step 5a. *If* v_{i+1} lies to right of $\overrightarrow{qv_i}$ (Figure 2.5(b)) *then* $i := i + 1$ *and goto* Step 4b.

Step 5b. Let m be the point of intersection of $\overrightarrow{qv_i}$ and the edge containing u. *If* v_{i+1} lies to the right of $\overrightarrow{v_{i-1}v_i}$ (Figure 2.6(a)) *then* push m on the stack *and goto* Step 1.

Step 5c. Scan from v_{i+1} in counterclockwise order until a vertex v_k is found such that $v_{k-1}v_k$ intersects mv_i (Figure 2.6(b)). Assign k to i *and goto* Step 4b.

Step 6. Let w be the vertex immediately below u on the stack. Let p be the point of intersection between $v_{i-1}v_i$ and uq. If $p \in qw$ (Figure 2.7(a)) or q, w and u are not collinear *then* pop the stack *and goto* Step 4b.

Step 7. Scan from v_{i+1} in counterclockwise order until a vertex v_k is found such that $v_{k-1}v_k$ intersects wp (Figure 2.7(b)). Push the intersection point on the stack, assign k to i *and goto* Step 1.

Step 8. Output $V(q)$ by popping all vertices and points on the stack *and* Stop.

Let us discuss the correctness of the algorithm. As stated earlier, $V(q)$ is a star-shaped polygon with its kernel containing q, i.e., vertices of $V(q)$ are in sorted angular order with respect to q. The algorithm maintains an invariant that the vertices and points on the stack at any stage are in sorted angular order with respect to q. When the algorithm terminates, the current visibility region $V_c(q)$ is $V(q)$.

The algorithm scans the vertices of P starting from v_0 in counterclockwise order and checks in Step 2 whether the current vertex v_i is in the sorted angular order with the vertices and points on the stack. If v_i satisfies this property (see Figure 2.4(a)), it means that v_i lies to the left of $\overrightarrow{qv_{i-1}}$ and v_i is pushed on the stack. Since v_i is pushed on the stack, the current region of $V(q)$ is enhanced by the triangle formed by q, v_{i-1} and v_i. If v_i is not in sorted angular order, v_i must lie to the right of $\overrightarrow{qv_{i-1}}$. Moreover, v_i may lie inside $V_c(q)$.

Consider the situation when v_i lies outside $V_c(q)$ and v_i also lies to the right of $\overrightarrow{qv_{i-1}}$. Observe that although v_i lies outside $V_c(q)$, the edge $v_{i-1}v_i$ may pass through $V_c(q)$ (see Figure 2.7(b)). In the other situation, $v_{i-1}v_i$ does not pass through $V_c(q)$ (see Figure 2.4(b)). Consider the later situation. Observe that qv_i is intersected by $bd(v_0, v_{i-1})$ and therefore, v_i cannot be visible from q. Let $v_{k-1}v_k$ be the first edge in counterclockwise order starting from v_i such that $v_{k-1}v_k$ intersects qv_{i-1} at some points (say, z). Since P is a closed and bounded region, such an edge $v_{k-1}v_k$ intersecting $\overrightarrow{qv_{i-1}}$ exists. Note that since P does not have winding by assumption, v_k satisfies sorted angular order along with the vertices and points on the stack. So, the algorithm correctly locates such a vertex v_k in Step 3, and $V_c(q)$ is enhanced by the triangle formed by q, z and v_k.

If $v_{i-1}v_i$ passes through $V_c(q)$ (see Figure 2.7(b)), it can be seen that $v_{i-1}v_i$ has intersected a constructed edge uw computed by the algorithm earlier, where w is a vertex of $bd(v_0, v_{i-1})$. So, v_i cannot be visible from q as $bd(v_0, w)$ intersects qv_i. Let p be the intersection point of $v_{i-1}v_i$ and uw. Let $v_{k-1}v_k$ be the first edge in counterclockwise order starting from v_i such that $v_{k-1}v_k$ intersects pw at some point (say, z). Since P is a closed and bounded region, such an edge $v_{k-1}v_k$ exists. Observe that all points of $bd(w, z)$ (excluding w and z) cannot be visible from q, and v_k is in sorted angular order with the vertices and points of $bd(v_0, w)$ on the stack. So,

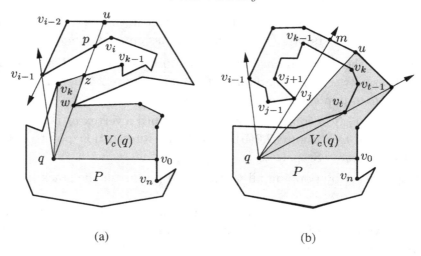

(a)   (b)

Figure 2.8 (a) Backtracking ends at v_k. (b) The edges $v_{j-1}v_j$ and $v_{k-1}v_k$ are two consecutive forward edges on $bd(v_{i-1}, v_t)$.

the algorithm correctly locates such a vertex v_k in Step 7. $V_c(q)$ is reduced triangle by triangle as vertices are popped off the stack till qw becomes a boundary edge of $V_c(q)$, and then $V_c(q)$ is enhanced by the triangle formed by q, z and v_k (see Figure 2.7(b) and Figure 2.8(a)).

Consider the other situation when v_i lies inside $V_c(q)$ (see Figure 2.5(a)). So, $v_{i-1}v_i$ blocks the visibility from q to some of the vertices and points currently on the stack. These vertices and points are popped off the stack in Step 4. While popping the stack, $V_c(q)$ is also reduced triangle by triangle until v_i no longer lies inside $V_c(q)$ (see Figure 2.5(b)). The vertex v_i is now in sorted angular order with the vertices and points on the stack. However, v_{i+1} may lie inside $V_c(q)$ (see Figure 2.5(b)) (which is checked in Step 5a) and therefore, backtracking continues. So, Step 4b is again executed with v_iv_{i+1} as the current forward edge.

Observe that two consecutive forward edges may not always be two consecutive edges on $bd(v_{i-1}, v_n)$. In Figure 2.8(b), $v_{j-1}v_j$ and $v_{k-1}v_k$ are two consecutive forward edges. It can happen when the next counterclockwise edge v_jv_{j+1} of the current forward edge $v_{j-1}v_j$ does not lie inside $V_c(q)$ but the visibility from q to v_{j+1} is blocked by forward edges on $bd(v_{i-1}, v_j)$. Let $v_{k-1}v_k$ be the first edge in counterclockwise order starting from v_{j+1} such that $v_{k-1}v_k$ intersects $\overrightarrow{qv_j}$. Since P is a closed and bounded region, such an edge $v_{k-1}v_k$ exists and it becomes the current forward edge. So, the algorithm correctly locates the next forward edge in Step 5c. Backtracking finally ends in Step 5b when the visibility of the next counterclockwise edge (say, v_tv_{t+1}) of the current forward edge $v_{t-1}v_t$ from q is not blocked by any forward edge of $bd(v_{i-1}, v_t)$ (see Figure 2.8(b)). So, v_{t+1} and v_t are

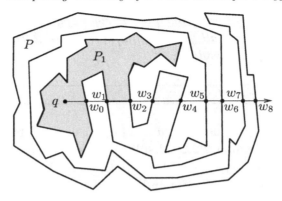

Figure 2.9 Alternate segments w_1w_2, w_3w_4, w_5w_6 and w_7w_8 have divided P into sub-polygons and the sub-polygon with w_0 as a boundary point contains both q and $V(q)$.

in sorted angular order with the vertices and points currently on the stack. $V_c(q)$ is first enhanced to v_t and then to v_{t+1}.

Finally, the algorithm reaches v_n and it outputs $V_c(q)$ in Step 8 as $V(q)$. It can be seen that every vertex of P is considered once by the algorithm while scanning from v_0 to v_n. If any vertex v_i is pushed on the stack, v_i remains on the stack unless it is removed during backtracking. Once v_i is removed of the stack, v_i is not considered again by the algorithm. Hence, the overall time complexity of the algorithm is $O(n)$. We state the result in the following theorem.

Theorem 2.2.1 *The visibility polygon $V(q)$ of a given point q inside an n-sided simple polygon P can be computed in $O(n)$ time.*

Exercise 2.2.2 *Let q be a point inside a given triangulated simple polygon P. Design a procedure for computing the visibility polygon of q in P whose running time is proportional to the number of triangles, partially or totally visible from q, in the triangulation of P.*

2.2.2 *Removing Winding: $O(n)$ Algorithm*

In this section, we present an $O(n)$ time algorithm of Bhattacharya *et al.* [49] to remove the winding of a simple polygon P with respect to a given point q inside P. Given a simple polygon P and a point $q \in P$, the problem is to compute a simple polygon $P_1 \subseteq P$ (called *a pruned polygon*) such that P_1 contains both $V(q)$ and q, and the angle subtended at q is at most 2π while the boundary of P_1 is scanned in clockwise or counterclockwise order (see Figure 2.9). This means that the revolution number of P_1 with respect to q is one. We have the following lemma.

Lemma 2.2.2 *Draw the half-line from q to the right of q intersecting $bd(P)$ at points $(w_0, w_1, ..., w_k)$ such that for all j, $w_j \in qw_{j+1}$ (Figure 2.9). Alternate segments $w_1 w_2$, $w_3 w_4$,..., $w_{k-1} w_k$ lie inside P.*

Exercise 2.2.3 *Prove Lemma 2.2.2.*

Partition P by adding segments $w_1 w_2$, $w_3 w_4$,..., $w_{k-1} w_k$ to P. Since these segments lie inside P by Lemma 2.2.2, P splits into several parts and the part with w_0 as a boundary point (say, P_1) contains both q and $V(q)$. Analogously, draw a horizontal line from q to the left of q and remove winding from P_1. Since the new P_1 does not have winding with respect to q, the revolution number of the new P_1 is one.

We know that points w_0, w_1,..., w_k can be computed in $O(n)$ time and then they can be sorted along the half-line in $O(n \log n)$ time. Using the property that w_0, w_1,..., w_k belong to the boundary of simple polygon, which is a closed and bounded region, Hoffmann *et al.* [195] showed that the sorting of w_0, w_1,..., w_k along the half-line can be done in $O(n)$ time. Hence, the pruned polygon P_1 containing both q and $V(q)$ can be computed in $O(n)$ time. However, the algorithm of Hoffmann *et al.* [195] is difficult to implement as it uses involved data structures called *level-linked search trees*.

Observe that the winding in the polygon P in Figure 2.9 can be removed by adding only the segments $w_1 w_2$ or $w_5 w_6$. This suggests that the winding in P can be removed by adding a few selected segments. We show that these segments can be identified in $O(n)$ time using only one stack without the sorting of all intersection points along the half-line as follows.

Let L denote the horizontal line passing through q. The portion of L to the right (or left) of q is denoted as L_r (respectively, L_l) (see Figure 2.10(a)). The closest point of q among the intersection points of $bd(P)$ with L_r (or L_l) is denoted as q_r (respectively, q_l). Since $q_l q_r$ lies inside P, two sub-polygons P_a and P_b are constructed by adding the segment $q_l q_r$ in P, where the boundary of P_a (or P_b) consists of $q_l q_r$ and the boundary of P from q_r to q_l in counterclockwise (respectively, clockwise) order.

It can be seen that there are four types of sub-segments of L lying inside P formed by pairs of intersection points of $bd(P_a)$ or $bd(P_b)$ with L_r or L_l (see Figure 2.10(a)). The algorithm identifies some of these sub-segments and by adding these sub-segments to P, the winding of P is removed. Among these sub-segments, the sub-segments formed by the intersection of L_r with P_a is located by scanning $bd(P_a)$ from q_r to q_l in counterclockwise order; the procedure is called $CC(P_a, q_r, q_l, L_r)$. The remaining sub-segments on L_r or L_l are identified by analogous procedures $C(P_a, q_l, q_r, L_l)$, $C(P_b, q_r, q_l, L_r)$ and $CC(P_b, q_l, q_r, L_l)$. In Figure 2.10(a), sub-segments $z_1 z_2$, $z_3 z_4$, $z_7 z_8$ and $z_5 z_6$ are identified by $CC(P_a, q_r, q_l, L_r)$,

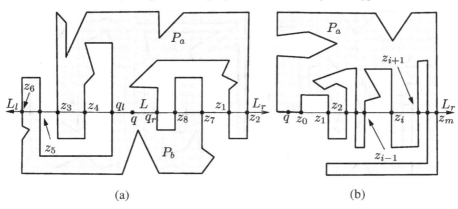

Figure 2.10 (a) Each procedure identifies one sub-segment on L. (b) Every pair of consecutive intersection points on L_r is of opposite type.

$C(P_a, q_l, q_r, L_l)$, $C(P_b, q_r, q_l, L_r)$ and $CC(P_b, q_l, q_r, L_l)$, respectively. Among these four procedures, only the procedure $CC(P_a, q_r, q_l, L_r)$ is presented here as other procedures are analogous.

Let us present $CC(P_a, q_r, q_l, L_r)$. An intersection point z between $bd(P_a)$ and L_r is called a *downward* (respectively, *upward*) point if the next counterclockwise vertex of z on $bd(P_a)$ is below (or above) L_r. For example, q_r is always an upward point. Two intersection points of $bd(P_a)$ and L_r are called *same type* if both of them are downward or upward points. Otherwise, they are *opposite type*. For example in Figure 2.10(a), z_1 and z_2 are downward and upward points, respectively, and therefore, (z_1, z_2) is a pair of opposite type. In the following lemma, we present properties of pairs of intersection points between L_r and $bd(P_a)$.

Lemma 2.2.3 *Let w and z be two intersection points between L_r and $bd(P_a)$.*

(i) If w and z are of same type, wz does not lie inside P_a.

(ii) If wz lies inside P_a, then w and z are of opposite type.

(iii) If w is a downward point, z is upward point and wz lies inside P_a, then w lies on qz.

(iv) If w is a downward point, z is an upward point and wz does not lie inside P_a, then wz contains a pair of opposite type.

Exercise 2.2.4 *Prove Lemma 2.2.3.*

The above lemma suggests that for locating sub-segments of L_r lying inside P_a, locate pairs of opposite type and then test whether a pair contains another pair of opposite type. Let $Z = (z_0, z_1, ..., z_m)$ be the intersection points from q_r to q_l along $bd(P_a)$ in counterclockwise order, where $q_r = z_0$ (see Figure 2.10(b)). We say that $(z_0, z_1, ..., z_{i-1})$ is in the *proper order* if for all k less than $i-1$, $z_k \in qz_{k+1}$ and

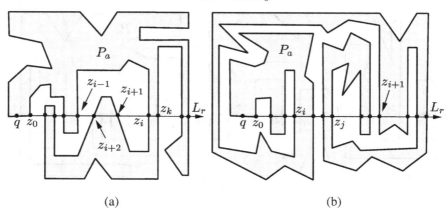

(a)   (b)

Figure 2.11 (a) The next pair is formed by z_i and z_k. (b) The next pair is formed by z_i and z_j.

(z_k, z_{k+1}) is a pair of opposite type. Observe that if there is no winding in P_a, all points in Z are in the proper order and therefore, segments connecting alternate pairs of points in Z lie inside P_a. We have the following properties on the proper order.

Lemma 2.2.4 *Assume that $(z_0, z_1, ..., z_{i-1})$ is in the proper order.*

(i) If z_i preserves the proper order, then $z_i \notin qz_{i-1}$ and (z_{i-1}, z_i) is a pair of opposite type.

(ii) If z_i violates the proper order, then $z_i \in qz_{i-1}$ or (z_{i-1}, z_i) is a pair of same type.

(iii) If there is a point $z_j \in z_k z_{k+1}$, where $k < i - 1$ and $j > i - 1$, then z_j is a subsequent point of z_{i-1} in Z.

Assume that $CC(P_a, q_r, q_l, L_r)$ has tested points $z_0, z_1, ..., z_{i-1}$ and they are in the proper order (see Figure 2.10(b)). This means that z_0 is an upward point, z_1 is a downward point, z_2 is a upward point and so on. We know that $z_0 z_1$, $z_2 z_3, ..., z_{i-3} z_{i-2}$ do not lie inside P_a. We assume that $(z_1, z_2), (z_3, z_4), ..., (z_{i-2}, z_{i-1})$ are pushed on the stack by the procedure with (z_{i-2}, z_{i-1}) on top of the stack. Note that z_{i-1} is an upward intersection point by assumption. The procedure checks whether $(z_0, z_1, ..., z_{i-1}, z_i)$ is in proper order. We have the following four cases depending upon the type and position of z_i.

Case 1. The point z_i is a downward point and $z_i \notin qz_{i-1}$ (see Figure 2.10(b)).
Case 2. The point z_i is a downward point and $z_i \in qz_{i-1}$ (see Figure 2.12(a)).
Case 3. The point z_i is an upward point and $z_i \in qz_{i-1}$ (see Figure 2.12(b)).
Case 4. The point z_i is an upward point and $z_i \notin qz_{i-1}$ (see Figure 2.14(b)).

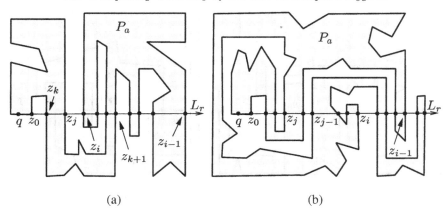

Figure 2.12 (a) The downward point z_i belongs to $z_k z_{k+1}$. (b) There is no pair in the stack whose segment contains the upward point z_i.

Consider Case 1. We know from Lemma 2.2.4 that z_i preserves the proper order as z_i is a downward point and $z_i \notin qz_{i-1}$. The procedure checks whether z_i and z_{i+1} form a pair of opposite type and z_{i+1} preserves the proper order. Consider the situation where $z_{i+1} \in qz_i$ (see Figure 2.11(a)). By Lemma 2.2.4, z_{i+1} has violated the proper order. Starting from z_{i+2}, scan Z to locate a point z_k such that $z_i \in qz_k$. Points $(z_{i+1}, \ldots, z_{k-1})$ are removed from Z and z_k becomes the new z_{i+1}. So, $z_i \in qz_{i+1}$. If z_{i+1} is an upward point (see Figure 2.10(b)), then $(z_0, z_1, \ldots, z_i, z_{i+1})$ is in the proper order by Lemma 2.2.4. So, the next pair of opposite type (z_i, z_{i+1}) is pushed on the stack. Otherwise, both z_i and z_{i+1} are downward points (see Figure 2.11(b)) and z_{i+1} has violated the proper order by Lemma 2.2.4. Since $bd(z_i, z_{i+1})$ has wound around q, scan Z starting from z_{i+2} and locate a point z_j such that $z_j \in z_i z_{i+1}$. Since z_j is an upward point and $z_i \in qz_j$, (z_i, z_j) becomes the next pair of opposite type by Lemma 2.2.4. Remove all points of Z that do not belong to qz_{i+1} and push (z_i, z_j) on the stack. Observe that if $z_i z_j$ lies inside P_a, $z_i z_j$ can be added to P_a to remove winding in $bd(z_i, z_{i+1})$. Otherwise, by Lemma 2.2.3, there exists a pair of opposite type in Z (see Figure 2.11(b)) lying on the $z_i z_j$, which is detected later.

Consider Case 2. By Lemma 2.2.4, z_i has violated the proper order (see Figure 2.12(a)) as z_i is a downward point and $z_i \in qz_{i-1}$. Pop the stack till the pair (say, (z_k, z_{k+1})) is on top of the stack such that $z_i \in z_k z_{k+1}$. We know from Lemma 2.2.3 that there is a pair of opposite type in Z lying on $z_k z_{k+1}$. Therefore scan Z from z_{i+1} and locate a point z_j such that $z_j \in z_k z_i$. It can be seen that z_j is an upward point. Therefore, (z_k, z_j) is a pair of opposite type. Hence, $(z_0, z_1, \ldots, z_k, z_j)$ is in the proper order by Lemma 2.2.4. Push (z_k, z_j) on the stack after (z_k, z_{k+1}) is popped from the stack.

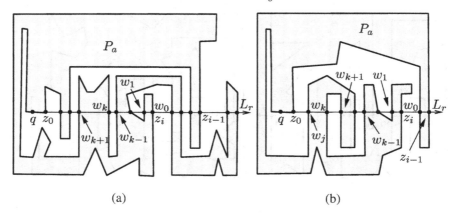

Figure 2.13 (a) The next pair formed by w_k and w_{k+1} is in the proper order. (b) The next pair in the proper order is formed by w_k and w_j.

Consider Case 3. By Lemma 2.2.4, z_i has violated the proper order as z_i is an upward point and $z_i \in qz_{i-1}$ (see Figure 2.12(b) and Figure 2.13(a)). Scan Z from z_i and locate two consecutive downward points $z_{j-1} \in qz_{i-1}$ and $z_j \in qz_{i-1}$ (see Figure 2.12(b)). Remove $(z_i, \ldots, z_{j-1})$ from Z and z_j becomes the new z_i. Execute Case 2. If no such points z_{j-1} and z_j exist (see Figure 2.13(a)), the segments formed by pairs in the stack are added to partition P_a. In the process, the stack becomes empty. Observe that $bd(z_{i-1}, z_i)$ still has winding (see Figure 2.13(a)) which has to be removed.

Using the same stack, $CC(P_a, q_r, q_l, L_r)$ locates the sub-segments of qz_i (from z_i toward q) lying inside P_a. Traverse $bd(P_a)$ in counterclockwise order starting from z_i, where $z_i = w_0$ (see Figure 2.13(a)) and compute intersection points $W = (w_0, w_1, \ldots, w_p)$ between $bd(z_i, q)$ and qz_i. Observe that although any two consecutive points w_{k-1} and w_k in W are of opposite type, w_k may not belong to qw_{k-1} for all k and therefore, W may not be in the proper order in the direction from w_0 towards q. The following lemma, which is analogous to Lemma 2.2.4, states the properties of the proper order of W.

Lemma 2.2.5 *Assume that $(w_0, w_1, \ldots, w_{k-1})$ is in the proper order.*
(i) If w_k preserves the proper order, then $w_k \notin w_0 w_{k-1}$.
(ii) If w_k violates the proper order, then $w_k \in w_0 w_{k-1}$.
(iii) If there is a point $w_j \in w_t w_{t+1}$, where $t < k-1$, then w_j is a subsequent point of w_{k-1} in W.

Assume that $CC(P_a, q_r, q_l, L_r)$ has tested points $w_0, w_1, \ldots, w_{k-1}$ and they are in proper order (see Figure 2.13(a)). We also assume that $(w_0, w_1), (w_2, w_3), \ldots, (w_{k-2}, w_{k-1})$ are pushed on the stack by the procedure. Note that w_0 is an upward point. If $w_k \notin w_0 w_{k-1}$, then $(w_0, w_1, \ldots, w_{k-1}, w_k)$ is in the proper order by Lemma

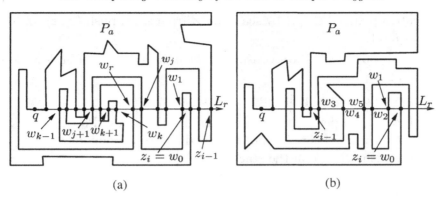

Figure 2.14 (a) The next pair in the proper order is formed by w_j and w_r. (b) P_a is partitioned by adding segments w_0w_1 and w_2w_5.

2.2.5. If $w_{k+1} \notin w_0w_k$ (see Figure 2.13(a)), then $(w_0, w_1, \ldots, w_k, w_{k+1})$ is also in the proper order by Lemma 2.2.5. So (w_k, w_{k+1}) is pushed on the stack as it is the next pair of opposite type. Otherwise, w_{k+1} has violated the proper order by Lemma 2.2.5 as $w_{k+1} \in w_0w_k$ (see Figure 2.13(b)). Scan W starting from w_{k+2} and locate a point w_j such that $w_j \notin w_0w_k$. So $(w_0, w_1, \ldots, w_k, w_j)$ is in the proper order by Lemma 2.2.5 and push (w_k, w_j) on the stack. If $w_k \in w_0w_{k-1}$ (see Figure 2.14(a)), w_k has violated the proper order by Lemma 2.2.5. Pop the stack till the pair (say, (w_j, w_{j+1})) is on top of the stack such that $w_k \in w_jw_{j+1}$. Scan W from w_{k+1} and locate a point $w_r \in w_jw_k$. It can be seen that w_r is a downward point and by Lemma 2.2.5, $(w_0, w_1, \ldots, w_j, w_r)$ is in the proper order. Push (w_j, w_r) on the stack.

Consider Case 4. By Lemma 2.2.4, z_i has violated the proper order as z_i is an upward point and $z_i \notin qz_{i-1}$ (see Figure 2.14(b)). Note that there is a winding around q in $bd(z_{i-1}, z_i)$. Traverse $bd(P_a)$ in counterclockwise order starting from z_i and compute intersection points $W = (w_0, w_1, ..., w_p)$, where $z_i = w_0$, between $bd(z_i, q)$ and $z_{i-1}z_i$. Clear the stack. Locate the pairs of opposite type in W from z_i toward z_{i-1} using the same method stated above for W. Partition P_a by adding segments corresponding to these pairs and the part containing q on its boundary is the new P_a. Execute $CC(P_a, q_r, q_l, L_r)$ with new P_a and new Z. Since Case 4 cannot occur again, $CC(P_a, q_r, q_l, L_r)$ terminates after the second round of execution. In the following, we state the major steps of the procedure $CC(P_a, q_r, q_l, L_r)$.

Step 1. Compute intersection points $Z = (z_0, z_1, ..., z_m)$ between L_r and $bd(P_a)$ in the order from q_r to q_l, where $z_0 = q_r$. Initialize i by 1 and h by 0.

Step 2. If z_i is a downward point not belonging to qz_h (see Case 1) *then*

Step 2a. Scan Z from z_{i+1} and locate a point z_k on qz_i.

Step 2b. *If* z_k is an upward point *then* push (z_i, z_k) on the stack and $i := k + 1$

else locate a point $z_j \in z_i z_k$ by scanning Z from z_{k+1}, push (z_i, z_j) on the stack and $i := j + 1$.

Step 2c. *If* all points of Z are considered *then goto* Step 10 *else* $h := i - 1$ and *goto* Step 2.

Step 3. *If* z_i is a downward point on qz_h (see Case 2) *then*

Step 3a. Let (z_k, z_r) denote the top element on the stack. Pop the stack until z_i is a point on $z_k z_r$. Scan Z from z_{i+1} and locate a point $z_j \in z_k z_i$. Pop the stack and push (z_k, z_j) on the stack.

Step 3b. *If* all points of Z are considered *then goto* Step 10 *else* $i := j+1$, $h := i-1$ and *goto* Step 2.

Step 4. *If* z_i is an upward point on qz_h (see Case 3) *then*

Step 4a. Scan Z from z_{i+1} and locate two consecutive downward points $z_j \in qz_h$ and $z_{j-1} \in qz_h$. *If* z_j and z_{j-1} are found *then* $i := j$ and *goto* Step 3.

Step 4b. Partition P_a by adding segments corresponding to pairs on the stack to P_a. Clear the stack.

Step 4c. Compute intersection points $W = (w_0, w_1, ..., w_p)$, where $w_0 = z_i$, between qz_i and $bd(z_i, q_l)$ in the order from z_i to q_l and *goto* Step 6.

Step 5. *If* z_i is an upward point not belonging to qz_h (see Case 4) *then*

Step 5a. Compute intersection points $W = (w_0, w_1, ..., w_p)$, where $w_0 = z_i$, between $z_h z_i$ and $bd(z_i, q_l)$ in the order from z_i to q_l.

Step 5b. Clear the stack.

Step 6. Initialize the stack by (w_0, w_1) and $k := 2$.

Step 7. *If* $w_k \notin w_0 w_{k-1}$ *then* locate a point $w_j \notin w_0 w_k$ by scanning W from w_{k+1}, push (w_k, w_j) on the stack, $k := j + 1$ and *goto* Step 9

Step 8. *If* $w_k \in w_0 w_{k-1}$ *then*

Step 8a. Let (w_j, w_t) denote the top element on the stack. Pop the stack till w_k is a point on $w_j w_t$.

Step 8b. Scan W from w_{k+1} and locate a point $w_r \in w_j w_k$. Pop the stack and push (w_j, w_r) on the stack.

Step 9. *If* all points of W are not considered *then goto* Step 7.

Step 10. Partition P_a by adding the segments corresponding to pairs on the stack to P_a and Stop.

The correctness of the procedure $CC(P_a, q_r, q_l, L_r)$ follows from Lemmas 2.2.3, 2.2.4 and 2.2.5. After the modification of P_a by $CC(P_a, q_r, q_l, L_r)$, P_a is again modified by the procedure $C(P_a, q_l, q_r, L_l)$, which gives the portion of the pruned polygon P_1 lying above the line L. Similarly, the portion of the pruned polygon P_1 lying below the line L is obtained by executing the procedures $C(P_b, q_r, q_l, L_r)$ and $CC(P_b, q_l, q_r, L_l)$. The union of these two portions gives P_1. Since each procedure

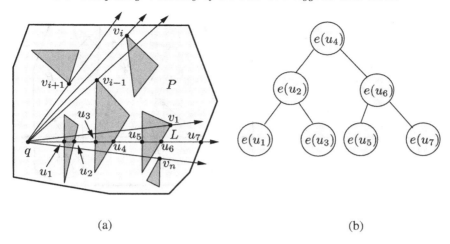

(a)   (b)

Figure 2.15 (a) The line L has intersected edges of P at u_1, u_2,..., u_7. (b) A balanced binary tree T is initialized by edges $e(u_1)$, $e(u_2)$,..., $e(u_7)$.

runs in $O(n)$ time, the algorithm takes $O(n)$ time. We summarize the result in the following theorem.

Theorem 2.2.6 *Given a point q inside a simple polygon P of n vertices, a sub-polygon P_1 of P containing both q and the visibility polygon of P from q can be computed in $O(n)$ time such that the boundary of P_1 does not wind around q.*

2.3 Computing Visibility of a Point in Polygons with Holes

In this section, we present the algorithm of Asano [27] for computing the visibility polygon $V(q)$ from a point q inside a polygon P with h holes with a total of n vertices. We first present an $O(n \log n)$ time algorithm based on *angular plane sweep*. Then we demonstrate how polygonal structures can be used to improve the time complexity of the algorithm to $O(n \log h)$.

The algorithm starts by drawing the horizontal line L from q to the right of q (see Figure 2.15(a)). Then it sorts the vertices of P based on their polar angles at q. The polar angle of a vertex v_j of P is the counterclockwise angle subtended by qv_j at q with L. Let $\theta(v_j)$ denote the polar angle of v_j. Vertices of P are labeled as v_1, v_2,..., v_n such that $\theta(v_{i-1}) < \theta(v_i) < \theta(v_{i+1})$ for all i (see Figure 2.15(a)).

Exercise 2.3.1 *A tree with a specific node as root is called a binary tree T if every node of T has either no child, a left child, a right child or both a left and a right child [15]. The height of T is the number of nodes in the longest path from the root to a leaf. Show that the maximum number of nodes in T of height h is $2^{h+1} - 1$.*

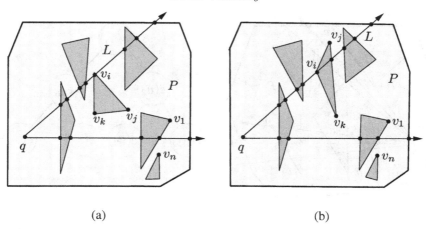

(a)   (b)

Figure 2.16 (a) Both edges of v_i are active edges and they are deleted from T. (b) The active edge $v_i v_k$ is replaced by the edge $v_i v_j$ in T.

Consider the intersection points of L with the edges of P (see Figure 2.15(a)). They can be ordered by sorting such that the distance from q to the intersection point u_i in the sorted list is less that of the intersection point u_j for all $i < j$. Accordingly, the polygonal edges $e(u_1)$, $e(u_2)$, ..., $e(u_k)$ are ordered from left to right along L, where $e(u_i)$ denotes the polygonal edge containing u_i. Let T denote a balanced binary tree, where $e(u_1)$, $e(u_2)$, ..., $e(u_k)$ are represented as nodes of T and if $e(u_i)$ is the left (or right) child of $e(u_j)$ in T, then $i < j$ (respectively, $j < i$) (see Figure 2.15(b)). So, $e(u_1)$ and $e(u_k)$ are the leftmost and rightmost leaves of T.

Suppose L is rotated around q in the counterclockwise direction. During the rotation, if an edge of P is intersected by the current position of L, the edge is called an *active edge* of P for that position of L. So, the list of active edges of P changes during the rotation (or angular sweep) of L and therefore, T also changes accordingly. Before we state the remaining steps for computing $V(q)$, we explain how the list of active edges of P changes during the angular sweep of L. We start with the following observation.

Lemma 2.3.1 *The list of active edges of P changes if and only if L sweeps a vertex of P.*

The above lemma suggests that T needs modification at each vertex of P during the angular sweep. Let us consider the situation when L passes through a vertex v_i. Let $v_i v_j$ and $v_i v_k$ be two polygonal edges incident at v_i. If both v_j and v_k lie to the right of $\overrightarrow{qv_i}$ (see Figure 2.16(a)), then $v_i v_j$ and $v_i v_k$ no longer remain active edges once L crosses v_i and therefore, the nodes of T containing $v_i v_j$ and $v_i v_k$ are deleted from T. Consider the situation when v_j and v_k lie to the opposite side of $\overrightarrow{qv_i}$ (see

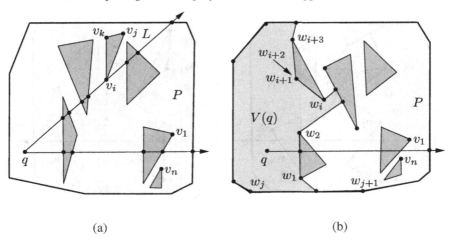

(a)   (b)

Figure 2.17 (a) Both edges v_iv_k and v_iv_j are not active edges and they are inserted in T. (b) Since $w_{i+1} = w_{i+2}$, no constructed edge is introduced at this vertex.

Figure 2.16(b)). Let v_k be the vertex lying to the right of $\overrightarrow{qv_i}$. It can be seen that v_iv_j becomes a new active edge. On the other hand, v_iv_k is not an active edge once L crosses v_i. So, v_iv_k is replaced by v_iv_j in T. If both v_j and v_k lie to the left of $\overrightarrow{qv_i}$ (see Figure 2.17(a)), then v_iv_j and v_iv_k become new active edges and therefore, two nodes representing them are inserted in T.

Let us return to the description of the algorithm. After initializing T, the algorithm traverses the sorted list $v_1, v_2,..., v_n$ starting from v_1. Suppose the algorithm has processed from v_1 to v_{i-1} and v_i is currently under consideration. It performs one of the three operations on T for v_i: $Delete(T, i)$, $Update(T, i)$ and $Insert(T, i)$. $Delete(T, i)$ is performed if both edges of v_i are active edges (see Figure 2.16(a)). So, the nodes corresponding to the edges of v_i are deleted from T. $Update(T, i)$ is performed when one of two edges of v_i is an active edge (see Figure 2.16(b)). So, the active edge of v_i in T is replaced by the other edge of v_i. $Insert(T, i)$ is performed if both edges of v_i are not active edges (see Figure 2.17(a)). $Insert(T, i)$ locates two nodes in T by binary search, where one node is the parent of other node in T, such that v_i lies between the two active edges represented by these two nodes in T. Then both edges of v_i are inserted as two new nodes in T in the position of T located by the binary search. Note that after each operation of $Insert(T, i)$ or $Delete(T, i)$, T is balanced again. We have the following lemma.

Lemma 2.3.2 *Any point z on a polygonal edge $e(z)$ is visible from q if and only if $e(z)$ is the left most leaf of T at some stage of the angular sweep of L.*

The above lemma can be used to construct $V(q)$ as follows. Let $W = (w_1w_2, w_3w_4, \ldots, w_jw_{j+1})$ be the ordered set of edges of P appeared in the leftmost leaf of

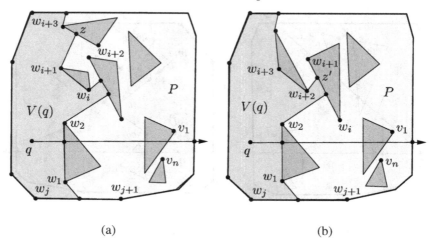

Figure 2.18 (a) The segment $w_{i+1}z$ is the constructed edge at w_{i+1}. (b) The segment $z'w_{i+2}$ is the constructed edge at w_{i+2}.

T during the angular sweep of L from its initial position to the final position (see Figure 2.17(b)). So, w_1w_2 is the first active edge in the leftmost leaf of T when T is initialized, and w_jw_{j+1} is the last active edge in the leftmost leaf of T. We have the following observation.

Lemma 2.3.3 *Two endpoints of every constructed edge of $V(q)$ belong to two consecutive edges w_iw_{i+1} and $w_{i+2}w_{i+3}$ of W and one of the endpoints of the constructed edge is either w_{i+1} or w_{i+2}.*

The above lemma can be used for computing constructed edges of $V(q)$. Consider any two consecutive edges w_iw_{i+1} and $w_{i+2}w_{i+3}$. If w_{i+1} is same as w_{i+2} (see Figure 2.17(b)), then no constructed edge is introduced. Otherwise, either w_{i+1} or w_{i+2} is the vertex of the constructed edge (see Figure 2.18). If the extension of the line segment qw_{i+1} from w_{i+1} meets $w_{i+2}w_{i+3}$ at some point (say, z), then $w_{i+1}z$ is the constructed edge (see Figure 2.18(a)). Otherwise, the extension of the line segment qw_{i+2} from w_{i+2} meets w_iw_{i+1} at some point (say, z'). So, $z'w_{i+2}$ is the constructed edge (see Figure 2.18(b)). Thus, all constructed edges of $V(q)$ can be computed by considering all pairs of consecutive edges of W. In the following, we present the major steps for computing $V(q)$.

Step 1. Draw the horizontal line L from q to the right of q and compute the intersection points of L with edges of P.

Step 2. Sort the intersection points from left to right along L. Let $(u_1, u_2, \ldots, u_k)$ be the sorted order of intersection points along L.

Step 3. Represent edges $e(u_1), e(u_2), \ldots, e(u_k)$ as nodes and connect them according to the sorted order $(u_1, u_2, \ldots, u_k)$ to form a balanced binary tree T.

Step 4. Sort the vertices of P based on their polar angle and label them accordingly as v_1, v_2,..., v_n. Initialize the index i by 1.

Step 5. *If* both edges of v_i are active edges *then*

Step 5a. *Delete*(T, i).

Step 5b. *If* there is a change in the leftmost leaf of T *then* compute the intersection point z of $\overrightarrow{qv_i}$ and the edge currently in the leftmost leaf of T *and* add $v_i z$ to the list of constructed edges.

Step 5c. *Goto* Step 8.

Step 6. *If* one edge of v_i is an active edge *then Update*(T, i) *and goto* Step 8.

Step 7. *If* both edges of v_i are not active edges *then*

Step 7a. *Insert*(T, i).

Step 7b. *If* there is a change in the leftmost leaf of T *then* compute the intersection point z' of $\overrightarrow{qv_i}$ and the edge previously in the leftmost leaf of T *and* add $z'v_i$ to the list of constructed edges.

Step 8. *If* $i \neq n$ *then* $i := i + 1$ *and goto* Step 5.

Step 9. Output $V(q)$ and Stop.

The correctness of the algorithm follows from Lemmas 2.3.1, 2.3.2 and 2.3.3. Let us now analyze the time complexity of the algorithm. Intersection points of the edges of P with L in Step 1 can be computed in $O(n)$ time. Sorting of intersection points based on their distance to q in Step 2 takes $O(n \log n)$ time. Step 3 takes $O(n)$ time to initialize T. Step 4 takes $O(n \log n)$ time to sort the vertices of P according to their polar angles. Since the height of T is $O(\log n)$, one operation of *Insert*(T, i) or *Delete*(T, i) can be done in $O(\log n)$ time [15]. Therefore, the total time taken for these two operations is $O(n \log n)$ as there can be at most n such operations. Since one operation of *Update*(T, i) takes $O(1)$ time, total time for this operation is $O(n)$. All constructed edges in $V(q)$ can be computed in $O(n)$ time as each constructed edge can be computed in $O(1)$ time. Therefore, Steps 5, 6 and 7 together take $O(n \log n)$ time. Hence, the overall time complexity of the algorithm is $O(n \log n)$. We summarize the result in the following theorem.

Theorem 2.3.4 *The visibility polygon $V(q)$ of a point q in a polygon P with holes with a total of n vertices can be computed in $O(n \log n)$ time.*

We modify the above algorithm to derive an $O(n \log h)$ time algorithm for computing $V(q)$. Let H_1, H_2,..., H_h be the holes inside P. For every hole H_i, compute the boundary of H_i that is externally visible from q (denoted as $BV(H_i, q)$) by the algorithm of Lee stated in Section 2.2. So, the line segment joining q and any point z of $BV(H_i, q)$ is not intersected by any edge of H_i as the vertices of $BV(H_i, q)$ are in the sorted angular order with respect to q. Since all holes of P except H_i are ignored while computing $BV(H_i, q)$, qz may be intersected by an edge of some other hole H_j for $i \neq j$.

We know that the boundary of P consists of boundaries of H_1, H_2,..., H_h and the outer boundary of P enclosing all holes. So the algorithm also computes the portion of the outer boundary of P internally visible from q ignoring all holes. Since this visible boundary is like the visible boundary of any other hole, we can consider that P has $h + 1$ holes. However, for simplicity of notation, we assume that no point of the outer boundary of P belongs to $V(q)$ and therefore, it is enough to consider holes H_1, H_2,..., H_h for computing $V(q)$. We have the following observation on $BV(H_i, q)$.

Lemma 2.3.5 *Let z be a point on the boundary of H_i for some i. If z belongs to the boundary of $V(q)$, then $z \in BV(H_i, q)$.*

The above lemma suggests that in order to compute $V(q)$, it is sufficient to consider $BV(H_i, q)$ for all i. This property can be used to design an $O(n \log h)$ time algorithm for computing $V(q)$ as follows. The algorithm starts by drawing the horizontal line L from q to the right of q and locates the edges of $BV(H_i, q)$ for all i that are intersected by L. Ordering these intersected edges from left to right along L takes $O(h \log h)$ time as L can intersect only one edge of $BV(H_i, q)$ for every i. These edges are represented as nodes of a balanced binary tree T as described in the earlier algorithm and it can be done in $O(h)$ time. Observe that L intersects only one edge of $BV(H_i, q)$ not only for the initial position of L but also for any position of L during the angular sweep, which suggests the following lemma.

Lemma 2.3.6 *The number of nodes in T is at most h during the angular sweep of L.*

Corollary 2.3.7 *Each $Delete(T, i)$ or $Insert(T, i)$ operation takes $O(\log h)$ time.*

Let S denote the list of union of vertices of $BV(H_1, q)$, $BV(H_2, q), \ldots, BV(H_h, q)$ in the sorted angular order around q in the counterclockwise direction. Since S can have $O(n)$ vertices, direct sorting takes $O(n \log n)$ time. To keep the time complexity of the algorithm bounded by $O(n \log h)$, we need a different approach for constructing S. Let S_i denote the list of vertices of $BV(H_i, q)$ in clockwise order. So, the first vertex and the last vertex of S_i make the minimum and maximum polar angles at q, respectively, among the vertices of S_i. We show that S can be obtained by merging $S_1, S_2, \ldots, S_h$ in $O(n \log h)$ time using a heap [15].

Initially, the heap contains all vertices of active edges in T that are above L. These vertices are placed in the heap based on their polar angles at q. So, the root of the heap contains the vertex (say w) whose polar angle at q is the smallest in the heap (see Figure 2.19). The heap is used to find the next vertex in S. After initializing

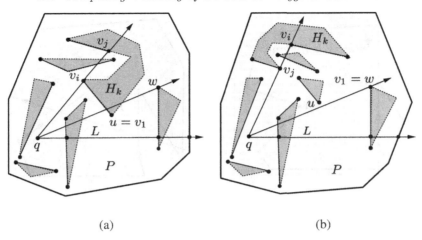

(a)   (b)

Figure 2.19 (a) The first vertex u in S' is v_1. (b) The vertex w in the root of the heap is v_1.

the heap, the algorithm takes only the first and last vertices from every S_i and sorts these $2h$ vertices according to their polar angles at q in $O(h \log h)$ time. Let us denote this sorted list by S'. Let u denote the first vertex in S'. If $\theta(u) < \theta(w)$ (see Figure 2.19(a)), then u is the first vertex v_1 in S. Let u belong to S_k for some k. So the next vertex of u in S_k is added to the heap. The new vertex in the root of the heap becomes the current w and the next vertex of u in S' becomes the current u. If $\theta(u) > \theta(w)$ (see Figure 2.19(b)), then w is the first vertex v_1 in S and w is removed from the heap. Then the new vertex currently in the root of the heap becomes w. The process is repeated till the entire S is constructed. Since there can be at most h vertices in the heap, it takes $O(\log h)$ time to find the vertex whose polar angle at q is the smallest in the heap. Therefore, S can be constructed in $O(n \log h)$ time.

After S is constructed, the algorithm performs the angular sweep of L and performs one of the three operations $Delete(T, i)$, $Update(T, i)$ and $Insert(T, i)$ on T at each vertex of S as in the the earlier algorithm. However, there is a small difference. $Delete(T, i)$ removes one edge from T instead of two edges. The same is true for $Insert(T, i)$. Then the algorithm constructs $V(q)$ from the active edges that appear in the leftmost leaf of T as before.

The above method constructs $V(q)$ correctly if there is no intersection between a constructed edge of $BV(H_k, q)$ with an edge of a hole H_p for $p \neq k$. If such an intersection takes place (see Figure 2.19), ordering of the active edges along L changes at the place of intersection. The correct order of active edges along L can be represented in T by modifying the operation $Update(T, i)$ as follows. Suppose $Update(T, i)$ is to be performed at some vertex v_i to replace the active edge of v_i by the other edge of v_i (say, $v_i v_j$) which is a constructed edge of $BV(H_k, q)$ for some k (see Figure 2.19). Without loss of generality, we assume that v_j is the next clockwise vertex of v_i in S_k. Note that one of v_i and v_j is actually a point on the

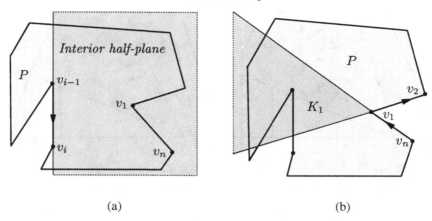

(a)   (b)

Figure 2.20 (a) The shaded region is the interior half-plane of $\overline{v_{i-1}v_i}$. (b) The common intersection region K_1 of the interior half-planes of $\overline{v_n v_1}$ and $\overline{v_1 v_2}$.

boundary of H_k and the point is treated as a vertex in S. Instead of replacing one edge of v_i by the other edge, the operation $Update(T, i)$ performs $Delete(T, i)$ and $Insert(T, j)$ operations. Thus, the ordering of active edges along L is correctly maintained without increasing the overall time complexity of the algorithm. We summarize the result in the following theorem.

Theorem 2.3.8 *The visibility polygon $V(q)$ of a point q in a polygon P with h holes with a total of n vertices can be computed in $O(n \log h)$ time.*

Corollary 2.3.9 *The visibility polygon of a point in a convex polygon P with h convex holes with a total of n vertices can be computed in $O(n + h \log h)$ time.*

2.4 Recognizing Simple Polygons Visible from a Point

In this section, we present the algorithm of Lee and Preparata [234] for computing the kernel of a simple polygon P of n vertices in $O(n)$ time. If the kernel of P is not empty, then P is the visibility polygon of P from any point of the kernel. We assume that the vertices of P are labeled $v_1, v_2, \ldots, v_n$ in counterclockwise order, where v_1 is a reflex vertex. We also assume that the given polygon P is a non-winding polygon (i.e., the revolution number of P is one) as the kernel of a winding polygon is always empty.

Suppose an edge $v_{i-1}v_i$ of P is extended from both ends and this line $\overleftrightarrow{v_{i-1}v_i}$ divides the plane into half-planes (see Figure 2.20(a)). The half-plane that lies to the left (or right) of $\overrightarrow{v_{i-1}v_i}$ is called the *interior half-plane* (respectively, *exterior half-plane*) of $\overline{v_{i-1}v_i}$. It can be seen that the interior half-plane of $\overline{v_{i-1}v_i}$ is same as the exterior half-plane of $\overline{v_i v_{i-1}}$. We have the following lemma.

Lemma 2.4.1 *The kernel of P is the intersection of the interior half-planes of $\overline{v_1 v_2}$, $\overline{v_2 v_3}, \ldots, \overline{v_n v_1}$.*

Exercise 2.4.1 *Prove Lemma 2.4.1.*

The above characterization immediately suggests an algorithm for computing the kernel of P in $O(n^2)$ time. Using the divide and conquer, the time complexity can be improved to $O(n \log n)$ [291].

Exercise 2.4.2 *Let Q_1 and Q_2 be two convex polygons (without holes) with a total of m vertices. Design an algorithm for computing the common intersection region of Q_1 and Q_2 in $O(m)$ time [291].*

Exercise 2.4.3 *Using Exercise 2.4.2, design an $O(n \log n)$ time algorithm for computing the common intersection region of n arbitrary half-planes by divide and conquer [291].*

The algorithm of Lee and Preparata incrementally constructs the kernel of P in $O(n)$ time taking advantage of the structure of a polygon as follows. The algorithm starts by constructing the common intersection region K_1 of the interior half-planes of $\overline{v_n v_1}$ and $\overline{v_1 v_2}$ (see Figure 2.20(b)). Then it constructs two tangents from v_1 to K_1, which are two rays from v_1, one in the direction of $\overrightarrow{v_n v_1}$ and the other in the direction of $\overrightarrow{v_2 v_1}$. Note that the two tangents are rays as K_1 is unbounded. Next, it constructs K_2 by computing the intersection of K_1 with the interior half-plane of $\overline{v_2 v_3}$. While computing K_2, tangents from v_2 to K_2 are also located. Then, it constructs K_3 by computing the intersection of K_2 with the interior half-plane of $\overline{v_3 v_4}$ and so on till K_{n-1} is computed, which is the kernel of P by Lemma 2.4.1. It can be seen that $K_1, K_2, \ldots, K_{n-1}$ are convex. We now describe the method for computing $K_1, K_2, \ldots, K_{n-1}$.

Assume that the algorithm has computed K_{i-1} by computing the intersection of interior half-planes of $\overline{v_n v_1}, \overline{v_1 v_2}, \ldots, \overline{v_{i-1} v_i}$. In the next stage, K_i is computed from the intersection of K_{i-1} and the interior half-plane of $\overline{v_i v_{i+1}}$. We also assume that two tangents from v_i to K_{i-1} have been computed. Let $v_i l_i$ and $v_i r_i$ denote the *left* and *right tangents* from v_i to K_{i-1} (see Figure 2.21), where l_i and r_i are two corner points of K_{i-1} such that no point of K_{i-1} lies to the left of $\overrightarrow{v_i l_i}$ and to the right of $\overrightarrow{v_i r_i}$. The following cases can arise depending upon the positions of l_i and r_i with respect to $\overline{v_i v_{i+1}}$.

Case 1. Both points l_i and r_i lie to the right of $\overrightarrow{v_i v_{i+1}}$ (see Figure 2.21(a)).
Case 2. Both points l_i and r_i lie to the left of $\overrightarrow{v_i v_{i+1}}$ (see Figure 2.21(b)).
Case 3. Points l_i and r_i lie on the opposite sides of $\overrightarrow{v_i v_{i+1}}$ (see Figure 2.22).

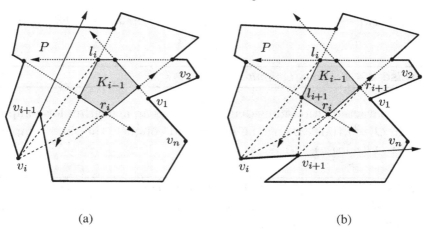

(a)   (b)

Figure 2.21 (a) The entire region K_{i-1} lies in the exterior half-plane of $\overline{v_i v_{i+1}}$. (b) The entire region K_{i-1} lies in the interior half-plane of $\overline{v_i v_{i+1}}$.

Consider Case 1. Since both points l_i and r_i lie to the right of $\overrightarrow{v_i v_{i+1}}$, the entire K_{i-1} lies in the exterior half-plane of $\overline{v_i v_{i+1}}$ (see Figure 2.21(a)). Hence, P is not a star-shaped polygon as the kernel of P is empty.

Consider Case 2. Since both points l_i and r_i lie to the left of $\overrightarrow{v_i v_{i+1}}$, the entire K_{i-1} lies in the interior half-plane of $\overline{v_i v_{i+1}}$ (see Figure 2.21(b)). So, $K_i = K_{i-1}$. Scan the boundary of K_{i-1} from l_i in counterclockwise order till a corner point u is reached such that no point of K_i lies to the left of $\overline{v_{i+1} u}$. Hence, $v_{i+1} u$ is the left tangent from v_{i+1} to K_i and l_{i+1} is u. Similarly, scan the boundary of K_{i-1} from r_i in counterclockwise order till a corner point w is reached such no point of K_i lies to the right of $\overline{v_{i+1} w}$. Hence, $v_{i+1} w$ is the right tangent from v_{i+1} to K_i and r_{i+1} is w.

Consider Case 3. Since l_i and r_i lie to the opposite sides of $\overrightarrow{v_i v_{i+1}}$, the line $\overrightarrow{v_i v_{i+1}}$ intersects K_{i-1} (see Figure 2.22). So, a part of K_{i-1} has to be removed to obtain K_i. Let z and z' be the intersection points of $\overline{v_i v_{i+1}}$ with the boundary of K_{i-1}, where $z \in z' v_i$. The following observations help in computing z and z'.

Lemma 2.4.2 *Assume that $\overline{v_i v_{i+1}}$ has intersected K_{i-1}. If v_i is a reflex vertex, l_i and r_i lie in the exterior and interior half-planes of $\overline{v_i v_{i+1}}$, respectively (Figure 2.22(a)).*

Lemma 2.4.3 *Assume that $\overline{v_i v_{i+1}}$ has intersected K_{i-1}. If v_i is a convex vertex, r_i and l_i lie in the exterior and interior half-planes of $\overline{v_i v_{i+1}}$, respectively (Figure 2.22(b)).*

The above lemmas suggest a simple way to compute z and z' by traversing the boundary of K_{i-1} as follows. Consider the situation when v_i is a reflex vertex (see Figure 2.22(a)). Scan the boundary of K_{i-1} from l_i in counterclockwise (or

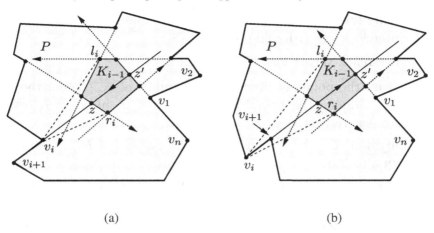

(a)   (b)

Figure 2.22 (a) Since v_i is a reflex vertex, the part of K_{i-1} containing l_i is removed. (b) Since v_i is a convex vertex, the part of K_{i-1} containing r_i is removed.

clockwise) order to locate the intersection point z (respectively, z'). Partition K_{i-1} using the segment zz'. By Lemma 2.4.2, the portion of K_{i-1} containing l_i does not belong to K_i. Therefore, the other part (which contains r_i) is K_i. Observe that z is l_{i+1}. The right tangent $v_{i+1}r_{i+1}$ can be located by scanning the boundary of K_i from r_i in counterclockwise order as stated earlier. Consider the situation when v_i is a convex vertex (Figure 2.22(b)). Again, scan the boundary of K_{i-1} from r_i in clockwise (respectively, counterclockwise) order to locate the intersection point z (respectively, z'). Note that z or z' may lie on the edge v_iv_{i+1} as v_i is convex. Partition K_{i-1} using the segment zz' and by Lemma 2.4.3, the portion of K_{i-1} containing r_i is removed to obtain K_i. Observe that z is r_{i+1}. The left tangent $v_{i+1}l_{i+1}$ can be located by scanning the boundary of K_i from l_i in counterclockwise order as stated earlier. In the following, we present the major steps for computing the kernel of P.

Step 1. Compute the intersection of the interior half-planes of $\overline{v_nv_1}$ and $\overline{v_1v_2}$ and assign it to K_1. Take a point z on $\overrightarrow{v_1v_2}$ lying outside the convex hull of P and assign z to l_2. Take a point z' on $\overline{v_nv_1}$ lying outside the convex hull of P and assign z' to r_2. Initialize the index i by 2.

Step 2. If both l_i and r_i lie to the right of $\overrightarrow{v_iv_{i+1}}$ (Figure 2.21(a)) *then* report that the kernel of P is empty and Stop.

Step 3. If both l_i and r_i lie to the left of $\overrightarrow{v_iv_{i+1}}$ *then* (Figure 2.21(b))

    Step 3a. Assign K_{i-1} to K_i.

    Step 3b. Locate the left tangent $v_{i+1}l_{i+1}$ by scanning the boundary of K_i from l_i in counterclockwise order.

Step 3c. Locate the right tangent $v_{i+1}r_{i+1}$ by scanning the boundary of K_i from r_i in counterclockwise order and *goto* Step 8.

Step 4. *If v_i is a reflex vertex then* (Figure 2.22(a))

Step 4a. Locate the points of intersection z and z' of $\overrightarrow{v_{i+1}v_i}$ and the boundary of K_{i-1} by scanning the boundary of K_{i-1} from l_i in counterclockwise and clockwise order, respectively.

Step 4b. Partition K_{i-1} by zz' and assign the portion of K_{i-1} containing r_i to K_i. Assign z to l_{i+1}.

Step 4c. Locate the right tangent $v_{i+1}r_{i+1}$ by scanning the boundary of K_i from r_i in counterclockwise order and *goto* Step 8.

Step 5. Locate the points of intersection z and z' of $\overrightarrow{v_iv_{i+1}}$ and the boundary of K_{i-1} by scanning the boundary of K_{i-1} from r_i in clockwise and counterclockwise order, respectively (see Figure 2.22(b)).

Step 6. Partition K_{i-1} by zz' and assign the portion of K_{i-1} containing l_i to K_i. Assign z' to r_{i+1}.

Step 7. Locate the left tangent $v_{i+1}l_{i+1}$ by scanning the boundary of K_i from l_i in counterclockwise order.

Step 8. *If $i \neq n-1$ then $i := i+1$* and *goto* Step 2.

Step 9. Report K_{n-1} as the kernel of P and Stop.

Let us discuss the correctness of the algorithm. For computing K_i from K_{i-1}, the algorithm checks whether $\overline{v_iv_{i+1}}$ intersects K_{i-1}. If there is no intersection, K_{i-1} lies entirely in the interior or exterior half-plane of $\overline{v_iv_{i+1}}$. If the entire K_{i-1} lies in the exterior half-plane of $\overline{v_iv_{i+1}}$ (see Figure 2.21(a)), the common intersection region of interior half-planes becomes empty and therefore, P is not a star-shaped polygon by Lemma 2.4.1. So, the algorithm terminates in Step 2. If the entire K_{i-1} lies in the interior half-plane of $\overline{v_iv_{i+1}}$ (see Figure 2.21(b)), the common intersection region of half-planes is same as K_{i-1}. So, K_{i-1} is assigned to K_i in Step 3. If $\overline{v_iv_{i+1}}$ intersects K_{i-1} (Figure 2.22), one part of K_{i-1} is the common intersection region of interior half-planes. The algorithm uses Lemmas 2.4.2 and 2.4.3 in Steps 4 and 6 to decide which part of K_{i-1} is the common intersection region of interior half-planes, and K_i is assigned accordingly. Thus the algorithm correctly computes K_{n-1} which is the kernel of P by Lemma 2.4.1.

The overall time complexity of the algorithm consists of (i) the time for computing $K_1, K_2, \ldots, K_{n-1}$, and (ii) the time for locating the left and right tangents for all vertices. It can be seen that two corner points can be introduced in the common intersection region by a half-plane and therefore, the total number of corner points that can be introduced is at most $2n$. Since the cost for computing K_i from K_{i-1} for all i is proportional to the number of corner points removed from K_{i-1}, the time taken for computing $K_1, K_2, \ldots, K_{n-1}$ is $O(n)$. The time for locating the left and right tangents for all vertices is $O(n)$, as the tangents move around the common intersection region of interior half-planes once in counterclockwise order. Hence, the overall time complexity of the algorithm is $O(n)$. We summarize the result in the following theorem.

Theorem 2.4.4 *The kernel of an n-sided simple polygon P can be computed in $O(n)$ time.*

Corollary 2.4.5 *Recognizing an n-sided simple polygon P visible from an internal point can be done in $O(n)$ time.*

2.5 Notes and Comments

Let us consider the parallel algorithms for point visibility problems investigated in this chapter. Computing the visibility polygon from a point in a polygon P with holes was first considered by Atallah and Goodrich [38]. Their algorithm runs in $O(\log n \log \log n)$ time using $O(n)$ processors in the CREW-PRAM model of computations. Using the cascading divide and conquer technique, Atallah *et al.* [37] showed that the visibility polygon of P from a point can be computed in $O(\log n)$ time using $O(n)$ processors in the CREW-PRAM model of computations. Independently, Bertolazzi *et al.* [45] gave another algorithm for this problem which also runs in $O(\log n)$ time using $O(n)$ processors in the CREW-PRAM model of computations.

Although the above algorithms also work for polygons without holes, Atallah and Chen [32] showed that a faster algorithm is possible for this problem if the given polygon P is simple. They showed that the visibility polygon of P from a point can be computed in $O(\log n)$ time using $O(n/\log n)$ processors in the CREW-PRAM model of computations. Finally, Atallah *et al.* [36] gave an optimal algorithm for this problem which runs in $O(\log n)$ time using $O(n/\log n)$ processors in the EREW-PRAM model of computations. Their algorithm starts by partitioning the boundary of P into chains. For each chain, it computes the portion of the chain whose vertices are in sorted angular order with respect to the given point. Then these chains are tested for intersections among themselves by exploiting polygonal properties. Finally, appropriate portions of these chains between intersection points are combined to form the visible boundary of P. If P is a star-shaped polygon, the visible boundary of P can be computed by a simple algorithm of Ghosh and Maheshwari [160], which also runs in $O(\log n)$ time using $O(n/\log n)$ processors in the EREW-PRAM model of computations.

Consider the problem of computing the kernel of a simple polygon P. We know that the sequential algorithm of Lee and Preparata [234] incrementally constructs the kernel of P. This means that their method does not directly lead to a parallel algorithm. Using a different approach, Chen [81] showed that the kernel of P can be computed in $O(\log n)$ time using $O(n/\log n)$ processors in the EREW-PRAM model of computations.

Let us mention results on the problems of visibility with reflections. Let q be a point light source inside a simple polygon P. Let $z \in P$ be a point such that z is not visible from q directly. If light rays from q are allowed to reflect on edges of P, z can become visible from q. This means that certain portions of P, which are not visible directly from q, may become visible due to one or more reflections on the edges of P. Observe that since rays after reflection may intersect each other, the boundary of visible portions of P may contain several intersection points of these rays.

There are two types of reflection. Reflection at a point is called *specular reflection* if the reflected ray follows the standard law of reflection; i.e., the angle of incidence is same as the angle of reflection. If reflecting edges are not perfect, another type of reflection called *diffuse reflection* can take place, where a light ray that is incident at a point is reflected in all possible directions toward the interior of P. Aronov *et al.* [25] studied the size of the visibility polygon for one specular or diffuse reflection. Corresponding problems for multiple specular or diffuse reflections were studied by Aronov *et al.* [24], Prasad *et al.* [289] and Pal *et al.* [281].

Exercise 2.5.1 *Draw a simple polygon P where there exists two points u and v in P such that if a light source is placed at u, no light ray from u reaches v by specular reflections on edges of P [328].*

Let us consider the visibility-based, pursuit-evasion problem in a polygon P. A point pursuer is assigned a task of locating moving evaders that are present in P. The evaders are also assumed to be points and are allowed to move in P continuously with unbounded speed. To solve the problem, the pursuer must move in P in such a way that every evader becomes visible to the pursuer eventually. This problem was first considered by Suzuki and Yamashita [323]. They gave algorithms for the movement of the pursuer in special classes of polygons having omni-directional visibility or flashlights. Guibas *et al.* [180] gave a complete solution for this problem for the case of omni-directional visibility. The variations of this problem in different types of polygons with one or more pursuers having omni-directional visibility or a given number of flashlights have been studied by Crass *et al.* [98], Lee *et al.* [236, 237], Park *et al.* [282], LaValle *et al.* [228], Suzuki *et al.* [322], Suzuki *et al.* [324] and Yamashita *et al.* [344]. For related problems, see LaValle [227] and Zhang [347].

Exercise 2.5.2 *Let Q be a set of m points inside a simple polygon P of n vertices. Design an algorithm for locating a point $z \in P$ (if it exists) in $O((n + m) \log(n + m))$ time such that all points of Q are visible from z in P [153].*

Exercise 2.5.3 *Let S be a subset of vertices of a polygon P with or without holes. Design a polynomial time algorithm to test whether every internal point of P is visible from some vertex of S [152].*

3

Weak Visibility and Shortest Paths

3.1 Problems and Results

The notion of weak visibility of a polygon from a segment was introduced by Avis and Toussaint [42] in the context of the art gallery problem. They considered a variation of the problem when there is only one guard and the guard is permitted to move along an edge of the polygon. They defined visibility from an edge $v_i v_{i+1}$ in a simple polygon P in three different ways.

(i) P is said to be *completely visible* from $v_i v_{i+1}$ if every point $z \in P$ and any point $w \in v_i v_{i+1}$, w and z are visible (Figure 3.1(a)).

(ii) P is said to be *strongly visible* from $v_i v_{i+1}$ if there exists a point $w \in v_i v_{i+1}$ such that for every point $z \in P$, w and z are visible (Figure 3.1(b)).

(iii) P is said to be *weakly visible* from $v_i v_{i+1}$ if each point $z \in P$, there exists a point $w \in v_i v_{i+1}$ (depending on z) such that w and z are visible (Figure 3.1(c)).

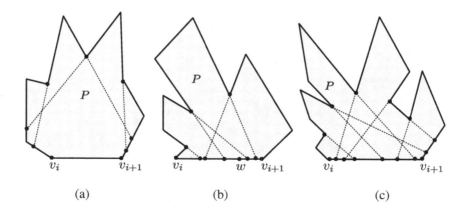

Figure 3.1 The polygon P is (a) completely, (b) strongly and (c) weakly visible from the edge $v_i v_{i+1}$.

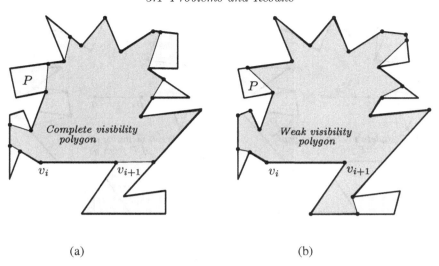

(a)   (b)

Figure 3.2 The (a) complete and (b) weak visibility polygons of P from the edge $v_i v_{i+1}$.

If P is completely visible from $v_i v_{i+1}$, the guard can be positioned at any point w on $v_i v_{i+1}$. In other words, P and the visibility polygon $V(w)$ of P from any point $w \in v_i v_{i+1}$ are same. If P is strongly visible from $v_i v_{i+1}$, there exists at least one point w on $v_i v_{i+1}$ from which the guard can see the entire P, i.e., $P = V(w)$. Finally, if P is weakly visible from $v_i v_{i+1}$, it is necessary for the guard to patrol along $v_i v_{i+1}$ in order to see the entire P.

> **Exercise 3.1.1** *Determine in $O(n)$ time whether a simple polygon P is completely or strongly visible from a given edge $v_j v_{j+1}$ of P [42].*

The above definitions for weak visibility also hold if P is a polygon with holes. It can be seen that there is no polygon with holes which is completely or strongly visible from an edge. However, the complete visibility polygon of P with or without holes can be defined as follows. A point $z \in P$ is called *completely visible* from an edge $v_i v_{i+1}$ if it is visible to every point of $v_i v_{i+1}$. The set of all points of P completely visible from $v_i v_{i+1}$ is called the *complete visibility polygon* of P from $v_i v_{i+1}$ (see Figure 3.2(a)). Similarly, a point $z \in P$ is said to be *weakly visible* from an edge $v_i v_{i+1}$ if it is visible to some point of $v_i v_{i+1}$. The set of all points of P weakly visible from $v_i v_{i+1}$ is called the *weak visibility polygon* of P from $v_i v_{i+1}$ (see Figure 3.2(b)). A more general notion of complete and weak visibility polygons allows visibility of P from an internal segment pq, not necessary an edge (see Figure 3.3).

Let us consider the problem of computing the complete visibility polygon from an internal segment pq in a polygon P with or without holes (see Figure 3.3(a)). Consider any point $z \in P$ that is visible from both endpoints p and q. If P is a

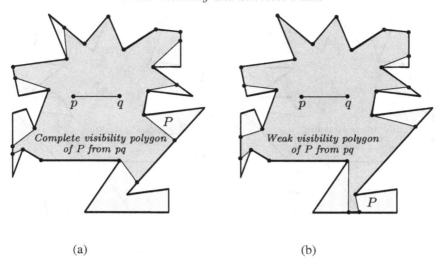

Figure 3.3 The (a) complete and (b) weak visibility polygons of P from an internal segment pq.

simple polygon, then z is completely visible from pq. If P contains holes, then the region enclosed by segments pq, qz and zp may contain a hole. In that case z may not be completely visible from pq. The following lemma suggests a way to compute the complete visibility polygon from pq inside P.

Lemma 3.1.1 *The complete visibility polygon from a line pq in a polygon P with or without holes is the visibility polygon from q inside the visibility polygon of P from p.*

   The above lemma suggests first to compute $V(p)$ inside P which can be done in $O(n \log n)$ time if P has holes (see Section 2.3) and in $O(n)$ time if P is a simple polygon (see Section 2.2). Then the visibility polygon from q inside $V(p)$ can be computed in $O(n)$ time to obtain the complete visibility polygon from pq inside P. On the other hand, it is not a straightforward task to compute the weak visibility polygon of a segment pq in a polygon P with or without holes (see Figure 3.3(b)). If P is a polygon without holes, ElGindy [127], Lee and Lin [232], and Chazelle and Guibas [76] gave $O(n \log n)$ time algorithms for this problem. Guibas *et al.* [178] showed that this problem can be solved in $O(n)$ time if a triangulation of P is given along with P. Since P can be triangulated in $O(n)$ time by the algorithm of Chazelle [71] (see Theorem 1.4.6), the algorithm of Guibas *et al.* [178] runs in $O(n)$ time. In Section 3.3.1, we present the algorithm of Lee and Lin [232] which computes the weak visibility polygon by scanning the boundary of P. We present the algorithm of Guibas *et al.* [178] in Section 3.3.2.

The relation between weak visibility polygons and *Euclidean shortest paths* was first observed by Guibas *et al.* [178] and Toussaint [330]. Their characterization was in terms of *Euclidean shortest paths* from p and q to every vertex of a weak visibility polygon, which was later used by them in computing the weak visibility polygon from pq. Ghosh *et al.* [163] generalized this characterization for any two vertices of a weak visibility polygon, which helped in recognizing weak visibility polygons. It has been shown by Icking and Klein [200], Das *et al.* [100] and Bhattacharya and Mukhopadhyay [50] that weak visibility polygons can also be characterized in terms of *non-redundant components*. In the next section (i.e., Section 3.2), we state these characterizations of weak visibility polygons along with some properties of *Euclidean shortest paths*.

The union of *Euclidean shortest paths* from a vertex to all vertices of a simple polygon is called the *shortest path tree* (see Figure 3.24(a)). The shortest path tree has been used extensively as a tool in computational geometry for computing visibility in a polygon. Guibas *et al.* [178] presented an $O(n)$ time algorithm for computing the shortest path tree in a triangulated simple polygon, which they also used in computing weak visibility polygon from a segment. We present their algorithm in Section 3.6.1 for computing the shortest path tree.

For computing the weak visibility polygon from a line segment in a polygon with holes, Suri and O'Rourke [321] presented an $O(n^4)$ time algorithm. The algorithm is worst-case optimal as there are polygons with holes whose weak visibility polygon from a given segment can have $O(n^4)$ vertices. In Section 3.4, we present the algorithm of Suri and O'Rourke [321].

In the paper introducing weak and complete visibility, Avis and Toussaint [42] gave an $O(n)$ time algorithm for recognizing a given simple polygon P that is weakly visible from a given edge $v_i v_{i+1}$ (see Figure 3.1(c)). Applying this algorithm to each edge of P, it can be tested in $O(n^2)$ time whether P is weakly visible from any edge of P. Sack and Suri [300] and Shin and Woo [311] improved this result by giving $O(n)$ time algorithms for determining whether P is weakly visible from an edge. Chen [83] presented an $O(n)$ time algorithm for computing the shortest sub-segment of an edge of P from which P is weakly visible.

Exercise 3.1.2 *Let uw be an edge of a simple polygon P of n vertices. Design an $O(n)$ time algorithm for testing whether P is weakly from the edge uw [42].*

Any line segment connecting two boundary points of P and lying inside P is called a *chord* of P. The general recognition problem is to construct a chord st (if it exists) inside a given simple polygon P such that P is weakly visible from st (see Figure 3.4(a)). The chord st is called a *visibility chord*. Ghosh *et al.* [163] gave an algorithm for this problem and their algorithm runs in $O(E)$ time, where E is the number of

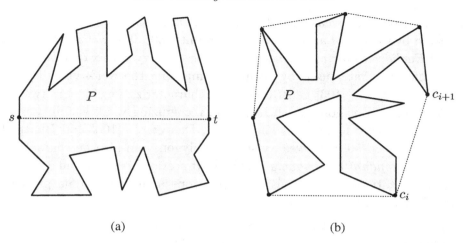

(a)   (b)

Figure 3.4 (a) The polygon P is weakly visible from the chord st but P is not weakly visible from any edge. (b) A weakly externally visible polygon P.

edges in the *visibility graph* of P. We present their algorithm in Section 3.5.1. For this problem, Doh and Chwa [114] and Kim *et al.* [215] presented $O(n \log n)$ time algorithms. For the same problem, Das *et al.* [100] and Bhattacharya and Mukhopadhyay [50] presented $O(n)$ time algorithms. The algorithm of Das *et al.* [100] can also report *all* visibility chords. Das and Narasimhan [103] presented an $O(n)$ time algorithm for computing the shortest segment from which P is weakly visible. In Section 3.5.2, we present the recognition algorithm given by Bhattacharya *et al.* [47], which is the combined results of Bhattacharya and Mukhopadhyay [50] and Das and Narasimhan [103].

Suppose a simple polygon P is given and the problem is to compute the shortest path tree from a vertex in P, if P has a visibility chord. It has been shown by Ghosh *et al.* [162] that the shortest path tree can be computed in P from any vertex in $O(n)$ time without the prior knowledge of any visibility chord. If the algorithm terminates without computing the shortest path tree, then P does not have a visibility chord. If the algorithm computes the shortest path tree, P may have a visibility chord. The algorithm computes the shortest path tree by scanning the boundary of P and it does not require a triangulation of P as a preprocessing step. In fact, a triangulation of P can be constructed once the shortest path has been computed. This algorithm has been used as a preprocessing step in recognizing weak visibility polygons in the algorithms of Ghosh *et al.* [163] and Bhattacharya and Mukhopadhyay [50]. We present the algorithm of Ghosh *et al.* [162] in Section 3.6.2.

Avis and Toussaint [42] first considered external visibility of a simple polygon P. A point z on the boundary of P is said to be *externally visible* from another point $z' \notin P$ if the line segment zz' does not intersect the interior of P. If every point

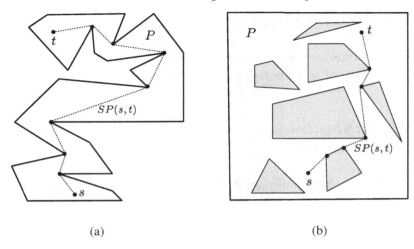

(a)   (b)

Figure 3.5 The Euclidean shortest path between s and t (a) in a simple polygon P and (b) in a polygon P with holes.

on the boundary of P is visible from some point outside the convex hull of P, P is called a *weakly externally visible* polygon (see Figure 3.4(b)). Let $c_1, c_2, \ldots, c_k$ be the vertices of the convex hull of P in counterclockwise order. Note that the convex hull of P can be computed in $O(n)$ time by the algorithm of Graham and Yao [175]. Using the algorithm of Avis and Toussaint [42], it can be tested whether the counterclockwise boundary of P from c_i to c_{i+1} is weakly visible from the convex hull edge $c_i c_{i+1}$ for all i. Thus, the external weak visibility of P can be determined in $O(n)$ time. A variation of this problem is to compute the shortest line segment for which the given simple polygon is weakly externally visible. This problem was solved in $O(n)$ time by Bhattacharya and Toussaint [54] when P is a convex polygon. Later, they extended this result along with Mukhopadhyay [52, 53] for arbitrary simple polygons. In Section 3.7, we present the algorithm of Bhattacharya *et al.* [53].

3.2 Characterizing Weak Visibility

We start this section with some properties of Euclidean shortest paths in a polygon P with and without holes. The Euclidean shortest path between two points s and t in P (denoted as $SP(s, t)$) is the path connecting s and t such that (i) the entire path lies totally inside P, and (ii) the length of the path is smaller than that of any path connecting s and t (see Figure 3.5). Observe that s and t can be connected by several paths inside P. In the following lemmas, we prove a few properties of $SP(s, t)$; some of these properties have been observed by Lozano-Perez and Wesley [249], Lee and Preparata [235] and Chein and Steinberg [79].

Lemma 3.2.1 $SP(s,t)$ *is a simple path in* P.

Proof. If $SP(s,t)$ intersects itself at some point u, by removing the sub-path from u to itself (i.e., the loop at u) a shorter path can be obtained, which is a contradiction. □

Lemma 3.2.2 *Let* $SP(s,t) = (s, ..., u, ..., v, ..., t)$. *Then,* $SP(u,t)$ *and* $SP(s,v)$ *pass through* v *and* u *respectively.*

Proof. If $SP(u,t)$ does not pass through v, then there exists a shorter path between s and t consisting of $SP(s,u)$ and $SP(u,t)$ contradicting the assumption that $SP(s,t)$ is the shortest path. Analogous argument shows that $SP(s,v)$ passes through u. □

Lemma 3.2.3 $SP(s,t)$ *turns only at vertices of* P.

Proof. Assume that $SP(s,t)$ has turned at some point u where u is not a vertex of P. Consider two points v and w on $SP(s,t)$ such that (i) they are arbitrary close to u, (ii) v is on $SP(s,u)$, and (iii) w is on $SP(u,t)$. If the segment vw does not lie inside P for any choice of v and w, then u is a vertex of P which contradicts the assumption that u is not a vertex of P. So, we assume that the segment vw lies inside P. By triangle inequality the length of vw is less than the sum of the length of $SP(v,u)$ and $SP(u,w)$. So, there exists a shorter path between s and t consisting of $SP(s,v)$, vw and $SP(w,t)$. Hence, if $SP(s,t)$ has turned at some point u, then u must be a vertex of P. □

Corollary 3.2.4 *The angle facing the exterior of the polygon at every vertex of* P *on* $SP(s,t)$ *is convex (called outward convex).*

Lemma 3.2.5 *If* P *does not contain a hole, then* $SP(s,t)$ *is a unique path in* P.

Proof. Assume that there are two paths between s and t inside P having the minimum length. Since both paths are shortest paths between s and t, they satisfy Lemmas 3.2.1 and 3.2.3. Without loss of generality, assume that both paths meet only at s and t. Since both paths lie inside P and P does not contains holes, the two paths form a simple polygon P'. Let m denote the number of vertices of P'. From Corollary 3.2.4, the internal angle at each vertex of P' is reflex except at s and t. Therefore, the sum of the internal angles of P' is more than $(m-2)\pi$, contradicting the fact that the sum of internal angles of a simple polygon of m vertices is $(m-2)\pi$. □

Corollary 3.2.6 *If P contains holes and there exists two paths between s and t having minimum length, then the region enclosed by these two paths must contain a hole.*

Let us state the relation in a simple polygon P between Euclidean shortest paths between vertices of P and weak visibility polygons from edges of P as observed by Guibas *et al.* [178] and Toussaint [330]. We assume that the vertices of P are labeled $v_1, v_2, \ldots, v_n$ in counterclockwise order. An edge $v_k v_{k+1}$ of P is called a *convex* edge if both v_k and v_{k+1} are convex vertices. As before, $bd(v_i, v_j)$ denote the counterclockwise boundary of P from a vertex v_i to another vertex v_j. In the following lemma, we state the relationship.

Lemma 3.2.7 *Let $v_k v_{k+1}$ be a convex edge of a simple polygon P. A vertex v_i of P is visible from some point of $v_k v_{k+1}$ if and only if $SP(v_k, v_i)$ makes a left turn at every vertex in the path and $SP(v_{k+1}, v_i)$ makes a right turn at every vertex in the path.*

Proof. If v_i is visible from a point u on $v_k v_{k+1}$ (see Figure 3.6(a)), then $SP(v_k, v_i)$ cannot intersect the segment uv_i. So all vertices in $SP(v_k, v_i)$ must belong to $bd(v_i, v_k)$. Therefore, $SP(v_k, v_i)$ can only make a left turn at every vertex in the path. Analogously, $SP(v_{k+1}, v_i)$ makes a right turn at every vertex in the path. Now we prove the converse. Let v_p and v_q denote the next vertex of v_i in $SP(v_k, v_i)$ and $SP(v_{k+1}, v_i)$, respectively (see Figure 3.6(a)). Since $SP(v_k, v_i)$ makes a left turn at every vertex in the path, v_k lies to the right of $\overrightarrow{v_i v_p}$. Analogously, since $SP(v_{k+1}, v_i)$ makes a right turn at every vertex in the path, v_{k+1} lies to the left of $\overrightarrow{v_i v_{k+1}}$. So, v_k and v_{k+1} lie on opposite sides of the wedge formed by rays $\overrightarrow{v_i v_p}$ and $\overrightarrow{v_i v_q}$. Therefore, the wedge intersects $v_k v_{k+1}$. Hence v_i is visible from any point of $v_k v_{k+1}$ lying in the wedge. □

Corollary 3.2.8 *If a vertex v_i of P is visible from some point of a convex edge $v_k v_{k+1}$, then $SP(v_k, v_i)$ and $SP(v_{k+1}, v_i)$ are two disjoint paths and they meet only at v_i.*

Corollary 3.2.9 *If a vertex v_i of P is visible from some point of a convex edge $v_k v_{k+1}$, then the region enclosed by $SP(v_k, v_i)$, $SP(v_{k+1}, v_i)$ and $v_k v_{k+1}$ (called funnel) is totally contained inside P.*

Exercise 3.2.1 *Draw a simple polygon showing that Lemma 3.2.7 does not hold if v_k or v_{k+1} is a reflex vertex.*

It can be seen that the properties in Lemma 3.2.7 are of the shortest paths from the vertices v_k and v_{k+1} to one other vertex v_i of P. The shortest path between any

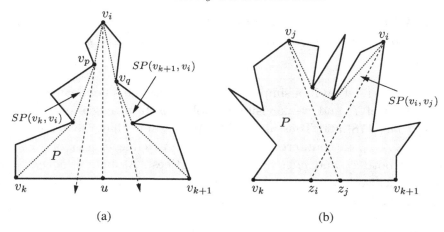

(a)   (b)

Figure 3.6 (a) The wedge formed by two rays intersects $v_k v_{k+1}$. (b) All vertices of $SP(v_i, v_j)$ belong to $bd(v_i, v_j)$.

two vertices v_i and v_j of P also satisfy certain properties as shown by Ghosh *et al.* [163]. We state these properties in the following lemmas.

Lemma 3.2.10 *Assume that P is weakly visible from a convex edge $v_k v_{k+1}$. Let v_i and v_j be two vertices of P such that $v_k v_{k+1}$ belongs to $bd(v_j, v_i)$. All vertices of $SP(v_i, v_j)$ belong to $bd(v_i, v_j)$.*

Proof. Since v_i is visible from some point z_i of $v_k v_{k+1}$ (see Figure 3.6(b)), $SP(v_i, v_j)$ does not intersect the segment $v_i z_i$ and therefore, $SP(v_i, v_j)$ cannot pass through any vertex of $bd(v_{k+1}, v_i)$. Again, since v_j is visible from some point z_j of $v_k v_{k+1}$ (see Figure 3.6(b)), $SP(v_i, v_j)$ does not intersect the segment $v_i z_j$ and therefore, $SP(v_i, v_j)$ cannot pass through any vertex of $bd(v_j, v_k)$. Hence $SP(v_i, v_j)$ passes only through vertices of $bd(v_i, v_j)$.   □

Lemma 3.2.11 *Let $v_k v_{k+1}$ be a convex edge of P. Let v_i and v_j be two vertices of P such that $v_k v_{k+1}$ belongs to $bd(v_j, v_i)$. If all vertices of $SP(v_i, v_j)$ belong to $bd(v_i, v_j)$, then $SP(v_i, v_j)$ makes a right turn at every vertex in the path.*

Proof. Consider any vertex v_q of $SP(v_i, v_j)$. Assume on the contrary that $SP(v_i, v_j)$ makes a left turn at v_q (see Figure 3.7(a)). If the convex angle at v_q is facing towards the interior of P, then by triangle inequality $SP(v_i, v_j)$ does not pass through v_q, which is a contradiction. If the convex angle at v_q is facing toward the exterior of P, then v_q belongs to $bd(v_j, v_i)$, which is also a contradiction. Therefore $SP(v_i, v_j)$ makes a right turn at v_q. Hence, $SP(v_i, v_j)$ makes a right turn at every vertex in the path.   □

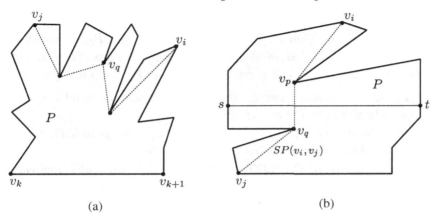

Figure 3.7 (a) The vertex v_q does not belong to $SP(v_i, v_j)$. (b) The edge $v_p v_q$ is an eave in $SP(v_i, v_j)$.

Lemma 3.2.12 *Let $v_k v_{k+1}$ be a convex edge of P. For every vertex v_i of P, if $SP(v_{k+1}, v_i)$ makes a right turn at every vertex in the path and $SP(v_k, v_i)$ makes a left turn at every vertex in the path, then P is weakly visible from $v_k v_{k+1}$.*

Proof. Proof follows along the line of the proof of Lemma 3.2.7. □

Using the above lemmas, Ghosh *et al.* [163] characterized simple polygons that are weakly visible from a convex edge. Their characterization is stated in the following theorem.

Theorem 3.2.13 *Let $v_k v_{k+1}$ be a convex edge of a simple polygon P. The following statements are equivalent.*

(i) *P is weakly visible from $v_k v_{k+1}$.*
(ii) *For any two vertices v_i and v_j of P, where $v_k v_{k+1}$ belongs to $bd(v_j, v_i)$, $SP(v_i, v_j)$ passes only through vertices of $bd(v_i, v_j)$.*
(iii) *For any two vertices v_i and v_j of P, where $v_k v_{k+1}$ belongs to $bd(v_j, v_i)$, $SP(v_i, v_j)$ makes a right turn at every vertex in the path.*
(iv) *For any vertex v_i of P, $SP(v_{k+1}, v_i)$ makes a right turn at every vertex in the path and $SP(v_k, v_i)$ makes a left turn at every vertex in the path.*

Proof. (i) implies (ii) by Lemma 3.2.10, (ii) implies (iii) by Lemma 3.2.11, (iii) implies (iv) as a special case and (iv) implies (i) by Lemma 3.2.12. □

Using Theorem 3.2.13, Ghosh *et al.* [163] characterized simple polygons that are weakly visible from a chord st. Their characterization is stated in the following theorem.

Theorem 3.2.14 *A simple polygon P is a weak visibility polygon if and only if there is a chord st inside P dividing P into sub-polygons P_1 and P_2, where the boundary of P_1 consists of $bd(t, s)$ and st, and the boundary of P_2 consists of $bd(s, t)$ and ts, such that the following equivalent conditions hold for P_1 and analogously for P_2.*

(i) *For any two vertices v_i and v_j of P_1 where v_i belongs to $bd(t, v_j)$, $SP(v_i, v_j)$ passes only through vertices of $bd(v_i, v_j)$.*

(ii) *For any two vertices v_i and v_j of P_1, where v_i belongs to $bd(t, v_j)$, $SP(v_i, v_j)$ makes a right turn at every vertex in the path.*

(iii) *For any vertex v_i of P_1, $SP(t, v_i)$ makes a right turn at every vertex in the path and $SP(s, v_i)$ makes a left turn at every vertex in the path.*

Proof.   If P is a weak visibility polygon from a chord st, then it follows from Theorem 3.2.13 that the three equivalent conditions hold for P_1 as well as for P_2 as st is a convex edge of both P_1 and P_2. Let us prove the converse. If there is a chord st in P such that the three equivalent conditions hold for P_1 and P_2, then it follows from Theorem 3.2.13 that both P_1 and P_2 are weakly visible from st. Therefore, P is weakly visible from st.   □

From Theorem 3.2.14, we know that the shortest path between any two vertices in a sub-polygon P_1 or P_2 is convex. However, the shortest path from a vertex v_i of one sub-polygon to another vertex v_j of an other sub-polygon may not be convex (see Figure 3.7(b)). In that case, there exists an edge $v_p v_q$ in $SP(v_i, v_j)$ such that $SP(v_i, v_j)$ makes a left turn (or, right turn) at v_p and makes a right turn (respectively, left turn) at v_q. Such edges $v_p v_q$ are called *eaves*. In the following lemmas, we present the properties of eaves given by Ghosh *et al.* [163].

Lemma 3.2.15 *If st is a visibility chord of a simple polygon P, then the shortest path between any two vertices in the same sub-polygon has no eaves.*

Proof.   Proof follows from Theorem 3.2.14.   □

Lemma 3.2.16 *If the shortest path between two vertices v_i and v_j in a weak visibility polygon P has an eave $v_p v_q$, then every visibility chord st of P intersects the eave $v_p v_q$.*

Proof.   Proof follows from Lemma 3.2.15.   □

Lemma 3.2.17 *In a weak visibility polygon P, the shortest path between any two vertices v_i and v_j of P has at most one eave.*

Proof.   Proof follows from Lemma 3.2.16.   □

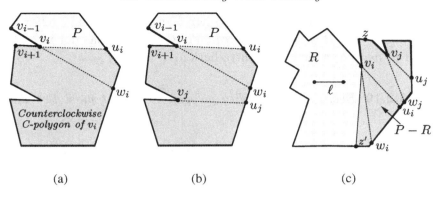

(a) (b) (c)

Figure 3.8 (a) The counterclockwise *C-polygon* of v_i. (b) The counterclockwise *C-polygon* of v_i is *redundant* as it contains the counterclockwise *C-polygon* of v_j. (c) The clockwise *C-polygons* of v_i and v_j lie inside the region $P - R$.

Exercise 3.2.2 *Draw a simple polygon P such that (i) there is no eave in the shortest path between any two vertices of P, and (ii) P is not weakly visible from any chord.*

Let us present the characterization of weak visibility polygons in terms of *non-redundant components* as stated in Bhattacharya *et al.* [47]. Let v_i be a reflex vertex of P. Extend the edge $v_{i+1}v_i$ (and $v_{i-1}v_i$) from v_i till it meets a point u_i (respectively, w_i) on the boundary of P (see Figure 3.8(a)). The clockwise boundary of P from v_i to w_i (i.e., $bd(w_i, v_i)$) is called the *clockwise component* of v_i. Similarly, the *counterclockwise component* of v_i is $bd(v_i, u_i)$. A *component* is *redundant* if it totally contains another *component* (see Figure 3.8(b)). Otherwise, it is called a *non-redundant component*. The region of P enclosed by the chord v_iw_i (or v_iu_i) and $bd(w_i, v_i)$ (respectively, $bd(v_i, u_i)$) is called the clockwise (respectively, counterclockwise) *C-polygon* of v_i (see Figure 3.8(a)). We have the following lemma.

Lemma 3.2.18 *P is weakly visible from an internal line segment ℓ if and only if ℓ intersects every non-redundant C-polygon of P.*

Proof. If ℓ does not intersect a *non-redundant C-polygon* of some vertex v_i, then ℓ cannot see v_{i-1} or v_{i+1}. Hence P is not weakly visible from ℓ. Let us prove the converse. Assume that ℓ intersects every *non-redundant C-polygon* of P but there exists a point z on the boundary of P that is not visible from ℓ (Figure 3.8(c)). So, ℓ lies in a region of P (denoted as R) that is not visible from z. Let $z'v_i$ be the constructed edge on the boundary of R, where the vertex v_i is reflex. Observe that $P - R$ totally contains either the clockwise or the counterclockwise *C-polygon* of v_i. Moreover, ℓ does not intersect the *C-polygon* of v_i. If the *C-polygon* of v_i lying inside $P - R$ is *non-redundant*, then ℓ has intersected all *non-redundant C-polygons*, which is a contradiction. So, we assume that the *C-polygon* of v_i lying inside $P - R$

is *redundant*. Therefore, there exists another *C-polygon* of some reflex vertex v_j lying totally inside $P - R$ which is *non-redundant*. Hence, ℓ has not intersected this *C-polygon* of v_j as well, which is a contradiction.   □

Corollary 3.2.19 *Every weak visibility polygon P has at most two disjoint C-polygons.*

Corollary 3.2.20 *If P has three or more mutually disjoint C-polygons, then P is not a weak visibility polygon.*

3.3 Computing Weak Visibility in Simple Polygons

3.3.1 Scanning the Boundary: $O(n \log n)$ Algorithm

In this section, we present an $O(n \log n)$ time algorithm of Lee and Lin [232] for computing the weak visibility polygon of a simple polygon P of n vertices from a line segment pq inside P (see Figure 3.3(b)). The weak visibility polygon of P from pq is denoted as $V(pq)$. So, $V(pq)$ contains all points of P that are visible from some point of pq.

Let u be the closest point to p among the intersection points of $\overrightarrow{qp}$ with $bd(P)$ (see Figure 3.9(a)) and let u lie on the edge v_iv_{i+1}. Similarly, let w be the closest point to q among the intersection points of $\overrightarrow{pq}$ with $bd(P)$ and let w lie on the edge v_kv_{k+1}. Cut P into two polygons P_1 and P_2 along uw. Let $P_1=(v_i, u, p, q, w, v_{k+1}, ..., v_{i-1}, v_i)$ and $P_2=(v_{i+1}, ..., v_k, w, q, p, u, v_{i+1})$. It can be seen that $V(pq)$ is the union of weak visibility polygons of P_1 and P_2 from pq. So the problem is now to compute the weakly visible polygons of P_1 and P_2 from the edge pq. Since pq has become a convex edge of both P_1 and P_2, the procedures for computing the weak visibility polygon from pq in P_1 and P_2 are analogous.

For simplicity, we assume that pq is a convex edge of the given polygon P and we present the procedure accordingly. We assume that the vertices of P are labeled $v_1, v_2, \ldots, v_n$ in counterclockwise order, where $q = v_1$ and $p = v_n$. If the revolution number of P with respect to p or q is more than one, the algorithm in Section 2.2.2 can be used to prune P. Hence, we assume that the revolution number of P with respect to p or q is one.

In our definition, $bd(a, b)$ denotes the counterclockwise boundary of P from a point a to another point b. We also denote $bd(a, b)$ as $bd_{cc}(a, b)$. In the same way, $bd_c(a, b)$ denotes the clockwise boundary of P from a to b.

Let $SP_{cc}(v_j, v_k)$ denote the convex path restricted to $bd_{cc}(v_j, v_k)$ (see Figure 3.9(b)) such that (i) intermediate vertices of the path belong to $bd_{cc}(v_j, v_k)$, and (ii) the path makes only right turns. In general, $SP(v_j, v_k)$ may not pass through only the vertices of $bd_{cc}(v_j, v_k)$ as it can also pass through vertices of $bd_c(v_j, v_k)$.

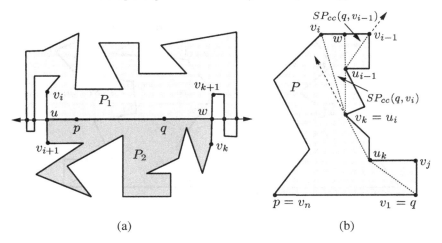

(a)   (b)

Figure 3.9 (a) P is divided by uw into two sub-polygons P_1 and P_2. (b) $SP_{cc}(v_j, v_k)$, $SP_{cc}(q, v_{i-1})$ and $SP_{cc}(q, v_i)$ make only right turns.

Therefore, $SP(v_j, v_k)$ and $SP_{cc}(v_j, v_k)$ can be different and hence, $SP_{cc}(v_j, v_k)$ may not always lie totally inside P. Again, $SP_c(v_j, v_k)$ denotes the convex path restricted to $bd_c(v_j, v_k)$ such that (i) intermediate vertices of the path belong to $bd_c(v_j, v_k)$, and (ii) the path makes only left turns. We have the following lemma.

Lemma 3.3.1 *A vertex v_i is weakly visible from pq if and only if $SP(p, v_i) = SP_c(p, v_i)$ and $SP(q, v_i) = SP_{cc}(q, v_i)$.*

Proof. Proof follows from Theorem 3.2.13. □

Based on the above lemma, the algorithm scans $bd_{cc}(v_2, v_{n-1})$ in counterclockwise order, and computes $SP_{cc}(q, v_2)$, $SP_{cc}(q, v_3)$,..., $SP_{cc}(q, v_{n-1})$. During the scan, if $SP_{cc}(q, v_i)$ does not make only right turns for some vertex v_i, $SP_{cc}(q, v_i)$ is removed. In this process, the algorithm computes $SP_{cc}(q, w)$ for all those vertices $w \in bd_{cc}(v_2, v_{n-1})$ such that $SP_{cc}(q, w)$ makes only right turns. Analogously, the algorithm scans $bd_c(v_{n-1}, v_2)$ in clockwise order and computes $SP_c(p, w)$ for all those vertices $w \in bd_c(v_{n-1}, v_2)$ such that $SP_c(p, w)$ makes only left turns. After both scans, those vertices v_i of P that have both $SP_{cc}(q, v_i)$ and $SP_c(p, v_i)$ are weakly visible from pq due to Lemma 3.3.1.

Let us explain the procedure for computing $SP_{cc}(q, v_2)$, $SP_{cc}(q, v_3)$, $SP_{cc}(q, v_4)$..., $SP_{cc}(q, v_{n-1})$. Assume that $SP_{cc}(q, v_2)$, $SP_{cc}(q, v_3)$,..., $SP_{cc}(q, v_{i-1})$ have been computed and the procedure wants to compute $SP_{cc}(q, v_i)$. The tree formed by the union of $SP_{cc}(q, v_2)$, $SP_{cc}(q, v_3)$,..., $SP_{cc}(q, v_{i-1})$ is denoted as $SPT_{cc}(q, v_{i-1})$. Let u_j denote the parent of v_j in $SPT_{cc}(q, v_{i-1})$, i.e., u_j is the previous vertex of v_j in $SP_{cc}(q, v_j)$. We have the following cases.

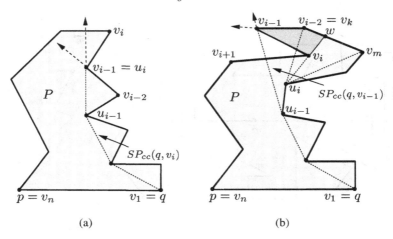

Figure 3.10 (a) $SP_{cc}(q, v_i) = (SP_{cc}(q, v_{i-1}), v_i)$. (b) Since there is a reverse turn at v_{i-1}, some vertices, including v_{i-1}, are not visible from pq.

Case 1. The vertex v_i lies to the left of $\overrightarrow{u_{i-1}v_{i-1}}$ (see Figure 3.9(b)).

Case 2. The vertex v_i lies to the right of $\overrightarrow{u_{i-1}v_{i-1}}$.

   Case 2a. The vertex v_i lies to the right of $\overrightarrow{v_{i-2}v_{i-1}}$ (see Figure 3.10(a)).

   Case 2b. The vertex v_i lies to the left of $\overrightarrow{v_{i-2}v_{i-1}}$ (see Figure 3.10(b)).

Consider Case 1. Since v_i lies to the left of $\overrightarrow{u_{i-1}v_{i-1}}$, it means that $SP_{cc}(q, v_i)$ makes only right turns. Let v_k be the previous vertex of v_i in $SP_{cc}(q, v_i)$. It can be seen that $v_i v_k$ is the tangent from v_i to $SP_{cc}(q, v_{i-1})$ (see Figure 3.9(b)). So, $SP_{cc}(q, v_i) = (SP_{cc}(v_1, v_k), v_i)$, where v_k is the first vertex of $SP_{cc}(q, v_{i-1})$ starting from v_{i-1} such that v_i lies to the right of $\overrightarrow{u_k v_k}$. Hence, v_k becomes the parent of v_i in $SPT_{cc}(q, v_i)$. In other words, v_k becomes u_i. The region enclosed by $v_{i-1}v_i$, $v_i u_i$ and $SP_{cc}(u_i, v_{i-1})$ are divided into triangles by extending each edge of $SP_{cc}(u_i, v_{i-1})$ to $v_{i-1}v_i$.

Consider Case 2a. Since v_i lies to the right of both $\overrightarrow{u_{i-1}v_{i-1}}$ and $\overrightarrow{v_{i-2}v_{i-1}}$ (see Figure 3.10(a)), it means that $SP_{cc}(q, v_i)$ makes only right turns, and v_{i-1} is the previous vertex of v_i in $SP_{cc}(q, v_i)$ as $v_i v_{i-1}$ is the tangent from v_i to $SP_{cc}(q, v_{i-1})$. So, $SP_{cc}(q, v_i) = (SP_{cc}(q, v_{i-1}), v_i)$.

Consider Case 2b. Since v_i lies to the right of $\overrightarrow{u_{i-1}v_{i-1}}$ and to the left of $\overrightarrow{v_{i-2}v_{i-1}}$ (see Figure 3.10(b)), $SP(q, v_{i-1})$ passes through vertices of $bd_{cc}(v_i, p)$ and therefore, $SP(q, v_{i-1})$ and $SP_{cc}(q, v_{i-1})$ are not the same. So v_{i-1} is removed from $SPT_{cc}(q, v_{i-1})$. We say that there is a *reverse turn* at v_{i-1}. Observe that there may be other vertices v_k like v_{i-1} in $SPT_{cc}(q, v_{i-1})$ such that $SP(q, v_k)$ and $SP_{cc}(q, v_k)$ are not the same. This means that the edge $v_{i-1}v_i$ has intersected some edges of $SP_{cc}(q, v_k)$. By checking the intersection with $v_{i-1}v_i$ (explained later), such vertices v_k are removed from $SPT_{cc}(q, v_{i-1})$. The edge $v_{i-1}v_i$ is called the *current inward*

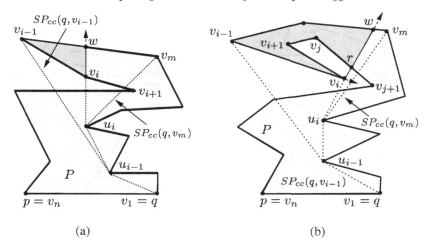

(a)　　　　　　　　　　　　　　　(b)

Figure 3.11 (a) Backtracking continues with $v_i v_{i+1}$ as the current inward edge. (b) Backtracking continues with $r v_{j+1}$ as the current inward edge.

edge. Let v_m be the first vertex from v_{i-1} on $bd_{cc}(q, v_{i-1})$ such that $v_{i-1} v_i$ does not intersect $SP_{cc}(q, v_m)$ (see Figure 3.10(b)). Locate u_i by drawing the tangent from v_i to $SP_{cc}(q, v_m)$ as stated in Case 1. If v_{i+1} lies to the right of $\overrightarrow{u_i v_i}$ (see Figure 3.11(a)), the process of backtracking as stated above for $v_{i-1} v_i$ continues with $v_i v_{i+1}$ as the current inward edge. Consider the other situation when v_{i+1} lies to the left of $\overrightarrow{u_i v_i}$ (see Figure 3.11(b) and Figure 3.13(a)). Let w denote the point of intersection of $v_m v_{m+1}$ and $\overrightarrow{u_i v_i}$. If v_{i+1} lies to the left of $\overrightarrow{v_{i-1} v_i}$ (see Figure 3.11(b)), scan $bd_{cc}(v_{i+1}, p)$ from v_{i+1} in counterclockwise order until an edge $v_j v_{j+1}$ is located such that $v_j v_{j+1}$ intersects $w v_i$ at some point r. So, backtracking continues with $r v_{j+1}$ as the current inward edge. If v_{i+1} lies to the right of $\overrightarrow{v_{i-1} v_i}$ (see Figure 3.13(a)), backtracking ends at v_i.

Let us explain the procedure for locating the parent u_i of v_i. Let xyz be a triangle (see Figure 3.13(a)) such that (i) y and z are two consecutive points or vertices on $bd_{cc}(q, v_{i-1})$, (ii) x is the parent of y in $SPT_{cc}(q, v_{i-1})$, and (iii) if z is a vertex (or a point), then x is the parent (respectively, grandparent) of z in $SPT_{cc}(q, v_{i-1})$. Note that if z is a point (created in Case 1), the parent of z (which is a vertex) is lying on xz. Observe that there exists one triangle xyz such that $v_{i-1} v_i$ has intersected xy but it has not intersected xz (see Figure 3.13(a)). So, x is the parent u_i of v_i in $SPT_{cc}(q, v_{i-1})$.

The above discussion suggests that the problem of locating u_i is to locate the triangle xyz containing v_i. The procedure initializes xyz by the triangle whose xy is $u_{i-1} v_{i-1}$. If xz of the current triangle xyz is not intersected by $v_{i-1} v_i$ (see Figure 3.13(a)), then the process of checking for intersections ends as xyz contains v_i. Otherwise, the procedure has to identify the next triangle for checking the

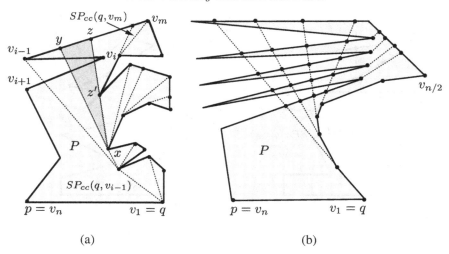

(a)   (b)

Figure 3.12 (a) The edge $v_{i-1}v_i$ has intersected the segment connecting z and its parent z'. (b) Number of extension points inserted on edges of P can be $O(n^2)$.

intersection. If z is not a vertex, then $v_{i-1}v_i$ intersects either xz' (see Figure 3.13(b)) or $z'z$ (see Figure 3.12(a)), where z' is the parent of z lying on the segment xz. If $v_{i-1}v_i$ intersects xz' (or, $z'z$), the other triangle of the segment xz' (respectively, $z'z$) becomes the current triangle xyz. If z is a vertex of P, then the other triangle of xz is unique. Observe that the cost of locating u_i is proportional to the number of triangles intersected by $v_{i-1}v_i$.

In the following, we formally present the procedure for computing $SPT_{cc}(q, v_{n-1})$. Initialize $SPT_{cc}(q, v_2)$ by assigning v_1 as the parent of v_2 and the index i by 2.

Step 1. *If v_i lies to the left of $\overrightarrow{u_{i-1}v_{i-1}}$ (Figure 3.9(b)) then*

    Step 1a. Scan $SP_{cc}(q, v_{i-1})$ from v_{i-1} till a vertex v_k is reached such that v_i lies to the right of $\overrightarrow{u_k v_k}$. Assign v_k as the parent u_i of v_i in $SPT_{cc}(q, v_i)$.

    Step 1b. *For* every intermediate vertex v_l in $SP_{cc}(u_i, v_{i-1})$, extend $u_l v_l$ from v_l to $v_{i-1}v_i$ meeting it at some point w, insert w on $v_{i-1}v_i$ and assign v_l as the parent of w in $SPT_{cc}(q, v_i)$. *Goto* Step 4

Step 2. *If v_i lies to the right of both $\overrightarrow{u_{i-1}v_{i-1}}$ and $\overrightarrow{v_{i-2}v_{i-1}}$ (Figure 3.10(a)) then* assign v_{i-1} as the parent u_i of v_i in $SPT_{cc}(q, v_i)$ and *goto* Step 4.

Step 3. *If v_i lies to the right of $\overrightarrow{u_{i-1}v_{i-1}}$ and to the left of $\overrightarrow{v_{i-2}v_{i-1}}$ (Figure 3.10(b)) then*

    Step 3a. Locate the parent u_i of v_i in $SPT_{cc}(q, v_{i-1})$ by checking for intersections with triangles. Extend $u_i v_i$ from v_i meeting the side of the triangle containing v_i at w (Figure 3.10(b)).

    Step 3b. *If v_{i+1} lies to the left of both $\overrightarrow{u_i v_i}$ and $\overrightarrow{v_{i-1}v_i}$ (Figure 3.11(b)) then* locate

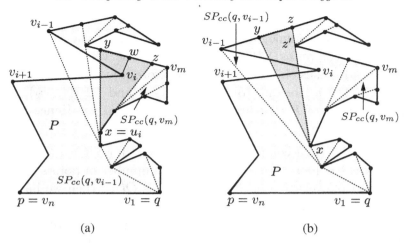

Figure 3.13 (a) Backtracking ends at v_i. (b) The edge $v_{i-1}v_i$ has intersected the segment connecting the parent z' and the grandparent x of z.

the edge $v_j v_{j+1}$ intersecting $w v_i$ at a point r by scanning $bd_{cc}(v_{i+1}, p)$ from v_{i+1} and treat r as v_i.

Step 3c. Connect u_i to v_i by an edge in $SPT_{cc}(q, v_i)$ and remove the region of P bounded by $v_i w$ and $bd_{cc}(w, v_i)$. Assign v_i as the parent of w in $SPT_{cc}(q, v_i)$ and treat w as v_{i-1}.

Step 3d. *If v_{i+1} lies to the right of $\overrightarrow{u_i v_i}$* (Figure 3.11(a)) *then* $i := i + 1$ *and goto* Step 3a.

Step 4. *If $i \neq n - 1$ then* $i := i + 1$ *and goto* Step 1.

Step 5. Report $SPT_{cc}(q, v_{n-1})$ and Stop.

It can be seen that the above procedure has removed some regions of P in Step 3c. Let P' denote the remaining polygon. Using the analogous procedure, $SPT_c(p, v_2)$ can be computed by scanning the boundary P' in clockwise order. The remaining portion of P' is $V(pq)$.

Let us discuss the correctness of the algorithm. As stated in Lemma 3.3.1, a vertex v_{i-1} of P is weakly visible from pq if and only if $SP(p, v_{i-1}) = SP_c(p, v_{i-1})$ and $SP(q, v_{i-1}) = SP_{cc}(q, v_{i-1})$. This means that if $SP(q, v_{i-1}) \neq SP_{cc}(q, v_{i-1})$, $SP(q, v_{i-1})$ makes both left and right turns and therefore there is an edge in $bd_{cc}(v_i, p)$ intersecting $SP_{cc}(q, v_{i-1})$. The procedure for computing $SPT_{cc}(q, v_{n-1})$ accepts the current vertex v_i in Steps 1 and 2 if v_i lies outside the region enclosed by $SP_{cc}(q, v_{i-1})$ and $bd_{cc}(q, v_{i-1})$, which ensures that $SP_{cc}(q, v_i)$ makes only right turns. However, if v_i lies inside the region enclosed by $SP_{cc}(q, v_{i-1})$ and $bd_{cc}(q, v_{i-1})$, the procedure locates the first vertex v_m in the clockwise order starting from v_{i-1} in Step 3 such that v_i lies outside the region enclosed by $SP_{cc}(q, v_m)$ and $bd_{cc}(q, v_m)$. By maintaining this invariant, the procedure for computing $SPT_{cc}(q, v_{n-1})$ computes $SP_{cc}(q, w)$ only for those vertices $w \in bd_{cc}(v_2, v_{n-1})$ such that $SP_{cc}(q, w)$ makes only right turns. Analogous arguments show that the procedure for computing $SPT_c(p, v_2)$ computes $SP_c(p, w)$ only for those vertices $w \in bd_c(v_{n-1}, v_2)$ such that $SP_c(p, w)$ makes only left turns. Therefore, the vertices v_i for which both $SP_{cc}(q, v_i)$ and $SP_c(p, v_i)$ belong to $SPT_{cc}(q, v_{n-1})$ and $SPT_c(p, v_2)$, respectively, are only those vertices of P that are weakly visible from pq. Hence the algorithm correctly computes $V(pq)$.

Let us analyze the time complexity of the algorithm. It can be seen that the algorithm runs in $O(n + m)$ time, where m is the number of points inserted on the boundary during the execution of Step 1b. If m is $O(n)$, then we have $O(n)$ time algorithm. Can m become $O(n^2)$? Yes, it can become $O(n^2)$ as shown in Figure 3.13(b). In this figure, $n/2$ points are removed during backtracking for one inward edge and then $n/2$ points are again inserted in the very next edge. The process can repeat for every pair of edges. Hence, the algorithm can take $O(n^2)$ time in the worst case.

Recall that the parent u_i of v_i is located in Step 1a by a linear search on $SP_{cc}(q, v_{i-1})$ starting from v_{i-1} and in the process, extension points are inserted on edges of P. Instead of a linear search, a binary search can be carried out on $SP_{cc}(q, v_{i-1})$ to locate u_i as $SP_{cc}(q, v_{i-1})$ is convex. On the other hand, the procedure needs the extension points to check the intersection of the current inward edge $v_{i-1}v_i$ with the triangles formed by these extension points in Step 3a. To overcome this difficulty, a binary search can be carried out to locate an edge $v_m v_{m+1}$ of P such that $v_{i-1}v_i$ intersects the tree edge $v_{m+1}u_{m+1}$ but does not intersect the tree edge $v_m u_m$. This means that v_i lies in the region bounded by $v_m v_{m+1}$, $v_{m+1}u_{m+1}$, $SP_{cc}(u_{m+1}, u_m)$ and $u_m v_m$. In other words, v_m is the first vertex from v_{i-1} in clockwise order such that $v_{i-1}v_i$ does not intersect $SP_{cc}(q, v_m)$. Another binary search can be carried out to locate u_i in $SP_{cc}(u_{m+1}, u_m)$. In this process, the parent u_i of v_i can be located. So, at most two binary searches are required for each vertex v_i to locate its parent u_i. Thus, the overall time complexity of the algorithm can be reduced to $O(n \log n)$.

To facilitate the above binary search, $SPT_{cc}(q, v_{i-1})$ can be stored in concatenable queues. Concatenable queues support binary search, split and merge operations [14]. After locating the parent u_i of v_i by binary search on $SP_{cc}(q, v_{i-1})$, a split operation is performed at u_i and then v_i is added to $SP_{cc}(q, u_i)$. Similarly, merge operations are performed at vertices during backtracking to obtain $SP_{cc}(u_{m+1}, u_m)$. We summarize the result in the following theorem.

Theorem 3.3.2 *The weak visibility polygon $V(pq)$ of an internal segment pq in an n-sided simple polygon can be computed in $O(n \log n)$ time.*

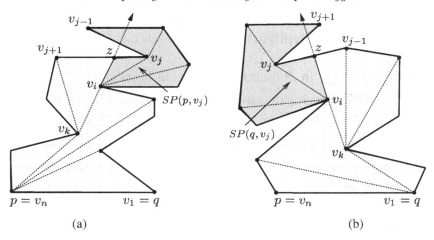

Figure 3.14 (a) $SP(p, v_j)$ makes a first right turn at v_i. (b) $SP(q, v_j)$ makes a first left turn at v_i.

3.3.2 *Using Shortest Path Trees:* $O(n)$ *Algorithm*

In this section, we present an $O(n)$ time algorithm of Guibas *et al.* [178] for computing the weak visibility polygon $V(pq)$ of a simple polygon P of n vertices from a line segment pq inside P. As in Section 3.3.1, we present the algorithm for computing $V(pq)$ from a convex edge pq of P. We assume that the vertices of P are labeled $v_1, v_2, \ldots, v_n$ in counterclockwise order, where $q = v_1$ and $p = v_n$.

Let $SPT(p)$ and $SPT(q)$ denote the shortest path trees in P rooted at p and q respectively. The union of *Euclidean shortest paths* from a vertex to all vertices of a simple polygon is called the *shortest path tree*. For more details on the shortest path tree, see Section 3.6.1. In the following lemmas, we present the main idea used in the algorithm.

Lemma 3.3.3 *Let v_i be the parent of v_j in $SPT(p)$ such that $SP(p, v_j)$ makes a first right turn at v_i (Figure 3.14(a)). Then all descendants of v_i in $SPT(p)$ are not visible from any point of pq.*

Proof. Proof follows from Theorem 3.2.13. □

Lemma 3.3.4 *Let v_i be the parent of v_j in $SPT(q)$ such that $SP(q, v_j)$ makes a first left turn at v_i (Figure 3.14(b)). Then all descendants of v_i in $SPT(q)$ are not visible from any point of pq.*

Proof. Proof follows from Theorem 3.2.13. □

Lemmas 3.3.3 and 3.3.4 suggest a simple algorithm to compute $V(pq)$ by traversing $SPT(p)$ and $SPT(q)$ using depth-first search (see [15]) as follows.

Step 1. Compute $SPT(p)$ in P by the algorithm in Section 3.6.1.

Step 2. Traverse $SPT(p)$ using depth-first search and check the turn at every vertex v_i in $SPT(p)$. If the path makes a right turn at v_i then (Figure 3.14(a))

   Step 2a. Find the descendant of v_i in $SPT(p)$ with the largest index j.

   Step 2b. Compute the intersection point z of $v_j v_{j+1}$ and $\overrightarrow{v_k v_i}$, where v_k is the parent of v_i in $SPT(p)$.

   Step 2c. Remove the counterclockwise boundary of P from v_i to z by inserting the segment $v_i z$.

Step 3. Let P' denote the remaining portion of P. Compute $SPT(q)$ in P' by the algorithm in Section 3.6.1.

Step 4. Traverse $SPT(q)$ using depth-first search and check the turn at every vertex v_i in $SPT(q)$. If the path makes a left turn at v_i then (Figure 3.14(b))

   Step 4a. Find the descendant of v_i in $SPT(q)$ with the smallest index j.

   Step 4b. Compute the intersection point z of $v_j v_{j-1}$ and $\overrightarrow{v_k v_i}$, where v_k is the parent of v_i in $SPT(q)$.

   Step 4c. Remove the clockwise boundary of P' from v_i to z by inserting the segment $v_i z$.

Step 5. Output the remaining portion of P' as $V(pq)$.

The correctness of the algorithm follows from Lemmas 3.3.3 and 3.3.4. We analyze the time complexity of the algorithm. The algorithm for computing $SPT(p)$ and $SPT(q)$ takes $O(n)$ time (see Section 3.6.1). Every vertex of $SPT(p)$ and $SPT(q)$ is traversed once and the remaining operations take constant time. So, the overall time complexity of the algorithm is $O(n)$. We summarize the result in the following theorem.

Theorem 3.3.5 *The weak visibility polygon $V(pq)$ from an internal segment pq in an n-sided simple polygon can be computed in $O(n)$ time.*

3.4 Computing Weak Visibility in Polygons with Holes

In this section, we present an $O(n^4)$ time algorithm of Suri and O'Rourke [321] for computing the weak visibility polygon $V(pq)$ of a polygon P with holes with a total of n vertices from a line segment pq inside P. We treat the line segment pq as a hole inside P. In the following lemma, we present the main idea used in the algorithm.

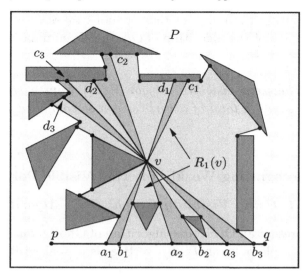

Figure 3.15 Regions $R_1(v)$, $R_2(v)$ and $R_3(v)$ are added to $V(pq)$.

Lemma 3.4.1 *If any point $u \in P$ is weakly visible from pq, then u is visible (i) from p or q, or (ii) from a point $y \in pq$ such that there exists a vertex v lying on the segment uy.*

Proof. The first part of the lemma follows from the fact that $V(p) \subset V(pq)$ and $V(q) \subset V(pq)$. Consider a point u that is not visible from p or q but is visible from some point z of pq. As z is moved along pq toward p or q, z continues to see u till z reaches either p or q or an internal point y of pq such that the segment uy touches the boundary of P at some vertex v. Since u is not visible from p or q by assumption, uy contains v. □

Corollary 3.4.2 *Both y and u belong to the visibility polygon $V(v)$.*

Let a_1b_1, a_2b_2,..., a_kb_k be the maximal intervals on pq that are visible from v (see Figure 3.15). For all i, extend va_i and vb_i from v to the boundary of $V(v)$ meeting at c_i and d_i, respectively. Let $R_i(v)$ denote the region of $V(v)$ lying between a_ic_i and b_id_i. For all i, $R_i(v)$ belongs to $V(pq)$ by Lemma 3.4.1. So, the algorithm computes all such regions $R_i(v)$ for every vertex v of P and then takes the union of all these regions to construct $V(pq)$. Note that the union of these regions also includes points that are visible from p or q.

Let us analyze the time complexity of the algorithm. For all vertices v of P, $V(v)$ can be computed in $O(n^2)$ time [28, 165, 339]. All regions $R_i(v)$ inside $V(v)$ can be computed in $O(n)$ time by scanning the boundary of $V(v)$ once. Since there can be $O(n)$ regions in each $V(v)$ to be added to $V(pq)$, the total number of such regions is $O(n^2)$. So, computing the union of these regions takes $O(n^4)$ time. Hence the overall time complexity of the algorithm is $O(n^4)$. We summarize the result in the following theorem.

Theorem 3.4.3 *The weak visibility polygon $V(pq)$ from a segment pq inside a polygon P with holes with a total of n vertices can be computed in $O(n^4)$ time.*

3.5 Recognizing Weakly Internal Visible Polygons

3.5.1 Using Visibility Graph: $O(E)$ Algorithm

In this section, we present an $O(E)$ time algorithm of Ghosh *et al.* [163] to determine whether the given simple polygon P of n vertices is a weak visibility polygon from some chord, where E is the number of visible pairs of vertices in P. The algorithm computes a visibility chord st in P by searching for the locations of s and t on the polygonal edges. The polygon in Figure 3.4(a) is weakly visible from the chord st but it is not weakly visible from any edge of the polygon. We assume that the vertices of P are labeled $v_1, v_2, \ldots, v_n$ in counterclockwise order. As before, $SPT(v_i)$ denotes the shortest path tree in P rooted at v_i. We also use the notation $bd(v_i, v_j)$ to denote the counterclockwise boundary of P from v_i to v_j. We start with the following lemma.

Lemma 3.5.1 *Let st be a visibility chord of P, where $s \in v_i v_{i+1}$ and $t \in v_j v_{j+1}$. The shortest path between any two vertices of $bd(v_{i+1}, v_j)$ (or $bd(v_{j+1}, v_i)$) is convex (i.e., makes only left turns or only right turns).*

Proof. The proof follows from Theorem 3.2.14.   □

In order to locate a visibility chord st in P, it is necessary to locate the pair of edges $v_i v_{i+1}$ and $v_j v_{j+1}$ (called *potential pair of edges*) of P that satisfy the above lemma. For every edge $v_i v_{i+1}$ of P, the algorithm identifies the set of edges E_i of P that can form a potential pair with $v_i v_{i+1}$. We call the edges in E_i as *potential edges* of $v_i v_{i+1}$. Observe that if $v_i v_{i+1}$ is a potential edge of an edge $v_j v_{j+1} \in E_i$, then $v_i v_{i+1}$ and $v_j v_{j+1}$ form a potential pair of edges by Lemma 3.5.1. The following observations on potential edges follow from Lemma 3.5.1.

Lemma 3.5.2 *If $v_j v_{j+1}$ is a potential edge of $v_i v_{i+1}$, then (i) for any vertex $v_k \in bd(v_{i+1}, v_j)$, $SP(v_{i+1}, v_k)$ makes only right turns, and (ii) for any vertex $v_k \in bd(v_{j+1}, v_i)$, $SP(v_i, v_k)$ makes only left turns.*

Lemma 3.5.3 *If no two edges of P are mutually potential edges of each other, then P is not a weak visibility polygon.*

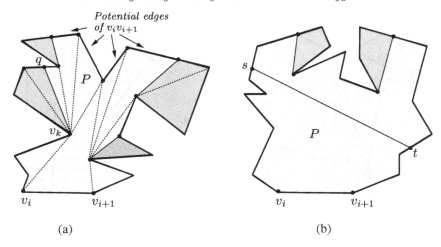

(a)   (b)

Figure 3.16 (a) Right and left constructed edges are in proper order. (b) P has a visibility chord st but there is no potential edge of $v_i v_{i+1}$.

The potential edges of $v_i v_{i+1}$ can be identified from constructed edges of the weak visibility polygon $V(v_i v_{i+1})$. A constructed edge $v_k q$ of $V(v_i v_{i+1})$ is called a *left* constructed edge (Figure 3.16(a)) if $bd(q, v_k)$ does not contain $v_i v_{i+1}$ and a *right* constructed edge, otherwise. We have the following lemma.

Lemma 3.5.4 *If $v_j v_{j+1}$ is a potential edge of $v_i v_{i+1}$, then all right constructed edges of $V(v_i v_{i+1})$ are on $bd(v_{i+1}, v_j)$ and all left constructed edges of $V(v_i v_{i+1})$ are on $bd(v_{j+1}, v_i)$.*

Proof. For any vertex $v_k \in bd(v_{i+1}, v_j)$ (or $bd(v_{j+1}, v_i)$), we know from Lemma 3.5.2 (see Figure 3.16(a)) that $SP(v_{i+1}, v_k)$ (respectively, $SP(v_i, v_k)$) makes only right turns (respectively, left turns). So, all right and left constructed edges of $V(v_i v_{i+1})$ belong to $bd(v_{i+1}, v_j)$ and $bd(v_{j+1}, v_i)$, respectively. □

Using the above lemma, the potential edges of $v_i v_{i+1}$ for all i can be identified by scanning the boundary of $V(v_i v_{i+1})$ (denoted as $bV(v_i v_{i+1})$) from v_{i+1} to v_i in counterclockwise order. The following three cases can arise during the scan.

Case 1. If there is no constructed edge, then $bV(v_i v_{i+1}) = bd(P)$. It means that the edge $v_i v_{i+1}$ is a visibility chord of P.

Case 2. If a left constructed edge is scanned before a right constructed edge, then there is no potential edge of $v_i v_{i+1}$ (Figure 3.16(b)).

Case 3. If all right constructed edges are scanned before all left constructed edges, then all edges of P between the last right constructed edge and the first left constructed edge are potential edges of $v_i v_{i+1}$ (Figure 3.16(a)). Note that the potential edges of $v_i v_{i+1}$ are consecutive edges on $bd(P)$.

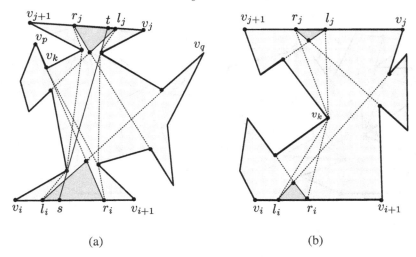

(a)   (b)

Figure 3.17 (a) Right and left intervals on $v_i v_{i+1}$ as well as on $v_j v_{j+1}$ are overlapping. (b) There is no visibility chord in P.

Once potential edges E_i of $v_i v_{i+1}$ are found, check whether $v_i v_{i+1}$ has already been found to be a potential edge of $v_j v_{j+1} \in E_i$. If so, $v_i v_{i+1}$ and $v_j v_{j+1}$ form a potential pair. Thus all potential pairs of edges in P can be located by scanning $bV(v_i v_{i+1})$ for $i = 1, 2, ..., n$. We have the following observation.

Lemma 3.5.5 *If $(v_i v_{i+1}, v_j v_{j+1})$ and $(v_i v_{i+1}, v_k v_{k+1})$ are potential pairs, where $j > k$, then for any edge $v_m v_{m+1} \in bd(v_{k+1}, v_j)$, $(v_i v_{i+1}, v_m v_{m+1})$ is also a potential pair.*

We need another property for a potential pair to contain a visibility chord st. Consider a potential pair $(v_i v_{i+1}, v_j v_{j+1})$. Let l_i denote the furthest point of v_{i+1} on $v_i v_{i+1}$ (Figure 3.17(a)) such that for every vertex $v_q \in bd(v_{i+1}, v_j)$, $SP(l_i, v_q)$ makes only right turns. The portion $l_i v_{i+1}$ is called the *right interval* of $v_i v_{i+1}$ for $v_j v_{j+1}$. Similarly, let r_i denote the furthest point of v_i on $v_i v_{i+1}$ such that for every vertex $v_p \in bd(v_{j+1}, v_i)$, $SP(r_i, v_p)$ makes only left turns. The portion $v_i r_i$ is called the *left interval* of $v_i v_{i+1}$ for $v_j v_{j+1}$. We have the following lemma.

Lemma 3.5.6 *Let $v_i v_{i+1}$ and $v_j v_{j+1}$ be the edges of a potential pair. Assume that there exists a chord st in P where $s \in v_i v_{i+1}$ and $t \in v_j v_{j+1}$. The chord st is a visibility chord of P if and only if s belongs to both left and right intervals of $v_i v_{i+1}$ for $v_j v_{j+1}$ and t belongs to both left and right intervals of $v_j v_{j+1}$ for $v_i v_{i+1}$.*

Proof. Assume that st is a visibility chord. Since st is a visibility chord, for any vertex $v_p \in bd(v_{j+1}, v_i)$, $SP(s, v_p)$ makes only left turns by Theorem 3.2.14 (see Figure 3.17(a)). So s lies in the left interval of $v_i v_{i+1}$ for $v_j v_{j+1}$. Similarly, for any vertex $v_q \in bd(v_{i+1}, v_j)$, $SP(s, v_q)$ makes only right turns. So s lies in the right interval of $v_i v_{i+1}$ for $v_j v_{j+1}$. Hence s belongs to both intervals of $v_i v_{i+1}$ for $v_j v_{j+1}$. Analogous arguments show that t belongs to both intervals of $v_j v_{j+1}$ for $v_i v_{i+1}$.

We now prove the converse. Assume that s belongs to both left and right intervals of $v_i v_{i+1}$ for $v_j v_{j+1}$ and t belongs to both left and right intervals of $v_j v_{j+1}$ for $v_i v_{i+1}$. Therefore, for any vertex $v_p \in bd(v_{j+1}, v_i)$, $SP(s, v_p)$ (respectively, $SP(t, v_p)$) makes only left (respectively, right) turns, and for any vertex $v_q \in bd(v_{i+1}, v_j)$, $SP(s, v_q)$ (respectively, $SP(t, v_q)$) makes only right (respectively, left) turns. Hence, st is a visibility chord of P by Theorem 3.2.14.

□

Let us state the procedure for computing left and right intervals of $v_i v_{i+1}$ for $v_j v_{j+1}$. For each vertex $v_p \in bd(v_{j+1}, v_i)$ and $bV(v_i v_{i+1})$, compute the intersection point of $v_i v_{i+1}$ and $\overrightarrow{v_p v_k}$, where v_k is the parent of v_p in $SPT(v_{i+1})$ (see Figure 3.17(a)). Among all the intersection points, the intersection point closest to v_i is the point r_i. So $v_i r_i$ is the left interval of $v_i v_{i+1}$ for $v_j v_{j+1}$. Analogously, the right interval of $v_i v_{i+1}$ for $v_j v_{j+1}$ can be computed. Observe that if $v_i v_{i+1}$ has two or more potential edges, the left and right intervals of $v_i v_{i+1}$ for all its potential edges (which are consecutive by Lemma 3.5.5) can be computed by scanning $bV(v_i, v_{i+1})$ once in clockwise order and once in counterclockwise order. We have the following lemmas.

Lemma 3.5.7 *Let $v_i v_{i+1}$ and $v_j v_{j+1}$ be the edges of a potential pair. Assume that the left interval $v_i r_i$ and the right interval $l_i v_{i+1}$ of $v_i v_{i+1}$ for $v_j v_{j+1}$ overlap, and the left interval $v_j r_j$ and the right interval $l_j v_{j+1}$ of $v_j v_{j+1}$ for $v_i v_{i+1}$ overlap. If $SP(l_i, r_j)$ and $SP(r_i, l_j)$ are disjoint, then there is a visibility chord st in P such that $s \in l_i r_i$ and $t \in l_j r_j$.*

Proof. Consider $SP(l_i, l_j)$. If $SP(l_i, l_j)$ is just the segment $l_i l_j$, then $s = l_i$ and $t = l_j$. Otherwise, $SP(l_i, l_j)$ contains an eave (see Figure 3.17(a)). Since $SP(l_i, r_j)$ and $SP(r_i, l_j)$ are convex and disjoint, the eave in $SP(l_i, l_j)$ is a cross-tangent between $SP(r_j, l_i)$ and $SP(l_j, r_i)$. Extend the eave in both directions meeting $l_i r_i$ and $l_j r_j$ at points s and t, respectively. Hence, st is a visibility chord of P by Lemma 3.5.6.

□

Lemma 3.5.8 *Let $v_i v_{i+1}$ and $v_j v_{j+1}$ be the edges of a potential pair. Assume that the left interval $v_i r_i$ and the right interval $l_i v_{i+1}$ of $v_i v_{i+1}$ for $v_j v_{j+1}$ overlap, and the left interval $v_j r_j$ and the right interval $l_j v_{j+1}$ of $v_j v_{j+1}$ for $v_i v_{i+1}$ overlap. If $SP(l_i, r_j)$ and $SP(r_i, l_j)$ share a vertex, then there is no visibility chord in P.*

Proof. Let v_k be a vertex common to $SP(l_i, r_j)$ and $SP(r_i, l_j)$ (see Figure 3.17(b)). Since both $SP(r_i, l_j)$ and $SP(l_i, r_j)$ pass through v_k, there is no chord between $l_i r_i$

and $l_j r_j$. If $v_k \in bd(v_{j+1}, v_i)$, then any visibility chord must have one endpoint on $bd(v_k, r_i)$ and the other on $bd(l_j, v_k)$, which is not possible. Analogous argument holds if $v_k \in bd(v_{i+1}, v_j)$. Hence, there is no visibility chord in P.   □

A visibility chord st in P can be computed between the edges in a potential pair if the edges satisfy Lemma 3.5.7. If no such pair exists or there is a potential pair of edges which satisfy Lemma 3.5.8, then P does not have a visibility chord. In the following, we state the major steps for computing a visibility chord st inside P.

Step 1. Compute $SPT(v_1)$ by the algorithm of Ghosh *et al.* [162] stated in Section 3.6.2.

Step 2. Compute $V(v_1 v_2)$, $SPT(v_2)$, $V(v_2 v_3)$, $SPT(v_3)$,..., $SPT(v_n)$, $V(v_n v_1)$ by the algorithm of Hershberger [186] stated in Section 5.2.

Step 3. *For* every edge $v_i v_{i+1}$ in P, locate the potential edges of $v_i v_{i+1}$ by scanning $bV(v_i v_{i+1})$ from v_{i+1} to v_i in counterclockwise order.

Step 4. *For* every pair of edges $v_i v_{i+1}$ and $v_j v_{j+1}$ that are mutually potential edges of each other, add $(v_i v_{i+1}, v_j v_{j+1})$ to the list of potential pairs.

Step 5. *For* every edge $v_i v_{i+1}$ in the list of potential pairs *do*

  Step 5a. Scan $bV(v_i v_{i+1})$ once in clockwise order and compute the left interval of $v_i v_{i+1}$ for each edge that has formed a potential pair with $v_i v_{i+1}$.

  Step 5b. Scan $bV(v_i v_{i+1})$ once in counterclockwise order and compute the right interval of $v_i v_{i+1}$ for each edge that has formed a potential pair with $v_i v_{i+1}$.

  Step 5c. *If* the left and right intervals of $v_i v_{i+1}$ do not overlap for an edge $v_j v_{j+1}$ *then* remove $(v_i v_{i+1}, v_j v_{j+1})$ from the list of potential pairs.

Step 6. *If* the list of potential pairs is empty or *if* $SP(l_i, r_j)$ and $SP(r_i, l_j)$ share a vertex for a potential pair $(v_i v_{i+1}, v_j v_{j+1})$ *then* report that P is not a weak visibility polygon and Stop.

Step 7. Take any potential pair $(v_i v_{i+1}, v_j v_{j+1})$ from the list of potential pairs, compute a visibility chord st by extending the eave in $SP(l_i, l_j)$ in both directions to $l_i r_i$ and $l_j r_j$, report st as a visibility chord of P and Stop.

The correctness of the algorithm follows from Lemmas 3.5.1, 3.5.4, 3.5.6, 3.5.7 and 3.5.8. We analyze the time complexity of the algorithm. The algorithm of Ghosh *et al.* [162] in Step 1 for computing $SPT(v_1)$ takes $O(n)$ time. The algorithm of Hershberger [186] for computing $V(v_1 v_2)$, $SPT(v_2)$, $V(v_2 v_3)$, $SPT(v_3)$,..., $SPT(v_n)$, $V(v_n v_1)$ in Step 2 takes $O(E)$ time. To find the list of potential pairs, the algorithm scans the boundary of each visibility polygon once. Since the sum of the sizes of $bV(v_i v_{i+1})$ for all i is $O(E)$, Step 3 and Step 4 run in $O(E)$ time. Then the algorithm scans $bV(v_i v_{i+1})$ twice to compute intervals for each $v_i v_{i+1}$. So, Step 5 also takes $O(E)$ time. Step 6 and Step 7 together run in $O(n)$ time. Hence, the overall time complexity of the algorithm is $O(E)$. We summarize the result in the following theorem.

Theorem 3.5.9 *A visibility chord st in a simple polygon P can be constructed in $O(E)$ time, where E is the number of visible pairs of vertices in P.*

3.5.2 Scanning the Boundary: $O(n)$ Algorithm

In this section, we present an $O(n)$ time algorithm of Bhattacharya *et al.* [47] for recognizing a weak visibility polygon P of n vertices. The algorithm constructs visibility chords of P and then computes the shortest segment from which P is weakly visible. Here we present only a part of their algorithm which locates a visibility chord in P in $O(n)$ time. In Section 3.2, weak visibility polygons have been characterized in terms of non-redundant *C-polygons*. This characterization stated in Lemma 3.2.18 is used here to compute a visibility chord of P. We also use here the algorithm of Ghosh *et al.* [162], presented in Section 3.6.2, for computing shortest path trees in P.

We know from Lemma 3.2.18 that it is enough to consider only non-redundant *C-polygons* of P as they determine the positions of visibility chords in P. On the other hand, Corollary 3.2.19 suggests that a weak visibility polygon can have at most two disjoint *C-polygons*. Let us first check whether the given simple polygon P has one, two or more disjoint *C-polygons*. We assume that the vertices of P are labeled $v_1, v_2, \ldots, v_n$ in counterclockwise order. Without loss of generality, we assume that v_1 is a reflex vertex. Compute $SPT(v_1)$ in P by the algorithm of Ghosh *et al.* [162]. If the algorithm does not succeed in computing $SPT(v_1)$, then P is not a weak visibility polygon. Henceforth we assume that $SPT(v_1)$ has been computed. Scan $bd(P)$ in counterclockwise order from v_2 (see Figure 3.18(a)) and locate the first vertex v_i such that v_{i+1} is the parent of v_i in $SPT(v_1)$. If no such vertex exists, scan $bd(P)$ in clockwise order from v_n and locate the first vertex v_i such that v_{i-1} is the parent of v_i in $SPT(v_1)$. If no such vertex exists, then the entire polygon P is visible from v_1 and the algorithm terminates.

Without loss of generality, we assume that v_i has been located during the counterclockwise scan (see Figure 3.18(a)). Locate the meeting point w_{i+1} by extending $v_i v_{i+1}$ from v_{i+1} (through the edges of $SPT(v_1)$) to $bd(v_1, v_i)$. So, $bd(w_{i+1}, v_{i+1})$ and the bounding chord $v_{i+1}w_{i+1}$ define a clockwise *C-polygon* (denoted as $poly_c(v_{i+1})$). Observe that this *C-polygon* does not contain any other clockwise *C-polygon*. However, it may contain a counterclockwise *C-polygon*. Scan from v_{i-1} in clockwise order to locate the first vertex v_j before reaching w_{i+1} such that (i) v_{j-1} is the parent of v_j in $SPT(v_1)$, and (ii) $\overrightarrow{v_j v_{j-1}}$ does not intersect the bounding chord $v_{i+1}w_{i+1}$. Locate the meeting point u_{j-1} by extending $v_j v_{j-1}$ from v_{j-1} to $bd(v_j, v_{i+1})$. So, the counterclockwise *C-polygon* with bounding chord $v_{j-1}u_{j-1}$ (denoted as $poly_{cc}(v_{j-1})$) is contained inside $poly_c(v_{i+1})$. It can be seen that $poly_{cc}(v_{j-1})$ is not contained in any clockwise or counterclockwise *C-polygon*. If no such vertex v_j is located before

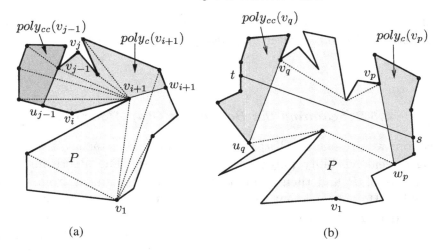

Figure 3.18 (a) The clockwise C-*polygon* with bounding chord $v_{i+1}w_{i+1}$ contains the counterclockwise C-*polygon* with bounding chord $v_{j-1}u_{j-1}$. (b) Two disjoint critical polygons with bounding chords v_pw_p and v_qu_q.

reaching w_{i+1}, $poly_c(v_{i+1})$ does not contain any C-*polygon*. Thus the algorithm locates the first disjoint C-*polygon*; call it a *critical polygon*.

Without loss of generality, we assume that the algorithm has located a clockwise C-*polygon* as the first critical polygon; call it $poly_c(v_p)$ (see Figure 3.18(b)). It can be seen that $poly_c(v_p)$ is weakly visible from its bounding chord v_pw_p. If v_pw_p can also see the remaining portion of P, then it is a visibility chord of P. This can be tested, as shown in Section 3.6, by traversing $SPT(v_p)$ and $SPT(w_p)$. These two trees can be computed directly by the algorithm of Ghosh *et al.* [162]. They can also be computed easily by scanning $bd(P)$ using $SPT(v_1)$.

> **Exercise 3.5.1** *Let v_k be a vertex of a simple polygon P of n vertices. Assume that $SPT(v_k)$ has been given along with P. Assume that any path in $SPT(v_k)$ has at most one eave. From any vertex v_m of P, compute $SPT(v_m)$ in $O(n)$ time by scanning the boundary of P using $SPT(v_k)$.*

We assume that v_pw_p is not a visibility chord and we have $SPT(v_p)$ and $SPT(w_p)$ in addition to $SPT(v_1)$. Scan $bd(v_p, w_p)$ and locate a C-*polygon* using $SPT(v_p)$ or $SPT(w_p)$ (as stated above) such that it does not contain another C-*polygon* and its bounding chord connects two points of $bd(v_p, w_p)$ (see Figure 3.18(b)). Without loss of generality, we assume that it is a counterclockwise C-*polygon*; call it $poly_{cc}(v_q)$. It can be tested again whether entire P is visible from the bounding chord v_qu_q. In the process, $SPT(v_q)$ and $SPT(u_q)$ have been computed. Assume that v_qu_q is not a visibility chord of P. It can be seen that $bd(P)$ has been partitioned into four chains $bd(v_p, v_q)$, $bd(v_q, u_q)$, $bd(u_q, w_p)$ and $bd(w_p, v_p)$ (see Figure 3.18(b)) and each of them has a particular structure as shown in the following lemmas.

Lemma 3.5.10 *Let $v_p w_p$ and $v_q u_q$ be bounding chords of two disjoint critical polygons $poly_c(v_p)$ and $poly_{cc}(v_q)$ in P, respectively, where $v_p \in bd(w_p, v_q)$. One endpoint of every visibility chord st belongs to $bd(w_p, v_p)$ and the other endpoint belongs to $bd(v_q, u_q)$.*

Proof. We know that every visibility chord must intersect both critical polygons $poly_c(v_p)$ and $poly_{cc}(v_q)$ by Lemma 3.2.18. Since $poly_c(v_p)$ and $poly_{cc}(v_q)$ are disjoint (see Figure 3.18(b)), one endpoint of every visibility chord st belongs to $bd(w_p, v_p)$ and the other belongs to $bd(v_q, u_q)$. □

Corollary 3.5.11 *Every visibility chord of P lies inside the visibility polygon of P from $v_p w_q$ as well as in the visibility polygon of P from $v_q u_q$.*

Lemma 3.5.12 *Let $v_p w_p$ and $v_q u_q$ be bounding chords of two disjoint critical polygons $poly_c(v_p)$ and $poly_{cc}(v_q)$ in P, respectively, where $v_p \in bd(w_p, v_q)$. If P is a weak visibility polygon, then for every vertex $v_k \in bd(u_q, w_p)$, (i) $SP(w_p, v_k)$ makes only left turns, (ii) $SP(u_q, v_k)$ makes only right turns and (iii) both $SP(w_p, v_k)$ and $SP(u_q, v_k)$ pass through only the vertices of $bd(u_q, w_p)$.*

Proof. If $SP(w_p, v_k)$ makes a right turn at some vertex $v_m \in bd(w_p, v_q)$, then there exists a critical polygon such that both endpoints of its bounding chord belong to $bd(u_q, w_p)$. It means that P has three disjoint critical polygons and therefore, P is not a weak visibility polygon by Corollary 3.2.20, which is a contradiction. Analogous arguments show that $SP(u_q, v_k)$ makes only right turns. If $SP(w_p, v_k)$ or $SP(u_q, v_k)$ pass through a vertex $v_m \in bd(v_p, v_q)$, then no point of $v_p w_p$ is visible from any point of $v_q u_q$ and vice versa. Therefore, there is no chord with one endpoint on $bd(w_p, v_p)$ and other endpoint on $bd(v_q, u_q)$, contradicting Lemma 3.5.10. So, $SP(w_p, v_k)$ and $SP(u_q, v_k)$ pass through only the vertices of $bd(w_p, v_q)$. □

Lemma 3.5.13 *Let $v_p w_p$ and $v_q u_q$ be bounding chords of two disjoint critical polygons $poly_c(v_p)$ and $poly_{cc}(v_q)$ in P, respectively, where $v_p \in bd(w_p, v_q)$. If P is a weak visibility polygon, then for every vertex $v_k \in bd(v_p, v_q)$, (i) $SP(v_p, v_k)$ makes only right turns, (ii) $SP(v_q, v_k)$ makes only left turns, and (iii) both $SP(v_p, v_k)$ and $SP(v_q, v_k)$ pass through only the vertices of $bd(v_p, v_q)$.*

From now on we assume that $bd(u_q, w_p)$ and $bd(v_p, v_q)$ satisfy Lemmas 3.5.12 and 3.5.13, respectively. Lemma 3.5.12 suggests that there is no critical polygon with the bounding chord ending at two points on $bd(u_q, w_p)$. However, it is possible to have a critical polygon, say $poly_{cc}(v_k)$, with bounding chord $v_k u_k$ such that $v_k \in bd(u_q, w_p)$ and $u_k \in bd(w_p, v_p)$ (see Figure 3.19(a)). Similarly, there can be a critical

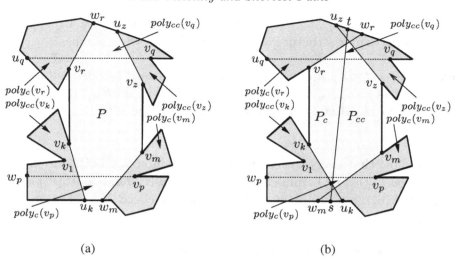

(a)   (b)

Figure 3.19 (a) Critical polygons $poly_{cc}(v_k)$, $poly_c(v_m)$ and $poly_{cc}(v_q)$ are disjoint. Similarly, critical polygons $poly_{cc}(v_z)$, $poly_c(v_r)$ and $poly_c(v_p)$ are disjoint. (b) The bounding chords $v_k u_k$ and $v_m w_m$ have intersected. Similarly, $v_z u_z$ and $v_r w_r$ have intersected.

polygon $poly_c(v_m)$ with bounding chord $v_m w_m$ such that $v_m \in bd(v_p, v_q)$ and $w_m \in bd(w_p, v_p)$. In the following lemma, we establish the relationship between $poly_{cc}(v_k)$ and $poly_c(v_m)$.

Lemma 3.5.14 *Let $v_p w_p$ and $v_q u_q$ be bounding chords of two disjoint critical polygons $poly_c(v_p)$ and $poly_{cc}(v_q)$ in P, respectively, where $v_p \in bd(w_p, v_q)$. Let $poly_{cc}(v_k)$ and $poly_c(v_m)$ be critical polygons with bounding chords $v_k u_k$ and $v_m w_m$, respectively, where $v_k \in bd(u_q, w_p)$ and $u_k \in bd(w_p, v_p)$, $v_m \in bd(v_p, v_q)$ and $w_m \in bd(w_p, v_p)$. If $v_k u_k$ and $v_m w_m$ do not intersect, then there is no visibility chord in P.*

Proof. If two bounding chords $v_k u_k$ and $v_m w_m$ do not intersect, then $poly_{cc}(v_k)$, $poly_c(v_m)$ and $poly_{cc}(v_q)$ are three disjoint critical polygons in P (see Figure 3.19(a)). Therefore, P cannot not have a visibility chord by Corollary 3.2.20. □

Corollary 3.5.15 *If P is a weak visibility polygon (Figure 3.19(b)), then $v_k u_k$ and $v_m w_m$ intersects and one endpoint of every visibility chord of P belongs to $bd(w_m, u_k)$.*

Let us check whether there exists two disjoint critical polygons $poly_{cc}(v_k)$ and $poly_c(v_m)$ as stated in Lemma 3.5.14. Scan $bd(u_q, w_p)$ from w_p in clockwise order (see Figure 3.20(a)) until a vertex v_{i+1} is located such that v_i is the parent of v_{i+1} in $SPT(v_p)$. Extend $v_{i+1}v_i$ from v_i through edges of $SPT(w_p)$ meeting $bd(w_p, v_p)$ at u_i. Continue the scan to locate another such vertex v_{k+1} such that (i) v_k is the parent of v_{k+1} in $SPT(v_p)$, and (ii) $\overrightarrow{v_{k+1}v_k}$ intersects $v_i u_i$. Then $v_k u_k$ becomes the current

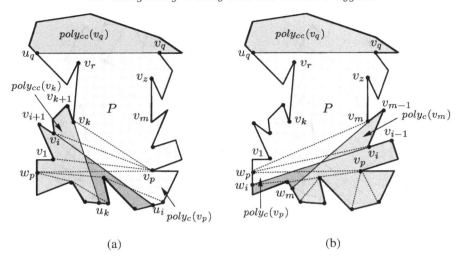

(a)   (b)

Figure 3.20 (a) By scanning $bd(u_q, w_p)$ from w_p in clockwise order, $poly_{cc}(v_k)$ is located. (b) By scanning $bd(v_p, v_q)$ from v_p in counterclockwise order, $poly_c(v_m)$ is located.

$v_i u_i$. This process is repeated till all vertices in $bd(u_q, w_p)$ are scanned. Note that to locate u_k, the algorithm first locates the edge of $SP(w_p, u_i)$ intersected by $\overrightarrow{v_{k+1}v_k}$ by traversing $SP(w_p, u_i)$ from u_i and then it traverses through the edges of $SPT(w_p)$ till u_k is found. Essentially, u_k moves in the clockwise direction on $bd(w_p, v_p)$ toward w_p. Analogously, w_m can be located by scanning $bd(v_p, v_q)$ from v_p in counterclockwise order and by moving w_m in the clockwise direction on $bd(w_p, v_p)$ (see Figure 3.20(b)). If $v_k u_k$ and $v_m w_m$ do not intersect, then there cannot be any visibility chord in P by Lemma 3.5.14 and the algorithm terminates. So we assume that $v_k u_k$ and $v_m w_m$ intersect in P. In the following lemma, we state the corresponding lemma to Lemma 3.5.14 for the bounding chord $v_q u_q$ (see Figure 3.19(a)).

Lemma 3.5.16 *Let $v_p w_p$ and $v_q u_q$ be bounding chords of two disjoint critical polygons $poly_c(v_p)$ and $poly_{cc}(v_q)$ in P, respectively, where $v_p \in bd(w_p, v_q)$. Let $poly_{cc}(v_z)$ and $poly_c(v_r)$ be critical polygons with bounding chords $v_z u_z$ and $v_r w_r$, respectively, where $v_z \in bd(v_p, v_q)$ and $u_z \in bd(v_q, u_p)$, $v_r \in bd(u_q, w_p)$ and $w_r \in bd(v_q, u_q)$. If $v_z u_z$ and $v_r w_r$ do not intersect, then there is no visibility chord in P.*

Corollary 3.5.17 *If P is a weak visibility polygon (Figure 3.19(b)), then $v_z u_z$ and $v_r w_r$ intersect and one endpoint of every visibility chord of P belongs to $bd(v_q, u_q)$.*

Corollaries 3.5.15 and 3.5.17 suggest that one endpoint, say s, of every visibility chord st belongs to $bd(w_m, u_k)$ and the other endpoint t belongs to $bd(w_r, u_z)$ (see Figure 3.19(b)). Locating s and t essentially means constructing two sub-polygons of P partitioned by st. Let P_c and P_{cc} denote these two sub-polygons, where $bd(P_c)$ consists of $bd(t, s)$ and st, and $bd(P_{cc})$ consists of $bd(s, t)$ and st. We know that

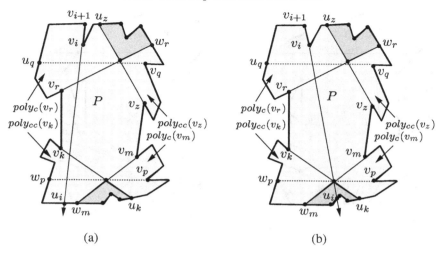

Figure 3.21 (a) The bounding chords $v_i u_i$ and $v_m w_m$ are non-intersecting. (b) The bounding chords $v_i u_i$, $v_k u_k$ and $v_m w_m$ are mutually intersecting.

$bd(u_q, w_p)$ can be included in $bd(P_c)$. Similarly, $bd(v_p, v_q)$ can be included in $bd(P_{cc})$. We also know that $bd(P_c)$ must include $bd(u_z, u_q)$ and $bd(w_p, w_m)$. Similarly, $bd(P_{cc})$ must include $bd(u_k, v_p)$ and $bd(v_q, w_r)$. Let us test whether $bd(P_c)$ can include $bd(u_z, u_q)$. Suppose there exists a counterclockwise *C-polygon* $poly_{cc}(v_i)$ (see Figure 3.21), where $v_i \in bd(u_z, u_q)$ and v_i is the parent of v_{i+1} in $SPT(v_p)$. We have the following cases.

Case 1. The ray $\overrightarrow{v_{i+1}v_i}$ has not intersected $v_m w_m$ (Figure 3.21(a)).
Case 2. The ray $\overrightarrow{v_{i+1}v_i}$ has intersected both $v_k u_k$ and $v_m w_m$ (Figure 3.21(b)).
Case 3. The ray $\overrightarrow{v_{i+1}v_i}$ has not intersected $v_k u_k$ (Figure 3.22(a)).

Consider Case 1. Since $\overrightarrow{v_{i+1}v_i}$ has not intersect $v_m w_m$ (see Figure 3.21(a)), then there is no visibility chord st in P by Lemma 3.2.18 as no st between $bd(w_m, u_k)$ and $bd(w_r, u_z)$ can intersect $v_i u_i$. So, the algorithm terminates. From now on, we assume that Case 1 has not occurred.

Consider Case 2. Since $\overrightarrow{v_{i+1}v_i}$ has intersected both $v_k u_k$ and $v_m w_m$ (see Figure 3.21(b)), $v_i u_i$ becomes the new $v_k u_k$ as any st between $bd(w_m, u_k)$ and $bd(w_r, u_z)$ must intersect $v_i u_i$. So, Case 2 changes u_k which means that some consecutive vertices of the previous $bd(w_m, u_k)$ have been excluded from the current $bd(w_m, u_k)$. Excluded vertices are automatically added to the current $bd(u_k, v_p)$. Computing the exact position of u_i in Case 2 can be done in the same way as u_k has been computed earlier.

Consider Case 3. Since $\overrightarrow{v_{i+1}v_i}$ has not intersected $v_k u_k$ (see Figure 3.22(a)), any st between $bd(w_m, u_k)$ and $bd(w_r, u_z)$ also intersects $v_i u_i$ satisfying Lemma 3.2.18. So $bd(w_m, u_k)$ remains unchanged.

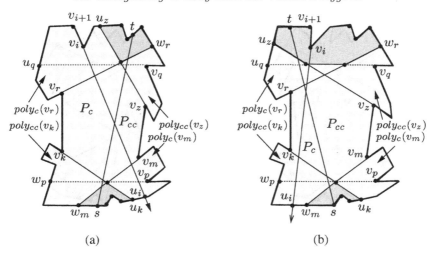

(a)   (b)

Figure 3.22 (a) The bounding chords $v_i u_i$ and $v_k u_k$ are non-intersecting. (b) The point t belongs to $bd(v_{i+1}, u_z)$.

The above process of testing is also carried out before including $bd(w_p, w_m)$ in P_c, $bd(u_k, v_p)$ in P_{cc} and $bd(v_q, w_r)$ in P_{cc}. Observe that this process of testing continues as long as some vertices of the previous $bd(w_m, u_k)$ or $bd(w_r, u_z)$ have been excluded. If the algorithm does not terminate, then this process of testing ends with new $bd(w_m, u_k)$ and $bd(w_r, u_z)$ and all the vertices excluded so far have been tested. It can be seen that if the testing is again carried out for the vertices in the present $bd(u_z, u_q)$, $bd(w_p, w_m)$, $bd(u_k, v_p)$ and $bd(v_q, w_r)$, Case 1 and Case 2 cannot arise and only Case 3 occurs. Observe that the process of testing always involves a new vertex that has not been tested earlier and it has been excluded only in the previous pass. This observation keeps the recognition algorithm linear.

It can be seen that the algorithm is yet to test the vertices of the present $bd(w_m, u_k)$ and $bd(w_r, u_z)$. Scan $bd(w_r, u_z)$ in clockwise order from u_z until a vertex v_i is found (see Figure 3.22(b)) such that (i) v_i is the parent of v_{i+1} in $SPT(v_p)$, and (ii) $\overrightarrow{v_{i+1}v_i}$ does not intersect $v_m w_m$. If no such vertex v_i exists, it means that st can intersect counterclockwise C-polygons of all reflex vertices in $bd(w_r, u_z)$. If such vertex v_i exists, then v_{i+1} can be viewed as the new w_r as t must belong to $bd(v_{i+1}, u_z)$. So, the excluded vertices between new w_r (i.e., v_{i+1}) and old w_r are now added to new $bd(v_q, w_r)$ which invokes the process of testing for inclusion of these vertices in P_{cc} as stated earlier. While including these excluded vertices in P_{cc}, both Case 1 and Case 2 can occur. If Case 1 occurs, the algorithm terminates. If Case 2 occurs, it changes the current w_m, which invokes the process of inclusion of vertices for P_c as stated earlier. Once the cascading process of testing for inclusion in both P_c and P_{cc} is over, it means that new $bd(w_m, u_k)$ and $bd(w_r, u_z)$ have been computed.

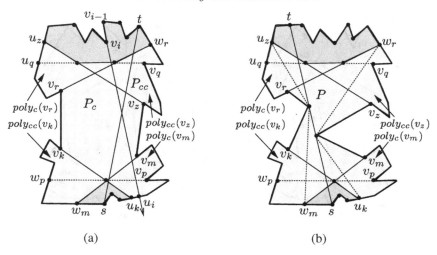

(a)   (b)

Figure 3.23 (b) The point t belongs to $bd(w_r, v_{i-1})$. (c) The visibility chord st is the extension of a cross-tangent between $SP(w_m, u_z)$ and $SP(w_r, u_k)$.

Once the clockwise scan is over, the algorithm scans the present $bd(w_r, u_z)$ in counterclockwise order from w_r (see Figure 3.23(a)) until a vertex v_i is found such that (i) v_i is the parent of v_{i-1} in $SPT(w_p)$, and (ii) $\overrightarrow{v_{i-1}v_i}$ does not intersect $v_k u_k$. If no such vertex v_i exists, it means that st can intersect clockwise C-*polygons* of all reflex vertices in $bd(w_r, u_z)$. If such vertex v_i exists, then v_{i-1} can be viewed as the new u_z as t must belong to $bd(w_r, v_{i-1})$. Then the analogous cascading process of testing for inclusion is carried out as stated earlier. If the algorithm does not terminate, it means that new $bd(w_m, u_k)$ and $bd(w_r, u_z)$ have been computed.

Analogous clockwise and counterclockwise scanning of $bd(w_m, u_k)$ followed by testing (if required) are carried out until the cascading process of testing for inclusion in both P_c and P_{cc} is over. Hence, the algorithm computes the final $bd(w_m, u_k)$ and $bd(w_r, u_z)$.

Let us now construct a visibility chord st in P. If $SP(w_m, u_z)$ or $SP(w_m, w_r)$ or $SP(u_k, u_z)$ or $SP(u_k, w_r)$ is a segment, then the segment is a visibility chord st. Otherwise, compute a cross-tangent between $SP(w_m, u_z)$ and $SP(w_r, u_k)$ (see Figure 3.23(b)) and extend its both ends to $bd(P)$, which is a visibility chord st in P. In the following, we state the major steps for computing a visibility chord st inside P.

Step 1. Compute $SPT(v_1)$ by the algorithm of Ghosh *et al.* [162].

Step 2. By traversing $SPT(v_1)$, locate two disjoint critical polygons $poly_c(v_p)$ and $poly_{cc}(v_q)$ with bounding chords $v_p w_p$ and $v_q u_q$, respectively.

Step 3. Compute $SPT(v_p)$, $SPT(w_p)$, $SPT(v_q)$ and $SPT(u_q)$.

Step 4. *For* each vertex v_k of $bd(u_q, w_p)$, test whether (i) $SP(w_p, v_k)$ makes only left turns, and (ii) $SP(u_q, v_k)$ makes only right turns.

Step 5. *For* each vertex $v_k \in bd(v_p, v_q)$, test whether (i) $SP(v_p, v_k)$ makes only right turns, and (ii) $SP(v_q, v_k)$ makes only left turns.

Step 6. Test whether $SP(u_q, w_p)$ passes through a vertex of $bd(v_p, v_q)$ or $SP(v_p, v_q)$ passes through a vertex of $bd(u_q, w_p)$.

Step 7. Locate two critical polygons $poly_{cc}(v_k)$ and $poly_c(v_m)$ with bounding chords $v_k u_k$ and $v_m w_m$, respectively, where $v_k \in bd(u_q, w_p)$ and $u_k \in bd(w_p, v_p)$, $v_m \in bd(v_p, v_q)$ and $w_m \in bd(w_p, v_p)$. Test whether $v_k u_k$ and $v_m w_m$ intersect.

Step 8. Locate two critical polygons $poly_{cc}(v_z)$ and $poly_c(v_r)$ with bounding chords $v_z u_z$ and $v_r w_r$, respectively, where $v_z \in bd(v_p, v_q)$ and $u_z \in bd(v_q, u_q)$, $v_r \in bd(u_q, w_p)$ and $w_r \in bd(v_q, u_q)$. Test whether $v_z u_z$ and $v_r w_r$ intersect.

Step 9. Using cascade testing, determine whether (i) $bd(u_z, w_m)$ can be included in $bd(P_c)$, and (ii) $bd(u_k, w_r)$ can be included in $bd(P_{cc})$.

Step 10. Scan $bd(w_r, u_z)$ and $bd(w_m, u_k)$ in both clockwise and counterclockwise order to compute the final $bd(w_r, u_z)$ and $bd(w_m, u_k)$.

Step 11. Compute a visibility chord in P by extending a cross-tangent between $SP(w_m, u_z)$ and $SP(w_r, u_k)$ to $bd(P)$ and report st.

Let us discuss the correctness of the algorithm. It follows from Lemma 3.2.18 that a visibility chord st must intersect all clockwise and counterclockwise *C-polygons*. At each stage, the algorithm considers a *C-polygon* C_i and checks whether it forms a disjoint critical polygon with any critical polygons $CP_{i-1} = (C_1, C_2,..., C_{i-1})$ located so far. The algorithm also maintains two common intersection regions implicitly by maintaining $bd(w_m, u_k)$ and $bd(w_r, u_z)$ formed by the bounding chords of CP_{i-1} such that one common intersection region can contain s and the other can contain t. If C_i is a disjoint critical polygon with two other mutually disjoint critical polygons C_j and C_k in CP_{i-1}, the algorithm terminates. If C_i does not intersect either of the two common intersection regions, the algorithm terminates. If C_i intersects one of the two common intersection regions, it updates that common intersection region. If C_i intersects both common intersection regions, it leaves both common intersection regions unchanged. Once all *C-polygons* are considered, the algorithm constructs st by ensuring that st intersects all *C-polygons* of P using a cross-tangent between $SP(w_m, u_z)$ and $SP(w_r, u_k)$.

Let us analyze the time complexity of the algorithm. It can be seen that all shortest paths computed in P in Steps 1 and 3 can be done in $O(n)$ time as it involves computing five shortest path trees. Two disjoint critical polygons $poly_c(v_p)$ and $poly_{cc}(v_q)$ in Step 2 can be located by traversing $SPT(v_1)$ at most four times. By traversing $SPT(v_p)$, $SPT(w_p)$, $SPT(v_q)$ and $SPT(u_q)$ once, turns at all vertices on $bd(u_q, w_p)$ and $bd(v_p, v_q)$ can be tested in Steps 4 and 5 in $O(n)$ time. Since u_k and u_z move only on the clockwise direction in two disjoint portions of the boundary of P, total cost for updating u_k and u_z is $O(n)$. Similarly, total cost for updating w_m and w_r is $O(n)$ as w_m and w_r move only in the counterclockwise direction on two disjoint portions of the boundary of P. Therefore, Steps 7 and 8 can be performed in $O(n)$ time. Similarly, Steps 9 and 10 take $O(n)$ time. The chord st in Step 11 can be constructed in $O(n)$ time. Therefore, the overall time complexity of the algorithm is $O(n)$. We summarize the result in the following theorem.

Theorem 3.5.18 *A visibility chord st in a simple polygon P of n vertices can be constructed in $O(n)$ time.*

3.6 Computing Shortest Path Trees

3.6.1 In Simple Polygons: $O(n)$ Algorithm

In this section, we present an $O(n)$ time algorithm of Guibas *et al.* [178] for computing Euclidean shortest paths inside a simple polygon P of n vertices from a given point s to all vertices of P. This algorithm is a generalization of the linear time algorithm of Lee and Preparata [235] for computing the shortest path from a point s to another point t inside P. Here, we also present the algorithm of Lee and Preparata.

It can be seen that the union of shortest paths from s to all vertices of P form a tree (see Figure 3.24(a)) and it is called the *shortest path tree* rooted at s (denoted as $SPT(s)$). Observe that the parent of a vertex v in $SPT(s)$ is the previous vertex u of v in $SP(s,v)$ (see Figure 3.24(a)). The algorithm for computing $SPT(s)$ first triangulates the given simple polygon P (denoted as $T(P)$). This can be done by the algorithm of Chazelle [71] in $O(n)$ time (see Theorem 1.4.6). Then the algorithm traverses triangle by triangle using the dual graph of $T(P)$ and it computes the shortest paths from s to the vertices of triangles in $T(P)$. Thus, the algorithm computes $SPT(s)$ in P. For properties of triangulations of P and their dual graphs, see Section 1.4.

Let T_s denote the triangle containing s. So, s can be connected to all three vertices of T_s in $SPT(s)$. Note that s is currently the *least common ancestor* of the vertices of T_s in $SPT(s)$. Assume that the algorithm has computed $SP(s,u)$ and $SP(s,v)$, where uv is an edge of $T(P)$ (Figure 3.24(b)). Let w be the least common ancestor of u and v in $SPT(s)$. The region of P bounded by $SP(w,u)$, $SP(w,v)$ and uv is called a *funnel F*, where w is the *apex* of the funnel, $SP(w,u)$ and $SP(w,v)$ are the *sides of the funnel*, and uv is the *base of the funnel*. Observe that $SP(w,u)$ and $SP(w,v)$ are convex paths facing toward the interior of F. Let $\triangle uvz$ be the next triangle of F in $T(P)$. So, z lies outside F and the diagonal uv is not a polygonal edge. The vertex z is called the *next vertex* of F in $T(P)$. We have the following observation.

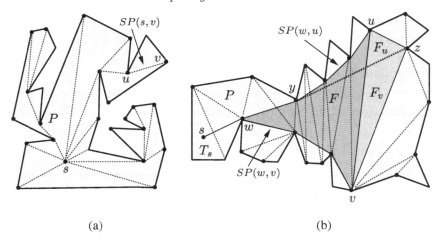

Figure 3.24 (a) The shortest path tree $SPT(s)$ from a point s to all vertices of P. The vertex u is the parent of the vertex v in $SPT(s)$. (b) The tangent yz splits the funnel F into two funnels F_u and F_v.

Lemma 3.6.1 *Let $\triangle uvz$ be the next triangle in $T(P)$ of a funnel F, where w is the apex of F and uv is the base of F. Let y be the vertex of F such that yz is the tangent to $SP(w,u)$ or $SP(w,v)$. The vertex y is the parent of z in $SPT(s)$.*

Proof. Since w is the least common ancestor of u and v in $SPT(s)$ (see Figure 3.24(b)), the line segment joining z and any vertex on $SP(s,w)$, excluding w, does not lie inside P. Therefore, the previous vertex of z on $SP(s,z)$ belongs to F. Since the internal angle at the previous vertex of z on $SP(s,z)$ is reflex by Corollary 3.2.4, the last edge in $SP(s,z)$ is the tangent yz from z to $SP(w,u)$ or $SP(w,v)$. Hence, y is the parent of z in $SPT(s)$. $\qquad\square$

Corollary 3.6.2 *If yz is the tangent to both $SP(w,u)$ and $SP(w,v)$, then $y = w$.*

The above lemma suggests a procedure for locating the parent of z in $SPT(s)$ as follows. Traverse F starting from u or v (see Figure 3.24(b)) till a vertex y is reached such that yz is the tangent to the side of the funnel at y. Once yz is added to F, F splits into two funnels F_u and F_v. If $y \in SP(w,u)$, then $F_u = (SP(y,u),z,y)$ and $F_v = (SP(w,z),SP(v,w))$ (see Figure 3.24(b)). Otherwise, $F_u = (SP(w,u),SP(z,w))$ and $F_v = (y,z,SP(v,w))$. Note that uz and zv are the bases of F_u and F_v, respectively.

It can be seen that after splitting F into two funnels F_u and F_v, both F_u and F_v may have their respective next vertices (see Figure 3.24(b)) and therefore, it is again necessary to split both F_u and F_v by drawing tangents from their respective next vertices. Repeat the process of splitting a funnel as long as it has a next vertex. In other words, the process of splitting funnels terminates when the base of each funnel is a polygonal edge. Thus, $SPT(s)$ is computed. In the following, we state the major steps of the algorithm for computing $SPT(s)$ in P.

Step 1. Triangulate P by the algorithm of Chazelle [71].

Step 2. Locate the given point s in a triangle T_s of $T(P)$. Assign s as the parent of all three vertices of T_s in $SPT(s)$. Initialize the list of funnels L by these three funnels.

Step 3. *While* a funnel F in L has a next vertex *then*

Step 3a. Let z the next vertex of F. Compute the tangent yz to F and assign y as the parent of z in $SPT(s)$.

Step 3b. Add yz to F and split F into two new funnels. Add these two funnels to L.

Step 4. Output $SPT(s)$ and Stop.

The correctness of the algorithm follows from Lemma 3.6.1. Let us analyze the time complexity of the algorithm. It can be seen that the algorithm runs in $O(n)$ time if the total cost for computing tangents in Step 3a for all funnels is $O(n)$. Suppose the algorithm uses a linear search to locate y in F in Step 3a. It means that y is located by traversing vertices in F starting from u or v. So, the cost for locating y is proportional to the number of vertices traversed in F. Suppose y is the adjacent vertex of v in F and the linear search is performed starting at u (see Figure 3.25(a)). If m is the number of vertices in F, the number of vertices traversed for locating y is $m - 1$. Now F_u has all vertices of F except v, and z is added to F_u. Hence the size of F_u is same as F. If the same situation again occurs while splitting the funnel F_u, the number of vertices traversed again is $m - 1$. If such a situation occurs repeatedly for subsequent splitting, the total time required for splitting all funnels can be $O(n^2)$.

Let us consider a special situation. Assume that the dual graph of $T(P)$ does not have any node of degree 3 (see Figure 3.25(b)). This means that whenever F is split into F_u and F_v by yz, uz or vz is a polygonal edge. Therefore, only one of F_u and F_v can have a next vertex which requires further splitting. If uz is a polygonal edge (see Figure 3.25(b)), a linear search in F can start from u. In that case, the cost for locating y in F is proportional to the size of F_u. Since F_u does not have a next vertex as uz is a polygonal edge, the vertices of F_u are not considered again for subsequent splitting of any other funnel. Similarly, if vz is a polygonal edge, a linear search in F for locating y can start from v instead of u. Using this strategy of choosing the starting vertex of a linear search, the total cost for splitting all funnels can be bounded by $O(n)$ in this special situation.

In light of above discussion, let us consider the problem of computing the shortest path $SP(s, t)$ between two given points s and t in P. Let T_s and T_t denote the triangles in $T(P)$ containing s and t, respectively. Let p_{st} denote the path from T_s

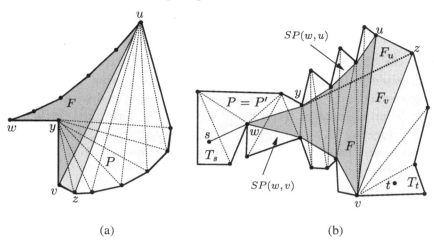

Figure 3.25 (a) Splitting all funnels takes $O(n^2)$ time by a linear search. (b) One side of every triangle in the triangulation of P is a polygonal edge.

to T_t in the dual of $T(P)$. Construct the sub-polygon P' of P consisting of only those triangle of $T(P)$ that are on p_{st}. In Figure 3.25(b), P' is same as P as one side of every triangle in $T(P)$ is a polygonal edge. Since $SP(s, t)$ lies inside P', P' can be considered for computing $SP(s, t)$ in place of P. Since the dual graph of $T(P')$ is a path, the above strategy of linear search can be used for computing $SP(s, t)$ in $O(n)$ time as shown by Lee and Preparata [235]. We have the following theorem.

Theorem 3.6.3 *The shortest path between two points inside a simple polygon P of n vertices can be computed in $O(n)$ time.*

Let us return to the discussion on the cost of computing tangent yz in F in Step 3a of the algorithm for computing $SPT(s)$. In order to obtain the desired linear time complexity for computing $SPT(s)$, a different searching strategy for locating y is required at the time of splitting F. Is it possible to perform binary search (instead of a linear search) on F to locate y? Before we answer this question affirmatively, we need a suitable representation of F.

Observe that the current funnel F can be maintained as a sorted list $[u_l, u_{l-1}, ..., u_1,$ $w, v_1, v_2, ..., v_k]$, where $u_0 = v_0 = w$ is the apex of F, and the sides of F are $SP(u_0, u_l) = [u_0, ..., u_l]$ and $SP(v_0, v_k) = [v_0, ..., v_k]$. The list representing F is stored in a search tree. To perform search for locating the vertex y, store two pointers with each vertex x of F appearing in the search tree, pointing to its two neighbors x' and x'' in F. This allows to calculate the slope of two edges xx' and xx'' of F in constant time. By comparing the slopes of xx' and xx'' with that of xz, it can be decided in constant time on which side of x the binary search should continue in order to locate y. Therefore, this data structures supports searching for

y in $O(\log(l + k + 1))$ time. Since there can be at most $O(n)$ operations of splitting funnels in P, the total time required for splitting all funnels is $O(n \log n)$.

Although the binary search gives a better time complexity than a linear search, it is still possible to improve the time complexity by storing F in *a finger search tree*. A finger search tree is essentially a search tree equipped with *fingers*. A finger is a pointer to an element of the list and searching is performed in the search tree between two fingers. In a search tree, searching starts from the root of the tree, whereas in a finger search tree the searching starts from a finger. For more details on finger search trees, see Mehlhorn [256].

In our application, the fingers are placed at the first and the last node of the tree in symmetric order, i.e., at u_l and v_k. We now discuss the procedure for locating y in our finger search tree. Let d be the distance from u_l to y in F. Observe that the number of nodes in the path A_u from u_l to y in the finger search tree is $O(\log d)$. The next node in the path can be determined from the current node by comparing slopes as stated earlier. If m is the size of F, then y is at a distance $m - d$ from v_k in F. So, the number of nodes in the path A_v from v_k to y in the finger search tree is $O(\log(m - d))$. Using both paths A_u and A_v, then y can be located as follows. Move from u_l to the next node in A_u. Move from v_k to the next node in A_v. Move from the current node to the next node in A_u. Move from the current node to the next node in A_v and so on, until y is reached either from u_l or from v_k. So y can be located in $O(\min(\log d, \log(m - d))$ time.

The finger search tree therefore supports searching for the tangent from the next vertex in time $O(\log \delta)$, where δ is the distance from y to the nearest finger. It also supports operations that split the tree into two sub-trees at y in amortized time $O(\log \delta)$.

To bound the time required for splitting all funnels recursively using finger search trees, we argue as follows. Let T denote the dual tree of a triangulation of P and it has $n - 2$ nodes. If s lies in one triangle T_s, take that triangle as the root of T. Otherwise, s is a vertex and lies in several triangles of the given triangulation. There exists at least one triangle with a polygonal edge incident to s and take that triangle as the root of T. Thus each node of T (including the root) has 0, 1, or 2 children. The algorithm is a depth-first traversal of T [15].

We know that the cost for processing the node of x is $O(\min(\log d, \log(m - d)))$, where m is the size of the funnel before the node of x is processed and, d and $m - d$ are the size of two funnels after splitting. Let $C^*(m)$ denote the cost of processing the sub-tree rooted at the node of x. So,

$$C^*(m) = C^*(d) + C^*(m - d) + O(\min(\log d, \log(m - d))),$$

where $C^*(d)$ and $C^*(m - d)$ denote the cost of processing the sub-trees rooted at the children of the node of x. Taking all possible partitions of m, we obtain the formula

$C^*(m) = \max_{1 \le d \le m-1}[C^*(d) + C^*(m-d) + O(\min(\log d, \log(m-d)))]$.

It can be shown by induction on m that $C^*(m)$ is maximum for $d = m/2$. Therefore, $C^*(m) \le C'(m) = 2C'(m/2) + O(\log m/2)$. So,

$C'(m) = O(m) + O(\log\{(m^1 . m^2 . m^4 ... m^{2^{\log m}})/(2^1 . 2^{2.2} . 2^{3.2^2} . 2^{4.2^3} ... 2^{\log m . 2^{\log m - 1}})\})$.

Assuming m is power of 2,

$$C'(m) = O(m) + O(\log\{(m^{m-1})/(2^{m \log m + 1 - m})\})$$
$$= O(m) + O(\log\{(m^{m-1})/(m^m 2^{1-m})\})$$
$$= O(m) + O(m - 1 - \log m).$$

Hence $C^*(m)$ is $O(m)$. So the total time required for splitting all funnels is $O(n)$. Thus the overall time complexity of the algorithm is $O(n)$. We summarize the result in the following theorem.

Theorem 3.6.4 *The shortest path tree rooted at a point inside a simple polygon P of n vertices can be computed in $O(n)$ time.*

3.6.2 In Weak Visibility Polygons: $O(n)$ Algorithm

In this section, we present an $O(n)$ time algorithm of Ghosh *et al.* [162] for computing the shortest path tree from a vertex in a simple polygon P of n vertices without the prior knowledge of a visibility chord in P. If the algorithm terminates without computing the shortest path tree, it means that P is not a weak visibility polygon because it does not satisfy the characterization of weak visibility polygons presented in Theorem 3.2.14. If the algorithm computes the shortest path tree, P may or may not have a visibility chord. The algorithm computes the shortest path tree by scanning the boundary of P using simple data structures. This algorithm can be viewed as a preprocessing step for recognizing weak visibility polygons as shown in Sections 3.5.1 and 3.5.2.

> **Exercise 3.6.1** *Assume that a simple polygon P of n vertices is given along with a visibility chord. Design an $O(n)$ time algorithm for computing the shortest path tree from a vertex of P by scanning the boundary of P [162].*

We assume that the vertices of the given simple polygon P are labeled $v_1, v_2, \ldots, v_n$ in counterclockwise order. The algorithm chooses v_1 as the root and then computes $SPT(v_1)$. In presenting the algorithm, we use the same notations and definitions introduced in Section 3.3.1. The algorithm starts by scanning $bd_{cc}(v_2, v_n)$ in counterclockwise order, and computes $SP_{cc}(v_1, v_2)$, $SP_{cc}(v_1, v_3)$,..., $SP_{cc}(v_1, v_{n-1})$ (see Figure 3.26(a)). During the counterclockwise scan, if it is found that $SP(v_1, v_{i-1})$ does not make only right turns for some vertex v_{i-1} (i.e., $SP(v_1, v_{i-1}) \ne SP_{cc}(v_1, v_{i-1})$),

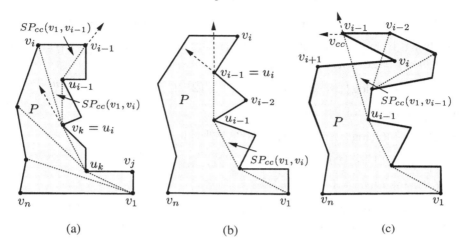

(a)   (b)   (c)

Figure 3.26 (a) $SP_{cc}(v_1, v_i) = (SP_{cc}(v_1, v_k), v_i)$. (b) $SP_{cc}(v_1, v_i) = (SP_{cc}(v_1, v_{i-1}), v_i)$. (c) There is a reverse turn at v_{i-1}.

then the algorithm marks the vertex v_{i-1} as v_{cc} (see Figure 3.26(c)), and starts the clockwise scan from v_n for computing $SP_c(v_1, v_{n-1})$, $SP_c(v_1, v_{n-2})$,..., $SP_c(v_1, v_2)$. During the clockwise scan, if it is found that $SP_c(v_1, v_{i-1})$ does not make only left turns for some vertex v_{i-1} (i.e., $SP(v_1, v_{i-1}) \neq SP_c(v_1, v_{i-1})$), then the algorithm marks the vertex v_{i-1} as v_c. If the counterclockwise scan reaches v_n, then $SPT_{cc}(v_1, v_n)$ is $SPT(v_1)$ (see Figure 3.26(a)). Similarly, if the clockwise scan reaches v_2, then $SPT_c(v_1, v_2)$ is $SPT(v_1)$. Otherwise, the algorithm has located v_{cc} and v_c. We say that there are reverse turns at v_{cc} and v_c.

Let us explain the procedure for locating v_{cc} during the counterclockwise scan. The vertex v_c can be located by the analogous procedure. Assume that $SP_{cc}(v_1, v_2)$, $SP_{cc}(v_1, v_3)$,..., $SP_{cc}(v_1, v_{i-1})$ have been computed and the procedure wants to compute $SP_{cc}(v_1, v_i)$. Let u_j denote the parent of v_j in $SPT_{cc}(v_1, v_{i-1})$. We have the following cases.

Case 1. The vertex v_i lies to the left of $\overrightarrow{u_{i-1}v_{i-1}}$ (Figure 3.26(a)).
Case 2. The vertex v_i lies to the right of $\overrightarrow{u_{i-1}v_{i-1}}$.

  Case 2a. The vertex v_i lies to the right of $\overrightarrow{v_{i-2}v_{i-1}}$ (Figure 3.26(b)).
  Case 2b. The vertex v_i lies to the left of $\overrightarrow{v_{i-2}v_{i-1}}$ (Figure 3.26(c)).

Consider Case 1. Since v_i lies to the left of $\overrightarrow{u_{i-1}v_{i-1}}$ (see Figure 3.26(a)), $SP_{cc}(v_1, v_i)$ makes only right turns. Let v_k be the first vertex of $SP_{cc}(v_1, v_{i-1})$ starting from v_{i-1} such that v_i lies to the right of $\overrightarrow{u_k v_k}$. Therefore, v_k becomes the parent u_i of v_i in $SPT_{cc}(v_1, v_i)$ as $v_i v_k$ is the tangent from v_i to $SP_{cc}(v_1, v_{i-1})$. Hence, $SP_{cc}(v_1, v_i) = (SP_{cc}(v_1, v_k), v_i)$.

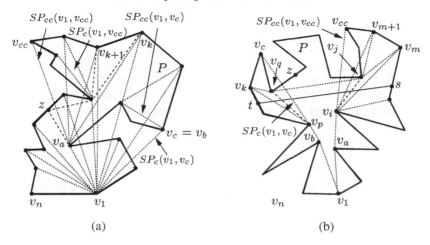

Figure 3.27 (a) The vertex v_c belongs to $bd_{cc}(v_1, v_{cc})$. (b) The vertex v_c does not belong to $bd_{cc}(v_1, v_{cc})$.

Consider Case 2a. Since v_i lies to the right of both $\overrightarrow{u_{i-1}v_{i-1}}$ and $\overrightarrow{v_{i-2}v_{i-1}}$ (see Figure 3.26(b)), it means that $SP_{cc}(v_1, v_i)$ makes only right turns, and v_{i-1} is the parent u_i of v_i in $SPT_{cc}(v_1, v_i)$ as $v_i v_{i-1}$ is the tangent from v_i to $SP_{cc}(v_1, v_{i-1})$. So, $SP_{cc}(v_1, v_i) = (SP_{cc}(v_1, v_{i-1}), v_i)$.

Consider Case 2b. Since v_i lies to the right of $\overrightarrow{u_{i-1}v_{i-1}}$ and to the left of $\overrightarrow{v_{i-2}v_{i-1}}$ (see Figure 3.26(c)), $SP(v_1, v_{i-1})$ passes through vertices of $bd_{cc}(v_i, v_{n-1})$ and therefore, $SP(v_1, v_{i-1})$ and $SP_{cc}(v_1, v_{i-1})$ are not same. The vertex v_{i-1} is marked as v_{cc}.

> **Exercise 3.6.2** *Let v be a vertex of a simple polygon P of n vertices. Assume that the shortest path from v to each vertex of P does not make a right turn at any vertex in the path. Design an $O(n)$ time algorithm to compute the shortest path tree in P from the next counterclockwise vertex of v by scanning the boundary of P.*

From now on we assume that the algorithm has located v_c and v_{cc}, and has computed $SPT_c(v_1, v_c)$ and $SPT_{cc}(v_1, v_{cc})$. We have the following two cases.

Case A. The vertex v_c belongs to $bd_{cc}(v_1, v_{cc})$ (Figure 3.27(a)).

Case B. The vertex v_c does not belong to $bd_{cc}(v_1, v_{cc})$ (Figure 3.27(b)).

It will be shown later that Case A can be solved using the method presented for Case B. Consider Case B. From the definitions of v_c and v_{cc}, it is clear that $SP_c(v_1, v_c)$ is not $SP(v_1, v_c)$ as $SP(v_1, v_c)$ passes through at least a vertex of $bd_{cc}(v_1, v_c)$. Similarly, $SP_{cc}(v_1, v_{cc})$ is not $SP(v_1, v_{cc})$ as $SP(v_1, v_{cc})$ passes through at least a vertex of $bd_c(v_1, v_{cc})$. We have the following observation on the relationship of v_c and v_{cc} with a visibility chord st in P.

Lemma 3.6.5 *Let v_1, v_c and v_{cc} be any three vertices of P such that $SP(v_1, v_{cc})$ and $SP(v_1, v_c)$ pass through a vertex of $bd_c(v_1, v_{cc})$ and $bd_{cc}(v_1, v_c)$, respectively. If P is weakly visible from a chord st, then one endpoint of st lies on $bd_{cc}(v_1, v_{cc})$ and the other endpoint of st lies on $bd_c(v_1, v_c)$.*

Proof. Since $SP(v_1, v_{cc})$ passes through a vertex of $bd_c(v_1, v_{cc})$ (see Figure 3.27(b)), st must intersect the eave $v_i v_j$ of $SP(v_1, v_{cc})$ by Lemma 3.2.16, where $v_i \in bd_{cc}(v_1, v_{cc})$ and $v_j \in bd_c(v_1, v_{cc})$. Therefore, one endpoint of st lies on $bd_{cc}(v_1, v_{cc})$. The arguments also hold for the special situation when $v_i = v_1$. Analogous arguments show that the other endpoint of st lies on $bd_c(v_1, v_c)$.   □

Corollary 3.6.6 *The vertex v_1 belongs to one sub-polygon of st, and vertices v_c and v_{cc} belong to the other sub-polygon of st.*

Corollary 3.6.7 *For any vertex $v_k \in bd_{cc}(v_{cc}, v_c)$, $SP(v_c, v_k)$ makes only left turns and $SP(v_{cc}, v_k)$ makes only right turns.*

Corollary 3.6.7 suggests the next step of the algorithm. Scan $bd_{cc}(v_{cc}, v_c)$ in counterclockwise order and compute $SPT_{cc}(v_{cc}, v_c)$. If a reverse turn is encountered during the scan, i.e., Corollary 3.6.7 does not hold, the algorithm terminates as there is no visibility chord in P. So, we assume that $SPT_{cc}(v_{cc}, v_c)$ has been computed. Analogously, scan $bd_c(v_c, v_{cc})$ in clockwise order and compute $SPT_c(v_c, v_{cc})$. Hence, four trees $SPT_{cc}(v_1, v_{cc})$, $SPT_{cc}(v_{cc}, v_c)$, $SPT_c(v_1, v_c)$ and $SPT_c(v_c, v_{cc})$ have been computed.

The above four partial trees computed by the algorithm can be merged to compute $SPT(v_1)$. We know that $SP_c(v_c, v_{cc})$ and $SP_{cc}(v_1, v_{cc})$ are intersecting (see Figure 3.27(b)). So, the two paths $SP_c(v_c, v_{cc})$ and $SP_{cc}(v_1, v_{cc})$ share a point other that v_{cc}. It can be seen in Figure 3.28(a) that $SP_c(v_c, v_{cc})$ and $SP_{cc}(v_1, v_{cc})$ meet only at v_{cc} but two paths cannot be called non-intersecting as the previous vertices of v_{cc} in the two paths are in the reverse order at v_{cc}. So, we need a proper definition of intersecting paths. For any vertex $v_k \in bd_{cc}(v_1, v_{cc})$, two convex paths $SP_c(v_c, v_k) = (v_c, ..., w_k, v_k)$, and $SP_{cc}(v_1, v_k) = (v_1, ..., u_k, v_k)$ are said to be *intersecting* if w_k lies to the right of $\overrightarrow{u_k v_k}$ (see Figure 3.28). In order to rectify the intersection of $SP_c(v_c, v_{cc})$ and $SP_{cc}(v_1, v_{cc})$, a vertex $v_m \in bd_{cc}(v_2, v_{cc})$ is located such that (i) $SP_c(v_c, v_m)$ and $SP_{cc}(v_1, v_m)$ are not intersecting, and (ii) $SP_c(v_c, v_{m+1})$ and $SP_{cc}(v_1, v_{m+1})$ are intersecting (see Figure 3.27(b)). Note that no such vertex v_m exists for the polygon in Figure 3.28(a) and therefore, this polygon does not have any visibility chord. From now on we assume that v_m always exists (see Figure 3.27(b)). We have the following observations.

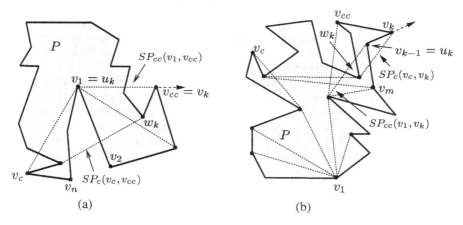

Figure 3.28 (a) Two paths $SP_{cc}(v_1, v_{cc})$ and $SP_c(v_c, v_{cc})$ intersect. (b) A reverse turn is encountered at v_k before v_m is reached.

Lemma 3.6.8 *Let v_k be a vertex of $bd_{cc}(v_1, v_{cc})$. If $SP_c(v_c, v_k)$ and $SP_{cc}(v_1, v_k)$ intersect, then $SP(v_1, v_k)$ contains an eave.*

Proof. Proof follows from the definition of intersecting paths. □

Lemma 3.6.9 *If st is a visibility chord of P, where $s \in bd_{cc}(v_1, v_{cc})$ and $t \in bd_c(v_1, v_c)$, then every path in $SPT_c(v_c, s)$ makes only left turns and every path in $SPT_{cc}(v_{cc}, t)$ makes only right turns.*

Proof. Proof follows from Theorem 3.2.13 (see Figure 3.27(b)). □

Lemma 3.6.9 suggests a method to locate v_m. The merging procedure scans $bd_c(v_{cc}, v_1)$ in clockwise order starting from v_{cc} and it computes $SP_c(v_c, v_k)$, where v_k is the current vertex under consideration. If $SP_c(v_c, v_k)$ and $SP_{cc}(v_1, v_k)$ are non-intersecting, then v_k is v_m (see Figure 3.27(b)). Otherwise, v_{k-1} becomes the current vertex under consideration. During the scan, if a reverse turn is encountered at v_k (see Figure 3.28(b)), s belongs to $bd_c(v_{cc}, v_k)$ by Lemmas 3.6.5 and 3.6.9. On the other hand, there is no chord connecting a point of $bd_c(v_{cc}, v_k)$ to another point of $bd_c(v_1, v_c)$ in P. Therefore, there is no visibility chord in P and the algorithm terminates. From now on we assume that v_m is reached by the algorithm by scanning $bd_c(v_{cc}, v_1)$.

Exercise 3.6.3 *Let Q_1 and Q_2 be two disjoint convex polygons of m_1 and m_2 vertices. Let $a \in Q_1$ and $b \in Q_2$ be two vertices such that Q_1 and Q_2 lie on the opposite sides of the line drawn through a and b. The segment ab is called a cross-tangent between Q_1 and Q_2. Design an algorithm for locating both cross-tangents between Q_1 and Q_2 in $O(m_1 + m_2)$ time [291].*

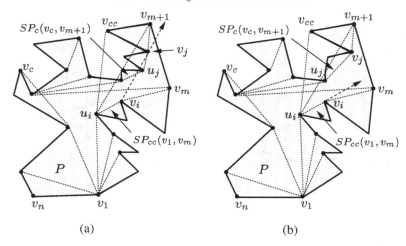

Figure 3.29 (a) The parent u_j of v_j in $SPT_c(v_c, v_{m+1})$ becomes the current v_j. (b) The parent u_i of v_i in $SPT_{cc}(v_1, v_m)$ becomes the current v_i.

After locating v_m, the merging procedure draws the cross-tangent $v_i v_j$ between $SP_c(v_c, v_{m+1})$ and $SP_{cc}(v_1, v_m)$, where $v_i \in SP_{cc}(v_1, v_m)$ and $v_j \in SP_c(v_c, v_{m+1})$ (see Figure 3.27b). So, v_i is the parent of v_j in $SPT_{cc}(v_1, v_j)$. Concatenate the subtree at v_j of $SPT_c(v_c, v_{m+1})$ as the subtree at v_j in $SPT_{cc}(v_1, v_j)$.

Let us explain how the cross-tangent $v_i v_j$ is computed. Assign v_{m+1} to v_j. Assign the parent of v_m in $SPT_{cc}(v_1, v_m)$ to v_i. If the parent u_j of v_j in $SPT_c(v_c, v_{m+1})$ lies to the right of $\overrightarrow{v_i v_j}$ (see Figure 3.29(a)), then assign u_j to v_j. Otherwise, if v_j lies to the left of $\overrightarrow{u_i v_i}$ (see Figure 3.29(b)), where u_i is the parent of v_i in $SPT_{cc}(v_1, v_m)$, assign u_i to v_i. This process is repeated till $v_i v_j$ becomes the cross-tangent, i.e., $SP_c(v_c, v_{m+1})$ and $SP_{cc}(v_1, v_m)$ lie on opposite sides of the line drawn through v_i and v_j.

After computing $SPT_{cc}(v_1, v_j)$, the merging procedure analogously locates the vertex $v_k \in bd_c(v_1, v_c)$ by scanning $bd_c(v_1, v_c)$ in clockwise order starting from v_c (see Figure 3.27(b)) such that (i) $SP_c(v_1, v_k)$ and $SP_{cc}(v_{cc}, v_k)$ are non-intersecting, and (ii) $SP_c(v_1, v_{k-1})$ and $SP_{cc}(v_{cc}, v_{k-1})$ are intersecting. Then the merging procedure locates the cross-tangent $v_p v_q$ between $SP_c(v_1, v_k)$ and $SP_{cc}(v_{cc}, v_{k-1})$, where $v_p \in SP_c(v_1, v_k)$ and $v_q \in SP_{cc}(v_{cc}, v_{k-1})$. Finally, $SPT_c(v_1, v_k)$ is extended to $SPT_c(v_1, v_q)$.

Exercise 3.6.4 *Draw a figure showing $SPT_{cc}(v_1, v_j)$ and $SPT_c(v_1, v_q)$ are overlapping.*

After computing $SPT_{cc}(v_1, v_j)$ and $SPT_c(v_1, v_q)$, the procedure checks whether they are disjoint or overlapping. Let v_a and v_b be the next vertex of v_1 in $SP_{cc}(v_1, v_j)$ and $SP_c(v_1, v_q)$, respectively. If v_b lies to the left of $\overrightarrow{v_1 v_a}$, then $SPT_{cc}(v_1, v_j)$ and

$SPT_c(v_1, v_q)$ are disjoint (see Figure 3.27(b)). Otherwise, they are overlapping. We have the following observations.

Lemma 3.6.10 *If $SPT_{cc}(v_1, v_j)$ and $SPT_c(v_1, v_q)$ are disjoint, then (i) for every vertex $v_d \in bd_c(v_1, v_q)$, $SP_c(v_1, v_d)$ is same as $SP(v_1, v_d)$, and (ii) for every vertex $v_d \in bd_{cc}(v_1, v_j)$, $SP_{cc}(v_1, v_d)$ is same as $SP(v_1, v_d)$.*

Lemma 3.6.11 *If $SPT_{cc}(v_1, v_j)$ and $SPT_c(v_1, v_q)$ are overlapping, then there is no visibility chord in P.*

Exercise 3.6.5 *Prove Lemma 3.6.11.*

From now on, we assume that $SPT_{cc}(v_1, v_j)$ and $SPT_c(v_1, v_q)$ are disjoint. Extend $v_i v_b$ from v_b to $bd_c(v_q, v_j)$ meeting it at z (see Figure 3.27(b)). The merging procedure scans $bd_{cc}(v_j, z)$ in counterclockwise order starting from v_j and computes $SPT_{cc}(v_1, z)$ by drawing a tangent from the current vertex v_r to $SP_{cc}(v_1, v_{r-1})$. Note that the tangent from v_r can be computed by the procedure stated earlier in Case 1 and Case 2a. A reverse turn in Case 2b can be avoided by computing the cross-tangent between $SP_c(v_c, v_r)$ and $SP_{cc}(v_1, v_{r-1})$ as stated earlier. Observe that while locating the cross-tangent, some vertices of $bd_{cc}(v_j, z)$ are skipped when the current vertex v_r is assigned to its parent in $SPT_c(v_c, v_r)$. As before, appropriate sub-trees of $SPT_c(v_c, v_j)$ at some of these skipped vertices are concatenated to complete the construction of $SPT_{cc}(v_1, z)$. Similarly, $SPT_c(v_1, v_q)$ is extended to $SPT_c(v_1, z)$ with the help of $SPT_{cc}(v_{cc}, v_q)$. Hence, the union of $SPT_c(v_1, z)$ and $SPT_{cc}(v_1, z)$ gives $SPT(v_1)$.

Consider Case A. In this case, v_c belongs to $bd_{cc}(v_1, v_{cc})$ (see Figure 3.27(a)). The algorithm checks whether $SPT_c(v_1, v_{cc})$ and $SPT_{cc}(v_1, v_c)$ are disjoint or overlapping. If they are disjoint, the algorithm locates the intersection point z as before by extending the first edge of $SP_c(v_1, v_{cc})$ to $bd_{cc}(v_c, v_{cc})$. Then the algorithm takes the union of $SPT_c(v_1, z)$ and $SPT_{cc}(v_1, z)$ to construct $SPT(v_1)$.

Consider the other situation when $SPT_c(v_1, v_{cc})$ and $SPT_{cc}(v_1, v_c)$ are overlapping (see Figure 3.27(a)). Let v_a and v_b be the next vertex of v_1 in $SP_{cc}(v_1, v_{cc})$ and $SP_c(v_1, v_c)$, respectively. It can be seen that if $bd(P)$ intersects both $v_1 v_a$ and $v_1 v_b$, then there is no visibility chord in P by Lemma 3.2.17 as there are more than one eave in $SP(v_1, v_{cc})$ or $SP(v_1, v_c)$. So, we assume that $bd(P)$ intersects either $v_1 v_b$ or $v_1 v_a$. Consider the situation when $bd(P)$ intersects $v_1 v_b$ but does not intersect $v_1 v_a$ (see Figure 3.27(a)). Scan $bd_c(z, v_c)$ in counterclockwise order until a vertex $v_k \in bd_c(v_{cc}, v_c)$ is found such that (i) $SP_c(z, v_k)$ and $SP_{cc}(v_1, v_k)$ are not intersecting, and (ii) $SP_c(z, v_{k+1})$ and $SP_{cc}(v_1, v_{k+1})$ are intersecting. If no such vertex v_k exists, it means that $SP_c(v_1, v_{cc})$ and $SP_{cc}(v_1, v_c)$ have overlapped more than once and therefore, there are two or more eaves in $SP(v_1, v_{cc})$ or $SP(v_1, v_c)$. By Lemma 3.2.17, there is no visibility chord in P. So, we assume that v_k exists.

Draw the cross-tangent between $SP_c(z, v_{k+1})$ and $SP_{cc}(v_1, v_k)$ and using the cross-tangent, complete the construction of $SPT(v_1)$ by choosing the appropriate sub-trees as discussed earlier. The other situation, i.e, when $bd(P)$ intersects $v_1 v_a$ but does not intersect $v_1 v_b$, can be handled analogously.

In the following, we state the major steps of the algorithm for computing $SPT(v_1)$ in P under the assumption that both v_c and v_{cc} exist, and $v_{cc} \in bd_{cc}(v_1, v_c)$ (i.e., Case B).

Step 1. Scan $bd(P)$ in counterclockwise order and compute $SPT_{cc}(v_1, v_{cc})$, where the reverse turn is encountered at the vertex v_{cc}.

Step 2. Scan $bd(P)$ in clockwise order and compute $SPT_c(v_1, v_c)$, where the reverse turn is encountered at the vertex v_c.

Step 3. Scan $bd_{cc}(v_{cc}, v_c)$ in counterclockwise order and compute $SPT_{cc}(v_{cc}, v_c)$. If a reverse turn is encountered at some vertex of $bd_{cc}(v_{cc}, v_c)$ *then goto* Step 12.

Step 4. Scan $bd_c(v_c, v_{cc})$ in clockwise order and compute $SPT_c(v_c, v_{cc})$. *If* a reverse turn is encountered at some vertex of $bd_c(v_c, v_{cc})$ *then goto* Step 12.

Step 5. Let v_m be a vertex of $bd_c(v_{cc}, v_1)$ such that (i) $SP_c(v_c, v_m)$ and $SP_{cc}(v_1, v_m)$ are non-intersecting, and (ii) $SP_c(v_c, v_{m+1})$ and $SP_{cc}(v_1, v_{m+1})$ are intersecting. Scan $bd_c(v_{cc}, v_1)$ in clockwise order and extend $SPT_c(v_c, v_{cc})$ to $SPT_c(v_c, v_m)$. If no such vertex v_m exists or a reverse turn is encountered before reaching v_m *then goto* Step 12.

Step 6. Compute the cross-tangent $v_i v_j$ between $SP_c(v_c, v_{m+1})$ and $SP_{cc}(v_1, v_m)$, where $v_i \in SP_{cc}(v_1, v_m)$ and $v_j \in SP_c(v_c, v_{m+1})$. Assign v_i as the parent of v_j in $SPT_{cc}(v_1, v_j)$. Concatenate the sub-tree at v_j of $SPT_c(v_c, v_{m+1})$ as the sub-tree rooted at v_j in $SPT_{cc}(v_1, v_j)$.

Step 7. Let v_k be a vertex of $bd_c(v_1, v_c)$ such that (i) $SP_c(v_1, v_k)$ and $SP_{cc}(v_{cc}, v_k)$ are non-intersecting, and (ii) $SP_c(v_1, v_{k-1})$ and $SP_{cc}(v_{cc}, v_{k-1})$ are intersecting. Scan $bd_c(v_c, v_1)$ in clockwise order and extend $SPT_{cc}(v_{cc}, v_c)$ to $SPT_{cc}(v_{cc}, v_k)$. If no such vertex v_k exists or a reverse turn is encountered before reaching v_k *then goto* Step 12.

Step 8. Compute the cross-tangent $v_p v_q$ between $SP_c(v_1, v_k)$ and $SP_{cc}(v_{cc}, v_{k-1})$, where $v_p \in SP_c(v_1, v_k)$ and $v_q \in SP_{cc}(v_{cc}, v_{k-1})$. Assign v_q as the parent of v_p in $SPT_c(v_1, v_q)$. Concatenate the sub-tree at v_q of $SPT_{cc}(v_{cc}, v_c)$ as the sub-tree rooted at v_q in $SPT_c(v_1, v_q)$.

Step 9. *If* $SPT_c(v_1, v_q)$ and $SPT_{cc}(v_1, v_j)$ are overlapping *then goto* Step 12.

Step 10. Extend the first edge of $SP_c(v_1, v_q)$ to $bd_c(v_q, v_j)$ meeting it at a point z. Extend $SPT_c(v_1, v_q)$ to $SPT_c(v_1, z)$ using $SPT_{cc}(v_{cc}, v_q)$. Extend $SPT_{cc}(v_1, v_j)$ to $SPT_{cc}(v_1, z)$ using $SPT_c(v_c, v_j)$.

Step 11. Output the union of $SPT_c(v_1, z)$ and $SPT_{cc}(v_1, z)$ as $SPT(v_1)$ and *Stop*.

Step 12. Report that there is no visibility chord in P and *Stop*.

Let us discuss the correctness of the algorithm. Steps 1 and 2 identify two vertices of P as v_{cc} and v_c in the counterclockwise and clockwise scans, respectively, where $v_{cc} \in bd_{cc}(v_1, v_c)$. As there are reverse turns at v_{cc} and v_c, one endpoint (say, s) of any visibility chord st in P belongs to $bd_{cc}(v_1, v_{cc})$ and the other endpoint t belongs to $bd_c(v_1, v_c)$ by Lemma 3.6.5. So, all vertices in $bd_{cc}(v_{cc}, v_c)$ belong to the same sub-polygon of st by Corollary 3.6.6. Therefore, the shortest paths from v_{cc} and v_c to any vertex of $bd_{cc}(v_{cc}, v_c)$ must be convex by Corollary 3.6.7, which are checked in Steps 3 and 4. Consider a vertex $v_{m+1} \in bd_{cc}(v_1, v_{cc})$ such that there is an eave in $SP(v_1, v_{m+1})$. Since st intersects every eave in $SPT(v_1)$ by Lemma 3.2.16, v_1 and v_{m+1} must belong to different sub-polygons of st. So, s belongs to $bd_{cc}(v_1, v_{m+1})$ and by Lemma 3.6.9, $SP(v_c, v_{m+1})$ makes only left turns. Step 5 locates the edge $v_m v_{m+1}$ by scanning $bd_c(v_{cc}, v_1)$ in clockwise order such that $SP_{cc}(v_1, v_m)$ is convex but $SP_{cc}(v_1, v_{m+1})$ is not convex. Step 6 locates the eave $v_i v_j$ in $SP_{cc}(v_1, v_{m+1})$ by drawing the cross-tangent between $SP_{cc}(v_1, v_m)$ and $SP_c(v_c, v_{m+1})$ and extends $SPT_{cc}(v_1, v_m)$ to $SPT_{cc}(v_1, v_j)$. Analogously, Steps 7 and 8 construct $SPT_c(v_1, v_q)$. Step 9 checks whether $SPT_{cc}(v_1, v_j)$ and $SPT_c(v_1, v_q)$ are overlapping. If they are overlapping, P cannot have a visibility chord by Lemma 3.6.11 since either $SP(v_1, v_{cc})$ or $SP(v_1, v_c)$ must have two or more eaves. If they are disjoint, then the paths in $SPT_{cc}(v_1, v_j)$ and $SPT_c(v_1, v_q)$ are the shortest paths in P by Lemma 3.6.10. The algorithm completes the construction of $SPT(v_1)$ in Steps 10 and 11. It can be seen that the algorithm runs in $O(n)$ time since the vertices of P are scanned at most four times. We summarize the result in the following theorem.

Theorem 3.6.12 *The shortest path tree rooted at a vertex of a simple polygon P of n vertices can be computed in $O(n)$ time without the prior knowledge of a visibility chord of P.*

3.7 Recognizing Weakly External Visible Polygons

In this section, we present an $O(n)$ time algorithm of Bhattacharya *et al.* [53] for computing a line segment pq outside a given simple polygon P such that P is weakly externally visible from pq. A polygon P is called *weakly externally visible* if every point on the boundary of P is visible from some point on the convex hull of P (see Figure 3.4(b)). This means that a ray can be drawn from each boundary point of P such that the ray does not intersect the interior of P. In the following, we present a recognition algorithm of P that runs in $O(n)$ time.

Step 1. Compute the convex hull of P by the algorithm of Graham and Yao [175] (see Figure 3.30(a)). Let $C = (c_1, c_2, ..., c_k)$ denote the convex hull of P where c_{i+1} is the next counterclockwise vertex of c_1.

Step 2. Scan $bd(P)$ in counterclockwise order (see Figure 3.30(a)) and compute the

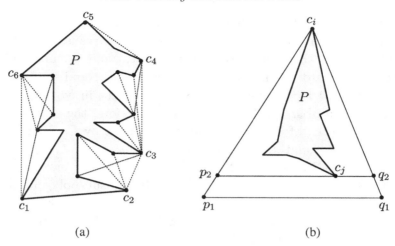

(a)   (b)

Figure 3.30 (a) The boundary of P is weakly visible from the convex hull edges of P. (b) The boundary of P is weakly visible from both $p_1 q_1$ and $p_2 q_2$.

shortest path tree $SPT_{cc}(c_1)$ rooted at c_1 by the scanning procedure mentioned in Section 3.6.2 as Case 1 and Case 2. Avis and Toussaint [42]. Analogously, scan $bd(P)$ in clockwise order (see Figure 3.30(b)) and compute $SPT_c(c_1)$.

Step 3. *If* any reverse turn is encountered during either scan *then* report that P is not weakly externally visible *else* report $SPT_{cc}(c_1)$ and $SPT_c(c_1)$.

Once we know that P is weakly externally visible, the problem is now to construct a segment pq such that P is also weakly externally visible from pq. Two vertices c_i and c_j are said to be *antipodal* if there exists two parallel lines passing through c_i and c_j such that they do not intersect the interior of P [291]. In the following lemma, we establish a property of pq.

Exercise 3.7.1 *Prove that there are at most $3m/2$ antipodal pairs of vertices in a convex polygon of m vertices [291].*

Lemma 3.7.1 *If P is weakly externally visible from a line segment $p_1 q_1$, then P is also weakly externally visible from another line segment $p_2 q_2$ which passes through a vertex of the convex hull of P.*

Proof. We prove only for the case when $p_1 q_1$ and the convex hull of P are disjoint (see Figure 3.30(b)). Let c_i be a vertex of the convex hull of P such that the triangle formed by three segments $p_1 q_1$, $p_1 c_i$ and $q_1 c_i$ contains P. Observe that such a vertex c_i always exists as P is weakly externally visible from $p_1 q_1$. Translate $p_1 q_1$ parallel to itself toward the interior of the triangle till it touches a vertex c_j of the convex hull of P. Let $p_2 \in p_1 c_i$ and $q_2 \in q_1 c_i$ be the endpoints of the translated segment

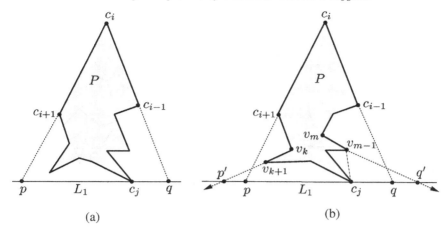

Figure 3.31 (a) P is weakly externally visible form pq. (b) The points p and q are moved to the points of intersection of the rays and L_1.

passing through c_j. It can be seen that P is also weakly externally visible from p_2q_2.

□

Corollary 3.7.2 *The vertices c_i and c_j are antipodal vertices of P.*

Suppose a line L_1 is given and it passes through a vertex c_j of the convex hull of P (see Figure 3.31(a)). Assume that P is weakly externally visible from L_1. We wish to locate the positions of p and q on L_1 closest to c_j such that P is weakly externally visible from pq.

Let c_i be an antipodal vertex of c_j such that a line parallel to L_1 touches c_i. Assign p to the intersection point of L_1 and $\overrightarrow{c_i c_{i+1}}$. Similarly, assign q to the intersection point of L_1 and $\overrightarrow{c_i c_{i-1}}$. If P is weakly externally visible from pq, then p and q are located correctly. Observe that the polygonal boundary $bd(c_j, c_i)$ is visible from qc_j and the remaining polygonal boundary $bd(c_i, c_j)$ is visible from pc_j. Note that pq satisfies Lemma 3.7.1.

Consider the other situation when P is not weakly externally visible from the current pq (see Figure 3.31(b)). This means that pc_j cannot see the entire polygonal boundary of $bd(c_i, c_j)$ or qc_j cannot see the entire polygonal boundary of $bd(c_j, c_i)$. Consider the later situation. Move q along L_1 away from c_j to the point q' such that $q'c_j$ sees the entire polygonal boundary of $bd(c_j, c_i)$ (see Figure 3.31(b)). It can be seen that q' is the intersection point of L_1 and $\overrightarrow{v_m v_{m-1}}$, where $v_m v_{m-1}$ is an edge on the polygonal boundary of $bd(c_j, c_i)$. Observe that v_{m-1} is the parent of v_m in $SPT_{cc}(c_j)$, where $SPT_{cc}(c_j)$ is the union of (i) the sub-tree of $SPT_{cc}(c_1)$ rooted at c_j, and (ii) the sub-tree of $SPT_c(c_1)$ rooted at c_j. Analogously, p can be moved along L_1 away from c_j till the point p' such that $p'c_j$ sees the entire polygonal boundary $bd(c_i, c_j)$ (see Figure 3.31(b)). This means that p' is the intersection point of L_1

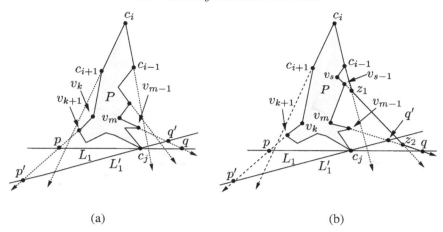

(a)   (b)

Figure 3.32 (a) The line L_1 is rotated around c_j in the counterclockwise direction to L_1'. (b) The *right envelope* (c_i, c_j) is the locus of the point q along rays.

and some $\overrightarrow{v_k v_{k+1}}$, where $v_k v_{k+1}$ is an edge on the polygonal boundary of $bd(c_i, c_j)$ and v_{k+1} is the parent of v_k in $SPT_c(c_j)$. The segment $p'q'$ becomes new pq as P is weakly externally visible from $p'q'$.

The above discussion shows how to locate the segment pq on a given line L_1. Let L_1' denote another line passing through c_j (see Figure 3.32(a)) such that there exists a line parallel to L_1' that passes through c_i and does not intersect the interior of P. So, L_1' can be viewed as the new position of L_1 after L_1 is rotated around c_j (say, in the counterclockwise direction) and c_i remains the antipodal vertex of c_j with respect to L_1'. Let p' (or q') denote the intersection point of $\overrightarrow{v_k v_{k+1}}$ (respectively, $\overrightarrow{v_m v_{m-1}}$) with L_1'. This rotation from L_1 to L_1' can also be achieved by moving p along $\overrightarrow{v_k v_{k+1}}$ away from v_k and q along $\overrightarrow{v_m v_{m-1}}$ toward v_m such that (i) the new segment $p'q'$ still passes through c_j, and (ii) c_i remains the antipodal vertex of c_j. Observe that though P is weakly externally visible from pq, P may not be weakly externally visible from $p'q'$. For example, P is weakly externally visible from $p'q'$ in Figure 3.32(a) but not in Figure 3.32(b). This can happen if the polygonal boundaries of $bd(c_i, c_j)$ and $bd(c_j, c_i)$ are not weakly visible from $p'c_j$ and $q'c_j$, respectively.

Suppose $q'c_j$ cannot see the entire polygonal boundary of $bd(c_j, c_i)$ (see Figure 3.32(b)). This means that q must move away from c_j along L_1' to the intersection point of L_1' with some ray $\overrightarrow{v_s v_{s-1}}$, where v_{s-1} is the parent of v_s in $SPT_{cc}(c_j)$ and $v_s v_{s-1}$ is an edge on $bd(v_m, c_i)$. Let z_2 be the intersection point of $\overrightarrow{v_s v_{s-1}}$ and $\overrightarrow{v_m v_{m-1}}$. In order to see the entire polygonal boundary of $bd(c_j, c_i)$ continuously, q must follow $\overrightarrow{v_m v_{m-1}}$ toward v_m till it reaches z_2 and then it has to follow $\overrightarrow{v_s v_{s-1}}$ toward v_s. Thus q can be moved along rays through their intersection points which gives the locus of q. In other words, the locus of q is the boundary of the intersection of the left half-planes of these rays $\overrightarrow{v_m v_{m-1}}$, $\overrightarrow{v_s v_{s-1}}$.... emitted from the vertices on

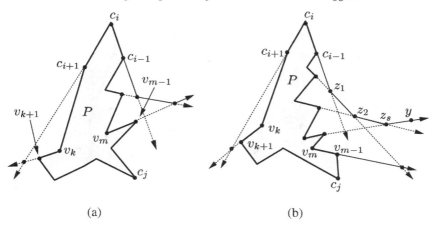

(a)   (b)

Figure 3.33 (a) P is not weakly externally visible from any segment. (b) The *right envelope* (c_i, c_j) consists of segments $c_i z_1$, $z_1 z_2$,..., $z_{s-1} z_s$, $z_s y$.

the polygonal boundary of $bd(c_j, c_i)$. Analogously the locus of p is the boundary of the right half-planes of rays like $\overrightarrow{v_k v_{k+1}}$ emitted from the vertices on the polygonal boundary of $bd(c_i, c_j)$.

The above discussion suggests a method to locate pq passing through c_j without any given line like L_1 or L_1'. Take any antipodal vertex c_i of c_j. Construct the envelope of the intersection of the left half-planes of the rays by traversing $bd(c_j, c_i)$ in clockwise order starting from c_i; call it *right envelope* (c_i, c_j). Analogously, construct the envelope of the intersection of the right half-planes of the rays by traversing $bd(c_i, c_j)$ in counterclockwise order starting from c_i; call it *left envelope* (c_i, c_j). We have the following lemma for locating pq.

Lemma 3.7.3 *Let c_i and c_j form an antipodal pair of vertices of P. Any segment through c_j which connects a point (say, q) of the right envelope (c_i, c_j) to a point (say, p) of the left envelope (c_i, c_j) is the segment pq from which P is weakly externally visible.*

Exercise 3.7.2 *Prove Lemma 3.7.3.*

Assume that no pair of points p and q satisfy Lemma 3.7.3 (see Figure 3.33(a)). Then the algorithm considers another antipodal pair and tries to construct pq by constructing *left* and *right envelopes* for this antipodal pair. By repeating the process for all antipodal pairs (c_i, c_j) of the convex hull of P, the algorithm can locate a segment pq (if it exists) from which P is weakly externally visible. Since there are at most $2n$ antipodal pairs in P and constructing the *left* and *right envelopes* for an antipodal pair takes $O(n)$ time as shown below, the algorithm takes $O(n^2)$ time in the worst case to construct pq.

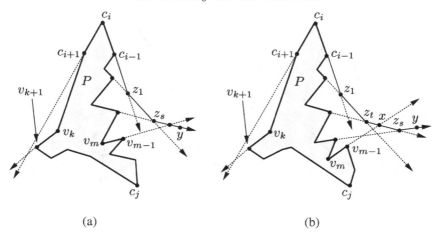

Figure 3.34 (a) The current ray intersects the last ray of *right envelope* (c_i, c_j). (b) The current ray intersects an intermediate segment of *right envelope* (c_i, c_j).

Let us explain the procedure for constructing the *right envelope* (c_i, c_j) (see Figure 3.33(b)). Initialize the *right envelope* (c_i, c_j) by $\overrightarrow{c_i c_{i-1}}$. Scan the polygonal boundary $bd(c_j, c_i)$ in clockwise order starting from c_i until a vertex v_m is located such that v_{m-1} is the parent of v_m in $SPT_{cc}(c_j)$. Let z_1 be the intersection point of $\overrightarrow{v_m v_{m-1}}$ and $\overrightarrow{c_i c_{i-1}}$. The current *right envelope* (c_i, c_j) is the segment $c_i z_1$ followed by $\overrightarrow{z_1 y}$, where z_1 lies on the segment $y v_m$. So the current *right envelope* (c_i, c_j) consists of segments starting for c_1, where the last segment ending at y represents a ray.

Assume that the current *right envelope* (c_i, c_j) consists of segments $c_i z_1$, $z_1 z_2$,..., $z_{s-1} z_s$, $z_s y$. Let $\overrightarrow{v_m v_{m-1}}$ be the current ray under consideration. We have the following cases.

Case 1. The point z_s lies to the left of $\overrightarrow{v_m v_{m-1}}$, and $\overrightarrow{z_s y}$ does not intersect $\overrightarrow{v_m v_{m-1}}$ (see Figure 3.33(b)). The *right envelope* (c_i, c_j) remains unchanged.

Case 2. Two rays $\overrightarrow{z_s y}$ and $\overrightarrow{v_m v_{m-1}}$ intersect (see Figure 3.34(a)). Call the intersection point as z_{s+1}. Update the current *right envelope* (c_i, c_j) by replacing $z_s y$ by $z_s z_{s+1}$. Choose a point y, where z_{s+1} lies on the segment $v_m y$. Append $z_{s+1} y$ to the *right envelope* (c_i, c_j).

Case 3. The point z_s lies to the right of $\overrightarrow{v_m v_{m-1}}$ (see Figure 3.34(b)). Scan the *right envelope* (c_i, c_j) from z_s till z_t is located such that $\overrightarrow{v_m v_{m-1}}$ intersect $z_t z_{t+1}$ at a point x. Delete all segments of the *right envelope* (c_i, c_j) from $z_{t+1} z_{t+2}$ to $z_s y$. Replace $z_t z_{t+1}$ by $z_t x$. Choose a point y, where x lies on the segment $v_m y$, and append xy to the *right envelope* (c_i, c_j).

Once all such vertices v_m on $bd(c_j, c_i)$ are considered, the procedure has constructed the *right envelope* (c_i, c_j). Analogously, the *left envelope* (c_i, c_j) can be constructed by scanning vertices on the polygonal boundary of (c_i, c_j). After constructing both envelopes of (c_i, c_j) the procedure locates pq, if it exists. Hence, constructing pq for an antipodal pair can be done in $O(n)$ time.

Instead of constructing the left and right envelopes in $O(n)$ time for each antipodal pair, both envelopes for all antipodal pairs can be constructed in $O(n)$ as follows. Assume that the algorithm could not find any segment pq passing through c_j for its antipodal vertex c_i, and the algorithm is currently considering the next antipodal vertex c_{i-1} of c_j. To construct the *right envelope* (c_{i-1}, c_j), the algorithm removes those segments from the *right envelope* (c_i, c_j) that are contributed by the rays emitted from the vertices of the polygonal boundary $bd(c_{i-1}, c_i)$. Observe that these segments, say, $c_i z_1, z_1 z_2,..., z_{t-1} z_t$ are consecutive segments starting from c_i. Assume that z_t and z_{t+1} lie on $\overrightarrow{v_m v_{m-1}}$. Let x be the point of intersection of $\overrightarrow{c_{i-1} c_{i-2}}$ and $\overrightarrow{v_m v_{m-1}}$. So the *right envelope* (c_{i-1}, c_j) consists of segments $c_{i-1} x$, $x z_{t+1}, z_{t+1} z_{t+2},..., z_s y$.

To construct the *left envelope* (c_{i-1}, c_j), the algorithm scans the polygonal boundary $bd(c_{i-1}, c_i)$ in counterclockwise order starting from c_{i-1} and construct a partial *left envelope* (c_{i-1}, c_j) up to c_i. Let x be the point of intersection of the *left envelope* (c_i, c_j) and the ray, which corresponds to the last segment in the partial *left envelope* (c_{i-1}, c_j). The *left envelope* (c_{i-1}, c_j) is the concatenation of the partial *left envelope* (c_{i-1}, c_j) up to x and the portion of the *left envelope* (c_i, c_j) from x to its end.

If c_{i-2} is also an antipodal vertex of c_j, the above method of updating can be used to construct the *left* and *right envelopes* (c_{i-2}, c_j). Otherwise, c_{i-1} is an antipodal vertex of c_{j-1}. Analogous method of updating can be used to construct the *left* and *right envelopes* (c_{i-1}, c_{j-1}). When the algorithm returns to the antipodal pair c_i and c_j after going around the boundary once in clockwise order, it can be seen that the total cost of updating both envelopes is proportional to the number of vertices of P. Thus the algorithm constructs both envelopes for all antipodal pairs in $O(n)$ time. In the following, we state the major steps of the algorithm.

Step 1. Compute the convex hull of P by the algorithm of Graham and Yao [175] and label the vertices of the convex hull as $c_1, c_2, ..., c_k$ in counterclockwise order.

Step 2. Scan $bd(P)$ in counterclockwise order and compute $SPT_{cc}(c_1)$. If there is any reverse turn *then goto* Step 9.

Step 3. Scan $bd(P)$ in counterclockwise order and compute $SPT_c(c_1)$. If there is any reverse turn *then goto* Step 9.

Step 4. Locate all antipodal pairs of vertices of the convex hull of P and add them in clockwise order to the list of antipodal pairs. Initialize (c_i, c_j) by the first antipodal pair in the list.

Step 5. Construct the *left* and *right envelope* (c_i, c_j) and *goto* Step 7.

Step 6. Assign (c_i, c_j) by the next antipodal pair of (c_i, c_j) in the list of antipodal pairs. Construct the *left* and *right envelope* (c_i, c_j) by updating the envelopes of the previous antipodal pair.

Step 7. *If* there is a point p on the *left envelope* (c_i, c_j) that can be connected through c_j to a point q on the *right envelope* (c_i, c_j) *then* report the segment pq and Stop.

Step 8. *If* all antipodal pairs of vertices have not been considered *then goto* Step 6.

Step 9. Report that P is not weakly externally visible from any segment and Stop.

Let us discuss the correctness of the algorithm. The algorithm first computes the convex hull of P in Step 1 and then checks in Steps 2 and 3 whether P is weakly externally visible from the boundary of the convex hull of P by computing $SPT_{cc}(c_1)$ and $SPT_c(c_1)$. Assume that that the given polygon P is weakly externally visible. We know from Lemmas 3.7.1 and 3.7.3 that P is also weakly externally visible from a segment if there is a segment pq and an antipodal pair (c_i, c_j) such that pq passes through c_j, and p and q are two points on the *left* and *right envelope* (c_i, c_j). So, the algorithm locates all antipodal pairs of P in Step 4 and then constructs both envelopes of each antipodal pair (c_i, c_j) in Steps 5 and 6 until a segment pq is found in Step 7 satisfying Lemmas 3.7.1 and 3.7.3. Hence the algorithm correctly locates a segment pq from which P is weakly externally visible. It has already been shown that the algorithm runs in $O(n)$ time as both envelopes for all antipodal pairs of vertices can be computed in $O(n)$ time. We summarize the result in the following theorem.

Theorem 3.7.4 *Recognizing a simple polygon P of n vertices weakly externally visible from a segment can be done in $O(n)$ time.*

3.8 Notes and Comments

We have presented algorithms in Section 3.5 for recognizing a weak visibility polygon P by constructing a chord st inside P. The first algorithm proposed for this problem was given by Ke [212]. However, it has been pointed out by Aleksandrov *et al.* [16] that Ke's algorithm is not correct.

Ghosh [155] studied the problem of computing the complete and weak visibility polygons of a set Q inside a simple polygon P. He presented $O(n + k)$ algorithms for both of these problems, where k is the number of corner vertices of Q. This problem has been studied by Briggs and Donald [66] for polygon with holes.

Exercise 3.8.1 *Let P be an n-sided, star-shaped polygon containing a convex set C. Assume that C is given in the form of a k-sided convex polygon where every extreme point of C is a vertex of the convex polygon. Two points of P or C are visible if the line segment joining them lies inside P. Design an O(n + k) time algorithm for computing the complete visibility polygon of P from C.*

A simple polygon P is said to be a *palm polygon* if there exists a point $z \in P$ such that the shortest path from z to any point $y \in P$ makes only left turns or only right turns. Palm polygons were introduced by ElGindy and Toussaint [131], and this class of polygons has been characterized in terms of eaves of shortest paths by Ghosh *et al.* [164] as follows. Let $v_i v_j$ be an eave in the shortest path between any two vertices of P. Extend $v_i v_j$ from v_i (or v_j) to $bd(P)$ meeting it at u_i (respectively, u_j). Cut P into two parts by the segment $u_i v_i$ (or $u_j v_j$). The portion of P not containing v_j (respectively, v_i) is called a *forbidden region* of the eave $v_i v_j$. We have the following lemma from Ghosh *et al.* [164].

Lemma 3.8.1 *A simple polygon P is a palm polygon if and only if there exists a point $z \in P$ such that z is not in the forbidden region of any eave in the shortest path between any two vertices of P.*

Using the above characterization, Ghosh *et al.* [164] presented an $O(E)$ time recognition algorithm for palm polygons where E is the number of visible pairs of vertices in P.

Exercise 3.8.2 *Design an O(E) time algorithm for recognizing a palm polygon P where E is the number of visible pairs of vertices in P [164].*

Let us mention parallel algorithms for weak visibility and shortest path problems considered in this chapter. Consider the problem of computing the shortest path $SP(s, t)$ between two given points s and t inside a simple polygon P. ElGindy and Goodrich [129] and Goodrich *et al.* [173, 174] showed that $SP(s, t)$ can be computed in $O(\log n)$ time using $O(n)$ processors in the CREW-PRAM model of computations. ElGindy and Goodrich also showed that the shortest path tree from a point inside a simple polygon P can be computed in $O(\log^2 n)$ time by keeping the number of processors and the model of computation the same. Later, Goodrich *et al.* showed that the running time can be reduced from $O(\log^2 n)$ to $O(\log n)$ for this problem. If the triangulation of P is given, the shortest path tree in P can be computed by the algorithm of Hershberger [187] in $O(\log n)$ time using $O(n/\log n)$ processors in the CREW-PRAM model of computations. Note that P can be triangulated in $O(\log n)$ time using $O(n)$ processors in the CREW-PRAM model of computations by the algorithm of Yap [345] or Goodrich [171].

Consider the problem of computing the weak visibility polygon of a simple polygon P from a segment inside P. Goodrich *et al.* [173, 174] designed an algorithm for this problem using their own algorithm for computing the shortest path tree in P. For computing the complete and weak visibility polygons of a set Q inside a simple polygon P of total n vertices, Chandru *et al.* [69] gave an algorithm for this problem, which also uses the algorithm of Goodrich *et al.* mentioned above, for computing the shortest path tree in P. Both these algorithms run in $O(\log n)$ time using $O(n)$ processors in the CREW-PRAM model of computations. If the triangulation of P is given, both these problems can be solved by the algorithm of Hershberger [187] in $O(\log n)$ time using $O(n/\log n)$ processors in the CREW-PRAM model of computations.

Consider the problem of detecting the weak visibility polygon of a simple polygon P from a given edge of P. We know that this problem can be solved using shortest path trees after P is triangulated. Chen [84] showed that without using the triangulation of P and shortest path trees, the problem can be solved in $O(\log n)$ time using $O(n/\log n)$ processors in the CREW-PRAM model of computations. Chen [82] also showed that whether P is weakly visible from an edge can be determined in $O(\log n)$ time using $O(n/\log n)$ processors in the CREW-PRAM model of computations. Once P is found to be weakly visible, triangulating P and computing the shortest path tree in P can be done in $O(\log n)$ time using $O(n/\log n)$ processors in the CREW-PRAM model of computations as shown by Chen [84].

Exercise 3.8.3 *Let S be a subset of edges of a polygon P with or without holes. Design a polynomial time algorithm to test whether every internal point of P is visible from some point on an edge of S [152].*

4

LR-Visibility and Shortest Paths

4.1 Problems and Results

A simple polygon P is said to be an *LR-visibility polygon* if there exists two points s and t on the boundary of P such that every point of the clockwise boundary of P from s to t (denoted as L) is visible from some point of the counterclockwise boundary of P from s to t (denoted as R) and vice versa (see Figure 4.1(a)). *LR*-visibility polygons can be viewed as a generalization of weak visibility polygons (discussed in Chapter 3). We know that a simple polygon P is a weak visibility polygon from a chord if there exists two points s and t on $bd(P)$ such that (i) s and t are mutually visible, and (ii) every point of the clockwise boundary from s to t is visible from some point of the counterclockwise boundary from s to t and vice versa. If the condition (i) is removed, then it defines *LR-visibility polygons*, which contains weak visibility polygons as a subclass. It can be seen that if a point moves along any path between s and t inside an *LR*-visibility polygon, it can see the entire polygon. *LR*-visibility polygons are also called *streets* and this class of polygons was first considered while studying the problem of walking in a polygon. For more details, see Icking and Klein [200] and Klein [219].

Like weak visibility polygons, *LR*-visibility polygons can also be characterized in terms of shortest paths and non-redundant *C-polygons*. Heffernan [184], and Bhattacharya and Ghosh [48] characterized *LR*-visibility polygons using shortest paths between vertices of the polygon, and their characterization is similar to the characterization of weak visibility polygons given by Ghosh *et al.* [163] presented in Section 3.2. It has been observed by Icking and Klein [200] that *LR*-visibility polygons can be characterized in terms of non-redundant *C-polygons*. In the next section (i.e., Section 4.2), we state these characterizations of *LR*-visibility polygons.

The *LR*-visibility polygon inside a simple polygon P for a pair of s and t is the set of all points of P that are visible from some point of $SP(s,t)$. The characterization of Heffernan [184], and Bhattacharya and Ghosh [48] gives a straightforward $O(n)$

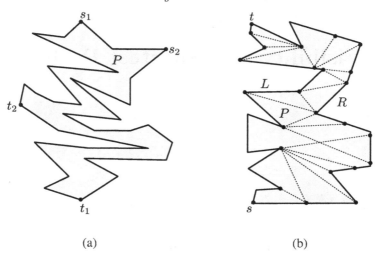

(a)   (b)

Figure 4.1 (a) P is a LR-visibility polygon with respect to s_1 and t_1 but not with respect to s_2 and t_2. (b) The polygon P is walkable but not straight walkable.

time algorithm for computing the LR-visibility polygon inside P. We present this algorithm in Section 4.3.

Heffernan [184], and Bhattacharya and Ghosh [48] presented a linear time algorithm for recognizing LR-visibility polygons with respect to a given s and t. The general problem of recognizing LR-visibility polygons is to locate s and t such that the given polygon is an LR-visibility polygon with respect to s and t. For this problem, Tseng *et al.* [332] presented an $O(n \log n)$ time algorithm and Das *et al.* [101] gave an $O(n)$ time algorithm. In fact, the algorithm of Das *et al.* [101] locates all pairs of points s and t that the polygon is LR-visible with respect to. In Section 4.4, we present an $O(n)$ time recognition algorithm for LR-visibility polygons, which follows a method similar to the algorithm in Section 3.5.2 for recognizing weak visibility polygons.

Bhattacharya and Ghosh [48] presented an $O(n)$ time algorithm for computing the shortest path tree from a vertex for a class of polygons which contains LR-visibility polygons as a subclass. If the algorithm terminates without computing the shortest path tree in a given polygon P, then P is not an LR-visibility polygon. If the algorithm computes the shortest path tree, then P may be an LR-visibility polygon. We present the algorithm of Bhattacharya and Ghosh [48] in Section 4.6. This algorithm is used here as a step in our recognition algorithm presented in Section 4.4 and it is also used in the algorithm for walking in an LR-visibility polygon presented in Section 4.5.

The algorithm of Bhattacharya and Ghosh [48] computes the shortest path tree by scanning the boundary of a given polygon P and it does not require a triangulation of P as a preprocessing step unlike the algorithm of Guibas *et al.* [178]. It may be noted that since the class of LR-visibility polygons contains many special classes of polygons such as spiral polygons, star-shaped polygons, weak visibility polygons, monotone polygons, etc., their algorithm can compute the shortest path tree in linear time in any of these special classes of polygons and therefore, triangulating these special classes of polygons is also possible in linear time.

Exercise 4.1.1 *Assume that a simple polygon P of n vertices is given along with the shortest path tree rooted at some vertex of P. Design an algorithm for constructing a triangulation of P in O(n) time from the shortest path tree.*

Suppose two police officers have to patrol a street and they walk along the opposite sides of the street. Can two officers proceed in such a way that they are always mutually visible? Formally, assume that a simple polygon P is given with two distinguished vertices s and t. Can two points be moved from s to t, one along the clockwise boundary of P and the other along the counterclockwise boundary of P, such that the line segment connecting them always lies totally inside P? The points are allowed to backtrack locally but they must arrive at t eventually. A movement subject to these constraints is called a *walk*. If P admits such a walk (see Figure 4.1(b)), P is called *2-guard walkable* (or, simply, *walkable*) and P is an LR-visibility polygon.

Icking and Klein [200] introduced this problem, and presented an $O(n \log n)$ time algorithm to test whether P is walkable for a given pair s and t. Later, Heffernan [184] gave an $O(n)$ time algorithm for this problem. One special case arises when the points do not backtrack during their walk. Such a walk is called *straight* (see Figure 4.2(a)). During a straight walk, the line segment connecting the points *sweeps* the polygon in an ordered way. To determine whether P is straight walkable for a given pair s and t, Heffernan [184] gave $O(n)$ time algorithm for this problem. Tseng *et al.* [332] presented an $O(n \log n)$ time algorithm for this problem when no pair s and t is given. They also showed within the same time bound how to generate all such pairs of s and t.

A straight walkable polygon P is said to be *discretely straight walkable* if only one of the two points is allowed to move at a time, while the other point remains stationary at a vertex (see Figure 4.2(b)). It has been observed by Arkin *et al.* [21] that P is discretely straight walkable if only if P has a Hamiltonian triangulation. A simple polygon P is said to have a *Hamiltonian triangulation* if it has a triangulation whose dual graph is a Hamiltonian path. Such triangulations are useful in fast rendering engines in computer graphics, since visualization of surfaces is normally done via triangulations [21]. It has been shown by Narasimhan [266] that testing discrete straight walkability and computing all discrete straight walkable pairs of s and t can be performed in $O(n \log n)$ time. Bhattacharya *et al.* [51] presented $O(n)$

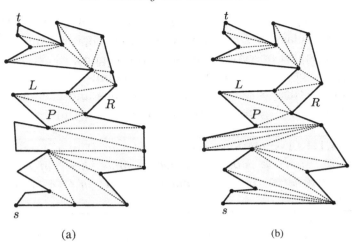

Figure 4.2 (a) The polygon P is straight walkable but not discretely straight walkable. (b) The polygon P is discretely straight walkable.

time algorithms for testing all pairs of s and t of P for which P is walkable, straight walkable and discretely straight walkable. In Section 4.5, we present their algorithm for testing whether a simple polygon P is walkable for any pair of boundary points s and t. In the same section, we also present an $O(n^2)$ time algorithm for constructing a walk between a pair of boundary points s and t of P based on the properties derived by Icking and Klein [200].

> **Exercise 4.1.2** *Let P be an LR-visibility polygon with respect to a given pair of points s and t on the boundary of P. Assume that $SPT(s)$ and $SPT(t)$ are given. Construct a Hamiltonian triangulation of P (if it exists) in $O(n)$ time, where n is the number of vertices of P.*

4.2 Characterizing *LR*-Visibility

In this section, we present the characterization of *LR*-visibility in polygons in terms of shortest paths and non-redundant *C-polygons*. We start with the characterization of Heffernan [184], and Bhattacharya and Ghosh [48] who used shortest paths between vertices to characterize *LR*-visibility polygons. For every point $z \in L$, the *same chain* and the *opposite chain* of z refer to L and R, respectively. Similarly, for every point $z \in R$, the *same chain* and the *opposite chain* of z refer to R and L respectively. In the following theorem, we characterize *LR*-visibility polygons.

Theorem 4.2.1 *Let P denote a simple polygon. The following statements are equivalent.*

(i) *P is an LR-visibility polygon with respect to vertices s and t.*

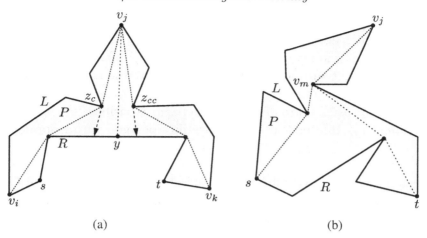

(a)   (b)

Figure 4.3 (a) Since $SP(v_i, v_j)$ and $SP(v_k, v_j)$ meet only at v_j, v_j is visible from the *opposite chain* of v_j. (b) $SP(s, v_j)$ and $SP(t, v_j)$ meet at a vertex v_m other than v_j.

(ii) *Let v_i, v_j and v_k be any three vertices of L (or R) (including s and t) such that they are in clockwise (respectively, counterclockwise) order while traversing L (respectively, R) from s to t. $SP(v_i, v_j)$ and $SP(v_k, v_j)$ meet only at v_j.*

(iii) *For any vertex $v_j \in L$ (or, $v_j \in R$), $SP(s, v_j)$ makes a left turn (respectively, a right turn) at every vertex of L (respectively, R) in the path. Analogously, for any vertex $v_j \in L$ (or, $v_j \in R$), $SP(t, v_j)$ makes a right turn (respectively, a left turn) at every vertex of R (respectively, L) in the path.*

Proof. Firstly, we show that (i) implies (ii). Since P is an LR-visibility polygon with respect to s and t, v_j is visible from some point y of the *opposite chain* of v_j (Figure 4.3(a)). So, the line segment yv_j partitions P into two polygons, one containing s and v_i, and the other containing t and v_k. So, $SP(v_i, v_j)$ and $SP(v_k, v_j)$ cannot cross the line segment yv_j and therefore, they meet only at v_j.

Secondly, we show (ii) implies (iii). We prove only for the case when v_j belongs to L (Figure 4.3(b)). Assume on the contrary that $SP(s, v_j)$ makes a right turn at some vertex $v_m \in L$. Consider the convex angle formed by $SP(s, v_j)$ at v_m. If the convex angle is *facing* toward the interior of P, then by triangle inequality $SP(s, v_j)$ does not pass through v_m, a contradiction. If the convex angle is *facing* toward the exterior of P, then $SP(s, v_j)$ and $SP(t, v_j)$ meet at the vertex v_m other than v_j contradicting (ii) (Figure 4.3(b)). Hence, $SP(s, v_j)$ makes a left turn at v_m. Analogous arguments show that $SP(t, v_j)$ makes a right turn at every vertex of L in the path.

Thirdly, we show that (iii) implies (i). It suffices to show that any vertex v_j of P is visible from some point of the *opposite chain* of v_j (Figure 4.3(a)). We prove only for the case when v_j belongs to L. Let z_c and z_{cc} be the vertices preceding v_j

on $SP(s, v_j)$ and $SP(t, v_j)$ respectively. If z_c or z_{cc} belongs to the *opposite chain* of v_j, then the claim holds. So we assume that z_c, z_{cc} and v_j belong to the *same chain*. From the condition (iii) we know that $SP(s, v_j)$ makes a left turn at z_c and $SP(t, v_j)$ makes a right turn at z_{cc}. It means that extensions of $v_j z_c$ and $v_j z_{cc}$ from z_c and z_{cc}, respectively, cannot meet the *same chain* of v_j. So, both extensions meet at points of the *opposite chain* of v_j. Therefore, v_j is visible for some point of the *opposite chain* of v_j. Hence, P is an LR-visibility polygon with respect to s and t.

$\square$

Let us characterize LR- visibility polygons in terms of non-redundant C-*polygons* as observed by Icking and Klein [200]. We use the same notions used in Section 3.5.2. The clockwise (or, counterclockwise) C-*polygon* of a vertex v_i is said to contain a point z if z lies on the clockwise (respectively, counterclockwise) boundary of the C-*polygon*. We have the following lemma.

Lemma 4.2.2 *A simple polygon P is an LR-visibility polygon with respect to boundary points s and t if and only if each non-redundant C-polygon of P contains s or t.*

Proof. If a *non-redundant C-polygon* of some vertex v_i does not contain s or t, then $SP(s, t)$ does not intersect the bounding chord of the C-*polygon*. Then v_{i-1} or v_{i+1} is not visible form any point of $SP(s, t)$. Therefore, P is not an LR-visibility polygon, which is a contradiction. We now prove the converse. Since every *non-redundant C-polygon* of P contains s or t, $SP(s, t)$ intersects the bounding chord of every *non-redundant C-polygon* of P. Therefore, every point of P is visible from some point of $SP(s, t)$. Hence, P is an LR-visibility polygon with respect to s and t.

$\square$

Corollary 4.2.3 *If an LR-visibility polygon P has two disjoint C-polygons, then one C-polygon contains s and the other contains t.*

Corollary 4.2.4 *If P has three or more mutually disjoint C-polygons, then P is not an LR-visibility polygon.*

4.3 Computing LR-Visibility Polygons

In this section, we present an $O(n)$ time algorithm for computing the LR-visibility polygon inside a simple polygon P for a given pair of boundary points s and t. The LR-visibility polygon inside P for a pair s and t is defined as the set of all points of P that are visible from some point of $SP(s, t)$. The algorithm is similar to the algorithm of Guibas *et al.* [178], presented in Section 3.3.2, for computing the weak visibility polygon of a simple polygon from an internal segment. We assume that

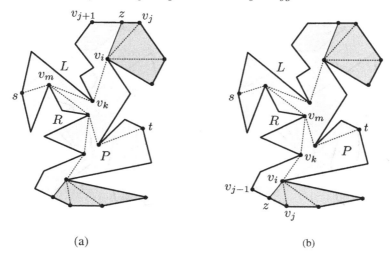

(a)   (b)

Figure 4.4 All descendants of v_i in $SPT(s)$ are not visible from any point of $SP(s,t)$.

P is given as a counterclockwise sequence of vertices $v_1, v_2, ..., v_n$ with two marked vertices s and t. In the following lemmas, we present the main idea used in the algorithm. The proofs of the lemmas follow from Theorem 4.2.1.

Lemma 4.3.1 *Let v_i, v_j and v_m be the three distinct vertices in $SPT(s)$ such that (i) v_i is the parent of v_j in $SPT(s)$, (ii) v_m is the least common ancestor of t and v_i in $SPT(s)$, (iii) $SP(v_m, v_i)$ makes a left turn at every intermediate vertex in the path, and (iv) $SP(s, v_j)$ makes a right turn at v_i (Figure 4.4(a)). If $v_i \in L$, then all descendants of v_i in $SPT(s)$ are not visible from any point of $SP(s,t)$.*

Lemma 4.3.2 *Let v_i, v_j and v_m be the three distinct vertices in $SPT(s)$ such that (i) v_i is the parent of v_j in $SPT(s)$, (ii) v_m is the least common ancestor of t and v_i in $SPT(s)$, (iii) $SP(v_m, v_i)$ makes a right turn at every intermediate vertex in the path, and (iv) $SP(s, v_j)$ makes a left turn at v_i (Figure 4.4(b)). If $v_i \in R$, then all descendants of v_i in $SPT(s)$ are not visible from any point of $SP(s,t)$.*

Lemma 4.3.3 *Let v_i, v_j and v_m be the three distinct vertices in $SPT(t)$ such that (i) v_i is the parent of v_j in $SPT(t)$, (ii) v_m is the least common ancestor of s and v_i in $SPT(t)$, (iii) $SP(v_m, v_i)$ makes a right turn at every intermediate vertex in the path, and (iv) $SP(t, v_j)$ makes a left turn at v_i (Figure 4.5(a)). If $v_i \in L$, then all descendants of v_i in $SPT(t)$ are not visible from any point of $SP(s,t)$.*

Lemma 4.3.4 *Let v_i, v_j and v_m be the three distinct vertices in $SPT(t)$ such that (i) v_i is the parent of v_j in $SPT(t)$, (ii) v_m is the least common ancestor of s and v_i in $SPT(t)$, (iii) $SP(v_m, v_i)$ makes a left turn at every intermediate vertex in the*

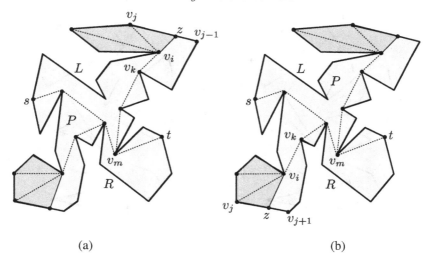

(a)   (b)

Figure 4.5 All descendants of v_i in $SPT(t)$ are not visible from any point of $SP(s,t)$.

path, and (iv) $SP(t, v_j)$ makes a right turn at v_i (Figure 4.5(b)). If $v_i \in R$, then all descendants of v_i in $SPT(t)$ are not visible from any point of $SP(s,t)$.

Exercise 4.3.1 *Prove Lemmas 4.3.1, 4.3.2, 4.3.3 and 4.3.4.*

Lemmas 4.3.1, 4.3.2, 4.3.3 and 4.3.4 suggest a simple procedure to compute the LR-visibility polygon as follows.

Step 1. Compute $SPT(s)$ in P by the algorithm of Guibas *et al.* [178]. Traverse $SPT(s)$ in depth first order and check the turn at every vertex v_i in $SPT(s)$.

Step 2. *If* it is a right turn at v_i and $v_i \in L$ (see Lemma 4.3.1) *then* (Figure 4.4(a))

    Step 2a. Find the descendant of v_i in $SPT(s)$ with the largest index j.

    Step 2b. Compute the intersection point z of $v_j v_{j+1}$ and $\overrightarrow{v_k v_i}$, where v_k is the parent of v_i in $SPT(s)$. Remove the counterclockwise boundary of P from v_i to z by inserting the segment $v_i z$.

Step 3. *If* it is a left turn at v_i and $v_i \in R$ (see Lemma 4.3.2) *then* (Figure 4.4(b))

    Step 3a. Find the descendant of v_i in $SPT(s)$ with the smallest index j.

    Step 3b. Compute the intersection point z of $v_j v_{j-1}$ and $\overrightarrow{v_k v_i}$, where v_k is the parent of v_i in $SPT(s)$. Remove the clockwise boundary of P from v_i to z by inserting the segment $v_i z$.

Step 4. Let P' denote the remaining portion of P. Compute $SPT(t)$ in P' by the algorithm of Guibas *et al.* [178]. Traverse $SPT(t)$ in depth first order and check the turn at every vertex v_i in $SPT(t)$.

Step 5. *If* it is a left turn at v_i and $v_i \in L$ (see Lemma 4.3.3) *then* (Figure 4.5(a))

Step 5a. Find the descendant of v_i in $SPT(t)$ with the smallest index j.

Step 5b. Compute the intersection point z of $v_j v_{j-1}$ and $\overrightarrow{v_k v_i}$, where v_k is the parent of v_i in $SPT(t)$. Remove the clockwise boundary of P' from v_i to z by inserting the segment $v_i z$.

Step 6. *If* it is a right turn at v_i and $v_i \in R$ (see Lemma 4.3.4) *then* (Figure 4.5(b))

Step 6a. Find the descendant of v_i in $SPT(t)$ with the largest index j.

Step 6b. Compute the intersection point z of $v_j v_{j+1}$ and $\overrightarrow{v_k v_i}$, where v_k is the parent of v_i in $SPT(t)$. Remove the counterclockwise boundary of P from v_i to z by inserting the segment $v_i z$.

Step 7. Let P'' denote the remaining portion of P'. Output P'' as the LR-visibility polygon.

The correctness of the algorithm follows from Lemmas 4.3.1, 4.3.2, 4.3.3 and 4.3.4. The algorithm for computing $SPT(s)$ and $SPT(t)$ takes $O(n)$ time [178]. Every vertex of $SPT(s)$ and $SPT(t)$ is traversed once and the remaining operations take constant time. So, the overall time complexity of the algorithm is $O(n)$. We summarize the result in the following theorem.

Theorem 4.3.5 *The LR-visibility polygon for a given pair of boundary points s and t inside a simple polygon P of n vertices can be computed in $O(n)$ time.*

4.4 Recognizing LR-Visibility Polygons

In this section, we present an $O(n)$ time algorithm for recognizing LR-visibility polygons. Given a simple polygon P, the problem is to locate two points s and t (if they exist) on $bd(P)$ such that P is an LR-visibility polygon with respect to s and t. The recognition algorithm follows steps similar to the algorithm for recognizing weak visibility polygons presented in Section 3.5.2. The algorithm uses the characterization of LR-visibility polygons presented in Lemma 4.2.2 and also uses the algorithm of Bhattacharya and Ghosh [48], presented in Section 4.6, for computing the shortest path tree in P by scanning $bd(P)$. We use the same notions used in Section 3.5.2 for presenting the algorithm here.

The algorithm starts by computing $SPT(v_1)$ by the algorithm of Bhattacharya and Ghosh [48]. By traversing $SPT(v_1)$, it locates two disjoint critical polygons $poly_{cc}(v_p)$ and $poly_c(v_q)$ with bounding chords $v_p w_p$ and $v_q u_q$ respectively (see Figure 4.6). Then, it computes $SPT(v_p)$, $SPT(w_p)$, $SPT(v_q)$ and $SPT(u_q)$. For each vertex v_k of $bd(u_q, w_p)$, it tests whether (i) $SP(w_p, v_k)$ makes only left turns, and (ii) $SP(u_q, v_k)$ makes only right turns. Similarly, for each vertex $v_k \in bd(v_p, v_q)$, it tests whether (i) $SP(v_p, v_k)$ makes only right turns, and (ii) $SP(v_q, v_k)$ makes only left turns. Note that LR-visibility polygons allow $SP(u_q, w_p)$ to pass through a vertex of $bd(v_p, v_q)$ and $SP(v_p, v_q)$ to pass through a vertex of $bd(u_q, w_p)$ (see Figure

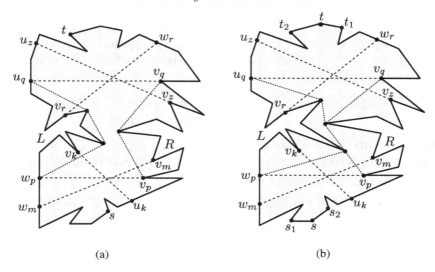

Figure 4.6 (a) Locations of s and t on $bd(P)$ when $SP(u_q, w_p)$ and $SP(v_p, v_q)$ are disjoint. (b) Locations of s and t on $bd(P)$ when $SP(u_q, w_p)$ and $SP(v_p, v_q)$ share vertices.

4.6(b)). It tests whether $v_k u_k$ and $v_m w_m$ intersect after locating two critical polygons $poly_{cc}(v_k)$ and $poly_c(v_m)$ with bounding chords $v_k u_k$ and $v_m w_m$, respectively, where $v_k \in bd(u_q, w_p)$ and $u_k \in bd(w_p, v_p)$, $v_m \in bd(v_p, v_q)$ and $w_m \in bd(w_p, v_p)$. Similarly, it tests whether $v_z u_z$ and $v_r w_r$ intersect after locating two critical polygons $poly_{cc}(v_z)$ and $poly_c(v_r)$ with bounding chords $v_z u_z$ and $v_r w_r$, respectively, where $v_z \in bd(v_p, v_q)$ and $u_z \in bd(v_q, u_p)$, $v_r \in bd(u_q, w_p)$ and $w_r \in bd(v_q, u_q)$. Then it performs cascade testing to determine whether (i) $bd(u_z, w_m)$ can be included in L, and (ii) $bd(u_k, w_r)$ can be included in R.

If $SP(u_q, w_p)$ and $SP(v_p, v_q)$ do not share a vertex (see Figure 4.6(a)), then the algorithm scans $bd(w_r, u_z)$ and $bd(w_m, u_k)$ in both clockwise and counterclockwise order to compute the final $bd(w_r, u_z)$ and $bd(w_m, u_k)$. The algorithm reports that P is an LR-visibility polygon with respect to pairs (i) w_m and w_r, and (ii) u_k and u_z. In Figure 4.6(a), the final u_k is taken as s and the final u_z is taken as t. If $SP(u_q, w_p)$ and $SP(v_p, v_q)$ share a vertex (see Figure 4.6(b)), it locates four vertices t_1, t_2, s_1 and s_2 as follows. The vertex t_1 belongs to $bd(w_r, u_z)$ and it is the first vertex in clockwise order from u_z whose parent in $SPT(w_p)$ is its next clockwise vertex. If no such vertex exists, t_1 is w_r. Similarly, the vertex t_2 also belongs to $bd(w_r, u_z)$ and it is the first vertex in counterclockwise order from w_r whose parent in $SPT(v_p)$ is its next counterclockwise vertex. If no such vertex exists, t_2 is u_z. If t_2 does not belong to $bd(t_1, u_z)$, then P is not an LR-visibility polygon. So, we assume that $t_2 \in bd(t_1, u_z)$. Any point of $bd(t_1, t_2)$ can be taken as the point t. Analogously, s_1 and s_2 can be located using $SPT(u_q)$ and $SPT(v_q)$ and then s is chosen appropriately. We summarize the result in the following theorem.

Theorem 4.4.1 *Two points s and t can be located in $O(n)$ time on the boundary of a simple polygon P of n vertices such that P is an LR-visibility polygon with respect to s and t.*

4.5 Walking in an *LR*-Visibility Polygon

In this section, we present an $O(n^2)$ time algorithm for constructing a walk between a pair of boundary points s and t of a simple polygon P. The algorithm is based on the properties derived by Icking and Klein [200]. We also present an $O(n)$ time algorithm given by Bhattacharya *et al.* [51] for testing whether or not a simple polygon P is walkable for a given pair of boundary points s and t. We assume that P is given as a counterclockwise sequence of vertices $v_1, v_2, ..., v_n$ with two marked vertices s and t. As in Section 3.5.2, for any reflex vertex v_i of P, let $poly_c(v_i)$ (or $poly_{cc}(v_i)$) denote the clockwise (respectively, counterclockwise) C-polygon of v_i, where $v_i u_i$ (respectively, $v_i w_i$) is the bounding chord of $poly_c(v_i)$ (respectively, $poly_{cc}(v_i)$).

Let g_c and g_{cc} be two moving points along the boundary of P starting from s such that (i) g_c moves along $bd(t, s)$ (denoted as L), and (ii) g_{cc} moves along $bd(s, t)$ (denoted as R). As stated in Section 4.1, P is 2-walkable if the line segment $g_c g_{cc}$ lies inside P during the entire movement of g_c and g_{cc} (see Figure 4.7(a)). We start with the following lemma from Icking and Klein [200].

Lemma 4.5.1 *If a simple polygon P is 2-walkable then P is an LR-visibility polygon.*

> **Exercise 4.5.1** *Prove Lemma 4.5.1.*

Using the recognition algorithm presented in Section 4.4, it can be determined whether P is an LR-visibility polygon. If P is an LR-visibility polygon, the recognition algorithm also locates a pair of points s and t on $bd(P)$. In fact, all pairs of points s and t, for which P is an LR-visibility polygon, can be located by the method presented by Tseng *et al.* [332]. They have shown that locating a pair of s and t is same as locating two *cut points* in a *2-cut circular arc* problem.

> **Exercise 4.5.2** *Let S be a set of $n \geq 2$ closed arcs on a unit circle K, where no arc totally contains another arc. Find pairs of intervals $((p, q), (r, s))$ in $O(n)$ time such that for every point $c_1 \in (p, q)$ and $c_2 \in (r, s)$, each arc of S contains a cut point c_1 or c_2 [332].*

From now on, we assume that P is an LR-visibility polygon. Observe that although P can have several pairs of s and t, P may be 2-walkable only for some pairs of s and t. The algorithm of Bhattacharya *et al.* [51] starts with a pair of s and t, and during the process of checking, if it encounters the next pair of s and t,

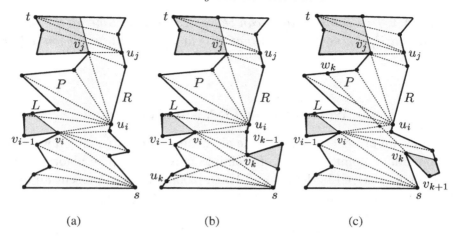

Figure 4.7 (a) The movements of g_c and g_{cc}: (i) g_c walks to v_i, (ii) g_{cc} walks to u_i, (iii) g_c walks to v_j, (iv) g_{cc} walks to u_j, (v) g_c walks to t and (vi) g_{cc} walks to t. (b) The vertex v_{k-1} is not visible from v_i. (c) The vertices v_i and v_k form an s-deadlock in P.

it switches to that pair, and continues the process until P is checked for all pairs of s and t. Thus, the algorithm identifies all pairs of s and t on $bd(P)$ for which P is 2-walkable. Here we consider only one pair of boundary points s and t in the presentation of their algorithm.

Suppose, g_c starts from s and moves along L as long as it is visible from g_{cc} which is currently waiting at s. Assume that g_c has reached a reflex vertex v_i (see Figure 4.7(a)) and it cannot move ahead without losing sight of g_{cc}. This means that there is a constructed edge in the visibility polygon $V(s)$ with v_i as one of its endpoints. Then, g_{cc} must move along R until the edge $v_i v_{i-1}$ is visible from g_{cc} so that g_c can move ahead from v_i. This means that g_{cc} must enter into the clockwise C-*polygon* of v_i whose bounding chord is $v_i u_i$. Therefore, g_{cc} must walk at least up to u_i and it should remain visible from g_c while walking from s to u_i. If the entire $bd(s, u_i)$ is visible from v_i, then g_{cc} can walk to u_i without losing sight of g_c. If some point of $bd(s, u_i)$ is not visible from v_i (see Figure 4.7(b) and Figure 4.7(c)), g_{cc} cannot remain visible from g_c while walking from s to u_i. This means that there exists a reflex vertex $v_k \in bd(s, u_i)$ such that v_k is visible from v_i but either v_{k+1} or v_{k-1} is not visible from v_i.

If v_{k-1} is not visible from v_i (see Figure 4.7(b)), g_c has to walk backward till it enters the clockwise C-*polygon* of v_k whose bounding chord is $v_k u_k$. So, g_c walks backward up to u_k and checks whether g_{cc} can walk up to v_k. If g_{cc} can walk up to v_k without losing sight of g_c who is waiting at u_k, then g_c can move forward after g_{cc} reaches v_k. If g_{cc} cannot walk up to v_k, then g_c walks backward as before until it enters the clockwise C-*polygon* of another reflex vertex $v_m \in bd(s, v_k)$. This discussion suggests that instead of g_c moving all the way up to v_i in greedy manner,

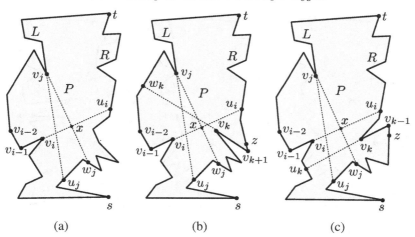

Figure 4.8 (a) The entire boundary $bd(w_j, u_i)$ is visible from x. (b) There is an s-deadlock in P as $v_i u_i$ and $v_k w_k$ have intersected. (c) There is a t-deadlock in P as $v_j w_j$ and $v_k u_k$ have intersected.

g_c should wait at one endpoint of the bounding chord until g_{cc} reaches the other endpoint. Since all bounding chords in P can be computed, g_c and g_{cc} can coordinate their walk as they encounter endpoints of bounding chords.

If v_{k+1} is not visible from v_i (see Figure 4.7(c)), g_{cc} cannot walk beyond v_k even if g_c moves backward toward s. This situation is called s-*deadlock*. A polygon P is said to have s-deadlock, if there exists two reflex vertices $v_i \in L$ and $v_k \in R$ such that the bounding chord $v_i u_i$ of $poly_c(v_i)$ intersects the bounding chord $v_k w_k$ of $poly_{cc}(v_k)$. Analogously, a polygon P is said to have t-deadlock, if there exists two reflex vertices $v_i \in L$ and $v_k \in R$ such that the bounding chord $v_i w_i$ of $poly_{cc}(v_i)$ intersects the bounding chord $v_k u_k$ of $poly_c(v_k)$. We have the following theorem from Icking and Klein [200].

Theorem 4.5.2 *A simple polygon P is 2-walkable if and only if P does not have an s-deadlock or a t-deadlock.*

Proof. Assume that P has an s-deadlock formed by the reflex vertices $v_i \in L$ and $v_k \in R$. Therefore, two bounding chords $v_i u_i$ and $v_k w_k$ intersect in P by definition. So, $v_i \in bd(w_k, s)$ and $v_k \in bd(s, u_i)$. Before g_c starts walking on the edge $v_i v_{i-1}$, g_{cc} must reach u_i so that g_c and g_{cc} remain mutually visible. Similarly, before g_{cc} starts walking on the edge $v_k v_{k+1}$, g_c must reach w_k so that g_c and g_{cc} remain mutually visible. This is a deadlock and hence, there is no walk between s and t in P. Analogous arguments show that if P has a t-deadlock, there is no walk between s and t in P.

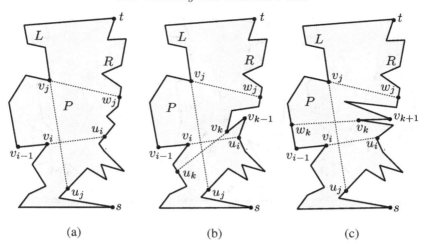

Figure 4.9 (a) The entire boundary $bd(u_i, w_j)$ is visible from v_i. (b) The vertex v_k is visible from v_i but not v_{k-1}. (c) The vertex v_k is visible from v_i but not v_{k+1}.

We now prove the converse. By assumption, P does not have an s-deadlock or t-deadlock. We show that there exists a walk from s to t in P. Assume that g_c and g_{cc} are currently at two endpoints of a bounding chord. Without loss of generality, assume that g_c has walked from s up to a reflex vertex $v_i \in L$ and g_{cc} has also walked from s up to the point $u_i \in R$, where $v_i u_i$ is the bounding chord of $poly_c(v_i)$ (see Figure 4.8). We also assume that they were mutually visible during the walk. They wish to walk to the endpoints of another bounding chord. Let $v_j \in L$ be the next reflex vertex while traversing from v_i to t. Consider the bounding chords $v_j u_j$ and $v_j w_j$ of $poly_c(v_j)$ and $poly_{cc}(v_j)$, respectively. There are three cases that can arise.

Case 1. The bounding chord $v_i u_i$ has intersected both $v_j u_j$ and $v_j w_j$ (see Figure 4.8).

Case 2. The bounding chord $v_i u_i$ has intersected $v_j u_j$ but has not intersected $v_j w_j$ (see Figure 4.9).

Case 3. The bounding chord $v_i u_i$ has not intersected $v_j u_j$ and $v_j w_j$ (see Figure 4.11(a)).

Consider Case 1 (see Figure 4.8). This condition suggests that g_c must walk ahead from v_i to v_j while g_{cc} walks backward from u_i to w_j. We show that g_c and g_{cc} can remain mutually visible during this walk. Let x be the point of intersection of $v_i u_i$ and $v_j w_j$. It is obvious that every point of $bd(v_j, v_i)$ is visible from x. If every point of $bd(w_j, u_i)$ is also visible from x (see Figure 4.8(a)), then g_c and g_{cc} can coordinate their walk in such a way that the segment $g_c g_{cc}$ always passes through x. We show that every point of $bd(w_j, u_i)$ is indeed visible from x. Suppose there is a point $z \in bd(w_j, u_i)$ which is not visible from x. Since z and x are not mutually visible by assumption, $SP(x, z)$ must pass through at least one reflex vertex v_k. If

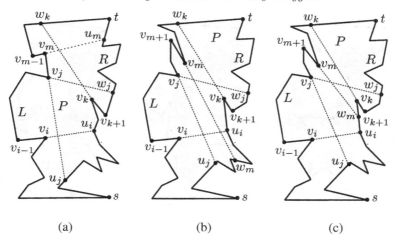

(a)   (b)   (c)

Figure 4.10 (a) There is an s-deadlock in P as $v_k v_m$ and $v_m u_m$ have intersected. (b) The bounding chords $v_k v_m$ and $v_i u_i$ have intersected. (c) The bounding chords $v_k v_m$ and $v_i u_i$ have not intersected.

$v_k \in bd(w_j, z)$ (see Figure 4.8(b)), then v_i and v_k form an s-deadlock in P as $v_i u_i$ intersects $v_k w_k$, a contradiction. If $v_k \in bd(z, u_i)$ (see Figure 4.8(c)), then v_j and v_k form a t-deadlock in P as $v_j w_j$ intersects $v_k u_k$, which is a contradiction. Therefore, the entire boundary $bd(w_j, u_i)$ is visible from x. Hence g_c can walk from v_i to v_j and g_{cc} can also walk from u_i to w_j while they remain mutually visible. Thus, g_c and g_{cc} can reach the endpoints of another bounding chord.

Consider Case 2. We know that $u_i \in bd(u_j, w_j)$ (see Figure 4.9). If the entire boundary $bd(u_i, w_j)$ is visible from v_i (see Figure 4.9(a)), g_{cc} walks from u_i to w_j and then g_c walks from v_i to v_j. So, g_c and g_{cc} have reached the endpoints of another bounding chord $v_j w_j$. Otherwise, if the entire boundary $bd(u_i, w_j)$ is visible from v_j, g_c walks to v_j and then g_{cc} walks to w_j. Again, g_c and g_{cc} are at the endpoints of the bounding chord $v_j w_j$. Consider the situation when the entire boundary $bd(u_i, w_j)$ is not visible either from v_i or from v_j (see Figure 4.9(b) and (c)). Let $v_k \in bd(u_i, w_j)$ be the first reflex vertex, while traversing from u_i to w_j, such that v_k is visible from v_i but either v_{k-1} or v_{k+1} is not visible from v_i. If v_{k-1} is not visible from v_i (see Figure 4.9(b)), then g_c moves backward from v_i to u_k while g_{cc} moves forward from u_i to v_k using the analogous method stated in Case 1. Thus g_c and g_{cc} move to the endpoints of another bounding chord $v_k u_k$. If v_{k+1} is not visible from v_i (see Figure 4.9(c)), then g_c walks to v_k and g_{cc} walks to w_k. Thus g_c and g_{cc} move to the endpoints of another bounding chord $v_k w_k$.

It may happen that w_k does not belong to $bd(v_j, v_i)$ (see Figure 4.10). In that case, g_c can still walk up to w_k if $bd(w_k, v_j)$ is entirely visible from v_k. Otherwise, the first reflex vertex $v_m \in bd(w_k, v_j)$ can be located while traversing from v_j to w_k (see Figure 4.10(a)) such that v_m is visible from v_k but either v_{m-1} or v_{m+1} is not visible

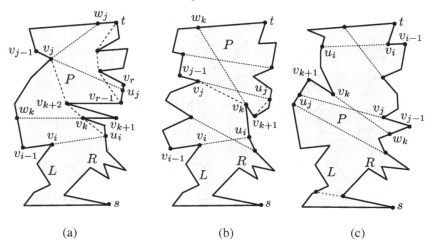

| (a) | (b) | (c) |

Figure 4.11 (a) The bounding chord $v_i u_i$ has not intersected both $v_j u_j$ and $v_j w_j$. (b) By scanning from s, P is partitioned into sub-polygons using non-intersecting bounding chords of same type. (c) By scanning from t, P is partitioned into similar sub-polygons.

from v_k. If v_{m-1} is not visible from v_k, then v_m and v_k form an s-deadlock in P as the bounding chords $v_m u_m$ and $v_k w_k$ intersect, which is a contradiction. Consider the other situation when v_{m+1} is not visible from v_k (see Figure 4.10(b) and (c)). If $v_m w_m$ intersects $v_i u_i$ (see Figure 4.10(b)), then it becomes Case 1 treating v_m as v_j. Thus g_c and g_{cc} move to the endpoints of another bounding chord $v_m w_m$. If $v_m w_m$ does not intersect $v_i u_i$ (see Figure 4.10(c)), then w_m belongs to $bd(u_i, v_k)$. We know that $bd(u_i, w_m)$ is entirely visible from v_i. So, g_{cc} walks from u_i to w_m and then g_c moves from v_i to v_m. Thus g_c and g_{cc} move to the endpoints of another bounding chord $v_m w_m$.

Consider Case 3. This is essentially Case 2 as w_k must belong to $bd(v_j, v_i)$ (see Figure 4.11(a)) otherwise there is an s-deadlock due to the intersection of bounding chords $v_j u_j$ and $v_k w_k$.

It can be seen that g_c and g_{cc} always walk from the endpoints of a bounding chord to another which has not been considered before. In this process of walking, g_c and g_{cc} walk from one clockwise C-*polygon* containing t to another C-*polygon* which is contained in the previous C-*polygon*. Thus, g_c and g_{cc} always succeed in reaching t keeping themselves mutually visible as there is no s-deadlock or t-deadlock in P.
□

The above theorem suggests that before any attempt is made to construct a walk from s to t, it is necessary to test whether P has any s-deadlock or t-deadlock. Let us proceed to test whether P has any s-deadlock. The main idea of the testing procedure given by Bhattacharya *et al.* [51] is to partition P into sub-polygons using non-intersecting bounding chords of the same type as follows. Scan L from s

to t till a reflex vertex v_i is located such that $u_i \in R$ (see Figure 4.11(b)). Continue the scan till another reflex vertex v_j is located such that $u_j \in R$ and $v_j u_j$ does not intersect $v_i u_i$. Treating v_j as v_i, repeat the process. We have the following lemma for s-deadlock.

Lemma 4.5.3 *Let P_i denote the sub-polygon of P bounded by two consecutive bounding chords $v_i u_i$ and $v_j u_j$, where $v_i \in L$, $v_j \in bd(t, v_i)$, $u_i \in R$ and $u_j \in bd(u_i, t)$ (Figure 4.11(b)). If there exists a reflex vertex $v_k \in bd(u_i, u_j)$ such that $v_k w_k$ intersects $v_j u_j$, then P has an s-deadlock formed by v_j and v_k.*

Using the above lemma, P can be tested whether there exists an s-deadlock formed by two reflex vertices in any sub-polygon P_i. If no sub-polygon of P has an s-deadlock, P does not have an s-deadlock. Then, the same process is used to test whether P has a t-deadlock. Starting from t (see Figure 4.11(c)), partition P using bounding chords $v_i u_i$, $v_j u_j$,... where v_i, v_j,... belong to R and u_i, u_j,... belong to L. For every sub-polygon bounded by two such consecutive bounding chords $v_i u_i$ and $v_j u_j$, check whether there exists a reflex vertex $v_k \in bd(u_i, u_j)$ forming a t-deadlock with v_j. If P does not have s-deadlock or t-deadlock, a walk can be constructed in P for g_c and g_{cc} from s to t using Cases 1 and 2 in the proof of Theorem 4.5.2. In the following, we present the major steps of the algorithm under the assumption that P does not have s-deadlock or t-deadlock.

Step 1. Locate two points s and t on $bd(P)$ such that P is an LR-visibility polygon with respect to s and t.

Step 2. Traverse L from s to t in clockwise order and partition P into sub-polygons using the non-intersecting bounding chords of clockwise C-polygons. Check whether any sub-polygon has a pair of reflex vertices forming an s-deadlock.

Step 3. Traverse R from t to s in clockwise order and partition P into sub-polygons using the non-intersecting bounding chords of counterclockwise C-polygons. Check whether any sub-polygon has a pair of reflex vertices forming a t-deadlock.

Step 4. Introduce a point $t' \in R$ arbitrarily close to t. Treat t as a reflex vertex of L and tt' as the clockwise bounding chord of C-polygon of the reflex vertex t. Also, treat t' as a reflex vertex of R and tt' as the counterclockwise bounding chord of the C-polygon of the reflex vertex t'. Introduce a point $s' \in R$ arbitrary close to s. Treat s as a reflex vertex of L and ss' as the clockwise bounding chord of the C-polygon of the reflex vertex s.

Step 5. Place g_c at s and g_{cc} at s'. Initialize v_i by s and u_i by s'.

Step 6. (Remark: g_c at v_i and g_{cc} at u_i). If g_c is currently at t and g_{cc} is currently at t' then goto Step 14.

Step 7. Initialize v_j by the next counterclockwise vertex of v_i. *While v_j is not a reflex vertex do $j := j - 1$.*

Step 8. *If $v_j w_j$ intersects $v_i u_i$ then* move simultaneously g_c and g_{cc} from their present positions to v_j and w_j respectively, $i := j$ and *goto* Step 11.

Step 9. *If $v_j u_j$ intersects $v_i u_i$ then*

   Step 9a. Initialize v_k by the next counterclockwise vertex of u_i.

   Step 9b. *While v_k is not a reflex vertex and $v_k \in bd(u_i, w_j)$ do* $k := k + 1$.

   Step 9c. *If $v_k \notin bd(u_i, w_j)$ then* move g_c from its present position to v_j and move g_{cc} from its present position to w_j, $i := j$ and *goto* Step 11.

   Step 9d. *If $v_k u_k$ intersects $v_i u_i$ then* move simultaneously g_c and g_{cc} from their present positions to u_k and v_k respectively (Figure 4.9(b)), $i := k$ and *goto* Step 12.

   Step 9e. *If $v_k w_k$ intersects $v_j w_j$ then* move g_{cc} from its present position to v_k, move g_c from its present position to w_k (Figure 4.10), $i := k$ and *goto* Step 13.

   Step 9f. *If $w_k \in bd(v_j, v_i)$ then* move g_{cc} from its present position to v_k, move g_c from its present position to w_k, $i := k$ and *goto* Step 13.

   Step 9g. *If $u_k \in bd(v_j, v_i)$ then* move g_{cc} from its present position to v_k, move g_c from its present position to u_k, $i := k$ and *goto* Step 12.

   Step 9h. Increment k by 1 and *goto* Step 9b.

Step 10. *If $v_j u_j$ does not intersect $v_i u_i$* (Figure 4.11(a)) *then* perform Step 9 by considering $bd(u_i, u_j)$ in place of $bd(u_i, w_j)$.

Step 11. *If g_c is currently at v_i and g_{cc} is currently at w_i then* perform Step 6 to Step 10 starting from the bounding chord $v_i w_i$ in place of $v_i u_i$.

Step 12. *If g_{cc} is currently at v_i and g_c is currently at u_i then* perform steps analogous to Step 6 to Step 11 by locating v_j in R and v_k in L.

Step 13. *If g_{cc} is currently at v_i and g_c is currently at w_i then* perform Step 12 starting from the bounding chord $v_i w_i$ in place of $v_i u_i$.

Step 14. Report the walk of g_c and g_{cc} from s to t and *Stop*.

The correctness of the algorithm follows from Theorem 4.5.2. Let us analyze the time complexity of the algorithm. The points s and t on $bd(P)$ can be located in $O(n)$ time by the recognition algorithm presented in Section 4.4. It has been shown by Bhattacharya *et al.* [51] that testing for s-deadlock and t-deadlock in Steps 2 and 3 can be done in $O(n)$ (explained later). Remaining steps of the algorithm can take $O(n^2)$ as g_c and g_{cc} can move back and forth along L and R, respectively. Hence the overall time complexity of the algorithm is $O(n^2)$ time. We summarize the result in the following theorem.

Theorem 4.5.4 *A walk between two boundary points s and t of a simple polygon P of n vertices can be constructed in $O(n^2)$ time.*

Let us explain how the testing for s-deadlock and t-deadlock in P can be done in $O(n)$ time using $SPT(s)$ and $SPT(t)$. Note that $SPT(s)$ and $SPT(t)$ can be computed in $O(n)$ time using the algorithm of Bhattacharya and Ghosh [48] presented in Section 4.6. We present here the procedure of Bhattacharya *et al.* [51] only for testing s-deadlock in P as the procedure for testing t-deadlock is analogous. Assume that the procedure has located the bounding chord $v_i u_i$ where $v_i \in L$ and $u_i \in R$. The procedure wishes to locate the first reflex vertex v_j by scanning L from v_{i-1} in clockwise order such that $u_j \in R$ and the bounding chord $v_j u_j$ does not intersect $v_i u_i$. We have the following lemma.

Lemma 4.5.5 *Let $v_i u_i$ be a bounding chord in P, where $v_i \in L$ and $u_i \in R$. Let v_j be a reflex vertex in $bd(t, v_i)$ such that v_j is the previous vertex of v_{j-1} on $SP(u_i, v_{j-1})$ (Figure 4.11(a)). Then the bounding chord $v_j u_j$ does not intersect $v_i u_i$.*

Based on the above lemma, the procedure for testing s-deadlock scans L from v_{i-1} in clockwise order and computes $SP(u_i, v_m)$ for every vertex v_m until v_j is located. It can be seen that $SP(u_i, v_m)$ follows $SP(u_i, t)$ from u_i up to a vertex $v_q \in R$ and then jumps to a vertex $v_p \in L$ of $SP(t, v_m)$ and then follows $SP(t, v_m)$ from v_p to v_m. Note that v_p and v_m may be the same vertex. For example, v_p is v_j and v_q is v_{k+2} in $SP(u_i, v_j)$ in Figure 4.11(a). It can be seen that $v_p v_q$ is a tangent from $v_p \in SP(t, v_m)$ to $SP(u_i, t)$ at v_q. Since all such tangents $v_p v_q$ computed until v_j is located are ordered from $v_i u_i$ to $v_j u_j$, the time required for computing all these tangents is proportional to the sum of the sizes of $bd(v_j, v_i)$ and $bd(u_i, u_j)$.

In order to locate u_j, the procedure scans R from u_i in counterclockwise order until it locates the first vertex v_r (see Figure 4.11(a)) such that $\overrightarrow{v_{j-1}v_j}$ does not intersect $SP(t, v_r)$. It can be seen that entire $SP(t, v_r)$ lies to the left of $\overrightarrow{v_{j-1}v_j}$ and $u_j \in v_r v_{r-1}$. The cost of locating v_r is proportional to the size of $bd(u_i, v_r)$. For more details on computing the intersection of a ray with the shortest path, see Section 3.5.2. As the sub-polygons are disjoint in P, all sub-polygons can be computed in $O(n)$ time. Once P is partitioned into sub-polygons, the procedure proceeds to test whether there is an s-deadlock in any sub-polygon P_i. We have the following lemma.

Lemma 4.5.6 *Let P_i denote the sub-polygon of P bounded by two consecutive bounding chords $v_i u_i$ and $v_j u_j$, where $v_i \in L$, $v_j \in bd(t, v_i)$, $u_i \in R$ and $u_j \in bd(u_i, t)$. If there exists a reflex vertex $v_k \in bd(u_i, u_j)$ (Figure 4.11(b)) such that (i) $SP(v_j, v_{k+1})$ and $SP(u_j, v_{k+1})$ meet only at v_{k+1} and (ii) v_k is the previous vertex of v_{k+1} on $SP(v_j, v_{k+1})$, then $v_k w_k$ intersects $v_j u_j$.*

Based on the above lemma, the procedure for testing s-deadlock scans R from u_j to u_i in counterclockwise order and computes $SP(v_j, v_m)$ for every vertex $v_m \in bd(u_i, u_j)$ by drawing tangents, as stated above, in time proportional to the sum of the size of $bd(v_j, v_i)$ and $bd(u_i, u_j)$. If any reflex vertex $v_k \in bd(u_i, u_j)$ satisfies

Lemma 4.5.6, then P has an s-deadlock. Thus, it can be determined in $O(n)$ whether P has an s-deadlock. We summarize the result in the following theorem.

Theorem 4.5.7 *Given a simple polygon P of n vertices, it can be determined in $O(n)$ time whether P is 2-walkable between two boundary points s and t.*

4.6 Computing Shortest Path Trees using LR-Visibility

In this section, we present an $O(n)$ time algorithm of Bhattacharya and Ghosh [48] for computing the shortest path tree from a vertex (say, v_1) in a simple polygon P if P satisfies the characterization of LR-visibility polygons presented in Theorem 4.2.1. If the algorithm terminates without computing the shortest path tree $SPT(v_1)$, it means that P is not an LR-visibility polygon with respect to any pair of boundary points of P. If the algorithm computes $SPT(v_1)$, P may be an LR-visibility polygon. If P is an LR-visibility polygon, the algorithm always succeeds in computing $SPT(v_1)$. Like the algorithm of Ghosh *et al.* [162] presented in Section 3.6.2, the algorithm computes $SPT(v_1)$ by scanning $bd(P)$ and it uses pointers and a doubly linked list as its data structures. In presenting this algorithm, we use the same notions of Sections 3.3.1 and 3.6.2. We assume that P is given as a counterclockwise sequence of vertices $v_1, v_2, ..., v_n$.

The algorithm starts by computing the visibility polygon $V(v_1)$ of P from v_1 by the algorithm of Lee [230] presented in Section 2.2.1 (see Figure 4.12). It can be seen that if constructed edges of $V(v_1)$ are used to partition P, they split P into disjoint regions of P. All such regions, except $V(v_1)$, are called *pockets* of $V(v_1)$. Since the vertices of $V(v_1)$ are visible from v_1, they are children of v_1 in $SPT(v_1)$. So, the remaining task for computing $SPT(v_1)$ is to compute the shortest path from v_1 to each vertex of every pocket. Since the shortest path from v_1 to any two vertices v_i and v_j of different pockets are disjoint, i.e., $SP(v_1, v_i)$ and $SP(v_1, v_j)$ meet only at v_1, the shortest path from v_1 to the vertices of one pocket can be computed independent of other pockets of $V(v_1)$. So, it is enough to state the procedure for computing $SPT(v_1)$ to all vertices in one pocket. We have the following lemma.

Lemma 4.6.1 *If P is an LR-visibility polygon with respect to some pair of boundary points s and t, then at most one of s and t can lie in a pocket of $V(v_1)$.*

Proof. If both s and t lie in one pocket of $V(v_1)$, then either the entire L or the entire R lies in the pocket of $V(v_1)$. If the entire R lies in the pocket, v_1 belongs to L. So, there is a point (i.e. v_1) of L which is not visible for any point of R. So, P is not an LR-visibility polygon, which is a contradiction. Analogous arguments hold if the entire L lies in the pocket. $\square$

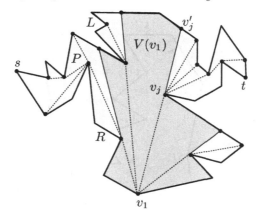

Figure 4.12 The disjoint regions of $P - V(v_i)$ are pockets of $V(v_1)$.

Corollary 4.6.2 *Let P be an LR-visibility polygon with respect to s and t. If both endpoints of a constructed edge of $V(v_1)$ belong to either L or R (Figure 4.12), then the entire pocket is weakly visible from the constructed edge.*

Corollary 4.6.3 *Let P be an LR-visibility polygon with respect to s and t. If one endpoint of a constructed edge of $V(v_1)$ belongs to L and the other belongs to R (Figure 4.12), then the pocket of $V(v_1)$ contains either s or t.*

After computing $V(v_1)$, the algorithm proceeds to compute the shortest paths to vertices of each pocket of $V(v_1)$ separately. Let $v_j v'_j$ be a constructed edge, where v_j is a vertex of P and v'_j is some boundary point of P (Figure 4.12). Note that v_1, v_j and v'_j are collinear. Without loss of generality, we assume that $bd(P)$ is traversed from v_1 to v'_j in counterclockwise order. So, v_j is encountered before reaching v'_j. The boundary of the pocket consists of the counterclockwise boundary of P from v_j to v'_j and the segment $v_j v'_j$. The counterclockwise (or clockwise) boundary from a boundary point z to another boundary point z' is denoted as $bd_{cc}(z, z')$ (respectively, $bd_c(z, z')$). Since the shortest path from v_1 to any vertex of this pocket passes through v_j, it is enough to compute $SPT(v_j)$ in the pocket of $V(v_1)$ bounded by $v_j v'_j$.

The procedure for computing $SPT(v_j)$ scans $bd_{cc}(v_j, v'_j)$ in counterclockwise order starting from v_{j+1} till it encounters a reverse turn at a vertex v_{cc} or it reaches v'_j. This procedure is similar to the procedure mentioned in Section 3.6.2 as two cases. Assume that $SP_{cc}(v_j, v_{j+1})$, $SP_{cc}(v_j, v_{j+2})$,..., $SP_{cc}(v_j, v_{i-1})$ have been computed and the procedure wants to compute $SP_{cc}(v_j, v_i)$. For any vertex $v_m \in bd_{cc}(v_j, v'_{i-1})$, let u_m denote the parent of v_m in $SPT_{cc}(v_j, v_{i-1})$, i.e., u_m is the previous vertex of v_m in $SP_{cc}(v_j, v_m)$. We have the following two cases.

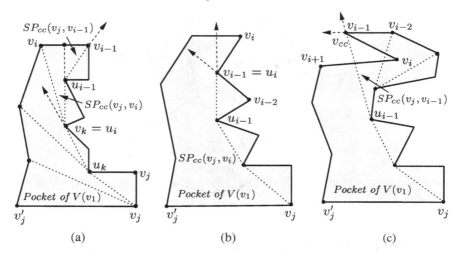

Figure 4.13 (a) $SP_{cc}(v_j, v_i) = (SP_{cc}(v_j, v_k), v_i)$. (b) $SP_{cc}(v_j, v_i) = (SP_{cc}(v_j, v_{i-1}), v_i)$. (c) There is a reverse turn at v_{i-1}.

Case 1. The vertex v_i lies to the left of $\overrightarrow{u_{i-1}v_{i-1}}$ (Figure 4.13(a)).

Case 2. The vertex v_i lies to the right of $\overrightarrow{u_{i-1}v_{i-1}}$.

Case 2a. The vertex v_i lies to the right of $\overrightarrow{v_{i-2}v_{i-1}}$ (Figure 4.13(b)).

Case 2b. The vertex v_i lies to the left of $\overrightarrow{v_{i-2}v_{i-1}}$ (Figure 4.13(c)).

Consider Case 1. Since v_i lies to the left of $\overrightarrow{u_{i-1}v_{i-1}}$ (see Figure 4.13(a)), $SP_{cc}(v_j, v_i)$ makes only right turns. Let v_k be the first vertex of $SP_{cc}(v_j, v_{i-1})$ starting from v_{i-1} such that v_i lies to the right of $\overrightarrow{u_k v_k}$. Therefore, v_k becomes the parent u_i of v_i in $SPT_{cc}(v_j, v_i)$ as $v_i v_k$ is the tangent from v_i to $SP_{cc}(v_j, v_{i-1})$. Hence, $SP_{cc}(v_j, v_i) = (SP_{cc}(v_j, v_k), v_i)$. The region enclosed by $v_{i-1}v_i$, $v_i u_i$ and $SP_{cc}(u_i, v_{i-1})$ is divided into triangles by extending each edge of $SP_{cc}(u_i, v_{i-1})$ to $v_{i-1}v_i$.

Consider Case 2a. Since v_i lies to the right of both $\overrightarrow{u_{i-1}v_{i-1}}$ and $\overrightarrow{v_{i-2}v_{i-1}}$ (see Figure 4.13(b)), it means that $SP_{cc}(v_j, v_i)$ makes only right turns, and v_{i-1} is the parent u_i of v_i in $SPT_{cc}(v_j, v_i)$ as $v_i v_{i-1}$ is the tangent from v_i to $SP_{cc}(v_j, v_{i-1})$. So, $SP_{cc}(v_j, v_i) = (SP_{cc}(v_j, v_{i-1}), v_i)$.

Consider Case 2b. Since v_i lies to the right of $\overrightarrow{u_{i-1}v_{i-1}}$ and to the left of $\overrightarrow{v_{i-2}v_{i-1}}$ (see Figure 4.13(c)), $SP(v_j, v_{i-1})$ passes through vertices of $bd_{cc}(v_i, v_j')$ and therefore, $SP(v_j, v_{i-1})$ and $SP_{cc}(v_j, v_{i-1})$ are not same. The vertex v_{i-1} is marked as v_{cc} as there is a reverse turn at v_{i-1}.

It can be seen that the above procedure of scanning $bd_{cc}(v_j, v_j')$ may not reach v_j' if Case 2b occurs. Otherwise the procedure has reached v_j', which means that $SPT_{cc}(v_j, v_j')$ has been computed. We have the following lemma.

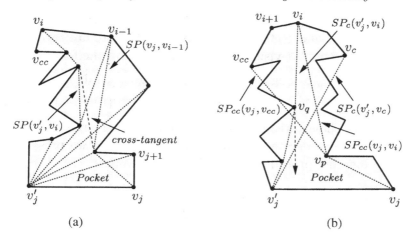

Figure 4.14 (a) The cross-tangent is drawn between $SP(v'_j, v_i)$ and $SP(v_j, v_{i-1})$. (b) The vertex v_c belongs to $bd_{cc}(v_j, v_{cc})$, and $SP_{cc}(v_j, v_i)$ and $SP_c(v'_j, v_i)$ meet only at v_i.

Lemma 4.6.4 *If no reverse turn is encountered during the counterclockwise scan of $bd_{cc}(v_j, v'_j)$ (Figure 4.13(a)), then $SPT_{cc}(v_j, v'_j)$ is same as $SPT(v_j)$.*

The above lemma suggests that if the scanning procedure does not terminate before reaching v'_j, it has computed $SPT(v_j)$. Otherwise, it has computed $SPT_{cc}(v_j, v_{cc})$. This means that (i) $SP(v_j, v_{cc})$ passes through vertices of $bd_c(v'_j, v_{cc+1})$, and (ii) s or t belongs to $bd_{cc}(v_j, v'_j)$ by Corollary 4.6.3. From now on, we assume that the procedure has not reached v'_j. The procedure scans $bd_c(v'_j, v_j)$ in clockwise order starting from the next clockwise vertex of v'_j by the analogous procedure of the above counterclockwise scan. We have following lemma.

Lemma 4.6.5 *If no reverse turn is encountered during the clockwise scan of $bd_c(v'_j, v_j)$, then $SPT_c(v'_j, v_j)$ is same as $SPT(v'_j)$ (Figure 4.14(a)).*

Exercise 4.6.1 *Prove Lemma 4.6.5.*

The above lemma suggests that if the clockwise scan reaches v_j, then it has computed $SPT(v'_j)$. Otherwise the clockwise scan has located a reverse turn at some vertex v_c (see Figure 4.14(b)). If $SPT(v'_j)$ has been computed, $SPT(v_j)$ can be computed from $SPT(v'_j)$ using the algorithm of Hershberger [186] presented in Section 5.2. The main step in computing $SPT(v_j)$ from $SPT(v'_j)$ (see Figure 4.14(a)) is to draw the cross-tangent between $SP(v'_j, v_i)$ and $SP(v_j, v_{i-1})$ for every vertex $v_i \in bd_{cc}(v_j, v'_j)$ starting from v_{j+1} (see Exercises 3.6.2 and 3.6.3). All cross-tangents in the pocket can be drawn in time proportional to the size of $SPT(v'_j)$.

From now on we assume that the procedure has located v_c and v_{cc}, and has computed $SPT_c(v_j', v_c)$ and $SPT_{cc}(v_j, v_{cc})$. Although there are reverse turns at v_c and v_{cc}, P can still be an LR-visibility polygon. We have the following two cases.

Case A. The vertex v_c belongs to $bd_{cc}(v_j, v_{cc})$ (Figure 4.14(b)).

Case B. The vertex v_c does not belong to $bd_{cc}(v_j, v_{cc})$ (Figure 4.15(a)).

Consider Case A. The algorithm computes $SPT(v_j)$ by merging $SPT_c(v_j', v_c)$ and $SPT_{cc}(v_j, v_{cc})$. Before we state the procedure for merging, we present the overall approach of the merging procedure in the following lemmas.

Lemma 4.6.6 *Let $v_j v_j'$ be a constructed edge of $V(v_1)$ in P satisfying Corollary 4.6.3. If $v_c \in bd_{cc}(v_j, v_{cc})$, then either s or t belongs to $bd_{cc}(v_c, v_{cc})$.*

Proof. We know from Corollary 4.6.3 that either s or t (say, s) must belong to $bd_{cc}(v_j, v_j')$. If $s \in bd_c(v_j', v_{cc+1})$, then there cannot be any reverse turn at v_{cc} as both v_{cc} and v_j belong to L. An analogous argument shows that s cannot belong to $bd_{cc}(v_j, v_{c-1})$. Hence, $s \in bd_{cc}(v_c, v_{cc})$. $\square$

Lemma 4.6.7 *Let v_p and v_q be the parents of a vertex $v_i \in bd_{cc}(v_c, v_{cc})$ in $SPT_{cc}(v_j, v_{cc})$ and $SPT_c(v_j', v_c)$, respectively. If v_p lies to the left of $\overrightarrow{v_i v_q}$, then $SP_{cc}(v_j, v_i)$ is same as $SP(v_j, v_i)$, and $SP_c(v_j', v_i)$ is same as $SP(v_j', v_i)$.*

Proof. If v_p lies to the left of $\overrightarrow{v_i v_q}$ (see Figure 4.14(b)), $SP_{cc}(v_j, v_i)$ and $SP_c(v_j', v_i)$ meet only at v_i because $SP_{cc}(v_j, v_i)$ makes only right turns and $SP_c(v_j', v_i)$ makes only left turns. So, v_i is visible from some point of $v_j v_j'$. By Theorem 4.2.1, $SP_{cc}(v_j, v_i)$ is same as $SP(v_j, v_i)$ and $SP_c(v_j', v_i)$ is same as $SP(v_j', v_i)$. $\square$

The above lemma suggests that if there exists such a vertex $v_i \in bd_{cc}(v_c, v_{cc})$, $SPT(v_j, v_i)$ is same as $SPT_{cc}(v_j, v_i)$. Similarly, $SPT(v_j', v_i)$ is same as $SPT_c(v_j', v_i)$. For each vertex v_k starting from v_{i+1} in counterclockwise order, draw the cross-tangent between $SP(v_j', v_k)$ and $SP(v_j, v_{k-1})$ as stated earlier, which gives $SPT(v_j)$. Consider the other situation when no vertex of $bd_{cc}(v_c, v_{cc})$ satisfies the above lemma (see Figure 4.15(b)). This means that for every vertex $v_i \in bd_{cc}(v_c, v_{cc})$, $SP(v_j, v_i)$ passes through vertices of $bd_c(v_j', v_i)$ or $SP(v_j', v_i)$ passes through vertices of $bd_{cc}(v_j, v_i)$. In order to identify all vertices of $SP(v_j, v_i)$ and $SP(v_j', v_i)$, we need the following lemmas.

Lemma 4.6.8 *For any vertex $v_i \in bd_{cc}(v_{j+1}, v_{cc})$, all vertices of $SP_{cc}(v_j, v_i)$ belong to $SP(v_j, v_i)$.*

Proof. If $SP_{cc}(v_j, v_i)$ is same as $SP(v_j, v_i)$, then the lemma holds. So, we assume that all edges of $SP_{cc}(v_j, v_i)$ do not lie inside P (see Figure 4.15(b)). Consider any edge $v_k v_m$ of $SP_{cc}(v_j, v_i)$ not lying inside P. This edge can be intersected only

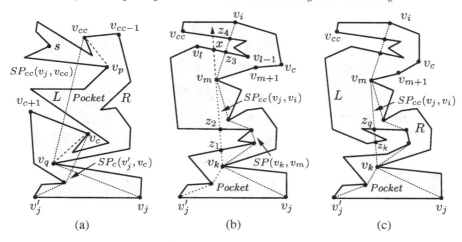

Figure 4.15 (a) The vertex v_c does not belong to $bd_{cc}(v_j, v_{cc})$. (b) $SP(v_j, v_i)$ and $SP(v'_j, v_i)$ pass through vertices of $bd_c(v'_j, v_i)$ and $bd_{cc}(v_j, v_i)$ respectively. (c) All points of $bd_c(z_q, z_k)$ are not visible from R.

by the edges of $bd_c(v'_j, v_i)$. So, $v_k v_m$ in $SP_{cc}(v_j, v_i)$ is replaced by $SP(v_k, v_m)$ in $SP(v_j, v_i)$. Hence, v_k and v_m remain in $SP(v_j, v_i)$. □

Lemma 4.6.9 *For any vertex $v_i \in bd_c(v'_j, v_c)$, all vertices of $SP_c(v'_j, v_i)$ belong to $SP(v'_j, v_i)$.*

Although Lemma 4.6.8 suggests that all vertices of $SP_{cc}(v_j, v_i)$ belong to $SP(v_j, v_i)$, all edges of $SP_{cc}(v_j, v_i)$ may not belong to $SP(v_j, v_i)$. In order to compute $SP(v_j, v_i)$, the problem is to replace each such edge $v_k v_m$ of $SP_{cc}(v_j, v_i)$ by $SP(v_k, v_m)$ (see Figure 4.15(b)). Observe that since $v_k v_m$ is intersected by edges of $bd_c(v'_j, v_i)$, $SP(v_k, v_m)$ must pass through some vertices of $bd_c(v'_j, v_i)$. Moreover, $SP(v_k, v_m)$ may pass through some more vertices of $bd_{cc}(v_j, v_i)$ (excluding v_k and v_m). Observe that there exists an order in which edges of $bd_c(v'_j, v_i)$ intersect edges of $SP_{cc}(v_j, v_i)$ in LR-visibility polygons (see Figure 4.15(b)) as shown in the following lemmas.

Lemma 4.6.10 *Assume that the pocket bounded by the constructed edge $v_j v'_j$ of $V(v_1)$ satisfies Lemma 4.6.6. Let v_i be a vertex of $bd_{cc}(v_c, v_{cc})$. Let $z_1, z_2, ..., z_p = v_i$ be the points of intersection of $bd_c(v'_j, v_i)$ with $SP_{cc}(v_j, v_i)$ in the order from v_j to v_i on $SP_{cc}(v_j, v_i)$ (Figure 4.15(b)). Let z_0 denote v_j. If P is an LR-visibility polygon, then for every intersection point z_k, where $0 < k < p$, z_k belongs to $bd_c(z_{k-1}, v_i)$.*

Proof. Assume on the contrary that there exist two intersection points z_k and z_q (Figure 4.15(c)), where $0 < k < q < p$, such that (i) z_k lies on $SP_{cc}(v_j, v_i)$ between v_j and z_q, and (ii) $z_k \in bd_c(z_q, v_i)$. If $v_i \in L$ or $s \in bd_c(z_k, v_i)$, then all points of $bd_c(z_q, z_k)$ are not visible from R. So, P is not an LR-visibility polygon, which is

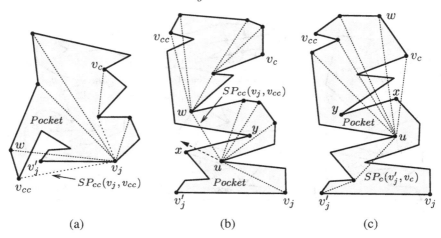

Figure 4.16 (a) All children of v_j in $SPT_{cc}(v_j, v_{cc})$ are not above $v_j v'_j$. (b) The inward edge xy is entering in the counterclockwise pocket bounded by uw and $bd_{cc}(u, w)$. (c) The inward edge xy is entering in the clockwise pocket bounded by uw and $bd_c(u, w)$.

a contradiction. If $s \in bd_c(v'_j, z_k)$, then s does not belong to $bd_{cc}(v_c, v_{cc})$, which contradicts Lemma 4.6.6.   □

Lemma 4.6.11 *Assume that the pocket bounded by the constructed edge $v_j v'_j$ of $V(v_1)$ satisfies Lemma 4.6.6. Let v_i be a vertex of $bd_{cc}(v_c, v_{cc})$. Let $z_1, z_2,..., z_p = v_i$ be the points of intersection of $bd_{cc}(v_j, v_i)$ with $SP_c(v'_j, v_i)$ in the order from v'_j to v_i on $SP_c(v'_j, v_i)$. Let z_0 denote v'_j. If P is an LR-visibility polygon, then for every intersection point z_k, where $0 < k < p$, z_k belongs to $bd_{cc}(z_{k-1}, v_i)$.*

Lemma 4.6.12 *Assume that the pocket bounded by the constructed edge $v_j v'_j$ of $V(v_1)$ satisfies Lemma 4.6.6. Let v_i be a vertex of $bd_{cc}(v_c, v_{cc})$. Let $v_k v_m$ be an edge of $SP_{cc}(v_j, v_i)$ where $v_k \in SP_{cc}(v_j, v_m)$. Let x the point of intersection of $\overrightarrow{v_k v_m}$ and $bd_c(v'_j, v_m)$ lying on an edge $v_l v_{l-1}$ of $bd_c(v'_j, v_m)$ (see Figure 4.15(b)) such that (i) x does not lie on $v_k v_m$, and (ii) x is the first point of intersection while traversing $bd_c(v'_j, v_m)$ in clockwise order from v'_j. If P is an LR-visibility polygon, then $bd_c(v_{l-1}, v_{m+1})$ does not intersect the segment $x v_m$.*

Proof. The proof follows along the line of the proof of Lemma 4.6.10.   □

Lemma 4.6.13 *Assume that the pocket bounded by the constructed edge $v_j v'_j$ of $V(v_1)$ satisfies Lemma 4.6.6. Let v_i be a vertex of $bd_{cc}(v_c, v_{cc})$. Let $v_k v_m$ be an edge of $SP_c(v'_j, v_i)$ where $v_k \in SP_c(v'_j, v_m)$. Let x the point of intersection of $\overrightarrow{v_k v_m}$ and $bd_{cc}(v_j, v_m)$ lying on an edge $v_l v_{l-1}$ of $bd_{cc}(v_j, v_m)$ such that (i) x does not lie on $v_k v_m$, and (ii) x is the first point of intersection while traversing $bd_{cc}(v_j, v_m)$ in*

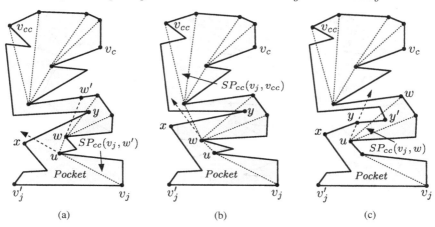

(a)   (b)   (c)

Figure 4.17 (a) The inward edge xy has intersected the extension ww'. (b) The inward edge xy has intersected the ray drawn from u through w. (c) The inward edge xy is updated to the next clockwise edge of xy.

counterclockwise order from v_j. If P is an LR-visibility polygon, then $bd_{cc}(v_l, v_{m-1})$ does not intersect the segment xv_m.

The ordered properties of intersection points in the above lemmas suggest a method for locating all edges of $bd_c(v'_j, v_i)$ intersecting $SP_{cc}(v_j, v_i)$ as follows. Let $v_j v_k$ be the first edge of $SP_{cc}(v_j, v_i)$. Scan $bd_c(v'_j, v_i)$ from v'_j until an edge of $bd_c(v'_j, v_i)$ intersects the current edge $v_j v_k$ or $\overrightarrow{v_j v_k}$. If $\overrightarrow{v_j v_k}$ is intersected, take the next edge of $v_j v_k$ in $SP_{cc}(v_j, v_i)$ as the current edge and repeat the process of checking the intersection. If an edge of $bd_c(v'_j, v_i)$ intersects $v_j v_k$, then continue the scan until another edge of $bd_c(v'_j, v_i)$ intersects $v_j v_k$. Once another edge is found intersecting $v_j v_k$, continue the scan as before to check for intersection with $v_j v_k$ or $\overrightarrow{v_j v_k}$. This method is used in the merging procedure for locating edges of $bd_c(v'_j, v_i)$ intersecting edges of $SP_{cc}(v_j, v_i)$ for all v_i using $SPT_{cc}(v_j, v_{cc})$.

The merging procedure maintains two current edges xy (called an *inward edge*), and uw (called a *lid*) and it checks the intersection between the current inward edge and the current lid. The merging procedure starts by assigning v'_j to x, the next clockwise vertex of x on $bd_c(v'_j, v_i)$ to y, v_j to u, and the next vertex of v_j on $SP_{cc}(v_j, v_{cc})$ to w. The above initialization of xy and uw is correct if all children of v_j in $SPT_{cc}(v_j, v_{cc})$ lie on the same side of $\overrightarrow{v_j v'_j}$. If children of v_j lie on both sides of $\overrightarrow{v_j v'_j}$ (see Figure 4.16(a)), w is assigned to the last child of v_j in counterclockwise order around v_j, lying to the right of $\overrightarrow{v_j v'_j}$.

Intuitively, the situation after initialization can be viewed as the inward edge xy entering the pocket induced by uw. In general, there are two situations: either the inward edge xy from $bd_c(v'_j, v_c)$ is entering in the counterclockwise pocket bounded

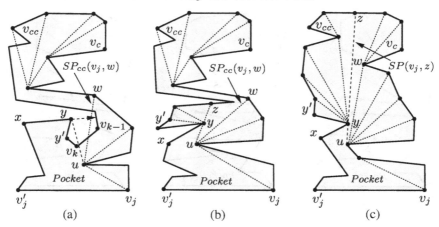

Figure 4.18 (a) The inward edge xy is updated to $v_k v_{k-1}$. (b) The point $z \in bd_c(y, v_{cc})$. (c) The point $z \in bd_{cc}(v_c, v_{cc})$.

by uw and $bd_{cc}(u, w)$ (see Figure 4.16(b)) or the inward edge xy from $bd_{cc}(v_j, v_{cc})$ is entering in the counterclockwise pocket bounded by uw and $bd_c(u, w)$ (see Figure 4.16(c)). Since these two cases are symmetric, we present the procedure only for the former situation, i.e., the inward edge xy from $bd_c(v'_j, v_c)$ is entering the counterclockwise pocket bounded by uw and $bd_{cc}(u, w)$ (see Figure 4.16(b)).

Step 1. *While xy intersects uw do* remove uw from $SPT_{cc}(v_j, v_{cc})$ and $w :=$ the next clockwise child of u in $SPT_{cc}(v_j, v_{cc})$ (see Figure 4.16(b)).

Step 2. *If xy intersects the extension ww' (if it exists) of uw (see Figure 4.17(a)) then* $u := w$, $w :=$ the next clockwise child of w in $SPT_{cc}(v_j, v_{cc})$ and *goto* Step 1.

Step 3. *If xy intersects $\overrightarrow{uw}$ (see Figure 4.17(b)) then* $u := w$, $w :=$ the next vertex of w on $SP_{cc}(v_j, v_{cc})$ and *goto* Step 1.

Step 4. Let y' be the next counterclockwise vertex of y. *If y' lies to the right of $\overrightarrow{uy}$ (see Figure 4.17(c)) then* $x := y$, $y := y'$ and *goto* Step 1.

Step 5. *If y' lies to the right of $\overrightarrow{xy}$ (see Figure 4.18(a)) then* scan the boundary in counterclockwise order starting from y' until an edge $v_k v_{k-1}$ intersecting uy is found, assign $v_k v_{k-1}$ as the inward edge xy and *goto* Step 1.

Step 6. (Remark: y' lies to the left of $\overrightarrow{xy}$). Extend uy from y to $bd(P)$ meeting it at a point z. Assign u as the parent of y in $SPT_{cc}(v_j, v_{cc})$.

Step 6a. *If z belongs to an edge of $bd_c(y, v_{cc})$ (see Figure 4.18(b)) then* concatenate the sub-tree of $SPT_c(v'_j, v_c)$ rooted at y to $SPT_{cc}(v_j, v'_j)$ by assigning u as the parent of y, assign the edge containing z as the inward edge xy and *goto* Step 1.

Step 6b. *If z belongs to an edge of $bd_{cc}(v_c, v_{cc})$ (see Figure 4.18(c)) then* concate-

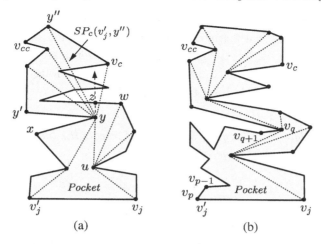

Figure 4.19 (a) The point $z \in bd_{cc}(v_j, v_c)$. (b) The parents of vertices v_{p-1}, $v_{p-2},...,$ v_{q+1} in $SPT_{cc}(v_j, v_j')$ are yet to be computed.

nate the sub-tree of $SPT_c(v_j', v_c)$ rooted at y to $SPT_{cc}(v_j, v_j')$ by assigning u as the parent of y and *goto* Step 7.

Step 6c. *If z belongs to an edge of $bd_{cc}(v_j, v_c)$ (see Figure 4.19(a)) then* locate the child y'' of y in $SPT_c(v_j', v_c)$ such that $\overrightarrow{uy}$ passes between y'' and its next sibling in clockwise order, $w := y''$, $u := y$, assign the edge containing z as the inward edge xy and call the analogous procedure for checking the intersection of inward edge xy entering into the clockwise pocket induced by uw.

Step 7. Let $v_p v_{p-1},...,$ $v_{q+1} v_q$ be the consecutive edges such that the parents of intermediate vertices v_{p-1}, $v_{p-2},...,$ v_{q+1} in $SPT_{cc}(v_j, v_j')$ are not yet computed (see Figure 4.19(b)). Compute the parent of every vertex $v_i \in bd_{cc}(v_{q+1}, v_{p-1})$ in $SPT_{cc}(v_j, v_j')$ starting from v_{q+1} by drawing the tangent from v_i meeting $SP_{cc}(v_j, v_p)$ or $SP_{cc}(v_j, v_{i-1})$. If $SPT_{cc}(v_j, v_j')$ is not computed completely *goto* Step 7.

Step 8. Output $SPT_{cc}(v_j, v_j')$ as $SPT(v_j)$ and Stop.

Consider Case B. We know that the vertex v_c does not belong to $bd_{cc}(v_j, v_{cc})$ (Figure 4.15(a)). We have the following lemma.

Lemma 4.6.14 *Let $v_j v_j'$ be a constructed edge of $V(v_1)$ in P satisfying Corollary 4.6.3. If v_c does not belong to $bd_{cc}(v_j, v_{cc})$, then the parent of v_{cc} in $SPT(v_j)$ is a vertex of $bd_c(v_j', v_c)$ or the parent of v_c in $SPT(v_j')$ is a vertex of $bd_{cc}(v_j, v_{cc})$.*

Proof. Let v_p and v_q be the parents of v_{cc} and v_c in $SPT(v_j)$ and $SPT(v_j')$, respectively (see Figure 4.15(a)). Since there is a reverse turn at v_{cc}, $v_p \in bd_c(v_j', v_{cc+1})$. If $v_p \in bd_c(v_j', v_c)$, then the lemma holds. So we assume that $v_p \in bd_c(v_c, v_{cc+1})$. In that case, $s \in bd_{cc}(v_j, v_{p-1})$. It means that there cannot be any reverse turn at any vertex v_c in $bd_c(v'_j, s)$ as both s and v'_j belong to L, which is a contradiction. So $s \in bd_{cc}(v_j, v_{cc})$ or $v_p \in bd_c(v'_j, v_c)$. Analogous arguments show that $s \in bd_c(v'_j, v_c)$ or $v_q \in bd_{cc}(v_j, v_{cc})$. If $s \in bd_{cc}(v_j, v_{cc})$, then v_q must belong to $bd_{cc}(v_j, v_{cc})$, or if $s \in bd_c(v'_j, v_c)$, then v_p must belong to $bd_c(v'_j, v_c)$.   □

Corollary 4.6.15 *The boundary $bd_{cc}(v_j, v_{cc})$ intersects the last edge of $SP_c(v'_j, v_c)$ or $bd_c(v'_j, v_c)$ intersects the last edge of $SP_{cc}(v_j, v_{cc})$.*

The above corollary suggests that by checking the intersection of $bd_c(v'_j, v_c)$ with $SP_{cc}(v_j, v_{cc})$, the parent of v_{cc} in $SPT_{cc}(v_j, v'_j)$ can be located. The intersection can be checked by the merging procedure stated as Step 1 to Step 8 in Case A. If the parent of v_{cc} in $SPT_{cc}(v_j, v_{cc})$ changes after checking the intersection (i.e. $v_{cc}v_{cc-1}$ becomes an inward edge), the procedure scans in counterclockwise order from v_{cc} till it finds a new v_{cc}. Again, the merging procedure is used to find the parent of the new v_{cc}. This process of scanning and merging is repeated till $SPT_{cc}(v_j, v'_j)$ is computed completely. Consider the other situation when the parent of v_{cc} in $SPT_{cc}(v_j, v_{cc})$ has not changed after v_{cc} is reached by the merging procedure. In that case, the analogous steps of the merging procedure is used to check the intersection between $bd_{cc}(v_j, v_{cc})$ with $SP_c(v'_j, v_c)$. If the parent of v_c changes in $SPT_c(v'_j, v_c)$, the procedure scans in clockwise order from v_c till it finds a new v_c, and the entire process is repeated with new v_c and v_{cc}. If the parent of v_c also does not change in $SPT_c(v'_j, v_c)$ after v_c is reached by the merging procedure, then P is not an LR-visibility polygon by Lemma 4.6.14. Finally, the procedure gives $SPT_{cc}(v_j, v'_j)$ or $SPT_c(v'_j, v_j)$. If the procedures gives $SPT_c(v'_j, v_j)$, $SPT_{cc}(v_j, v'_j)$ can be constructed from $SPT_c(v'_j, v_j)$ by drawing cross-tangents as stated earlier.

The correctness of the merging procedure follows from Lemmas 4.6.6, 4.6.10, 4.6.11, 4.6.12, 4.6.13 and 4.6.14. Let us analyze the time complexity of the merging procedure. For each constructed edge $v_j v'_j$, $SPT_{cc}(v_j, v_{cc})$ and $SPT_c(v'_j, v_c)$ can be computed in time proportional to the number of vertices of $bd_{cc}(v_j, v'_j)$. The merging procedure considers each edge of $SPT_{cc}(v_j, v_{cc})$ and $SPT_c(v'_j, v_c)$ at most twice. Note that all such points z in Step 6 of the merging procedure can be computed using $SPT_{cc}(v_j, v_{cc})$ and $SPT_c(v'_j, v_c)$ in a time that is proportional to the sum of sizes of $SPT_{cc}(v_j, v_{cc})$ and $SPT_c(v'_j, v_c)$. Therefore, $SPT(v_j)$ can be computed in a time that is proportional to the number of vertices in $bd_{cc}(v_j, v'_j)$. Therefore, the merging takes $O(n)$ time for all pockets of $V(v_1)$. We summarize the result in the following theorem.

Theorem 4.6.16 *The shortest path tree from a vertex inside an n-sided simple polygon P can be computed in $O(n)$ time if P is a LR-visibility polygon.*

4.7 Notes and Comments

In the recent years, several on-line algorithms have been designed for LR-visibility polygons (also called *streets*) in the context of robot path planning. These algorithms are designed for situations where a robot moves in an environment without completely knowing the geometry of the environment, navigating on the basis of *local* information provided by acoustic, visual or tactile sensors. A natural scenario in robotics is that of searching for a goal in an unknown polygonal region, i.e., a robot with an on-board vision system is placed at a starting point s in a polygon and it must traverse a path to some target point t in the polygon. A problem in the above scenario is to design efficient algorithms which a robot can use to search for the target. Any such algorithm is on-line in the sense that decisions must be made based only on what the robot has seen so far.

For target-searching problems (searching a point t from a starting point s), researchers have designed algorithms that minimize the Euclidean distance traveled by a robot in reaching the target point. They have also investigated this problem for streets for which better performance could be obtained. In the spirit of analyzing on-line algorithms by following the concept introduced by Sleator and Tarjan [312] for problems in computer science in general, the efficiency of such algorithms is determined by their *competitive ratio*: the worst-case ratio of the length of the path from s to t traversed by the on-line algorithm to the length of the Euclidean shortest path between s and t.

Klein [219] proposed an on-line algorithm with competitive ratio $1 + 3\pi/2$ for the target-searching problem in a street. He also showed for this problem that $\sqrt{2}$ is the lower bound on the competitive ratio. Since then, several on-line algorithms have been designed improving the upper bound of the competitive ratio [105, 220, 246, 247] and finally, an optimal on-line algorithm has been designed by Icking *et al.* [202]. For the corresponding problem of minimizing the number of links in the link path between s and t, Ghosh and Saluja [166] proposed an optimal on-line algorithm whose competitive ratio is $1 + 1/m$, where m is the link distance between s and t. For the target-searching problem in a generalized street, on-line algorithms were proposed by Datta and Icking [106] and Lopez-Ortiz and Schuierer [247]. There are on-line algorithms also for the target-searching problem in an unknown star-shaped polygon, where t is any point in the kernel of the star-shaped polygon [201, 238, 248].

5

Visibility Graphs

5.1 Problems and Results

The visibility graph is a fundamental structure in computational geometry; some early applications of visibility graphs include computing Euclidean shortest paths in the presence of obstacles [249] and in decomposing two-dimensional shapes into clusters [306]. The *visibility graph* (also called the *vertex visibility graph*) of a polygon P with or without holes is the undirected graph of the visibility relation on the vertices of P. The visibility graph of P has a node for every vertex of P and an edge for every pair of visible vertices in P. Figure 5.1(b) shows the visibility graph of the polygon in Figure 5.1(a). We sometimes draw the visibility graph directly on the polygon, as shown in Figure 5.1(c). It can be seen that every triangulation of P corresponds to a sub-graph of the visibility graph of P. The visibility graph of a line segment arrangement is defined similarly, where the endpoints of the line segments are represented as the nodes of the visibility graph.

Consider the problem of computing the visibility graph of a polygon P (with or without holes) having a total of n vertices. The visible pairs of vertices in P can

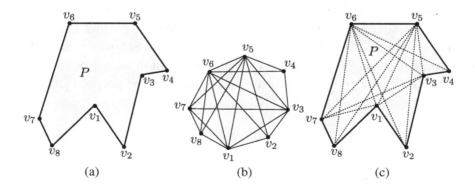

Figure 5.1 (a) A polygon. (b) The visibility graph of the polygon. (c) The visibility graph drawn on the polygon.

136

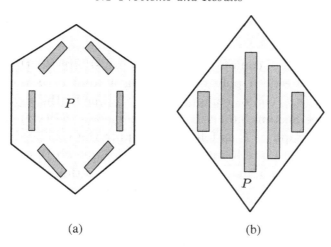

Figure 5.2 (a) The visibility graph of this polygon with holes has $O(n^2)$ edges. (b) The visibility graph of this polygon with holes has $O(n)$ edges.

be computed by checking intersections of segments connecting pairs of vertices in P with each polygonal edge of P. This naive method takes $O(n^3)$ time as in the first algorithm for computing the visibility graph given by Lozano-Perez and Wesley [249]. Lee [229] and Sharir and Schorr [307] improved the time complexity by designing $O(n^2 \log n)$ time algorithms. Asano *et al.* [28] and Welzl [339] later developed $O(n^2)$ time algorithms for this problem. Since, at its largest, the visibility graph can be of size $O(n^2)$ (see Figure 5.2(a)), the algorithms of Asano *et al.* and Welzl are worst-case optimal. In Section 5.3.1, we present the algorithm of Welzl [339].

Exercise 5.1.1 *Draw a simple polygon of n vertices whose visibility graph has 2n − 3 edges (including n polygonal edges) [271].*

The visibility graph may be much smaller than its worst-case size of $O(n^2)$ (in particular, it can have $O(n)$ edges (see Figure 5.2(b)) and therefore, it is not necessary to spend $O(n^2)$ time to compute it. In other words, the lower bound on the time to compute a visibility graph can be expressed as $\Omega(n^2)$, but a more exact lower bound is $\Omega(E)$, where E is the number of edges in the visibility graph. Matching this lower bound, Hershberger [186] developed an $O(E)$ algorithm for computing the visibility graph of a simple polygon which we present in Section 5.2. An algorithm that takes time depending on its output size E is called *output-sensitive*. Overmars and Welzl [278] gave an $O(E \log n)$ time, $O(n)$ space algorithm for computing the visibility graph for a polygon with holes. Ghosh and Mount [165] presented $O(n \log n + E)$ time, $O(E + n)$ space algorithm for this same problem; we present this algorithm in Section 5.3.2. Keeping the same time complexity, Pocchiola and Vegter [286] improved the space complexity to $O(n)$. Kapoor and Maheshwari [209] proposed another algorithm for this problem for a polygon with h holes that runs in $O(h \log n + T + E)$ time, where T is the time for triangulating a polygon. Note that a polygon with h holes can be triangulated in $O(n + h \log^{1+\epsilon} h)$ time [43].

Consider the problem of computing the Euclidean shortest path $SP(s,t)$ between two points s and t inside a polygon P having a total of n vertices. If P is a simple polygon, $SP(s,t)$ can be computed in $O(n)$ time by the algorithm of Lee and Preparata [235] (see Section 3.6.1). If P contains holes, $SP(s,t)$ can be computed using the visibility graph of P as follows. Compute the visibility graph of P using the algorithm of Ghosh and Mount [165] in $O(n \log n + E)$ time. Represent s as a node in the visibility graph and connect it by edges to those nodes in the visibility graph whose corresponding vertices in P are visible from s. This can be done in $O(n \log n)$ time using the algorithm of Asano [27] (see Section 2.3). Similarly, the node corresponding to t is connected to the visibility graph of P. Once the visibility graph of $n+2$ nodes is constructed, the Euclidean distance between every visible pair of vertices in P are assigned as the weight to the corresponding edge in the visibility graph. Thus a weighted visibility graph is constructed, and using the algorithm of Fredman and Tarjan [143], the shortest path from the node corresponding to s to all nodes in the weighted visibility graph can be computed in $O(n \log n + E)$ time. We have the following theorem.

Theorem 5.1.1 *The Euclidean shortest path between two points inside a polygon P with holes of total n vertices can be computed in $O(n \log n + E)$ time, where E is the number of edges in the visibility graph of P.*

Suppose a partial visibility graph of P is computed such that all edges of $SP(s,t)$ belong to the partial visibility graph. So, $SP(s,t)$ can still be computed from the partial visibility graph using the algorithm of Fredman and Tarjan [143]. It is better to compute such a partial visibility graph of P because it reduces the running time of the algorithm of Fredman and Tarjan [143]. This approach of computing a partial visibility graph of P (also called the *tangent visibility graph* [285]) has been taken by Rohnert [298] and Kapoor *et al.* [210]. Rohnert [298] has proposed an $O(n+h^2 \log h)$ time algorithm for computing the tangent visibility graph of P, where P contains h convex holes. If the holes in P are non-convex, the graph can still be computed in the same time complexity as shown by Kapoor *et al.* [210]. We present the algorithm of Rohnert [298] in Section 5.4.1 and the algorithm of Kapoor *et al.* [210] in Section 5.4.2.

5.2 Computing Visibility Graphs of Simple Polygons

In this section, we present the algorithm of Hershberger [186] for computing the visibility graph of a given simple polygon P in $O(E)$ time, where E is the number of edges in the visibility graph of P. We assume that P is given as a counterclockwise sequence of vertices $v_1, v_2, \ldots, v_n$.

Suppose, for every vertex $v_i \in P$, the visibility polygon $V(v_i)$ of P is computed using the algorithm of Lee presented in Section 2.2. For every vertex v_j belongs to $V(v_i)$, the corresponding nodes of v_i and v_j are connected by an edge in the visibility graph of P. We call such segment v_iv_j as *visible segment* in P. Since every visible segment v_iv_j for all i and j in P occurs in two visibility polygons $V(v_i)$ and $V(v_j)$, the union of all visible segments in $V(v_1)$, $V(v_2)$,..., $V(v_n)$ gives the visibility graph of P. Since, the algorithm of Lee runs in $O(n)$ time, this process of computing the visibility graph of P by computing $V(v_1)$, $V(v_2)$,..., $V(v_n)$ takes $O(n^2)$ time. Suppose, the shortest path trees $SPT(v_1)$, $SPT(v_2)$,..., $SPT(v_n)$ are computed in P instead of computing $V(v_1)$, $V(v_2)$,..., $V(v_n)$. Since each visible segment must appear at least in two such trees, the visibility graph of P can also be computed by computing $SPT(v_1)$, $SPT(v_2)$,..., $SPT(v_n)$. If these trees are computed independently, this process again takes $O(n^2)$ time, as the algorithm of Guibas *et al.* [178] for computing the shortest path tree from a vertex in P takes $O(n)$ time (see Section 3.3.2). It has been shown by Hershberger that $SPT(v_1)$, $SPT(v_2)$,..., $SPT(v_n)$ can be computed in $O(E)$ time.

Assume that $SPT(v_i)$ has been computed and the procedure wants to compute $SPT(v_{i+1})$. In order to compute $SPT(v_{i+1})$, it is enough to locate those vertices v_j of P such that the parents of v_j in $SPT(v_i)$ and $SPT(v_{i+1})$ are different. For the remaining vertices of P, the parents are the same in both $SPT(v_i)$ and $SPT(v_{i+1})$. Hence, the cost of computing $SPT(v_{i+1})$ is same as the cost of locating such vertices v_j and their parents in $SPT(v_{i+1})$. We show later that the sum of these costs for computing $SPT(v_{i+1})$ for all i is $O(E)$. In the following lemma, we present the main idea used by the algorithm for locating such vertices v_j.

Lemma 5.2.1 *For every vertex v_j of P, the parents of v_j in $SPT(v_i)$ and $SPT(v_{i+1})$ are different if and only if v_j is visible from some internal point of the edge v_iv_{i+1}.*

Proof. If v_j is visible from some internal point u on v_iv_{i+1} (see Figure 5.3(a)), then both $SP(v_i, v_j)$ and $SP(v_{i+1}, v_j)$ cannot intersect the segment uv_j (except at v_j). So, all vertices in $SP(v_i, v_j)$ must lie on the clockwise boundary from v_i to v_j (i.e., $bd(v_j, v_i)$). Hence, the parent of v_j in $SPT(v_i)$ belongs to $bd(v_j, v_i)$. Analogously, all vertices in $SP(v_{i+1}, v_j)$, including the parent of v_j in $SPT(v_{i+1})$, belong to $bd(v_{i+1}, v_j)$. Therefore, the parents of v_j in $SPT(v_i)$ and $SPT(v_{i+1})$ are different.

Now we prove the converse. Assume on the contrary that v_j is not visible from any internal point of the edge v_iv_{i+1} but the parents of v_j in $SPT(v_i)$ and $SPT(v_{i+1})$ are different. Let v_p and v_q denote the parents of v_j in $SPT(v_i)$ and $SPT(v_{i+1})$, respectively (see Figure 5.3(a)). Consider $\overrightarrow{v_jv_p}$ and $\overrightarrow{v_jv_q}$. If $SP(v_i, v_p)$ intersects $\overrightarrow{v_jv_p}$ other than at v_p, then v_p cannot be the parent of v_j in $SPT(v_i)$. So, $SP(v_i, v_p)$ does not intersect $\overrightarrow{v_jv_p}$. Analogously, $SP(v_{i+1}, v_q)$ does not intersect $\overrightarrow{v_jv_q}$ (except at v_q). So, v_i and v_{i+1} lie on opposite sides of the wedge formed by rays $\overrightarrow{v_jv_p}$ and

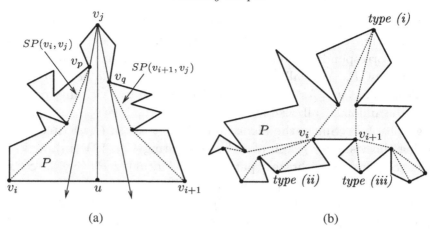

Figure 5.3 (a) The vertex v_j is visible from an internal point u of v_iv_{i+1}. (b) There are three types of vertices in $V(v_iv_{i+1})$.

$\overrightarrow{v_jv_q}$. Therefore, the wedge intersects v_iv_{i+1}. Hence v_j is visible from some internal point u of v_iv_{i+1}, which is a contradiction. $\square$

The above lemma suggests that the parents of those vertices of P, that do not belong to the weak visibility polygon $V(v_iv_{i+1})$ of P from v_iv_{i+1}, remain unchanged while computing $SPT(v_{i+1})$ from $SPT(v_i)$. This means that once $SPT(v_{i+1})$ is computed within $V(v_iv_{i+1})$, the entire $SPT(v_{i+1})$ has been computed. The task is now to compute $SPT(v_{i+1})$ within $V(v_iv_{i+1})$ using the structure of $SPT(v_i)$.

Observe that there can be three types of vertices in $V(v_iv_{i+1})$ (see Figure 5.3(b)): (i) the vertices of $V(v_iv_{i+1})$ that are visible from some internal point of v_iv_{i+1} satisfying Lemma 5.2.1, (ii) the vertices of $V(v_iv_{i+1})$ that are only visible from v_i (if v_i is a reflex vertex), and (iii) the vertices of $V(v_iv_{i+1})$ that are only visible from v_{i+1} (if v_{i+1} is a reflex vertex). For vertices of type (ii), the shortest path from v_{i+1} to any such vertex passes through v_i. So, the sub-tree rooted at v_i in $SPT(v_i)$ containing vertices of type (ii) and their descendants becomes the sub-tree of $SPT(v_{i+1})$ with v_{i+1} as the parent of v_i. For vertices of type (iii), the sub-tree rooted at v_{i+1} in $SPT(v_i)$ becomes the sub-tree of $SPT(v_{i+1})$.

The parent of vertices of type (i) in $SPT(v_{i+1})$ can be computed using the *shortest path map* of $SPT(v_i)$ as follows (see Figure 5.4(a)). It can be seen that $SPT(v_i)$ partitions the internal region of P into funnels, where the edges of P are the bases of funnels. The apex of a funnel F with base v_jv_{j+1} is the least common ancestor (say, v_k) of v_j and v_{j+1} in $SPT(v_i)$. So, $SP(v_k, v_j)$ and $SP(v_k, v_{j+1})$ are two sides of F. For more details on the properties of a funnel, see Section 3.6.1. If F is not a triangle, then extend each edge of $SP(v_k, v_j)$ and $SP(v_k, v_{j+1})$ to v_jv_{j+1} and insert the extension points on v_jv_{j+1}. It can be seen that these extensions partition F into

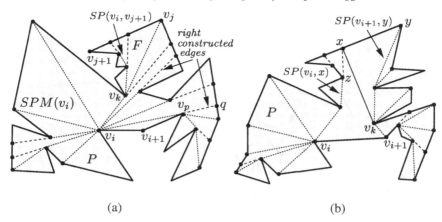

Figure 5.4 (a) The shortest path map $SPM(v_i)$ gives the right constructed edges of $V(v_iv_{i+1})$. (b) The segment xv_k is the tangent from x to $SP(v_{i+1}, y)$.

triangles. Similarly, partition all funnels in P into triangles and it gives the *shortest path map* of $SPT(v_i)$ (denoted as $SPM(v_i)$). The extensions of the sides of a funnel are called *extension edges* of $SPM(v_i)$.

We know that only the endpoints of a constructed edge of $V(v_iv_{i+1})$ lie on $bd(P)$, and one of them is a vertex of P. For a constructed edge v_pq, if v_p precedes q in clockwise order on the boundary of $V(v_iv_{i+1})$, then we say v_pq is a *left* constructed edge and a *right* constructed edge (see Figure 5.4(a)), otherwise. We have the following observation.

Lemma 5.2.2 *The right and left constructed edges of $V(v_iv_{i+1})$ are extension edges of $SPM(v_i)$ and $SPM(v_{i+1})$, respectively.*

Exercise 5.2.1 *Prove Lemma 5.2.2.*

The above lemma suggests that the right constructed edges of $V(v_iv_{i+1})$ can be identified from $SPM(v_i)$. However, the left constructed edges of $V(v_iv_{i+1})$ are not readily available as $SPM(v_{i+1})$ is yet to be constructed. So the task is to construct $SPM(v_{i+1})$, which can be done by traversing $SPM(v_i)$ and using Lemma 5.2.1 as follows.

Assume that the procedure has computed $SPT(v_{i+1})$ up to a vertex or point y by traversing $bd(P)$ in counterclockwise order starting from v_{i+1}. Initially, y is v_{i+1}. Let x denote the current vertex or point under consideration. If v_{i+1} is a convex vertex, x is initialized to the next counterclockwise vertex or point of v_{i+1} on $bd(P)$. Otherwise, x is initialized to the endpoint of the extension edge of $SPM(v_i)$ whose other endpoint is v_{i+1}. So, the segment xy is partially or totally an edge of P, or a right constructed edge of $V(v_iv_{i+1})$. If x is a vertex, then z denotes the parent

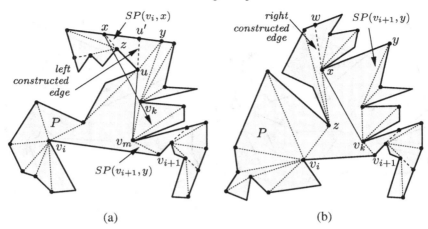

(a)   (b)

Figure 5.5 (a) The visible segment uv_m is the cross-tangent between $SP(v_i, x)$ and $SP(v_{i+1}, y)$. (b) The vertex x is not a leaf of $SPT(v_i)$.

of x in $SPT(v_i)$. Otherwise, zx denotes the extension edge of $SPM(v_i)$. We have following steps for computing $SPT(v_{i+1})$ and $SPM(v_{i+1})$ for vertices of type (i).

Step 1. Scan $SP(v_{i+1}, y)$ starting from y until a vertex v_k is reached such that xv_k is either the tangent from x to $SP(v_{i+1}, y)$ (Figure 5.4(b)) or z lies to the left of $\overrightarrow{xv_k}$ (Figure 5.5(a)).

Step 2. *If z lies to the left of $\overrightarrow{xv_k}$ then*

   Step 2a. Draw the cross-tangent uv_m between $SP(v_i, z)$ and $SP(v_{i+1}, v_k)$ where $u \in SP(v_i, z)$ and $v_m \in SP(v_{i+1}, v_k)$ (Figure 5.5(a)).

   Step 2b. Add uu' as an extension edge of $SPM(v_{i+1})$, where u' is the intersection point of $\overrightarrow{v_m u}$ and xy.

   Step 2c. Connect the sub-tree of $SPT(v_i)$ rooted at u (along with the map) to $SPT(v_{i+1})$ by assigning v_m as the parent of u.

   Step 2d. Extend each edge of $SP(v_m, y)$ to xy to form the extension edges of $SPM(v_{i+1})$.

   Step 2e. Assign u to y and *goto* Step 7.

Step 3. Extend each edge of $SP(v_k, y)$ to xy to form extension edges of $SPM(v_{i+1})$.

Step 4. *If x is a point or a leaf of $SPT(v_i)$ then* assign v_k as the parent of x in $SPT(v_{i+1})$, assign x to y and *goto* Step 7.

Step 5. Add the extension edge xw of $SPM(v_i)$ as an extension edge of $SPM(v_{i+1})$ (Figure 5.5(b)).

Step 6. Connect the sub-tree of $SPT(v_i)$ rooted at x (along with the map) to $SPT(v_{i+1})$ by assigning v_k as the parent of x. Assign w to y.

Step 7. Assign the next counterclockwise vertex or point of y on $bd(P)$ to x. If x is not v_i *then goto* Step 1.

Step 8. Assign v_{i+1} as the parent of v_i. Remove from $bd(P)$ the endpoints of the extension edges of $SPM(v_i)$ that are on the boundary of $V(v_1 v_{i+1})$ and Stop.

Once $SPT(v_1)$ is computed, the above procedure can be used to compute $V(v_1 v_2)$, $SPT(v_2)$, $V(v_2 v_3)$, $SPT(v_3)$,..., $V(v_{n-1} v_n)$, $SPT(v_n)$. Using the algorithm of Guibas et al. [178] (see Section 3.3.2), $SPT(v_1)$ can be computed in $O(n)$ time.

The correctness of the algorithm follows from Lemmas 5.2.1 and 5.2.2. We analyze the time complexity of the algorithm. Consider a visible segment $v_j v_k$. It is obvious that $v_j v_k$ appears as an edge in $SPT(v_j)$ and $SPT(v_k)$. Let $v_j v_j'$ and $v_k v_k'$ denote the two extension edges of $v_j v_k$, where $v_j' \in v_p v_{p+1}$ and $v_k' \in v_q v_{q+1}$. So, $v_j v_k$ appears as an edge in at least two trees among $SPT(v_p)$, $SPT(v_{p+1})$, $SPT(v_q)$ and $SPT(v_{q+1})$. Therefore, the algorithm considers a visible segment and its extension edges at most four times while computing tangents inside a weak visibility polygon. Hence, the overall time complexity of the algorithm is $O(E)$. We summarize the result in the following theorem.

Theorem 5.2.3 *The visibility graph of a simple polygon P can be computed in $O(E)$ time, where E is the number of edges in the visibility graph of P.*

5.3 Computing Visibility Graphs of Polygons with Holes

5.3.1 Worst-Case: $O(n^2)$ Algorithm

In this section, we present the algorithm of Welzl [339] for computing the visibility graph of a set S of n disjoint line-segments in $O(n^2)$ time. The endpoints of the line-segments $s_1, s_2, \ldots, s_n$ are marked as $v_1, v_2, \ldots, v_{2n}$, where v_{2i-1} and v_{2i} are endpoints of s_i. Any segment $v_i v_j$ is said to be a *visible segment* if $v_i v_j$ does not intersect any line-segment in S. We know that the visibility polygon $V(v_i)$ from each vertex v_i can be computed in $O(n \log n)$ time by the algorithm of Asano [27] presented in Section 2.3. Once $V(v_i)$ is known, then all visible segments with v_i as one endpoint are also known. Hence, the visibility graph of S can be computed in $O(n^2 \log n)$ time. Welzl [339] has shown that $V(v_i)$ can be computed in $O(n)$ time once slopes of all segments between v_i and all other endpoints in S are given in the sorted angular order around v_i. We show later that this sorted angular order for all vertices can be computed in $O(n^2)$.

Let L_i denote the list of all segments connecting v_i with every other endpoint of S. Assume that the segments in L_i are given in the counterclockwise angular order around v_i. The problem is to identify those segments in L_i that are visible segments. Let s_k be the first line-segment in S intersected by the ray emanating from v_i in the vertical direction downward (see Figure 5.6(a)). In other words, s_k is the current

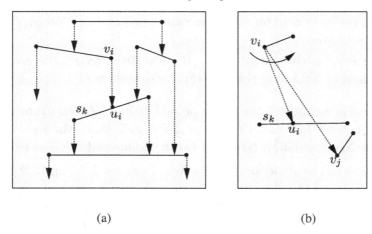

(a)   (b)

Figure 5.6 (a) The vertical ray is drawn from each endpoint of line-segments of S. (b) The segment $v_i v_j$ is not a visible segment.

line-segment visible from v_i in the direction vertically downward from v_i. Let u_i denote the current point on the boundary of $V(v_i)$ visible from v_i. Initialize u_i by the intersection point of s_k and the downward vertical ray from v_i.

In general, let $v_i v_j$ be the next counterclockwise segment of $v_i u_i$ in L_i. Without loss of generality, we assume that v_{j+1} is the other endpoint of v_j of the same line-segment in S. We have the following cases.

Case 1. The segment $v_i v_j$ intersects s_k (Figure 5.6(b)).
Case 2. The segment $v_i v_j$ does not intersect s_k.

     Case 2a. The vertex v_{j+1} is the vertex v_i (Figure 5.7(a)).
     Case 2b. The vertex v_{j+1} lies to the left of $\overrightarrow{v_i v_j}$ (Figure 5.7(b)).
     Case 2c. The vertex v_{j+1} lies to the right of $\overrightarrow{v_i v_j}$ (Figure 5.7(c)).

In Case 1, $v_i v_j$ is not a visible segment. So, s_k remains the same and the intersection point of $v_i v_j$ and s_k is assigned to u_i. Consider Case 2. We know that $v_i v_j$ is a visible segment (see Figure 5.7). If $v_i v_j$ itself is a line-segment in S (i.e., Case 2a), then it is not a new visible segment and the intersection point of $\overrightarrow{v_i v_j}$ and s_k is assigned to u_i. Otherwise, $v_i v_j$ is added to the list of visible segments of v_i. If v_{j+1} lies to the left of $\overrightarrow{v_i v_j}$ (i.e., Case 2b), then $v_j v_{j+1}$ becomes the current visible line-segment in place of s_k and v_j becomes the current u_i. If v_{j+1} lies the right of $\overrightarrow{v_i v_j}$ (i.e., Case 2c), locate the line-segment s_m intersecting $\overrightarrow{v_i v_j}$ such that the intersection point on s_m is the closest to v_i among all other intersection points on $\overrightarrow{v_i v_j}$. If $\overrightarrow{v_i v_j}$ does not intersect any line-segment in S, we assume that there is a line-segment s_{n+1} at infinity and s_m is s_{n+1}. Once the testing of $v_i v_j$ is over, the algorithm takes the next counterclockwise segment of $v_i u_i$ in L_i and proceeds as before. This process of rotation at v_i is repeated till all segments in L_i have been

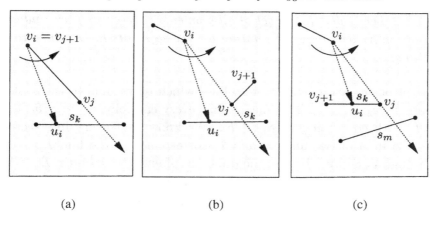

(a)   (b)   (c)

Figure 5.7 (a) The vertex v_{j+1} is the vertex v_i. (b) The vertex v_j is visible from v_i. (c) The segment $v_j v_{j+1}$ is the line-segment s_k.

considered. It can be seen that each $v_i v_j$ of L_i can be tested in $O(1)$ time provided locating s_m in Case 2c can also be done in $O(1)$ time. We have the following observation.

Lemma 5.3.1 *Let $v_i v_j$ be the next segment of $v_i u_i$ in the counterclockwise order around v_i, where u_i is a point on the current visible line-segment s_k of v_i (Figure 5.7(c)). If v_j is an endpoint of s_k, then the next visible line-segment s_m of v_i is the current visible line-segment of v_j in the direction $\overrightarrow{v_i v_j}$.*

The above lemma suggests that if the current visible line-segment in the direction $\overrightarrow{v_i v_j}$ is known for all v_j at the time of processing L_i, then each $v_i v_j$ of L_i can be tested in $O(1)$ time. Suppose, starting from the initial vertical direction, the algorithm has also processed all segments in L_j up to a segment $v_j v_p$ where $\overrightarrow{v_i v_j}$ is lying between $v_j v_p$ and its next segment in L_j. In that case s_m is the current visible line-segment of v_j. So, $v_j v_p$ should be processed before processing $v_i v_j$, which suggests an order of processing. It can be seen that the segments in L_i and L_j can be merged into one list, say L_{ij}, according to their angle with the initial vertical directions at v_i and v_j respectively. Then, the rotation can be done at either v_i or v_j depending upon the next segment in L_{ij}. In the same way, a combined merged list L can be constructed by merging $L_1, L_2, \ldots, L_{2n}$. We call L as the *order of rotation* for S. The merging of $2n$ sorted lists having n elements in each list takes $O(n^2 \log n)$ time using pair-wise merging. This can be improved to $O(n^2)$ by computing L directly from S without going through merging, using duality of lines and points as shown in the following lemma.

Lemma 5.3.2 *Let D denote the set of all segments between any two endpoints of n line-segments in S. The order of rotation for the segments in D can be constructed in $O(n^2)$ time.*

Proof. Let A be the arrangement of $2n$ lines which is the dual to the configuration of endpoints $v_1, v_2, \ldots, v_{2n}$. This means that every endpoint $v_i = (a_i, b_i)$ is mapped to a line T_i with equation $y = a_i x + b_i$. We know that every intersection point $w_{ij} = (a_{ij}, b_{ij})$ in A of two lines T_i and T_j corresponds to the line $y = -a_{ij} x + b_{ij}$ passing through v_i and v_j. Hence, the direction of every segment in D with slope k corresponds to an intersection in A with x-coordinate $-k$ and vice versa. Consider all intersection points on T_i in the order along T_i. It can be seen that this order is same as the angular order around v_i of all segments in D with endpoint v_i. For any two consecutive intersection points w_{ij} and w_{ik} on every T_i, a direction can be assigned from w_{ij} to w_{ik} if w_{ij} is to the right of w_{ik}. Let G represent an acyclic directed graph, where every intersection point in A is represented as a node in G and every direction assigned in A is represent as a corresponding directed edge in G. It has been shown by Chazelle *et al.* [77] and Edelsbrunner *et al.* [120] that G can be constructed from A in $O(n^2)$ time. Once G is constructed, topological sorting of G gives the order of rotation for S, which can also be computed in $O(n^2)$ time (see Kozen [221]).   □

In the following, we state the major steps of the algorithm.

Step 1. Compute the order of rotation for all segments between any two endpoints of the given n line-segments in S.

Step 2. Traverse the order of rotation and test whether the current segment $v_i v_j$ in the order is a visible segment.

Step 3. Output the visibility graph of S.

The correctness of the algorithms follows from Lemmas 5.3.1 and 5.3.2. We summarize the result in the following theorem.

Theorem 5.3.3 *The visibility graph of a set of n disjoint line-segments can be computed in $O(n^2)$ time.*

Exercise 5.3.1 *Design an algorithm for computing the visibility graph of a polygon with holes with a total of n vertices in $O(n^2)$ time.*

5.3.2 Output-Sensitive: $O(n \log n + E)$ Algorithm

In this section, we present an $O(n \log n + E)$ time algorithm given by Ghosh and Mount [165] for computing the visibility graph of a polygon P with holes, where n

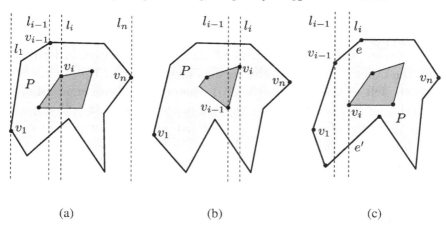

(a)   (b)   (c)

Figure 5.8 (a) The edges of v_i are on the opposite side of l_i. (b) Both edges of v_i are on the left of l_i. (c) Both edges of v_i are on the right of l_i.

and E are the number of vertices and edges of the visibility graph of P, respectively. This algorithm uses four key ideas. The first is a *plane-sweep triangulation* of P. The second is the *funnel sequence* of every edge in the triangulation of P. The third is the funnel sequence enhanced with appropriate data structures, which is called the *enhanced visibility graph*. The final one is the fast traversal of the enhanced visibility graph to locate *visible segments* in P.

Plane-Sweep Triangulation

Let us present the procedure for plane-sweep triangulation of P. This triangulation procedure can be viewed as the generalization of the algorithm described by Mehlhorn [257] for triangulating a simple polygon. We assume that the interior of P lies to the left of every edge of P. This means that the outer boundary of P has counterclockwise orientation and the boundaries of holes have clockwise orientation. Like any plane-sweep algorithm, the vertices of P are sorted by increasing order of their x-coordinates. Let $v_1, v_2, \ldots, v_n$ be the sorted list of the vertices of P. For every vertex v_i, draw the vertical line l_i through v_i. It can be seen that l_1 and l_n do not intersect any polygonal edge except at v_1 and v_n, respectively (see Figure 5.8(a)). Remaining vertical lines $l_2, l_3, \ldots, l_{n-1}$ intersects some polygonal edges and the intersection points on each line l_i can be ordered along l_i. The order of polygonal edges corresponding to their intersection points on l_i is called *the vertical ordering of l_i*.

The vertical ordering on each line l_i can be computed (or updated) by sweeping a vertical line over P from left to right by stopping at each vertex v_i. It starts by constructing the vertical ordering of l_1 by inserting both polygonal edges incident at v_1. The clockwise edge of v_1 is inserted above the counterclockwise edge of v_1 in the vertical ordering of l_1. Assume that vertical ordering of $l_1, l_2, \ldots, l_{i-1}$ have been computed and the sweep-line has currently stopped at v_i. If two edges incident at v_i are on the opposite side of l_i (see Figure 5.8(a)), the vertical ordering of l_i is the same as l_{i-1}, except that the edge incident on v_i in the vertical ordering of l_{i-1} is replaced by the other edge of v_i in the vertical ordering of l_i. If both edges incident on v_i are on the left of l_i (see Figure 5.8(b)), then remove both edges of v_i from the vertical ordering of l_{i-1} to obtain the vertical ordering of l_i. If both edges incident on v_i are on the right of l_i (see Figure 5.8(c)), then locate two edges e and e' by binary search in the vertical ordering of l_{i-1} such that e is the nearest edge above v_i and e' is the nearest edge below v_i. Insert two edges incident on v_i between e and e' in the vertical ordering of l_{i-1} to obtain the vertical ordering of l_i. Note that if no such edge e (or e') exists, it means that two edges of v_i are inserted at the top (respectively, bottom) of the vertical ordering of l_{i-1}. For more details on plane-sweep techniques, see Preparata and Shamos [291].

While updating the vertical ordering of l_i from l_{i-1}, the triangles can be added to the existing triangulation T_{i-1} (of the polygonal region P_{i-1}) to form the triangulation T_i, by adding diagonals between v_i and the vertices on the outer boundary of T_{i-1} that are visible from v_i. As before, we have three situations.

Consider the first situation when two edges of v_i are on opposite sides of l_i (see Figure 5.9(a)). Let v_j be the vertex such that the edge $v_j v_i$ is in the vertical ordering of l_{i-1}. Let $v_p v_q$ be the nearest edge below (or above) $v_j v_i$ such that there are an odd (respectively, even) number of edges below (respectively, above) $v_j v_i$ in the vertical ordering of l_{i-1}, where v_p is to the left of l_i. To construct T_i, add diagonals between v_i and the vertices on the boundary of T_{i-1} (facing v_i) between v_j and v_p, that are visible from v_i. Observe that the boundary of T_{i-1} between v_j and v_p (say, $chain(v_j, v_p)$) is convex. Starting from v_j, traverse $chain(v_j, v_p)$ until a vertex v_t is reached such that $v_t v_i$ is a tangent to $chain(v_j, v_p)$. Diagonals are added from v_i to all vertices of $chain(v_j, v_t)$. Note that the new triangles form one connected sequence about v_i and they are called the *interior triangles of* v_i. The edges of $chain(v_j, v_t)$ are called *windows* of v_i as v_i can see vertices of P_{i-1} only through these windows. Note that some of these windows may be polygonal edges.

Consider the second situation when both edges of v_i are on the left of l_i (see Figure 5.9(b)). Let $v_m v_i$ and $v_k v_i$ be two edges of v_i, where $v_m v_i$ is above $v_k v_i$ in the vertical ordering of l_{i-1}. Treating $v_m v_i$ and $v_k v_i$ separately as $v_j v_i$, add diagonals to construct T_i from T_{i-1} as stated above. Observe that the new triangles form two connected sequences about v_i, one is above $v_m v_i$ and the other is below $v_k v_i$. Note that if v_i is same as v_n, then T_i is same as T_{i-1} and T_i is the triangulation of the entire polygon P.

Consider the third situation when both edges of v_i are on the right of l_i (see Figure 5.9(c)). Let $v_p v_q$ and $v_j v_k$ be the nearest edge below and above v_i in the vertical ordering of l_i, where v_p and v_j lie on the left of l_i. If there are an odd number of edges below v_i in the vertical ordering of l_i, then construct T_i from T_{i-1} by adding

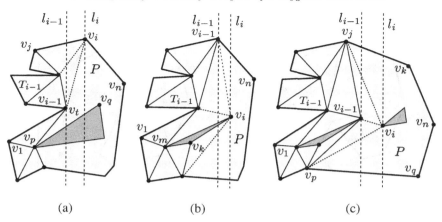

(a)   (b)   (c)

Figure 5.9 Diagonals are added between v_i and the visible vertices on the boundary of T_{i-1}.

diagonals between v_i and the visible vertices of $chain(v_j, v_p)$ on the boundary of T_{i-1} as stated earlier. Observe that the new triangles form one connected sequence about v_i.

It can be seen that diagonals can be added in time proportional to the number of diagonals in T_n, which is $O(n)$. The vertical ordering can be maintained in a height-balanced tree. Therefore, searching in the vertical ordering for nearest edges on both sides of the current vertex v_i takes $O(\log n)$ time. Since there are n vertical orderings, the time taken to update vertical orderings is $O(n \log n)$. Sorting of n vertices takes $O(n \log n)$ time. We have the following theorem.

Theorem 5.3.4 *Using plane-sweep techniques, a polygon P with holes with a total of n vertices can be triangulated in $O(n \log n)$ time.*

Exercise 5.3.2 *Given n line segments in the plane, design an $O(n \log n)$ time algorithm for detecting whether there is an intersection between any two segments using vertical orderings [291].*

The Funnel Sequence

Before we define the structure and properties of a funnel sequence, we explain the need for a funnel structure. As defined in earlier sections, a segment v_iv_j is called a *visible segment* if it lies inside P. We start with the following observations.

Lemma 5.3.5 *Let v_i and v_j be two vertices of P such that $j < i$. If v_jv_i is a visible segment, then v_j is weakly visible from a window of v_i.*

Proof. It can be seen that the segment joining v_j and v_i intersects one of the windows of v_i and therefore, v_j is weakly visible from a window of v_i.   □

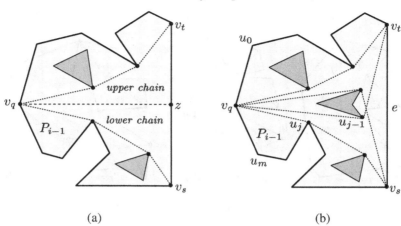

Figure 5.10 (a) The unique funnel (with v_q as the apex and $v_s v_t$ as the base) contains the segment $z v_q$. (b) Two funnels sharing a single apex v_q with common base $v_s v_t$.

Lemma 5.3.6 *Let v_i and v_j be two vertices of P such that $j < i$. If v_j is not weakly visible from a window of v_i, then the segment $v_j v_i$ does not lie inside P.*

The above lemmas suggest that in order to locate all such visible segments $v_j v_i$ in P, it is enough to consider those vertices of P_{i-1} that are weakly visible from windows of v_i. Once weakly visible vertices of P_{i-1} are known, they can be tested for visibility from v_i. After this process of testing for visibility has been carried out for all vertices of P in sorted order, all visible segments between the vertices in P are located.

Let us explain the structure of the funnel sequence. Let $v_s v_t$ be a window of v_i. Let v_q be a vertex of P_{i-1} that is weakly visible from some point z on $v_s v_t$. So, the segment $z v_p$ lies inside P. The *lower chain* of v_q with respect to $v_s v_t$ is defined as the unique convex chain from v_q to v_s inside P (see Figure 5.10(a)) such that the region enclosed by this chain and by the segments $z v_q$ and $z u_s$ does not contain any hole. The *upper chain* of v_q with respect to $v_s v_t$ is defined analogously. The region of P bounded by these two chains and $v_s v_t$ is called a *funnel*. The vertex v_q is called the *apex* of the funnel and $v_s v_t$ is called the *base* of the funnel. The upper and lower chains are also referred to as *upper* and *lower sides* of the funnel. Unlike funnels that arise in polygons without holes (see Section 3.6), there may be several funnels sharing a single apex with common base in a polygon with holes. In Figure 5.10(b), one funnel goes below the hole in the middle and the other funnel goes above it. These apexes may be viewed as being distinct vertices occupying the same physical location in the polygon.

Consider all vertices of P that are visible from a vertex v_q. Let $u_0, u_1, ..., u_m$ be the clockwise sequence of vertices around v_p that are visible from v_q, where $v_q u_0$

and $v_q u_m$ are edges of P. For every pair of adjacent vertices u_{j-1} and u_j (see Figure 5.10(b)), there is a unique edge e of P that can be seen from v_q looking between these vertices. Thus there is a unique funnel with apex v_q such that its base is e, its upper chain starts with $v_q u_{j-1}$ and its lower chain starts with $v_q u_j$. Hence, a funnel is uniquely determined by the first (directed) segment $v_q u_j$ of its lower chain. As a consequence of this, we have the following lemma.

Lemma 5.3.7 *The total number of funnels in the visibility graph of P with E undirected edges is at most $2E$.*

For a given window $v_s v_t$ of v_i, let $FNL(v_s v_t)$ denote the set of all funnels with $v_s v_t$ as their common base. Since the apexes of these funnels are assumed to be on the left of $v_s v_t$, these funnels are also on the left of $v_s v_t$. We have the following observation.

Lemma 5.3.8 *If v_q is the apex of a funnel F in $FNL(v_s v_t)$ and $v_q v_p$ is the first segment on the lower chain of F, then the region of F contains another funnel with v_p as the apex.*

Proof. The proof follows from the convexity of funnels. □

The above observation suggests that if we consider the apex v_p as the parent of the apex v_q, then the lower chains of all funnels in $FNL(v_s v_t)$ form a tree rooted at v_s and each path from the root to a leaf in this tree is a convex chain that makes only counterclockwise turns (see Figure 5.11(a)). We call this tree the *lower tree* for $v_s v_t$. Analogously, the *upper tree* rooted at v_t consists of the upper chains of all funnels in $FNL(v_s v_t)$ (see Figure 5.11(b)). Note that each path from the root to a leaf in the upper tree makes only clockwise turns. We differentiate vertices from apexes because a vertex can appear many times as an apex in $FNL(v_s v_t)$ but each apex appears only once.

Consider the clockwise preorder traversal of the lower tree rooted at v_s. It can be seen that the sequence of this traversal gives a natural linear ordering on the funnels of $FNL(v_s v_t)$, whose first element is the degenerate funnel with apex at v_s, and whose last element is the degenerate funnel with apex at v_t. We call this clockwise ordering of funnels as the *funnel sequence* for $v_s v_t$. Similarly, a natural linear ordering on the funnels of $FNL(v_s v_t)$ can be obtained by considering the clockwise postorder traversal of the upper tree rooted at v_t. We have the following observation.

Lemma 5.3.9 *The linear orders on $FNL(v_s v_t)$ arising from a clockwise preorder traversal of the lower tree and a clockwise postorder traversal of the upper tree are the same.*

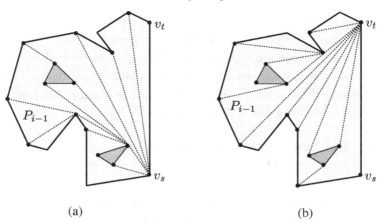

$$(a) \qquad\qquad\qquad\qquad\qquad (b)$$

Figure 5.11 (a) The lower tree rooted at v_s. (b) The upper tree rooted at v_t.

Exercise 5.3.3 *Prove Lemma 5.3.9.*

The Enhanced Visibility Graph

Once $FNL(v_s v_t)$ is computed for the window $v_s v_t$ of v_i, for every vertex v_j of $FNL(v_s v_t)$, it can be tested to determine whether $v_j v_i$ is a visible segment. It can be seen that if $v_j v_i$ is a visible segment, then the segment $v_j v_i$ lies inside the region bounded by the triangle $\triangle v_s v_t v_i$ and the funnel F in $FNL(v_s v_t)$ with the apex v_j and the base $v_s v_t$. This means that the segment $v_j v_i$ lies between two first segments of F and this criteria can be used for testing whether $v_j v_i$ is a visible segment.

Observe that there may be vertices in $FNL(v_s v_t)$ that are not visible from v_i. If such vertices are also traversed, then the running time of the algorithm cannot be output sensitive. In order to keep the running time of the algorithm proportional to the number of visible segments, all vertices of $FNL(v_s v_t)$ cannot be traversed during the process of locating such visible segments $v_j v_i$. This difficulty can be overcome using the *enhanced visibility graph* for v_{i-1}, which is the union of the enhanced visibility graph for v_{i-2} and all visible segments $v_k v_{i-1}$ where $v_k \in P_{i-2}$, with a few pointers at v_k and v_i. These pointers are used in traversing only those vertices of $FNL(v_s v_t)$ that form visible segments with v_i. Note that these visible vertices of v_i form sequences of consecutive vertices on the sides of the funnels in $FNL(v_s v_t)$ due to the convexity of the funnels.

Let us define these pointers for visible segments incident on a vertex v_q in the entire visibility graph of P. Let $u_0, u_2, ..., u_m$ be the clockwise sequence of vertices around v_q that are visible from v_q in P, where $v_q u_0$ and $v_q u_m$ are edges of P (see Figure 5.12). For any u_j, let $CCW(v_q u_j)$ denote the *counterclockwise successor* of $v_q u_j$. This means that $CCW(v_q u_j)$ is the next counterclockwise visible segment of $v_q u_j$ around v_q, which is $v_q u_{j-1}$. Analogously, the *clockwise successor* $CW(v_q u_j)$ of

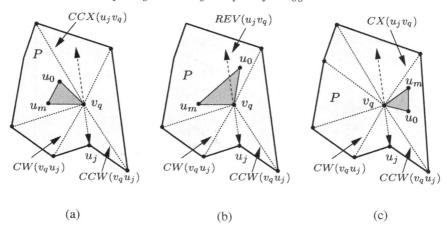

Figure 5.12 The pointers $CCW(v_qu_j)$, $CW(v_qu_j)$, $CCX(u_jv_q)$, $CX(u_jv_q)$ and $REV(u_jv_q)$ are shown in the figures.

v_qu_j is v_qu_{j+1}. The *counterclockwise extension* of v_qu_j, denoted as $CCX(u_jv_q)$, is defined as follows (see Figure 5.12(a)). Rotate $\overrightarrow{v_qu_j}$ counterclockwise by $180°$ about v_q. During the rotation, if $\overrightarrow{v_qu_j}$ remains entirely inside the interior of P locally about v_q, then the extension is the very next visible segment incident on v_q after the $180°$ rotation. Otherwise, there is no counterclockwise extension of v_qu_j (see Figure 5.12(b)). The clockwise extension $CX(u_jv_q)$ of v_qu_j is defined analogously by rotating $\overrightarrow{v_qu_j}$ clockwise around v_q (see Figure 5.12(c)). Finally, the reversal $REV(u_jv_q)$ of (directed) segment v_qu_j is the (directed) segment u_jv_q.

We observe that the enhanced visibility of P, consisting of funnel structures for every edge of the triangulation of P equipped with the pointers mentioned above for each visible segment of P, permits traversal of the lower and upper trees, which is proved in the following lemma.

Lemma 5.3.10 *Let v_pv_q be a directed segment in the lower tree (or upper tree) for a window v_sv_t of v_i in the enhanced visibility graph of P_{i-1} such that v_p is the parent of v_q. The following relatives of v_p and v_q in the lower tree (respectively, upper tree) can be computed in constant time: (i) the parent of v_p, (ii) the extreme clockwise and counterclockwise children of v_q, and (iii) the clockwise and counterclockwise siblings of v_q.*

Proof. We prove the lemma only for the lower tree as the proof for the upper tree is analogous. We know that v_pv_q is the first segment of a funnel F with apex v_q and v_sv_t as the base (see Figure 5.13(a)). Let v_lv_p be the next segment of v_pv_q on the same side of F. So, v_l is a parent of v_p in the lower tree. To prove (i), it is enough to show that v_pv_l is the same as $CX(v_qv_p)$ (i.e., $CW(REV(v_qv_p))$). If $CX(v_qv_p)$ is not v_pv_l, it means that v_pv_q belongs to both sides of F and therefore, the line

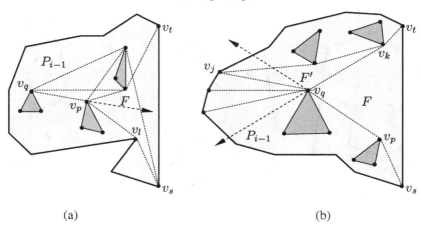

(a)   (b)

Figure 5.13 (a) Locating the next edge on the same side of a funnel F. (b) Locating the children of v_q in the lower tree.

segment joining v_q with any point of the base of F does not lie inside F, which is a contradiction. Hence, $v_p v_l$ is same as $CX(v_q v_p)$.

To prove (ii), let $CCW(v_q v_p)$ be $v_q v_k$ (see Figure 5.13(b)). So, $v_q v_k$ is the first segment on the other side of F, and v_k is a parent of v_q in the upper tree. It can be seen that all children of v_q in the lower tree lie between $\overrightarrow{v_p v_q}$ and $\overrightarrow{v_k v_q}$ because for any child v_j, the funnel F' with v_j as the apex must contain F by Lemma 5.3.8. So, $CCX(v_p v_q)$ is the edge connecting v_q with one of its extreme children. The edge connecting v_q with its other extreme child is $CW(CCX(v_k v_q))$.

To prove (iii), observe that $CW(v_p v_q)$ is the edge connecting v_p with the clockwise sibling of v_q. A symmetric statement holds for the counterclockwise sibling of v_q.
□

Corollary 5.3.11 *Clockwise and counterclockwise traversals of the lower and upper trees in the enhanced visibility graph of P_{i-1} can be executed in time proportional to the number of vertices in the trees.*

Corollary 5.3.12 *A funnel in the enhanced visibility graph of P_{i-1} can be traversed in time proportional to the number of vertices in the funnel.*

Traversal of Enhanced Visibility Graph

The enhanced visibility graph of P can be build up by successively incorporating visible segments of each vertex v_i with the enhanced visibility graph of P_{i-1}. Assume that the enhanced visibility graph of P_{i-1} has been computed and the algorithm wants to locate all visible segments $v_j v_i$, where $j < i$. For every window $v_s v_t$ of v_i, the algorithm traverses $FNL(v_s v_t)$ in the enhanced visibility graph of P_{i-1} to

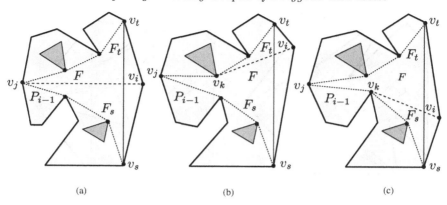

Figure 5.14 (a) The apex v_j is weakly visible from both $v_s v_i$ and $v_t v_i$. (b) The apex v_j is weakly visible only from $v_s v_i$. (c) The apex v_j is weakly visible only from $v_t v_i$.

locate such vertices v_j that can be seen from v_i through window $v_s v_t$. We have the following observation.

Lemma 5.3.13 *Let v_j be the apex of a funnel in $FNL(v_s v_t)$, where $v_s v_t$ is a window of v_i. The apex v_j is visible from both edges $v_s v_i$ and $v_t v_i$ if and only if v_j is visible from v_i.*

Corollary 5.3.14 *If v_j is visible from v_i, then all vertices in the lower and upper chains of the funnel with apex v_j are also visible from v_i.*

The above lemma suggests that the visible segments from v_i can be added to only those apexes in $FNL(v_s v_t)$ that are weakly visible from both $v_s v_i$ and $v_t v_i$; they are referred to as *visible apexes*. Adding a visible segment from v_i to a visible apex v_j amounts to splitting this funnel F into two funnels F_s and F_t (see Figure 5.14(a)), where F_s is for $FNL(v_s v_i)$ and F_t is for $FNL(v_i v_t)$. The lower chain of F_s is the lower chain of F, and the upper chain of F_s is only the visible segment $v_j v_i$. On the other hand, the lower chain of F_t is the visible segment $v_j v_i$, and the upper chain of F_t is the upper chain of F.

Consider the situation when the apex v_j is weakly visible only from $v_s v_i$ (see Figure 5.14(b)). Let $v_i v_k$ be the tangent from v_i to the upper chain of F. So, $v_k v_i$ splits F into two funnels F_s and F_t. The lower chain of F_s is the lower chain of F and the upper chain of F_s is the upper chain of F between the apex v_j and v_k and the visible segment $v_k v_i$. On the other hand, the lower chain of F_t is the visible segment $v_j v_i$, and the upper chain of F_t is the upper chain of F between v_k and v_t. If the apex v_j is weakly visible only from $v_t v_i$, the new funnels F_s and F_t can be defined analogously (see Figure 5.14(c)). This procedure of splitting a funnel is referred as $SPLIT$.

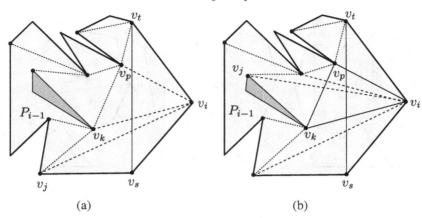

Figure 5.15 (a) SPLIT is called for the window $v_s v_t$ of v_i. (b) SPLIT is called for the window $v_k v_p$ of v_i.

The recursive procedure $SPLIT$ traverses the lower tree rooted at v_s in the linear order (see Lemma 5.3.9 for this order) from v_s to v_t in $FNL(v_s v_t)$, and it locates the next visible apex in $FNL(v_s v_t)$ from the current visible apex. Initially, v_s is the current visible apex as $SPLIT(v_s v_t v_i)$ is called for $\triangle v_s v_t v_i$. Let v_j be the next vertex of v_s in the linear order (see Figure 5.15(a)). Assume that v_j is a visible apex. So, the segments from v_i to all vertices of the upper chain between v_j and v_t are visible segments by Corollary 5.3.14 and therefore, they can be added to the enhanced visibility graph of P_{i-1}. For every such visible segment $v_k v_i$, $SPLIT(v_s v_t v_i)$ adds the pointers $CW(v_k v_i)$, $CCW(v_k v_i)$, $CX(v_i v_k)$, $CCX(v_i v_k)$. It is shown later that the cost of adding these pointers for every visible segment can be amortized to $O(1)$ time. Each edge $v_k v_p$ in the upper chain between v_j and v_t can be viewed as a window of v_i (see Figure 5.15(a)) and therefore, $SPLIT(v_s v_t v_i)$ calls $SPLIT(v_k v_p v_i)$ for each $v_k v_p$. Note that if any $v_k v_p$ happens to be a polygonal edge, $SPLIT$ is not called for this edge as it does not serve as a window of v_i.

Consider any recursive call $SPLIT(v_k v_p v_i)$ (see Figure 5.15(b)). We know that $v_k v_p$ is a window of v_i, v_p is the parent of v_k in the upper tree rooted at v_t and $v_k v_p$ is not a polygonal edge. We also know the pointers of $v_k v_p$ and $v_k v_i$. The task is to locate the next visible apex of v_k in the linear order. Let v_j be the next vertex of v_k in the linear order. We have the following cases.

Case 1. The vertex v_j is a visible apex (Figure 5.15(b)).

Case 2. The vertex v_j is not a visible apex and it lies to the right of $\overrightarrow{v_i v_k}$ (Figure 5.16(a)).

Case 3. The vertex v_j is not a visible apex and it lies to the left of $\overrightarrow{v_i v_k}$ (Figure 5.16(b)).

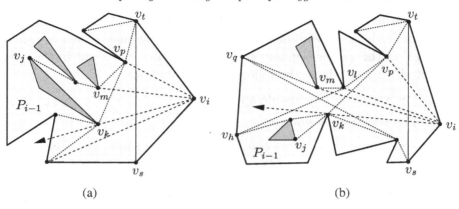

Figure 5.16 The next vertex v_j of v_k in the linear order is not a visible apex.

In Case 1, $SPLIT(v_k v_p v_i)$ carries out its task for this funnel with visible apex v_j as stated above for $SPLIT(v_s v_t v_i)$. Consider Case 2. Let v_m be the next visible apex of v_k in the linear order (see Figure 5.16(a)). Note that there may be several vertices between v_k and v_m in linear order and they are not visible from v_i. This means that once v_j is found not to be visible from v_i, $SPLIT(v_k v_p v_i)$ has to "jump" from v_j to v_m in $O(1)$ amortized time. It can be seen that the vertex v_m lies in upper chain between v_j and v_p as $v_i v_m$ is the tangent from v_i to the upper chain of the funnel with apex v_j. So, $SPLIT(v_k v_p v_i)$ traverses the upper chain from v_p toward v_j till it locates v_m. Note that all vertices from v_p to v_m in the path are visible from v_i. Observe that this traversal from v_p toward v_j in the upper chain can be done by using the pointer CX successively as v_k and v_j are two consecutive vertices in the linear order. Note that the vertices from v_j to the previous vertex of v_m in linear order, which form the sub-tree of upper tree rooted at v_m, are visible only from $v_s v_i$ and therefore, they are incorporated in $FNL(v_s v_i)$. In case v_p and v_m are same, then no vertex of P_{i-1} is visible from v_i through window $v_k v_p$.

Exercise 5.3.4 *Let F_k and F_j be two funnels of $FNL(v_s v_t)$ with apexes v_k and v_j, respectively, such that v_j is the next apex of v_k in the linear order of $FNL(v_s v_t)$. Prove that the region (which is called a hourglass) bounded by (i) the lower chain of F_k, (ii) the visible segment $v_k v_j$, (iii) the upper chain of F_j, and (iv) the window $v_t v_s$, does not contain any hole.*

Consider Case 3. Locate the first sibling (say, v_q) of v_j in the clockwise order in the lower tree such that v_q lies to the right of $\overrightarrow{v_i v_k}$ (see Figure 5.16(b)). If no such vertex v_q exists, i.e., all siblings of v_j lie to the left of $\overrightarrow{v_i v_k}$, then the next clockwise sibling of v_k in the lower tree is the vertex v_q. If v_k does not have a clockwise sibling, then take the parent of v_k in the lower tree and check its next clockwise sibling. By repeating this process, v_q can be located. If v_q is same as v_p, then no vertex of P_{i-1} is visible from v_i through window $v_k v_p$. So, we assume that v_p is not same as v_q. This implies that the visible segment connecting v_q and its parent in the lower tree has intersected $v_k v_p$. We have the following two sub-cases.

Case 3a. The vertex v_q is a visible apex.

Case 3b. The vertex v_q is not a visible apex (see Figure 5.16(b)).

Consider Case 3a. The vertex v_q is the next visible apex v_m of v_k and $SPLIT(v_k v_p v_i)$ has located v_m. Then, $SPLIT(v_k v_p v_i)$ carries out its task for this funnel with visible apex v_q as stated earlier. It can be seen that the vertices between v_k and v_q in the linear order are vertices that are visible only from $v_i v_t$ and therefore, they are incorporated in $FNL(v_i v_t)$.

Consider Case 3b. The next visible apex v_m lies in the upper chain between v_q and v_p as $v_m v_i$ is the tangent from v_i to the upper chain. Observe that v_k and v_q are not adjacent vertices in the linear order and therefore, the upper chain from v_p toward v_q cannot be traversed to locate v_m using the pointer CX successively as in Case 2. Let v_h be the previous vertex of v_q in the linear order. Let v_l be the parent of v_h in the upper tree. Observe that v_l is visible from v_i and it lies in the upper chain between v_m and v_p. So, all vertices in the upper chain between v_l and v_p are visible from v_i and all vertices from v_l to v_m in the upper chain are also visible from v_i. The upper chain from v_l to v_p can be traversed using the parent pointer in the upper tree successively. The upper chain from v_l to v_q can now be traversed using the pointer CX successively as v_h and v_q are adjacent vertices in the linear order. This traversal toward v_q stops once v_m is found and hence, $SPLIT(v_k v_p v_i)$ has located v_m. It can be seen that the vertices between v_k and v_q in the linear order, which form the sub-tree of the lower tree rooted at v_k, are visible only from $v_i v_t$ and therefore, they are incorporated in $FNL(v_i v_t)$. Similarly, the vertices between v_h and v_m in the linear order, which form the sub-tree of the upper tree rooted at v_m, are visible only from $v_i v_s$ and therefore, they are incorporated in $FNL(v_s v_i)$. We have the following lemma.

Lemma 5.3.15 *The recursive procedure $SPLIT(v_s v_t v_i)$ correctly locates all vertices of P_{i-1} that are visible from v_i through window $v_s v_t$.*

Exercise 5.3.5 *Prove Lemma 5.3.15.*

Once $SPLIT(v_s v_t v_i)$ is executed, $FNL(v_s v_t)$ splits into the lower funnel sequence $FNL(v_s v_i)$ and the upper funnel sequence $FNL(v_i v_t)$. It can be seen that SPLIT produces two such funnel sequences for each window of v_i. All lower funnel sequences are concatenated to form one lower funnel sequence for v_i and this can be done easily as a funnel sequence is maintained in a doubly linked list which permits

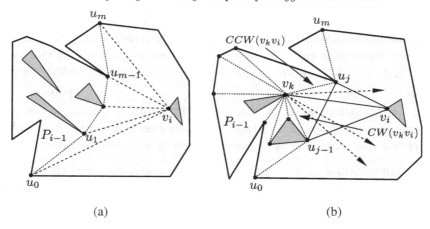

Figure 5.17 (a) The vertices $u_0, u_2, \ldots, u_m$ are visible from v_i. (b) Figure shows the visible segments and their extensions in the sorted angular order around v_k.

concatenation in $O(1)$ time. Similarly, all upper funnel sequences are concatenated to form one upper funnel sequence for v_i.

The Overall Algorithm

We present the overall algorithm for computing the enhanced visibility graph of P_n. We assume that the vertices of P are numbered $v_1, v_2, \ldots, v_n$ from left to right in the sorted order. Compute the enhanced visibility graph of P_1 and initialize the index i by 2. We have the following steps for computing the enhanced visibility graph of P_n.

Step 1. Add v_i to P_{i-1}.

Step 2. *For* each convex chain $u_0, u_1, \ldots, u_m$ of vertices of P_{i-1} visible to v_i (Figure 5.17(a)), add diagonals $u_0 v_i, u_1 v_i, \ldots, u_m v_i$ to form the triangulation of P_i.

Step 3. *For* each window $u_{j-1} u_j$ of v_i, call $SPLIT(u_{j-1} u_j v_i)$.

Step 4. Concatenate the lower funnel sequences $FNL(u_0 v_i)$, $FNL(u_1 v_i), \ldots,$ $FNL(u_{m-1} v_i)$ to form $FNL(u_0 v_i)$.

Step 5. Concatenate the upper funnel sequences $FNL(v_i u_1)$, $FNL(v_i u_2), \ldots,$ $FNL(v_i u_m)$ to form $FNL(v_i u_m)$.

Step 6. *If* $i \neq n$ then $i := i + 1$ and *goto* Step 1.

Step 7. Output the enhanced visibility graph of P_n and Stop.

The correctness of the algorithm essentially follows from Theorem 5.3.4 and Lemma 5.3.15. Let us analyze the time complexity of the algorithm. We know from Theorem 5.3.4 that P can be triangulated in $O(n \log n)$ time. In the following, we show that all visible segments in P can be computed in $O(E)$ time.

Consider the cost of adding visible segments to the enhanced visibility graph of P_{i-1} by the recursive procedure $SPLIT(u_{j-1}u_jv_i)$. The cost consists of two parts. The first part is the time taken to locate the visible segments and the second part is the time taken to add pointers to these visible segments. Since $SPLIT(u_{j-1}u_jv_i)$ moves from one visible apex to the next visible apex in $FNL(u_{j-1}u_j)$, the time taken in the first part is proportional to the number of visible segments located by $SPLIT(u_{j-1}u_jv_i)$. For estimating the time taken in the second part, we need a particular data structure at each vertex of P.

The algorithm maintains a doubly linked adjacency list for each vertex v_k of P such that the visible segments incident on v_k and their extensions are stored in the sorted angular order around v_k (see Figure 5.17(b)). Consider any visible segment v_kv_i added by $SPLIT(u_{j-1}u_jv_i)$, where $k < i$. Since v_k is a visible apex of some funnel F with base $u_{j-1}u_j$, the first segment in the lower (or upper) chain of F is $CW(v_kv_i)$ (respectively $CCW(v_kv_i)$). So, the pointers $CW(v_kv_i)$ and $CCW(v_kv_i)$ can be added in $O(1)$ time. It can be seen that the extensions of $CX(v_iv_k)$ and $CCX(v_iv_k)$ are two neighbors of v_kv_i at v_k. So, the position of v_kv_i in the angular order at v_k has to be located among the extensions of the visible segments incident on v_k that are lying between $CW(v_kv_i)$ and $CCW(v_kv_i)$ (see Figure 5.17(b)). We show later that the cost of searching for locating the position of v_kv_i at v_k can be amortized to $O(1)$ time. Let us now look at the cost of adding all such visible segments v_kv_i at v_i. It can be seen that the procedure $SPLIT$ inserts visible segments at v_i according to their position in the sorted angular order at v_i. Therefore, their extensions are also in sorted angular order around v_i. Hence every visible segment v_kv_i and its extension can be inserted in the linked list at v_i in amortized $O(1)$ time. So, we can conclude that the cost of the second part for adding all pointers to a visible segment is $O(1)$ time.

Let us now calculate how two neighbors of a visible segment v_kv_i among the extension of visible segments incident at v_k can be located in amortized $O(1)$ time. Let m and d be the numbers of extensions of visible segments incident on v_k that are lying between $CW(v_kv_i)$ and $CCW(v_kv_i)$, and between v_kv_i and $CCW(v_kv_i)$ respectively. So, the position of v_kv_i can be located in $\min(\log d, \log(m-d))$ using binary search from both directions. It has been shown in Section 3.6.1 how to carry out this search using finger search trees. However, the same binary search can also be carried out using SPLIT-FIND operation developed by Gabow and Tarjan [146] once integers (i.e. the slopes of visible segments incident on v_k) are stored in the data structure at v_k. If this cost is added over all visible segments in P, we get the following recurrence,

$$T(m) = \max_{1 \leq d \leq m-1}[T(d) + T(m-d) + O(\min(\log d, \log(m-d)))].$$

It has been shown in Section 3.6.1 by induction on m that $T(m)$ is $O(m)$. Therefore, the time required to locate the position of v_kv_i among the extensions is amortized $O(1)$. Hence, the total time taken by the algorithm to locate all visible seg-

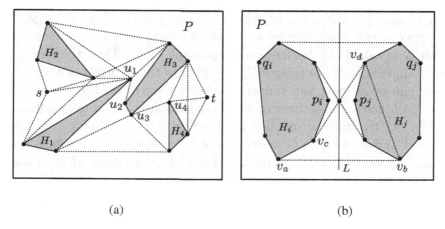

Figure 5.18 (a) $SP(s,t){=}(s, u_1, u_2, u_3, u_4, t)$ consists of tangents and polygonal edges. (b) Four tangents can be constructed between two convex holes H_i and H_j.

ments in P and add pointers to these visible segments is $O(E)$. We summarize the result in the following theorem.

Theorem 5.3.16 *The visibility graph of a polygon P with holes with a total of n vertices can be computed in $O(n \log n + E)$ time and $O(E + n)$ space, where E is the number of edges in the visibility graph of P.*

5.4 Computing Tangent Visibility Graphs

5.4.1 *Convex Holes:* $O(n + h^2 \log h)$ *Algorithm*

In this section, we present an $O(n + h^2 \log h)$ time algorithm given by Rohnert [298] for computing the tangent visibility graph inside a convex polygon P with h convex holes with a total of n vertices. This graph contains all those edges of the visibility graph of P that are relevant in computing the Euclidean shortest path $SP(s,t)$ between two given points s and t inside P.

A line segment $v_i v_j$ is called *a tangent* between two convex holes, where vertices v_i and v_j belong to different holes, if the line passing through v_i and v_j meets the holes only at v_i and v_j. Let $SP(s,t){=}(s, u_1, ..., u_k, t)$. Observe that (i) su_1 is a tangent from s to some vertex u_1 of a convex hole, (ii) $u_k t$ is a tangent from t to some vertex u_k of a convex hole, and (iii) for any edge $u_i u_{i+1}$, $u_i u_{i+1}$ is either an edge of a convex hole or a tangent between two convex holes (Figure 5.18(a)). This observation helps in defining the tangent visibility graph of P.

Let G be the partial visibility graph of P such that s, t and every vertex of holes in P are represented as nodes in G and two nodes w_i and w_j are connected by an edge in G if and only if (i) the corresponding vertices of w_i and w_j are mutually visible in P, and (ii) the segment corresponding $w_i w_j$ in P is an edge of P or a tangent between two convex holes or a tangent from s or t to some convex hole. The graph G is called the *tangent visibility graph* of P. Then the length of these edges and tangents in P are assigned as weights to their corresponding edges in G. Since there can be at most four tangents between two convex holes (Figure 5.18(b)) and there are h holes, the total number of tangents between convex holes can be at most $O(h^2)$. So, the number of edges in G is $O(n + h^2)$. Running the algorithm of Fredman and Tarjan [143] on G, $SP(s, t)$ can be computed in $O(n \log n + h^2)$ time. Assuming h^2 greater than n, the running time for computing $SP(s, t)$ can also be written as $O(n + h^2 \log n)$.

Observe that the tangents from s (or t) to convex holes can be computed from the visibility polygon of P from s (respectively, t) in $O(n)$ time. The visibility polygons of P from s and t can be computed by the algorithm of Asano [27] in $O(n + h \log h)$ time (see Section 2.3). Let us explain how to construct tangents between convex holes $H_1, H_2, \ldots, H_h$. The algorithm of Rohnert first constructs four tangents between each pair of convex holes and then checks whether or not these tangents are lying inside P. Let H_i and H_j be two convex holes of P (Figure 5.18(b)). Let $p_i \in H_i$ and $p_j \in H_j$ denote the closest pair of points between H_i and H_j. Draw the line L perpendicular to the segment $p_i p_j$. Let $q_i \in H_i$ be the furthest point of H_i from L. The clockwise and counterclockwise boundaries of H_i from q_i to u_i are referred to as the *upper* and *lower chains* of H_i, respectively. Analogously, let $q_j \in H_j$ be the furthest point of H_j from L. The clockwise and counterclockwise boundaries of H_j from q_j to u_j are referred to as the *lower* and *upper chains* of H_j, respectively. Tangents are drawn between the lower chain of H_i and the upper chain of H_j, between the lower chains of H_i and H_j, between the upper chains of H_i and H_j, and between the upper chain of H_i and the lower chain of H_j. It has been shown by Edelsbrunner [116] that these four tangents between H_i and H_j can be drawn in $O(\log n_i + \log n_j)$ time, where n_i and n_j are the number of vertices of H_i and H_j, respectively. So, the total time required to compute four tangents between $O(h^2)$ pairs of convex holes is bounded by $O(h^2 \log(n/h))$.

Exercise 5.4.1 *Prove that the sum of* $(\log n_i + \log n_j)$ *for* $1 \leq i, j \leq h$ *and* $i \neq j$ *is* $O(h^2 \log(n/h))$, *where* $n = n_1 + n_2 + \ldots + n_h$.

After constructing four tangents between every pair of holes in P, it is tested whether these tangents lie inside P. If we test for intersection of each tangent with every polygonal edge, the naive method takes $O(nh^2)$ time. We show that this can be improved to $O(h^2 \log h)$ time as follows. Observe that the lower chain of H_i for H_j is different from the lower chain of H_i for another hole H_k as the closest points between H_i and H_j are different from that of H_i and H_k. Two tangents between H_i and H_j touching the lower chain of H_i are called *lower tangents* of H_i for H_j. In Figure 5.18(b), $v_a v_b$ and $v_c v_d$ are two lower tangents of H_i for H_j. The other

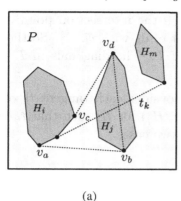
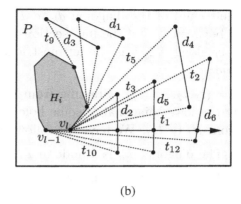

(a)   (b)

Figure 5.19 (a) Tangent t_k between holes H_i and H_m has intersected hole H_j. (b) Lower diagonals of holes for H_i are drawn as segments $(d_1, d_2, \ldots, d_6)$ along with the ray drawn from v_{l-1} through v_l. Lower tangents of H_i are $(t_1, t_2, \ldots, t_{12})$ in counterclockwise order.

two tangents touching the upper chain of H_i are called *upper tangents* of H_i for H_j. So there are $2(h-1)$ lower tangents (or upper tangents) of H_i in P. The segment connecting two vertices of H_j touched by the lower tangents of H_i is called the *lower diagonal* of H_j for H_i. The segment $v_b v_d$ in Figure 5.18(b) is the lower diagonal of H_j for H_i. The upper diagonal of H_j for H_i is defined analogously. In the following lemma, we state how to identify the lower tangents of H_i that are lying inside P.

Lemma 5.4.1 *Let $v_a v_b$ and $v_c v_d$ be the lower tangents of H_i for H_j (Figure 5.19(a)), where (i) v_a and v_c are vertices of H_i, (ii) v_b and v_d are vertices of H_j, and (iii) H_j lies to the left of $\overrightarrow{v_a v_b}$. Let t_k be a lower tangent of H_i for a hole H_m where $m \neq j$. The tangent t_k intersects H_j if and only if t_k intersects the lower diagonal $v_b v_d$ of H_j.*

Exercise 5.4.2 *Prove Lemma 5.4.1.*

Corollary 5.4.2 *If any lower tangent t_k of H_i intersects H_j, then the vertex of t_k belonging to H_i lies in the counterclockwise boundary from v_a to v_c.*

The above lemma and its corollary suggest a procedure for identifying lower tangents of H_i (for all i) lying inside P. Traverse the boundary of H_i in counterclockwise order starting from any vertex v_l of H_i, and at each vertex v_p of H_i, add the lower tangents of H_i incident at v_p to the ordered list L_i according to their counterclockwise angle at v_q with the clockwise edge of H_i at v_p. Consider $\overrightarrow{v_{l-1} v_l}$, where v_{l-1} is the next clockwise vertex of v_l in H_i (see Figure 5.19(b)). Compute the intersection points of $\overrightarrow{v_{l-1} v_l}$ with the lower diagonal of every hole for H_i and sort these diagonals along $\overrightarrow{v_{l-1} v_l}$ according to the distance of their intersection points from v_l. Construct a balanced binary tree T with nodes representing these diagonals and if a diagonal

d_j is the left child of the diagonal d_k in T, then the intersection point of d_j with $\overrightarrow{v_{l-1}v_l}$ lies between v_l and the intersection point of d_k with $\overrightarrow{v_{l-1}v_l}$. So the diagonal closest to v_l along $\overrightarrow{v_{l-1}v_l}$ is the leftmost leaf of T. The diagonals in T are called *active diagonals*.

Let $L_i = (t_1, t_2, \ldots, t_f)$. Starting from t_1, consider each tangent t_k of L_i. Let d_m denote the lower diagonal of some hole (say, H_q) for H_i such that t_k is a lower tangent from H_i to H_q. We have the following two cases.

Case 1. The diagonal d_m is a node in T.

Case 2. The diagonal d_m is not a node in T.

Consider Case 1. If d_m is not the diagonal in the leftmost leaf of T, then remove t_k from L_i because t_k has intersected the lower diagonal in the leftmost leaf of T. Remove the node of T containing d_m from T as d_m is no longer an active edge and balance T.

Consider Case 2. Insert d_m as a node in T such that t_k intersects only the diagonals in the left sub-tree of d_m in T. Balance T. If d_m is not the leftmost leaf of T, then remove t_k from L_i as t_k intersects the lower diagonal in the leftmost leaf of T.

In the following, we state the major steps of the algorithm for computing the tangent visibility graph G of P.

Step 1. Compute the visibility polygons of P from s and t by the algorithm of Asano [27] and traverse them to locate the tangents from s and t to the holes of P.

Step 2. Draw the four tangents between every pair of holes in P.

Step 3. *For* every hole H_i of P do

   Step 3a. Traverse the boundary of H_i in counterclockwise order and form the ordered list L_i of all lower tangents of H_i in the order they are incident at H_i.

   Step 3b. Traverse the ordered list L_i and remove the tangents in L_i that are intersected by any diagonal of a hole in P.

   Step 3c. Traverse the boundary of H_i in clockwise order and form the ordered list R_i of all upper tangents of H_i in the order they are incident at H_i.

   Step 3d. Traverse the ordered list R_i and remove the tangents in R_i that are intersected by any diagonal of a hole in P.

   Step 3e. Output the remaining tangents in L_i and R_i.

Step 4. Form the tangent visibility graph G and Stop.

The correctness of the algorithm follows from Lemma 5.4.1 and its corollary. Let us analyze the time complexity of the algorithm. We know that Step 1 takes $O(n + h \log h)$ time and Step 2 takes $O(h^2 \log(n/h))$. Steps 3a and 3c are problems of sorting and they can be performed in $O(h \log h)$ time. Insert or delete operations in T take $O(\log h)$ time as the size of the tree T is at most h. Since there are $4(h-1)$

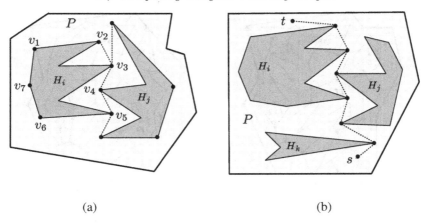

(a)   (b)

Figure 5.20 (a) The vertices of the relative convex hull of H_i are v_1, v_2, v_3, v_4, v_5, v_6 and v_7. (b) $SP(s,t)$ passes through edges of relative convex hulls of holes and tangents between holes.

such operations in T for the lower and upper tangents of H_i, Steps 3b and 3d can be performed in $O(h \log h)$. Hence the overall time complexity of the algorithm is $O(n + h^2 \log h)$. We state the results in the following theorems.

Theorem 5.4.3 *The tangent visibility graph of a polygon P with h convex holes with a total of n vertices can be computed in $O(n + h^2 \log h)$ time.*

Theorem 5.4.4 *The Euclidean shortest path between two given points inside a polygon P with h convex holes with a total of n vertices can be computed in $O(n + h^2 \log n)$ time.*

5.4.2 Non-Convex Holes: $O(n + h^2 \log h)$ Algorithm

In this section, we present an $O(n + h^2 \log h)$ time algorithm given by Kapoor *et al.* [210] for computing the tangent visibility graph inside a polygon P with h non-convex holes and a total of n vertices. This graph contains a subset of edges of the visibility graph of P, relevant for computing the Euclidean shortest path $SP(s,t)$ between two given points s and t inside P (see Section 5.4.1).

We assume that holes $H_1, H_2, \ldots, H_h$ inside P are arbitrary simple polygons. Suppose the convex hull of every hole is computed and each of these convex hulls lies inside P. Then the problem of computing the tangent visibility graph in P is reduced to that of computing the tangent visibility graph in a polygon containing only convex holes. Therefore, the algorithm of Rohnert [298] stated in Section 5.4.1 can be used to solve the problem.

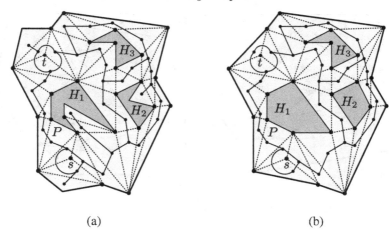

(a)   (b)

Figure 5.21 (a) The dual graph G_T of the triangulation of P after including s and t. (b) All triangles corresponding to the nodes of degree 1 in G_T are removed from the triangulation of P.

In general, convex hulls of holes do not lie inside P. Suppose the relative convex hull of every hole is computed (see Figure 5.20(a)). The *relative convex hull* of a hole H_i is the smallest perimeter polygon containing H_i. In other words, for any convex hull vertex v_j of H_i, the region enclosed by the shortest path from v_j inside P that goes around H_i and terminates at v_j is called the relative convex hull of H_i. Observe that $SP(s,t)$ passes through the edges of relative convex hulls of holes and tangents between holes (see Figure 5.20(b)). So, the tangent visibility graph G can be constructed such that (i) the edges of relative convex hulls of holes, (ii) tangents from s and t to holes, and (iii) tangents between holes, are represented as edges in G. Once G is constructed, the algorithm of Fredman and Tarjan [143] can be used on G for computing $SP(s,t)$.

The algorithm of Kapoor *et al.* starts by triangulating P in $O(n + h\log^{1+\epsilon} h)$ time by the algorithm of Bar-Yehuda and Chazelle [43]. Let T_s and T_t denote the triangles containing s and t, respectively. Connect s and t to all three vertices of T_s and T_t, respectively. Let T denote the resulting triangulation and let G_T denote the dual graph of T (Figure 5.21(a)). For more details on the dual graph of a triangulation, see Section 1.4. We have the following observation on G_T.

Lemma 5.4.5 *The dual graph G_T is a planar graph with $O(n)$ nodes, $O(n)$ edges and $h + 1$ faces (including the outer face), and at least one of three nodes of G_T incident on each of s and t has degree 3.*

It can be seen that $SP(s,t)$ does not pass through a triangle if the degree of the corresponding node of the triangle in G_T is one. So, all nodes in G_T corresponding to such triangles are deleted from G_T. Two polygonal edges forming the sides of

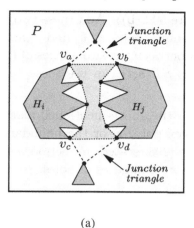
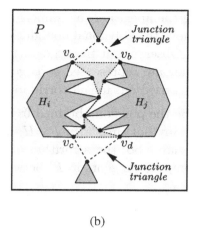

(a)   (b)

Figure 5.22 (a) The corridor is a hourglass bound by $v_a v_b$, $SP(v_a, v_c)$, $v_c v_d$ and $SP(v_b, v_d)$. (b) The corridor consists of two funnels with bases $v_a v_b$ and $v_c v_d$, and the shortest path between the apexes of these two funnels.

each of these triangles are replaced by the third edge of the triangle, which is treated as a polygonal edge for the subsequent computation. This process is repeated until all remaining nodes in G_T have degree 2 or 3 (see Figure 5.21(b)). The triangles corresponding to the nodes of degree 3 in G_T are called *junction triangles*. If all junction triangles are removed from P, P is divided into simple polygons which are called *corridors*. Corridors are *sleeves* in P because the nodes in G_T corresponding to the triangles in a corridor have degree 2.

Let C be a corridor bounded by the triangulating edges $v_a v_b$ and $v_c v_d$ of two different junction triangles (see Figure 5.22). Since no triangle inside C is a junction triangle, two vertices of v_a, v_b, v_c and v_d belong to one hole and other two vertices belong to another hole. Without loss of generality, we assume that v_a and v_c belong to one hole and v_b and v_d belong to another hole. Since C is a sleeve, the algorithm of Lee and Preparata [235] (see Section 3.6.1) can be used to compute $SP(v_a, v_c)$ and $SP(v_b, v_d)$. We have the following two cases.

Case 1. $SP(v_a, v_c)$ and $SP(v_b, v_d)$ are disjoint (Figure 5.22(a)).

Case 2. $SP(v_a, v_c)$ and $SP(v_b, v_d)$ are not disjoint (Figure 5.22(b)).

Consider Case 1. Since $SP(v_a, v_c)$ and $SP(v_b, v_d)$ are disjoint, the segment $v_a v_b$, $SP(v_a, v_c)$, the segment $v_c v_d$ and $SP(v_b, v_d)$ form a *hourglass* (see Figure 5.22(a)). Replace the polygonal boundary of C between v_a and v_c by $SP(v_a, v_c)$ in P. Analogously, replace the polygonal boundary of C between v_b and v_d by $SP(v_b, v_d)$ in P.

Consider Case 2. Since $SP(v_a, v_c)$ and $SP(v_b, v_d)$ are not disjoint, the union of $SP(v_a, v_c)$ and $SP(v_b, v_d)$ forms two funnels with bases $v_a v_b$ and $v_c v_d$, and a path connecting the apexes of the funnels (see Figure 5.22(b)). Add these two funnels in P and remove the polygonal boundaries of C from P between v_a and v_c and between v_b and v_d. Observe that the edges in the path between the two apexes of the funnels in a corridor are represented as edges in G as $SP(s,t)$ can use these edges. This process is carried out for all corridors in P.

Let P' be the polygon obtained from P after the above-mentioned modifications. Let H_i be any hole in P. In P', H_i is a convex polygon or the boundary of H_i is a convex chain. So, the algorithm of Rohnert [298] stated in Section 5.4.1 can be used to compute tangents in P' between convex boundaries of holes.

In the following, we state the major steps of the algorithm for computing the tangent visibility graph G of P.

Step 1. Triangulate P by the algorithm of Bar-Yehuda and Chazelle [43]. Connect s and t to all three vertices of the triangles containing them. Form the dual graph G_T.

Step 2. *While* G_T has a node of degree 1 *do* remove the triangle corresponding to the node from the triangulation of P.

Step 3. Generate corridors by removing junction triangles from P.

Step 4. Construct two funnels or a hourglass for each corridor in P and use them to replace the corridor.

Step 5. Compute the tangents between the convex chains of every pair of holes by the algorithm of Rohnert [298].

Step 6. Form the tangent visibility graph G and Stop.

The correctness of the algorithm directly follows from the properties of $SP(s,t)$ and the dual graph of a triangulation of P. Let us analyze the time complexity of the algorithm. The algorithm of Bar-Yehuda and Chazelle [43] for triangulating P in Step 1 takes $O(n+h\log^{1+\epsilon} h)$ time. Since G_T can be constructed in $O(n)$ time from the triangulation of P, Step 1 takes $O(n+h\log^{1+\epsilon} h)$ time. Steps 2 and 3 take $O(n)$ time. Since the corridors are disjoint and the time for computing the shortest paths between two pairs of vertices in a corridor is proportional to the number of vertices in a corridor, the time required in Step 4 to replace all corridors in P by funnels and hourglasses is $O(n)$. Since there can be at most h convex boundaries of holes in the modified polygon P', the algorithm of Rohnert in Step 5 runs in $O(h^2 \log h)$ time. Hence the tangent visibility graph G can be computed in $O(n + h^2 \log h)$ time. We state the results in the following theorems.

Theorem 5.4.6 *The tangent visibility graph of a polygon P with h non-convex holes with a total of n vertices can be computed in $O(n + h^2 \log h)$ time.*

Theorem 5.4.7 *The Euclidean shortest path between two given points inside a polygon P with h non-convex holes with a total of n vertices can be computed in $O(n + h^2 \log n)$ time.*

5.5 Notes and Comments

Goodrich *et al.* [173, 174] have given the only parallel algorithm for computing visibility graphs of simple polygons. Their algorithm computes the visibility graph by exploiting a duality relationship between a visibility graph and intersections of segments, and runs in $O(\log n)$ time using $O(n \log n + E/\log n)$ processors in the CREW-PRAM model of computations, where E is the number of edges of the visibility graph. There is no parallel algorithm for computing visibility graphs of polygons with holes.

In the beginning of this chapter, we have shown how visibility graphs help in computing the Euclidean shortest path $SP(s,t)$ between two given points s and t inside a polygon P with holes. $SP(s,t)$ can also be computed without computing the visibility graph of P partially or totally. Using the 'continuous Dijkstra' paradigm, Mitchell [259] presented an $O(n^{1.5+\epsilon})$ time algorithm for computing $SP(s,t)$. Using the same paradigm, Hershberger and Suri [189] first presented an $O(n \log^2 n)$ time algorithm for computing $SP(s,t)$ and then improved the time complexity of their algorithm to $O(n \log n)$ [192], which is optimal. Recently, Wein *et al.* [338] showed that a short and smooth path from s to t in P can be constructed by combining the visibility graph with the Voronai diagram of P. The path may not be $SP(s,t)$ but it keeps a fixed amount of clearance with holes in P wherever possible.

Euclidean shortest paths in a polygon are also called *geodesic paths*. The length of a geodesic path between two points is called the *geodesic distance* of the path. The *geodesic diameter* of a simple polygon P is the maximum geodesic distance among all pairs of vertices of P. The geodesic diameter can be computed in $O(n)$ time by the algorithm of Hershberger and Suri [191]. The *geodesic center* of a simple polygon P is a point in P which minimizes the maximum geodesic distance to any point in P; such a point can be located in $O(n \log^2 n)$ time by the algorithm of Pollack *et al.* [288]. Earlier, Asano and Toussaint [31] proposed an $O(n^4 \log n)$ time algorithm for this problem. It is still open whether the problem can be solved in $O(n)$ time [260]. For related problems on geodesic paths, see the review article of Mitchell [260].

Let us mention some results on shortest paths in L_1 metric. For any two points $p = (x_p, y_p)$ and $q = (x_q, y_q)$, the distance between p and q in L_m metric is defined by $(|x_p - x_q|^m + |y_p - y_q|^m)^{1/m}$. So, the length of a polygonal path in L_m metric is the sum of the lengths in L_m metric of edges in the path. A polygonal path is called a *rectilinear path* if each edge of the path is parallel to a coordinate axis. Observe that the length of a rectilinear path is the same in both L_1 and L_2 metric.

The problem of computing a shortest rectilinear path in L_1 metric in polygons P has been studied by several researchers including Clarkson [92], de Rezende *et al.* [109], Larson and Li [225] and Mitchell [258]. Clarkson *et al.* [92] showed a method for constructing a sparse graph which contains a shortest rectilinear path between any two vertices of P. Then a shortest rectilinear path in P can be computed from the sparse graph treating it as the visibility graph of P. Their algorithm runs in $O(n \log^2 n)$ time and $O(n \log n)$ space. Using the 'continuous Dijkstra' paradigm, Mitchell [258] improved the time complexity by showing that a shortest rectilinear path in P can be computed in $O(n \log n)$ time and $O(n)$ space.

> **Exercise 5.5.1** *Let Q be a set of m ·points inside a simple polygon P of n vertices. Design an algorithm to identify all pairs of points of Q that are mutually visible in P in $O(n + m \log m \log mn + k \log m)$ time, where k is the total number of visible pairs [44].*

Consider the problem of locating the closest visible pair of vertices between two disjoint simple polygons P and Q. The problem is to locate two vertices $u \in P$ and $v \in Q$ such that the segment uv does not intersect the interior of P or Q. Take a convex polygon C containing both P and Q and compute the visibility graph of C treating P and Q as holes in C. The problem of closest visible pair can now be solved by locating the shortest edge of the visibility graph connecting a vertex u of P with a vertex v of Q, and the entire process can be done in $O(n \log n + E)$, where n is the total number of vertices of P and Q.

The problem can directly be solved without computing the visibility graph. If both P and Q are convex polygons, the problem can be solved in $O(n)$ time by the algorithms of Chin *et al.* [88], McKenna and Toussaint [255] and Toussaint [329]. If either P or Q is a convex polygon, the problem can also be solved in $O(n)$ time by the algorithm of Chin *et al.* [88]. If both P and Q are non-convex polygons, Wang and Chan [337] gave an $O(n \log n)$ time algorithm for this problem. Later, optimal $O(n)$ time algorithms for this problem were given by Aggarwal *et al.* [13], and Hershberger and Suri [191]. Following the method of Aggarwal *et al.* [13], Hsu *et al.* [199] designed a parallel algorithm for this problem. Using a different method, Amato [19] also gave a parallel algorithm for this problem and the method of this algorithm gives another $O(n)$ time optimal sequential algorithm for this problem.

> **Exercise 5.5.2** *Design an $O(n)$ time algorithm for computing the closest visible pair of vertices between two disjoint convex polygons P and Q of total n vertices [88, 255].*

> **Exercise 5.5.3** *Design an $O(n \log n)$ time algorithm for computing the closest visible pair of vertices between two disjoint non-convex polygons P and Q of total n vertices [337].*

6

Visibility Graph Theory

6.1 Problems and Results

In the previous chapter we discussed how to compute the visibility graph of a polygon P with or without holes. Consider the opposite problem: let G be a given graph. The problem is to determine whether there is a polygon P whose visibility graph is the given graph G. This problem is called the visibility graph *recognition* problem. The problem of actually drawing one such polygon P is called the visibility graph *reconstruction* problem. The visibility graph recognition and reconstruction problems are long-standing open problems. So far, only partial results have been achieved. It has been shown by Everett [133] that visibility graph reconstruction is in *PSPACE*. This is the only upper bound known on the complexity of either problem.

Ghosh [154] presented three necessary conditions in 1986 for recognizing visibility graphs of simple polygons under the assumption that a Hamiltonian cycle of the given graph, which corresponds to the boundary of the simple polygon, is given as input along with the graph. It has been pointed out by Everett and Corneil [133, 135] that these conditions are not sufficient as there are graphs that satisfy the three necessary conditions but they are not visibility graphs of any simple polygon. These counter-examples can be eliminated once the third necessary condition is strengthened. It has been shown by Srinivasraghavan and Mukhopadhyay [314] that the stronger version of the third necessary condition proposed by Everett [133] is in fact necessary. On the other hand, the counter-example given by Abello *et al.* [4] shows that the three necessary conditions of Ghosh [154] are not sufficient even with the stronger version of the third necessary condition. In a later paper by Ghosh [157], another necessary condition is identified which circumvents the counter-example of Abello *et al.* [4]. These four necessary conditions are presented in Section 6.2.1. It has been shown more recently by Streinu [316, 317] that these four necessary conditions are also not sufficient.

In Section 6.2.2, we present the algorithm given by Ghosh [157] for testing his first two necessary conditions which runs in $O(n^2)$ time. The time complexity for checking the other two necessary conditions is not known. Earlier, Everett [133] gave an $O(n^3)$ time algorithm for testing the first necessary condition.

Let us state other results on the problems of recognizing and reconstructing visibility graphs for special classes of simple polygons. The earliest result is from ElGindy [126] who showed that every *maximal outerplanar graph* is a visibility graph of a simple polygon, and he suggested an $O(n \log n)$ algorithm for reconstruction. If all reflex vertices of a simple polygon occur consecutively along its boundary, the polygon is called a *spiral polygon*. Everett and Corneil [133, 134] characterized visibility graphs of spiral polygons by showing that these graphs are a subset of *interval graphs*, which leads to an $O(n)$ time algorithm for recognition and reconstruction. We present their characterization and recognition algorithm in Section 6.4.1. Choi *et al.* [89] characterized funnel-shaped polygons called *towers* and they gave an $O(n)$ time recognition algorithm. Visibility graphs of towers have also been characterized by Colley *et al.* [95] and they have shown that visibility graphs of towers are bipartite permutation graphs with an added Hamiltonian cycle. We present their characterization and their $O(n)$ time recognition algorithm in Section 6.4.2. If the internal angle at each vertex of a simple polygon is either 90° or 270°, then the polygon is called a *rectilinear polygon*. If the boundary of a rectilinear polygon is formed by a staircase path with two other edges, the polygon is called a *staircase polygon*. Visibility graphs of staircase polygons have been characterized by Abello *et al.* [1]. Lin and Chen [243] have studied visibility graphs that are *planar*.

The above-mentioned results show that there are characterizations of visibility graphs for some special classes of polygons. However, the problem of characterizing visibility graphs of arbitrary simple polygons is still an open problem. Ghosh has shown that visibility graphs do not possess the characteristics of *perfect graphs*, *circle graphs* or *chordal graphs*. On the other hand, Coullard and Lubiw [97] have proved that every triconnected component of a visibility graph satisfies *3-clique ordering*. This property suggests that structural properties of visibility graphs may be related to well-studied graph classes, such as *3-trees* and *3-connected graphs*. Everett and Corneil [133, 135] have shown that there is no finite set of forbidden induced sub-graphs that characterize visibility graphs. Abello and Kumar [2, 3] have suggested a set of necessary conditions for recognizing visibility graphs. However, it has been shown in [157] that this set of conditions follow from the last two necessary conditions of Ghosh. The efforts to characterize the visibility graphs are presented in Section 6.3.

Let us mention some of the later approaches on the visibility graph reconstruction problem. Abello and Kumar [3] studied the relationship between visibility graphs and oriented matroids, Lin and Skiena [244] studied the equivalent order types, and Streinu [316, 317] and O'Rourke and Streinu [274] studied psuedo-line arrangements. The reconstruction problem with added information has been studied by Coullard and Lubiw [97], Everett *et al.* [137, 138] and Jackson and Wismath [203].

There are other types of visibility graphs. *Vertex-edge visibility graphs* are graphs that represent the visibility relationship between the vertices and edges of a polygon. O'Rourke and Streinu [275] studied the properties of vertex-edge visibility graphs which are presented in Section 6.6. A one-directional variation of this graph was studied earlier by Fournier and Montuno [142]. *E*dge-edge visibility graphs are graphs indicating which edges see which edges; these have been studied by O'Rourke [271] and Srinivasaraghavan and Mukhopadhyay [315]. *Point visibility graphs* are infinite visibility graphs, where each point of a polygon is represented as a vertex of the graph. This graph has been studied by Bremner [64], Bremner and Shermer [65] and MacDonald and Shermer [251], The representation of visibility graphs has been studied by Agarwal *et al.* [7], Kant [208] and Tamassia and Tollis [325].

The *segment visibility graph* is a graph whose $2n$ vertices represent the endpoints of n disjoint segments and whose edges represent visible segments between the endpoints (see Figure 6.15(a)). Everett *et al.* [136] have characterized those segment visibility graphs that do not have K_5, the complete graph of 5 vertices, as a *minor*. This characterization leads to a polynomial time algorithm for recognizing this special class of segment visibility graphs. We present their characterization in Section 6.5. Segment visibility graphs have also been studied for different problems under various conditions by Andreae [20], Hoffmann and Toth [196, 197], Kirkpatrick and Wismath [218], O'Rourke and Rippel [273], Rappaport [292], Rappaport *et al.* [293], Shen and Edelsbrunner [308], and Wismath [340, 341].

Exercise 6.1.1 *Draw n disjoint line segments whose segment visibility graph has $5n - 4$ edges (including n given segments) [308].*

Let us consider the standard graph-theoretic problems on visibility graphs. The minimum dominating set problem in visibility graphs corresponds to the art gallery problem in polygons. Lee and Lin [231] showed that the problem is NP-hard. Independent sets in visibility graphs are known as *hidden vertex sets*. Shermer [309] proved that the maximum hidden vertex set problem on visibility graphs is also NP-hard. If the Hamiltonian cycle corresponding to the boundary of the simple polygon is given as an input along with the visibility graph, Ghosh *et al.* [167] showed that it is possible to compute in $O(nE)$ time the maximum hidden vertex set in the visibility graph of a very special class of simple polygons called *convex fans*, where n and E are the number of vertices and edges of the input visibility graph of the convex fan, respectively. We present this algorithm in Section 6.8. Hidden vertex sets have also been studied by Eidenbenz [124, 125], Ghosh *et al.* [163] and Lin and Skiena [244].

In visibility graphs of simple polygons, the problems of finding a minimum vertex cover and a maximum dominating set are NP-hard as shown by Lin and Skiena [244]. Everett [133] proved that the problem of determining whether the visibility graphs of two polygons with holes are isomorphic is isomorphic-complete. This problem remains isomorphic-complete even for the visibility graphs of two simple polygons as shown by Lin and Skiena [244]. In Section 6.9, we discuss isomorphic visibility graphs and similar polygons.

The problem of computing the maximum clique in the visibility graph is not known to be NP-hard. Observe that the maximum clique in a visibility graph corresponds to the largest empty convex polygon inside the corresponding polygon. Ghosh *et al.* [167] have recently presented an $O(n^2E)$ time algorithm for computing the maximum clique in the visibility graph of a simple polygon, under the assumption that the Hamiltonian cycle in the visibility graph corresponding to the boundary of the polygon is given along with the visibility graph as an input. We present the algorithm of Ghosh *et al.* [167] in Section 6.7.

6.2 Recognizing Visibility Graphs of Simple Polygons

6.2.1 Necessary Conditions

In this section, we present the four necessary conditions of Ghosh [157] for recognizing visibility graphs of simple polygons. During the presentation of these conditions, we have included the counter-examples given by Everett and Corneil [133, 135], Abello *et al.* [4] and Streinu [316, 317].

Given a graph G and a Hamiltonian cycle C of G, the recognition problem is to determine if G is the visibility graph of a simple polygon P whose boundary corresponds to the cycle C. This problem is easier than the actual recognition problem as the edges of G that correspond to the boundary edges of P have already been identified. We assume that the vertices of G are labeled with $v_1, v_2, \ldots, v_n$ and the cycle $C = (v_1, v_2, \ldots, v_n)$ is in counterclockwise order. A *cycle* is a simple and closed path in G. An edge in G connecting two non-adjacent vertices of a cycle is called a *chord* of the cycle. A cycle $u_1, u_2, \ldots, u_k$ in G is said to be *ordered* if the vertices $u_1, u_2, \ldots, u_k$ follow the order in C. The Hamiltonian cycle C is an ordered cycle of all n vertices in G. We make the following observations on the structure of an ordered cycle.

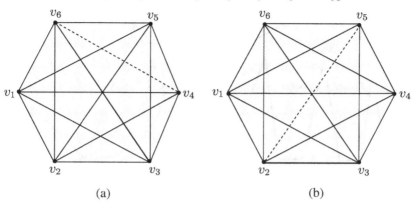

Figure 6.1 (a) The blocking vertex for the invisible pair (v_4, v_6) is v_5. (b) There is no blocking vertex for the invisible pair (v_2, v_5).

Necessary condition 1. *Every ordered cycle of $k \geq 4$ vertices in a visibility graph has at least $k - 3$ chords.*

Proof. Since an ordered cycle of k vertices in a visibility graph of a simple polygon P corresponds to a sub-polygon P' of k vertices in P, the ordered cycle has at least $k - 3$ chords in the visibility graph as P' requires $k - 3$ diagonals for triangulation of P'. □

A pair of vertices (v_i, v_j) in G is a *visible pair* (or *invisible pair*) if v_i and v_j are connected (respectively, not connected) by an edge in G. Without loss of generality, we assume i is always less than j for an invisible pair (v_i, v_j). For any two vertices v_i and v_j in G, the vertices from v_i to v_j on C, including v_i and v_j, in clockwise and counterclockwise order are called the *upper* and *lower chain* of (v_i, v_j), respectively. The vertices from v_i to v_j on C in counterclockwise order are also referred to as $chain(v_i, v_j)$.

A vertex v_a is a *blocking vertex* for an invisible pair (v_i, v_j) if no two vertices $v_k \in chain(v_i, v_{a-1})$ and $v_m \in chain(v_{a+1}, v_j)$ are connected by an edge in G. Since the line of sight between v_i and v_j in P can be blocked using v_a, v_a is called a blocking vertex. In Figure 6.1(a), v_5 is the blocking vertex for the invisible pair (v_4, v_6). On the other hand, the invisible pair (v_2, v_5) in Figure 6.1(b) does not have any blocking vertex and therefore, this graph is not a visibility graph of any simple polygon. Intuitively, blocking vertices are meant to correspond to reflex vertices of the polygon. However, all blocking vertices in G may not be reflex vertices in P. On the other hand, the reflex vertices in P are always blocking vertices in G as they introduce pockets on the boundary of P with the property that every pair of pockets are not mutually visible (see Figure 6.2(a)). This observation suggests the following necessary condition.

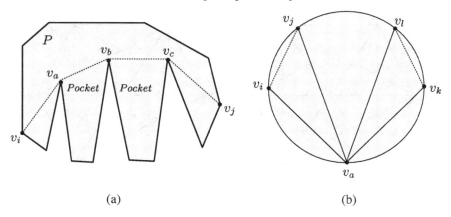

(a)   (b)

Figure 6.2 (a) No two pockets are mutually visible. (b) Two invisible pairs (v_i, v_j) and (v_k, v_l) are separable with respect to a blocking vertex v_a.

Necessary condition 2. *Every invisible pair in a visibility graph has at least one blocking vertex.*

Proof. For an invisible pair (v_i, v_j), the *Euclidean shortest path* in P between v_i and v_j makes turns at one or more reflex vertices, and each of these reflex vertices is a blocking vertex for (v_i, v_j) in G. $\qquad\square$

The above proof suggests that an invisible pair (v_i, v_j) can have more than one blocking vertex as the Euclidean shortest path in P between v_i and v_j may turn at more than one reflex vertex. It means that blocking vertices in the lower chain or upper chain of an invisible pair form a chain of consecutive reflex vertices in P (see Figure 6.2(a)). This observation leads to the following lemmas on the structure of blocking vertices.

Lemma 6.2.1 *Let v_a and v_b be the blocking vertices in the lower chain (or upper chain) for an invisible pair (v_i, v_j), where $i < a < b < j$ (Figure 6.2(a)). Vertices v_a and v_b are also blocking vertices for the invisible pairs (v_i, v_b) and (v_a, v_j), respectively.*

Lemma 6.2.2 *Let v_a and v_b be the blocking vertices in the lower chain (or upper chain) for invisible pairs (v_i, v_b) and (v_a, v_j), respectively, where $i < a < b < j$ (Figure 6.2(a)). Vertices v_a and v_b are also blocking vertices for the invisible pair (v_i, v_j).*

The above lemmas suggest that it is sufficient to consider only those invisible pairs in G which have one blocking vertex in the lower chain or one blocking vertex in the upper chain or one blocking vertex in each chain. Henceforth, we consider only such invisible pairs of G and they are called *minimal invisible pairs*.

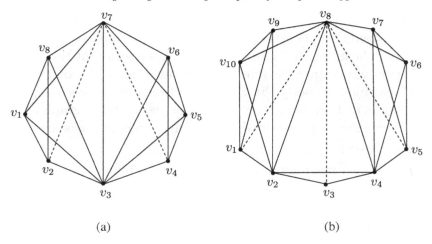

(a)   (b)

Figure 6.3 (a) The visibility of separable invisible pairs (v_2, v_7) and (v_4, v_7) cannot be simultaneously blocked by the blocking vertex v_3. (b) This graph was proposed by Everett and Corneil as a counter-example to Ghosh's earlier conjecture for sufficiency.

Exercise 6.2.1 *Let v_a and v_b be the blocking vertices of G in the lower and upper chains of a minimal invisible pair (v_i, v_j) respectively. If there is an edge in G connecting a vertex of $chain(v_{a+1}, v_{b-1})$ to another vertex of $chain(v_{b+1}, v_{a-1})$, then prove that both v_a and v_b are reflex vertices in the polygon [157].*

Let v_a be a blocking vertex in G for two invisible pairs (v_i, v_j) and (v_k, v_l) (see Figure 6.2(b)). Consider the situation when the Hamiltonian cycle C is traversed from v_a in counterclockwise order. If v_k and v_l are encountered before v_i and v_j during the traversal, then (v_i, v_j) and (v_k, v_l) are called *separable* with respect to v_a. In Figure 6.3(a), v_3 is the blocking vertex for both invisible pairs (v_2, v_7) and (v_4, v_7). Since (v_2, v_7) and (v_4, v_7) are separable with respect to v_3 and v_3 is the only blocking vertex, v_3 cannot simultaneously block the visibility of both (v_2, v_7) and (v_4, v_7). We have the following necessary conditions.

Necessary condition 3. *Two separable invisible pairs in a visibility graph must have distinct blocking vertices.*

Proof. Let v_a be the only blocking vertex for two separable invisible pairs (v_i, v_j) and (v_k, v_l). We prove only for the case when v_a belongs to the lower chain of (v_i, v_k) (see Figure 6.2(b)). Observe that v_a is a reflex vertex in P because the visibility in P between v_i and v_j as well as between v_k and v_l can only be blocked by v_a. Since the sub-polygons of P corresponding to ordered cycles $v_i, v_a, v_j, \ldots, v_i$ and $v_a, v_k, \ldots, v_l, v_a$ are disjoint, v_a cannot simultaneously block the visibility between v_i and v_j and between v_k and v_l in P. $\square$

Ghosh conjectured in the earlier version of his work [154] that if G satisfies these three necessary conditions, G is the visibility graph of a simple polygon P. However, it is not true for the graph in Figure 6.3(b). It can be seen that this graph satisfies the three necessary conditions of Ghosh. On the other hand, blocking vertices v_2 and v_4 cannot block simultaneously the visibility between three invisible pairs (v_1, v_8), (v_3, v_8) and (v_5, v_8). Therefore, the graph is not the visibility graph of any simple polygon. This counter-example to Ghosh's earlier conjecture was given by Everett and Corneil [133, 135].

An *assignment* is a mapping from vertices of G to minimal invisible pairs in G such that:

- a vertex assigned to any minimal invisible pair must be one of its blocking vertices,
- every minimal invisible pair has been assigned by one of its blocking vertices, and
- if a vertex v_a is assigned to a minimal invisible pair (v_i, v_j), then v_a is also assigned to every minimal invisible pair (v_k, v_m) where $v_k \in chain(v_i, v_{a-1})$ and $v_m \in chain(v_{a+1}, v_j)$.

Everett [133] proposed the following stronger version of Necessary condition 3, which is in fact necessary as shown by Srinivasraghavan and Mukhopadhyay [314].

Necessary condition 3'. *There is an assignment in a visibility graph such that no blocking vertex v_a is assigned to two or more minimal invisible pairs that are separable with respect to v_a.*

Exercise 6.2.2 *Prove Necessary condition 3'.*

Abello *et al.* [4] gave another counter-example as shown in Figure 6.4(a) to Ghosh's earlier conjecture of sufficiency [154]. This graph satisfies Necessary conditions 1 and 2, and there exists an unique assignment of blocking vertices v_1, v_2, v_5 and v_8 to all minimal invisible pairs in G as follows. The vertex v_1 is assigned to (v_2, v_9) and (v_2, v_{10}), the vertex v_2 is assigned to (v_1, v_3) and (v_1, v_4), the vertex v_5 is assigned to (v_1, v_6), (v_2, v_6), (v_3, v_6), (v_4, v_6), (v_4, v_7) and (v_4, v_8), and the vertex v_8 is assigned to (v_1, v_7), (v_2, v_7), (v_5, v_9), (v_6, v_9), (v_7, v_9) and (v_7, v_{10}). This assignment shows that no blocking vertex is assigned to two or more of its separable invisible pairs and therefore, this graph also satisfies Necessary condition 3'. However, the graph is not the visibility graph of any simple polygon.

Consider the ordered cycle $(v_1, v_2, v_4, v_5, v_8, v_9, v_1)$ in the same graph of Figure 6.4(a). Let P' be the sub-polygon corresponding to this ordered cycle. Observe that the blocking vertices v_1, v_2, v_5, v_8 are reflex vertices in P'. Therefore, there are four reflex vertices in P' with a total of six vertices, which is not possible. This observation suggests the following necessary condition.

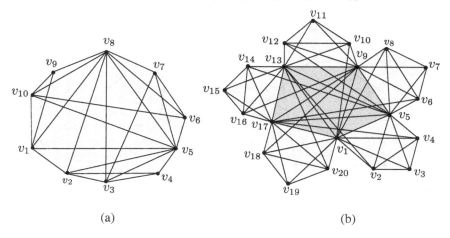

Figure 6.4 (a) Abello *et al.* gave this graph as a counter-example to Ghosh's earlier conjecture for sufficiency. (b) Streinu gave this graph as a counter-example to Ghosh's new conjecture for sufficiency.

Necessary condition 4. *Let D be any ordered cycle of a visibility graph. For any assignment of blocking vertices to all minimal invisible pairs in the visibility graph, the total number of vertices of D assigned to the minimal invisible pairs between the vertices of D is at most $|D| - 3$.*

Proof. Assume on the contrary that there is an assignment in the visibility graph which maps $|D| - 2$ or more vertices of D to the minimal invisible pairs that are between the vertices of D. Let P' be the sub-polygon which corresponds to D. Since every blocking vertex v_a is assigned to some minimal invisible pair between vertices of D, v_a is a reflex vertex in P'. So, the sum of internal angles of P' is more than $(|D| - 2)180°$ contradicting the fact that the sum of internal angles of any simple polygon of $|D|$ vertices is $(|D| - 2)180°$. □

Ghosh again conjectured in [157] that these four necessary conditions $(1, 2, 3',$ and 4) are sufficient to recognize the visibility graphs of simple polygons.. Recently, Streinu [316, 317] has given a counter-example to his new conjecture by providing the graph shown in Figure 6.4(b). This graph can be viewed as five symmetric ordered cycles each sharing an edge with the ordered cycle $(v_1, v_5, v_9, v_{13}, v_{17})$ in the middle. This graph satisfies all four necessary conditions but it is not the visibility graph of any simple polygon. It is not clear whether either another necessary condition is required to circumvent this counter-example or there is a need to strengthen the existing necessary conditions.

We hope that the visibility graph recognition problem will be settled in the near future.

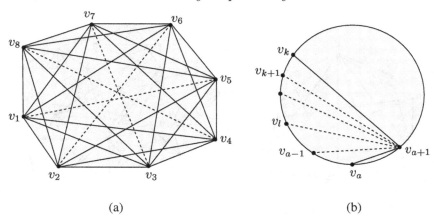

(a)   (b)

Figure 6.5 (a) The graph does not satisfy Necessary condition 1. (b) The vertices v_a and v_k are two consecutive visible vertices of v_{a+1}.

6.2.2 Testing Necessary Conditions: $O(n^2)$ Algorithm

We present an $O(n^2)$ time algorithm of Ghosh [157] for testing his first two necessary conditions (see Section 6.2.1), where n is the number of vertices of the given graph G. As in the previous section, we assume that the vertices of G are labeled with $v_1, v_2, \ldots, v_n$ and the Hamiltonian cycle $C = (v_1, v_2, \ldots, v_n)$ is in counterclockwise order. We also assume that G is stored in an adjacency matrix. We use the notions and definitions of Section 6.2.1 in presenting the algorithm.

It can be seen that Necessary condition 1 can be tested by checking the number of chords in every ordered cycle in G. As the number of vertices in an ordered cycle varies from 4 to n, visibility graphs have an exponential number of ordered cycles. Hence, this naive algorithm for testing Necessary condition 1 is an exponential-time algorithm. Consider any three vertices v_i, v_j and v_k of G, where $v_k \in chain(v_j, v_i)$. If (v_i, v_j) and (v_i, v_k) are visible pairs in G and (v_i, v_l) is an invisible pair for every $v_l \in chain(v_{j+1}, v_{k-1})$, then v_j and v_k are called *consecutive visible* vertices of v_i in G. For example, v_6 and v_4 are consecutive visible vertices of v_1 in Figure 6.5(a). Intuitively, v_j and v_k are two consecutive vertices on the boundary of the visibility polygon of P from v_i. We have the following lemma.

Lemma 6.2.3 *If the given graph G satisfies Necessary condition 1, then any two consecutive visible vertices of every vertex in G are connected by an edge in G.*

Proof. Let v_j and v_k be two consecutive visible vertices of v_i. If (v_j, v_k) is a visible pair in G, then the lemma holds. So, we assume that (v_j, v_k) is an invisible pair and $v_k \in chain(v_j, v_i)$. Let D be an ordered cycle of minimum number of vertices in G such that D passes through v_k, v_i, v_j and vertices of $chain(v_j, v_k)$. Since (v_j, v_k) is an invisible pair, $|D| \geq 4$. Moreover, there is no diagonal between vertices on D

because D is the smallest ordered cycle. Since D is an ordered cycle without any diagonal, G does not satisfy Necessary condition 1, which is a contradiction. Hence (v_j, v_k) is a visible pair in G. ☐

Consider the graph in Figure 6.5(a). This graph does not satisfy Necessary condition 1 as there is an ordered cycle (v_1, v_3, v_5, v_7) without any diagonal. On the other hand, the graph satisfies the condition that any two consecutive visible vertices of every vertex are connected by an edge. Observe that there is no blocking vertex for invisible pairs (v_1, v_5) and (v_3, v_7). Therefore, the graph does not satisfy Necessary Condition 2. We have the following lemma.

Lemma 6.2.4 *If the given graph G satisfies the condition that any two consecutive visible vertices of every vertex in G are connected by an edge in G, but G does not satisfy Necessary condition 1, then G fails to satisfy Necessary condition 2.*

Exercise 6.2.3 *Prove Lemma 6.2.4.*

For testing Necessary condition 1, the above lemmas suggest that it is enough to check whether or not any two consecutive visible vertices of every vertex in G are adjacent in G. Since G is stored in an adjacency matrix, the time required to check this condition for any vertex is $O(n)$.

For every invisible pair (v_i, v_j) in G, Necessary condition 2 can be tested by checking whether there exists a blocking vertex v_a in the lower (or upper) chain of (v_i, v_j). Since this checking for each invisible pair in G can be performed in $O(n^2)$ time, and the number of invisible pairs in G can be $O(n^2)$, this naive method takes $O(n^4)$ time. Using another approach, the time complexity for checking Necessary condition 2 can be improved to $O(n^2)$. The new approach is to locate those invisible pairs in G that can be blocked by a particular vertex v_a. We have the following lemma.

Lemma 6.2.5 *Let v_k and v_a be two consecutive visible vertices of v_{a+1} in G (Figure 6.5(b)). For every vertex $v_l \in chain(v_{k+1}, v_{a-1})$, v_a is a blocking vertex for the invisible pair (v_{a+1}, v_l).*

Corollary 6.2.6 *If v_k is the next clockwise vertex of v_a in C (i.e., $k = a - 1$), then v_a is not a blocking vertex for any invisible pair in G.*

Corollary 6.2.7 *If v_a is a blocking vertex for any invisible pair in G, then one of the vertices of such an invisible pair belongs to $chain(v_{k+1}, v_{a-1})$.*

The above lemma suggests a method for locating all invisible pairs in G that can be blocked by v_a by traversing C in counterclockwise order starting from v_{a+1}. At v_{a+1}, the procedure takes two consecutive visible vertices v_a and v_k of v_{a+1} (see

Figure 6.5(b)). A variable *span* for v_a is maintained which is initialized by k. So, v_a is a blocking vertex for all invisible pairs (v_{a+1}, v_l), where $v_l \in chain(v_{span+1}, v_{a-1})$. Let v_m and v_a be two consecutive visible vertices of v_{a+2} in G. If v_m belongs to $chain(v_{span}, v_{a-1})$, assign m to *span*. So, v_a is a blocking vertex for all invisible pairs (v_{a+2}, v_l), where $v_l \in chain(v_{span+1}, v_{a-1})$. This process is repeated till *span* becomes $a - 1$. Thus, all invisible pairs in G can be located whose v_a is a blocking vertex. In the following, we state the major steps of the algorithm for testing Necessary conditions 1 and 2. The variables i is initialized by 1.

Step 1. *For* each of the consecutive visible vertices v_m and v_k of v_i in G, *if* (v_m, v_k) is not a visible pair in G *then goto* Step 8.

Step 2. Initialize j by $i + 1$. Initialize *span* by the index of some vertex which is adjacent to v_j.

Step 3. Initialize l by $i - 1$. *While* (v_l, v_j) is an invisible pair in G and $v_l \in chain(v_{span+1}, v_i)$, assign v_i as a blocking vertex to (v_l, v_j) and $l := l - 1$.

Step 4. *If* $v_l \in chain(v_{span+1}, v_i)$ *then* $span := l$.

Step 5. *If* (v_{i-1}, v_{j+1}) is an invisible pair in G *then* $j := j + 1$ and *goto* Step 3.

Step 6. *If* $i \neq n$ *then* $i := i + 1$ and *goto* Step 1.

Step 7. *If* every minimal invisible pair in G has a blocking vertex *then* report that G satisfies Necessary conditions 1 and 2 and *goto* Step 9.

Step 8. Report that G does not satisfy Necessary conditions 1 and 2.

Step 9. Stop.

The correctness of the testing algorithm follows from Lemmas 6.2.3, 6.2.4 and 6.2.5. Let us analyze the time complexity of the algorithm. Step 1 takes $O(n)$ time as G is stored in an adjacency matrix. Let q_i denote the number of invisible pairs located in Step 3 for v_i. It can be seen that all invisible pairs in G, which can be blocked by v_i, are located in time proportional to q_i. Since Step 3 is executed for all vertices of G, blocking vertices for all invisible pairs in G can be located in time proportional to $(q_1 + q_2 + \ldots + q_n)$. If G has only minimal invisible pairs, then this sum is bounded by $O(n^2)$ as each invisible pair is consider once for its upper chain and once for its lower chain.

Consider the situation when G has invisible pairs that are not minimal. In such a situation, $(q_1 + q_2 + \ldots + q_n)$ may not be bounded by $O(n^2)$ as the same invisible pair (v_l, v_j) is considered once for each of its blocking vertices. This repetition can be avoided by restricting the variable l in Step 3 up to the blocking vertex located last. Thus, all of the invisible pairs in G that are not minimal are also considered at most twice. Hence, Necessary conditions 1 and 2 can be tested in $O(n^2)$ time. We have the following theorem.

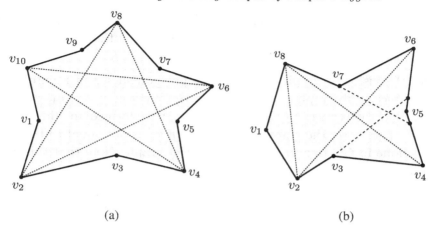

Figure 6.6 (a) The vertices v_2, v_8, v_4, v_{10} and v_6 have formed a chordless cycle. (b) The vertices v_2, v_6, v_5, v_4 and v_8 have formed a chordless cycle.

Theorem 6.2.8 *Given a graph G of n vertices and a Hamiltonian cycle in G, Necessary conditions 1 and 2 can be tested in $O(n^2)$ time.*

6.3 Characterizing Visibility Graphs of Simple Polygons

As mentioned in Section 6.1, the problem of characterizing visibility graphs of simple polygons is still an open problem in spite of the efforts made by several researchers over the last two decades. In this section, we present the properties and counter-examples that have evolved out of the studies of Ghosh [154, 157], Coullard and Lubiw [97], Everett and Corneil [133, 135] and Abello and Kumar [2, 3] in their attempts to characterize visibility graphs of simple polygons.

Special Classes of Graphs

Necessary conditions presented in Section 6.2.1 show that visibility graphs of simple polygons have natural structures. It appears from Ghosh's Necessary condition 1 that visibility graphs may fall into one of the well known special classes of graphs, e.g., perfect graphs, circle graphs, or chordal graphs. However, Ghosh [154, 157] has found counter-examples in all cases. In the following, we present these counter-examples.

We say that a graph G' is a *sub-graph* of another graph G if G' consists of a subset of vertices and edges of G. If G' consists of a subset of vertices V' of G and all edges of G between these vertices in V', then G' is called an *induced sub-graph* of G'. If all vertices of an induced sub-graph G' of G are adjacent to each other, then G' is called a *clique*. The chromatic number of a graph G is the smallest number of colors required to color vertices of G such that two vertices of every edge in G have different colors. An undirected graph G is called a *perfect graph* [170] if for every induced sub-graph G' of G (including G itself), the size of the maximum cardinality clique of G' is the chromatic number of G'.

Consider the visibility graph G of a simple polygon shown in Figure 6.6(a). Let G' be the induced sub-graph of G formed by the vertices v_2, v_8, v_4, v_{10} and v_6. It can be seen that the vertices v_2, v_8, v_4, v_{10} and v_6 have formed an odd cycle without chord in G'. Therefore, the chromatic number of G' is not equal to the size of the maximum clique in G'. Hence, G is not a perfect graph. Note that this cycle is an unordered cycle in G.

An undirected graph G is called a *chordal graph* if every cycle having four or more vertices has a chord [170]. The above counter-example also shows that visibility graphs of simple polygons are not chordal graphs as the visibility graph contains an unordered cycle v_2, v_8, v_4, v_{10} and v_6 without a chord.

Consider a simple polygon such that its visibility graph G does not have any unordered cycle of four or more vertices without a chord. In that case, G is a chordal graph because by Necessary Condition 1 in Section 6.2.1, every ordered cycle of four or more vertices in G has a chord. Therefore, visibility graphs of this class of simple polygons are chordal graphs. On the other hand, any chordal graph having a Hamiltonian cycle may not be the visibility graph of a simple polygon. For example, the graph in Figure 6.1(b) is a chordal graph but the graph is not the visibility graph of a simple polygon. We state this observation in the following lemma.

Lemma 6.3.1 *If every unordered cycle of four or more vertices in the visibility graph of a simple polygon has a chord, then the visibility graph is a chordal graph.*

A simple polygon P is called a *fan* if there is a vertex in P which can see all other vertices of P. Such a vertex of P is called a *fan vertex*. Note that a fan is a star-shaped polygon but a star-shaped polygon need not be a fan. If the internal angle at a fan vertex is convex, the polygon is called a *convex fan*. Visibility graphs are not perfect graphs even for convex fans. Consider the convex fan shown in Figure 6.6(b). Since the vertices v_2, v_6, v_5, v_4 and v_8 have formed an odd cycle without a chord, the visibility graph of a convex fan is not a perfect graph.

An undirected graph G is called a *circle graph* [68, 145] if every vertex of G can be represented as a chord of a circle C such that two chords in C intersect if and only if the corresponding vertices are adjacent in G. A graph H is not a circle graph if there exists a vertex in H which is adjacent to all vertices of any cycle having five or more vertices [68]. In the visibility graph of the convex fan shown in Figure 6.6(b), the vertex v_1 is adjacent to all vertices of the cycle v_2, v_6, v_5, v_4 and v_8. Hence, visibility graphs of simple polygons are not circle graphs. We state these facts in the following lemma.

Lemma 6.3.2 *Visibility graphs of simple polygons do not belong to the union of perfect graphs and circle graphs.*

Clique Ordering

A graph G is *3-connected* if there is no set of fewer than three vertices whose removal disconnects G. In other words, there exists three or more disjoint paths in G between any two vertices of G. A *3-clique ordering* of a graph G is an ordering of vertices of G (say, $v_1, v_2, \ldots, v_n$) such that the first three vertices (i.e., v_1, v_2 and v_3) form a clique and for every vertex v_i for $i > 3$, there exists a clique of three vertices v_j, v_k and v_l such that (i) v_j, v_k and v_l are adjacent to v_i in G, and (ii) $j < i$, $k < i$ and $l < i$. We have the following condition from Coullard and Lubiw [97].

Lemma 6.3.3 *Each 3-connected component of the visibility graph of a simple polygon has a 3-clique ordering starting from any 3-clique.*

Although the above property shows some structure in the visibility graph of a simple polygon, it does not lead to the characterizing of a visibility graph as any graph satisfying this condition is not necessarily the visibility graph of a simple polygon [4, 97, 135].

Exercise 6.3.1 *Draw a graph G such that (i) G satisfies Lemma 6.3.3 and (ii) G is not the visibility graph of any simple polygon.*

Forbidden Induced Sub-graphs

A graph H is said to be *forbidden* for a class of graphs if H is not an induced sub-graph of any graph in this class. The readers may know that the planar graphs can be characterized in terms of forbidden induced sub-graphs. In the same spirit, Everett and Corneil [133, 135] have asked the following question: is there a finite set of forbidden induced sub-graphs that characterize visibility graphs? They have shown that there is no such set that characterize visibility graphs. We start with a lemma of Everett and Corneil [133, 135], which follows from Necessary condition 1 of Ghosh presented in Section 6.2.1.

Lemma 6.3.4 *Let H be a graph containing an ordered chordless cycle of length at least 4 for every Hamiltonian cycle in H. Then, H is a forbidden induced sub-graph of visibility graphs of simple polygons.*

Consider the graph in Figure 6.7(a), which is known as Grötsch graph. It can be seen that this graph is a forbidden induced sub-graph of a visibility graph as it

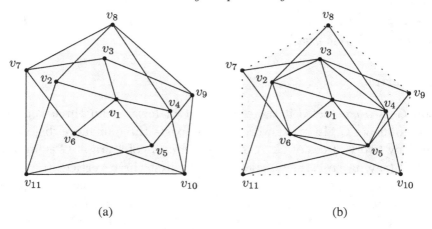

Figure 6.7 (a) Grötsch graph. (b) A variation of Grötsch graph.

satisfies Lemma 6.3.4. This graph can be shown to be minimal using an exhaustive search by considering all induced sub-graphs of this graph. Starting from a variation of this graph which is obtained by replacing the outer cycle of Grötsch graph by an inner cycle (see Figure 6.7(b)), Everett and Corneil have suggested a method for constructing an infinite family of minimal forbidden sub-graphs of visibility graphs. For more details of this construction, see [133, 135]. We state the result in the following lemma.

Lemma 6.3.5 *There exists an infinite family of minimal forbidden induced sub-graphs of visibility graphs of simple polygons.*

Euclidean Shortest Paths

Abello and Kumar [2, 3] have introduced a class of graphs called *quasi-persistent* graphs, which is equivalent to the class of graphs satisfying Necessary conditions 1 and 2 of Ghosh [154, 157] presented in Section 6.2.1. This equivalence also suggests that this class of graph can be recognized by the testing algorithm of Ghosh for Necessary conditions 1 and 2 (see Section 6.2.2).

Abello and Kumar [2, 3] have suggested four necessary conditions for quasi-persistent graphs to be visibility graphs of simple polygons. Their first necessary condition, which is called *locally-inseparable*, is essentially same as Necessary Condition 3' presented in Section 6.2.1. The second, third and fourth necessary conditions correspond to the properties of Euclidean shortest paths between vertices in a simple polygon. Here we state these three necessary conditions of Abello and Kumar [2, 3] under the assumption that the given graph G is a quasi-persistent graph. We follow the same notions used in Section 6.2.1 for presenting these conditions. For an invisible pair (v_i, v_j) in G and an assignment β of blocking vertices to invisible pairs in G, an *occluding path* between v_i and v_j under β (denoted as $path_\beta(v_i, v_j)$) is defined as the path from v_i to v_j in G consisting of vertices assigned by β such that only the adjacent vertices in the path is connected by an edge in G.

Necessary condition 2. *If a quasi-persistent graph G can be realized as a simple polygon under an assignment β of blocking vertices to invisible pairs in G, then for every invisible pair (v_i, v_j) in G, $path_\beta(v_i, v_j)$ is the same as $path_\beta(v_j, v_i)$ in the reverse order.*

Necessary condition 3. *If a quasi-persistent graph G can be realized as a simple polygon under an assignment β of blocking vertices to invisible pairs in G, and if $v_k \in path_\beta(v_i, v_l)$ and $v_l \in path_\beta(v_k, v_j)$, then $v_k, v_l \in path_\beta(v_i, v_j)$.*

Necessary condition 4. *If a quasi-persistent graph G can be realized as a simple polygon under an assignment β of blocking vertices to invisible pairs in G, and if $v_p \in path_\beta(v_i, v_j)$ is a blocking vertex of (v_i, v_j), then for all v_k on $chain(v_i, v_p)$ and v_l on $chain(v_p, v_j)$, $v_p \in path_\beta(v_k, v_l)$.*

We know from Lemma 3.2.5 that the Euclidean shortest path in a simple polygon is unique and it follows from the fact that the sum of the internal angles of a simple polygon of n vertices is $(n-2)180°$. Therefore, the above three conditions of Abello and Kumar, which correspond to the uniqueness property of Euclidean shortest paths, naturally follow from Ghosh's Necessary condition 4.

Exercise 6.3.2 *Prove that Necessary conditions 2, 3 and 4 of Abello and Kumar follow from Ghosh's Necessary condition 4 [157].*

6.4 Recognizing Special Classes of Visibility Graphs

6.4.1 Spiral Polygons: $O(n)$ Algorithm

In this section, we present an $O(n)$ time algorithm of Everett and Corneil [133, 134] for recognizing visibility graphs of spiral polygons. Given a graph G, the recognition problem is to determine whether G is the visibility graph of a spiral polygon S. The recognition algorithm is based on their characterization of visibility graphs of spiral polygons as interval graphs, which we also present in this section. It may be noted that although visibility graphs of simple polygons are not perfect graphs (see Lemma 6.3.2), it is not true for all special classes of polygons such as spiral polygons. We assume that the vertices of G are labeled with $v_1, v_2, \ldots, v_n$.

In a spiral polygon, all reflex vertices occur consecutively along its boundary. So, the problem of recognizing the visibility graph of a spiral polygon S_n is to identify

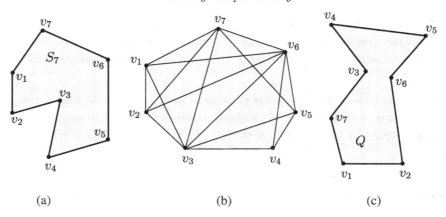

(a)   (b)   (c)

Figure 6.8 (a) A spiral polygon S_7. (b) The visibility graph G of S_7. (c) A non-spiral polygon Q.

a Hamiltonian cycle $C = (v_1, v_2, \ldots, v_n)$ (in counterclockwise order) in the given graph G such that there exists two special vertices v_i and v_j in S_n with the property that $v_i, v_{i+1}, \ldots, v_j$ are convex vertices in S_n and $v_{j+1}, v_{j+2}, \ldots, v_{i-1}$ are reflex vertices in S_n. A spiral polygon S_7 is shown in Figure 6.8(a) and its visibility graph G is shown in Figure 6.8(b). Consider the non-spiral polygon Q in Figure 6.8(c). It can be seen that the visibility graph of Q is also G. However, the boundary of Q corresponds to another Hamiltonian cycle $C = (v_1, v_2, v_6, v_5, v_4, v_3, v_7)$ in G. So, the choice of a Hamiltonian cycle in G is crucial in recognizing the visibility graph of a spiral polygon.

Let L denote the boundary of S_n from v_i to v_j (including v_i and v_j) containing a convex chain of vertices $v_i, v_{i+1}, \ldots, v_j$ (see Figure 6.9). Similarly, let R denote the boundary of S_n from v_j to v_i (including v_i and v_j) containing reflex vertices v_{j+1}, $v_{j+2}, \ldots, v_{i-1}$. Suppose v_i is removed from S_n by adding the diagonal $v_{i+1}v_{i-1}$ in S_n. This gives another spiral polygon S_{n-1}. If the angle at v_{i-1} is convex in S_{n-1} (see Figure 6.9(a)), then L in S_{n-1} consists of vertices $v_{i-1}, v_{i+1}, v_{i+2}, \ldots, v_j$ and R in S_{n-1} consists of $v_j, v_{j+1}, \ldots, v_{i-1}$. Note that the role of v_{i-1} in S_{n-1} is the same as the role of v_i in S_n. In the other situation, the angle at v_{i-1} in S_{n-1} is reflex (see Figure 6.9(b)). Therefore, L in S_{n-1} consists of vertices $v_{i+1}, v_{i+2}, \ldots, v_j$ and R in S_{n-1} consists of $v_j, v_{j+1}, \ldots, v_{i-2}, v_{i+1}$. Note that the role of v_{i+1} in S_{n-1} is same as the role of v_i in S_n. If this process of deletion is carried out recursively on S_n (see Figure 6.9(c)), we get a numbering of vertices of S_n starting from v_i in the order they are removed from the polygon. Observe that the similar process of deletion can also be carried out starting from v_j in S_n. The diagonals that are used to construct $S_{n-1}, S_{n-2}, \ldots, S_3$ along with the boundary of S_n form a Hamiltonian triangulation of S_n as the dual of this triangulation is a path. We have the following lemmas.

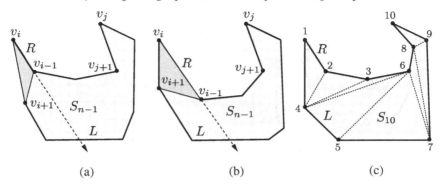

Figure 6.9 (a) The angle at v_{i-1} in S_{n-1} is convex. (b) The angle at v_{i-1} in S_{n-1} is reflex. (c) The vertices are numbered in the order they are deleted.

Lemma 6.4.1 *There exists a Hamiltonian triangulation for every spiral polygon.*

Lemma 6.4.2 *In a spiral polygon, there exists two vertices v_i and v_j such that the vertices of the polygon visible from either v_i or v_j form a clique in the visibility graph of the polygon.*

The above properties can be used for deriving properties in visibility graphs of spiral polygons. A vertex v_k in a graph is called *simplicial* if the adjacent vertices of v_k in the graph form a clique. The adjacent vertices of any vertex v_k in a graph are called *neighbors* of v_k. Locate a simplicial vertex v_k in G and mark it as u_1. Construct the graph $G - \{u_1\}$ by removing the vertex u_1 from G and all edges incident on u_1 in G. Again, locate a simplicial vertex v_p in $G - \{u_1\}$ such that v_p is a neighbor of u_1 in G, and mark it as u_2. Construct the graph $G - \{u_1, u_2\}$ by removing the vertex u_2 from $G - \{u_1\}$ and all edges incident on u_2 in $G - \{u_1\}$. Repeat this process until all vertices are numbered. If the given graph G is the visibility graph of a spiral polygon, then this process of deletion always succeeds due to Lemma 6.4.1. Any ordering of vertices $\{u_1, u_2, \ldots, u_n\}$ of G is called a *perfect vertex elimination scheme* if each u_i is simplicial in the induced sub-graph $G - \{u_1, u_2, \ldots, u_{i-1}\}$. A graph is called *chordal* if it has no chordless cycle of length greater than or equal to 4 [170]. We have the following lemmas.

Lemma 6.4.3 *The visibility graph of a spiral polygon admits a perfect vertex elimination scheme.*

Lemma 6.4.4 *A graph is chordal if and only if it has a perfect vertex elimination scheme [144].*

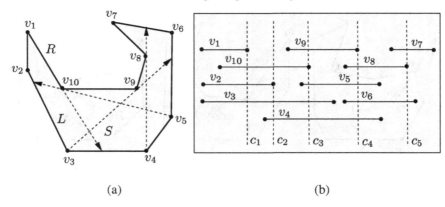

(a)   (b)

Figure 6.10 (a) A spiral polygon S. (b) The visibility graph of S is drawn as an interval graph with the ordering of maximal cliques $\{c_1, c_2, c_3, c_4, c_5\}$.

Lemma 6.4.5 *The visibility graph of a spiral polygon is a chordal graph.*

Proof. Proof follows from Lemmas 6.4.3 and 6.4.4. □

Consider three mutually non-adjacent vertices v_p, v_q and v_k in G. If v_p, v_q and v_k cannot be ordered such that every path in G from the first vertex v_p to the third vertex v_k passes through a neighbor of the second vertex v_q, then v_p, v_q and v_k are called an *asteroidal triple* in G. We have the following lemma.

Lemma 6.4.6 *A graph G is an interval graph if and only if G is a chordal graph containing no asteroidal triple [240].*

Consider a graph G that can be represented as a set of intervals of a linearly ordered set such that (i) every vertex of G is represented as a distinct interval and (ii) two intervals overlap if and only if their corresponding vertices are connected by an edge in G. The graph G is called an *interval graph* [170]. Figure 6.10(a) shows a spiral polygon and its visibility graph is drawn in Figure 6.10(b) as an interval graph. We have the following necessary condition.

Necessary condition 1. If G is the visibility graph of a spiral polygon S, then G is an interval graph.

Proof. We know from Lemma 6.4.5 that G is a chordal graph. Let v_p, v_q and v_k be any three pairwise non-adjacent vertices of G. Consider the sub-graph G' of G which corresponds to a Hamiltonian triangulation $T(S)$ of S. By Lemma 6.4.1, $T(S)$ always exists. Since the dual of $T(S)$ is a path, v_p, v_q and v_k can always be ordered in such a way that any path in G' between the first and the third vertex (say, v_p and v_k, respectively) must pass through vertices of G corresponding to a triangle in

$T(s)$, one of whose vertices is v_q. Therefore, G does not have any asteroidal triple. Hence, G is an interval graph by Lemma 6.4.6. $\square$

Exercise 6.4.1 *Design a linear time algorithm for recognizing interval graphs [59].*

Using the recognition algorithm of Booth and Lueker [59], it can be tested in $O(n)$ time whether the given graph G is an interval graph. From now on, we assume that G is an interval graph. A clique in G is called *maximal* if it is not a sub-graph of any other clique of G. In the following lemma, we present a property on the ordering of maximal cliques in an interval graph, which is used to identify vertices of G belonging to L or R.

Lemma 6.4.7 *For every vertex v_k of an interval graph, the maximal cliques of the graph can be linearly ordered such that the maximal clique containing v_k occur consecutively [169].*

During the process of testing for interval graphs, the algorithm of Booth and Lueker [59] computes an ordering of maximal cliques $\{c_1, c_2, \ldots, c_m\}$. Figure 6.10(b) shows an ordering of maximal cliques $\{c_1, c_2, \ldots, c_5\}$ in the visibility graph for a spiral polygon S. A vertex $v_l \in c_i$ for all i is called a *conductor* of a clique c_i, if v_l also appears in the clique c_{i+1}. It can be seen that for any three consecutive vertices v_{k-1}, v_k and v_{k+1} in either R or L, the middle vertex v_k is a conductor in G. Moreover, if $v_{k-1} \in c_i$ and $v_{k+1} \in c_j$ in the ordering of maximal cliques in G, then v_k belongs to all maximal cliques between c_i and c_j by Lemma 6.4.7. In order to find a Hamiltonian cycle C in G which corresponds to the boundary of a spiral polygon, we have to find an order of conductors in G from c_1 to c_m and then split the conductors according to their own properties so that one part forms L and the other part forms R. We have the following observations on the conductors that belong to $R = (v_j, v_{j+1}, \ldots, v_{i-1}, v_i)$.

Lemma 6.4.8 *The vertex v_i belongs only to the first maximal clique c_1 in G and the vertex v_j belongs only to the last maximal clique c_m in G.*

Corollary 6.4.9 *The vertices v_i and v_j are not conductors in G.*

Lemma 6.4.10 *If G is the visibility graph of a spiral polygon, then*

   (i) *each maximal clique in G has at most two vertices of R,*
   (ii) *all vertices in $R - \{v_i, v_j\}$ are conductors in G, and*
   (iii) *every maximal clique in G has a vertex of R and a vertex of L.*

Corollary 6.4.11 *If two vertices of R belong to any maximal clique, then one of them can be a conductor of that clique.*

It can be seen that the path between v_i to v_j in G corresponding to R is a path where no two non-adjacent vertices in the path is connected by an edge in G. In other words, $v_k \in R$ is the sole blocking vertex for the minimal invisible pair (v_{k-1}, v_{k+1}). For the definition of a blocking vertex, see Section 6.2.1. An induced path in G between vertices v_i and v_j *covers* an interval graph G if (i) $v_i \in c_1$ and $v_j \in c_m$, (ii) all vertices in the path excluding v_i and v_j are conductors in G, and (iii) the path contains only one conductor from each maximal clique between c_1 and c_{m-1}. An induced path in the graph of Figure 6.10(b) is the path formed by v_1, v_{10}, v_9, v_8, and v_7. We have the following lemma.

Lemma 6.4.12 *If G is the visibility graph of a spiral polygon, then an induced path in G, which corresponds to R in the spiral polygon, covers G.*

Proof. Proof follows from Lemma 6.4.8 and Corollaries 6.4.9 and 6.4.11.   □

Let us consider the path in G that corresponds to L. It can be seen that $v_4 \in L$ is a conductor of c_3 in the graph shown in Figure 6.10(b) but $v_3 \in L$ is not a conductor of c_3. So, v_3 must precede v_4 in L. Let b_i denote the conductors of c_i, i.e., b_i is the set of vertices that belong to both c_i and c_{i+1}. In the interval graph of Figure 6.10(b), $b_1 = \{v_2, v_3, v_{10}\}$, $b_2 = \{v_3, v_4, v_{10}\}$, $b_3 = \{v_4, v_5, v_9\}$, $b_4 = \{v_6, v_8\}$. Note that if $|b_i| < 2$ for $1 \le i \le m - 1$, then G does not have any Hamiltonian cycle. A path in an interval graph G is called *straight* if (i) all vertices of $c_i - b_i$ precedes the vertices of b_i in the path, where $1 \le i \le m$ and, (ii) all vertices of $c_i - b_{i-1}$ succeeds the vertices of b_{i-1} in the path, where $1 \le i \le m$. For any vertex v_k in G, let $low(v_k)$ denote the smallest index clique containing v_k. Similarly, $high(v_k)$ denotes the largest index clique containing v_k. We have the following lemma.

Lemma 6.4.13 *If G is the visibility graph of a spiral polygon, then a path in G which corresponds to either L or R is straight.*

Corollary 6.4.14 *If there is no edge in G between any two non-adjacent vertices in a straight path in G, then the path corresponds to R.*

Corollary 6.4.15 *(i) For every vertex v_k of L in G, $low(v_k) \le low(v_{k+1})$ and $high(v_k) \le high(v_{k+1})$. (ii) For every vertex v_k of R in G, $low(v_k) \le low(v_{k-1})$ and $high(v_k) \le high(v_{k-1})$.*

Consider a vertex v_k in G such that $low(v_k) < high(v_k) - 1$ (see Figure 6.11). Consider another vertex v_p such that $low(v_k) < low(v_p)$ and $high(v_p) < high(v_k)$. Intuitively, the interval of v_p is properly contained in the interval of v_k in the interval graph G. It can be seen that if (i) $low(v_p) = high(v_p)$ (see Figure 6.11(a)) or (ii) v_p belongs to L (see Figure 6.11(b)), then G cannot be the visibility graph of a spiral

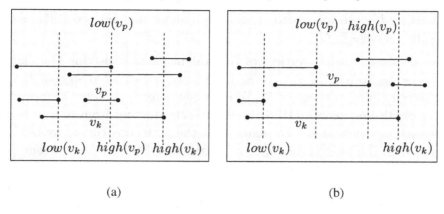

(a)   (b)

Figure 6.11 (a) The vertex v_p belongs to only one clique. (b) The vertex v_p must belong to R.

polygon. Such a vertex v_p is called *overlaying* vertex. Note that the second condition suggests a way to identify some vertices of G that must belong to R. Observe that if there exists such a vertex v_p with respect to v_k, then v_p must belong to R provided $low(v_p) \neq high(v_p)$ (see Figure 6.11(b)). However, for every reflex vertex v_p in R, there may not always be a corresponding vertex v_k. So, using this condition, not all reflex vertices of R may be identified. We have the following lemma.

Lemma 6.4.16 *If G is the visibility graph of a spiral polygon, then G does not have any overlaying vertex.*

The above three lemmas constitute the following necessary condition.

Necessary condition 2. If G is the visibility graph of a spiral polygon S, then (i) an induced path in G, which corresponds to R in S, covers G, (ii) a path in G, which corresponds to L of S, is straight, and (iii) G does not have any overlaying vertex.

Exercise 6.4.2 *Prove Necessary condition 2.*

Assume that the given graph G has satisfied Necessary Conditions 1 and 2, and some vertices of R (say, $u_2, u_3, \ldots, u_{q-1}$) have been identified. Take any vertex from $c_1 - b_1$ as u_1. Take any vertex from $c_m - b_{m-1}$ as u_q. So, u_1 is v_i and u_q is v_j. Let $U = (u_1, u_2, \ldots, u_q)$. Assume that for any vertex $u_i \in U$, $low(u_i) \leq low(u_{i+1})$ and $high(u_{i-1}) \leq high(u_i)$, i.e., the vertices of U are ordered in the same way they are identified. Observe that if any two vertices of U are conductors of the same clique, then G is not the visibility graph of a spiral polygon by Corollary 6.4.11. If every pair of two consecutive vertices of U are connected by an edge in G, then the path formed by U corresponds to R. So, we assume that no two vertices of U are connected by an edge in G.

In order to identify other vertices of R, straight paths satisfying Corollary 6.4.14 from u_1 to u_2, u_2 to $u_3, \ldots$, u_{q-1} to u_q have to be constructed so that these paths contain the remaining vertices of R. To construct such a path between u_i and u_{i+1} for all i, a depth-first search (DFS) method [221] starting from u_i can be used to construct such a path to u_{i+1}. To ensure that the path constructed by DFS satisfies Corollary 6.4.14, the next vertex v_{k-1} is chosen by DFS from the current vertex v_k satisfies the conditions that The path constructed in this manner is added between u_i and u_{i+1}. By concatenating these paths, the entire path in G, which corresponds R, is constructed. The remaining vertices of G are added to L preserving the order of $c_i - b_i$ precedes b_i in L for all i. Once the paths corresponding to R and L are identified, the reverse order of the perfect vertex elimination scheme can be used to construct spiral polygons $S_3, S_4, \ldots, S_n$. For more details of this polygon construction, see [133, 134]. We have the following theorem.

Theorem 6.4.17 *A graph G is the visibility graph of a spiral polygon if and only if G satisfies Necessary conditions 1 and 2.*

Exercise 6.4.3 *Let G be a given graph satisfying Necessary conditions 1 and 2. Design a polynomial-time algorithm for drawing a spiral polygon such that G is its visibility graph [133, 134].*

In the following, we state the major steps of the algorithm for identifying two paths in the given graph G, which correspond to L and R of an n-sided spiral polygon.

Step 1. Using the algorithm of Booth and Lueker [59], construct an interval graph representation of G and compute the ordered set of maximal cliques $\{c_1, c_2, \ldots, c_m\}$.

Step 2. Construct the ordered set of conductors $\{b_1, b_2, \ldots, b_{m-1}\}$.

Step 3. *For* every vertex v_k of G, compute $low(v_k)$ and $high(v_k)$.

Step 4. Check whether the paths in G are straight.

Step 5. Check whether G has any overlaying vertex.

Step 6. Locate the ordered set of those vertices U of G that must belong to R.

Step 7. Construct a straight path between two consecutive vertices of U using the modified DFS and concatenate these paths to form the path corresponding to R.

Step 8. Construct another path in G, corresponding to L, consisting of the remaining vertices of G in the proper order.

Step 9. Report both paths which correspond to L and R.

Step 10. Stop.

Let us analyze the time complexity of the algorithm. Step 1 takes $O(n)$ time as the recognition algorithm of Booth and Lueker [59] runs in $O(n)$ time. Since the number of maximal cliques in a chordal graph is proportional to n [213], we use this fact in our analysis of the remaining steps. Since the total number of conductors in G is $n-2$ and a maximal clique is considered twice, Step 2 takes $O(n)$ time. For every vertex v_k of c_i in the order from c_1 to c_m, assign i to $high(v_k)$. If v_k does not belong to c_{i-1} or v_k belongs to c_1, then assign i also to $low(v_k)$. Considering each maximal clique once in the order, Step 3 can be performed in $O(n)$ time. Step 4 and Step 5 can also be performed in $O(n)$ time using the order of the cliques. Constructing two paths corresponding to L and R in Steps 7 and 8 take $O(n)$ time as DFS runs in $O(n)$ time [221]. Hence, the overall time complexity of the recognition algorithm is $O(n)$. We summarize the result in the following theorem.

Theorem 6.4.18 *The visibility graph of a spiral polygon of n vertices can be recognized in $O(n)$ time.*

6.4.2 Tower Polygons: $O(n)$ Algorithm

In this section, we present an $O(n)$ time algorithm of Colley *et al.* [95] for recognizing visibility graphs of tower polygons. Given a graph G, the recognition problem is to determine if G is the visibility graph of a tower polygon F. Their recognition algorithm is based on the characterization that visibility graphs of tower polygons are bipartite permutation graphs with an added Hamiltonian cycle. We assume that the vertices of G are labeled with $v_1, v_2, \ldots, v_n$.

A *tower* polygon F is a simple polygon formed by two reflex chains of vertices with only one boundary edge connecting two convex vertices (see Figure 6.12(a)). The polygon F is also called a *funnel*. The convex vertex of F shared by two reflex chains is called the apex of F and the edge connecting two convex vertices of F is called the base of F. Let v_j denote the apex of a tower polygon F (see Figure 6.12(a)). Let v_i and v_{i+1} denote the other two convex vertices of F. Let us denote two reflex chains of vertices of F as R_1 and R_2, where $R_1 = (v_j, v_{j+1}, \ldots, v_i)$, $R_2 = (v_{i+1}, v_{i+2}, \ldots, v_j)$, and vertices in R_1 and R_2 are in counterclockwise order. Let V_1 and V_2 denote the vertices, excluding v_j, of R_1 and R_2, respectively. It can be seen that v_j is always visible from some point z on the boundary edge $v_i v_{i+1}$. Since V_1 and V_2 are on opposites sides of zv_j, every visible segment in F connecting a vertex of V_1 to a vertex of V_2 intersects zv_j. We have the following properties on V_1 and V_2 in F.

Lemma 6.4.19 *If a vertex v_p of V_1 (or V_2) is visible from two vertices v_l and v_m of V_2 (respectively, V_1), then v_p is also visible from all vertices of V_2 (respectively, V_1) between v_l and v_m (Figure 6.12(a)).*

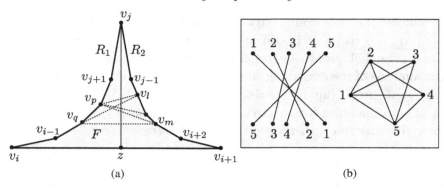

Figure 6.12 (a) A tower polygon F. (b) A permutation graph and its geometric representation.

Corollary 6.4.20 *If a vertex v_p of V_1 (or V_2) is visible from a vertex v_l of V_2 (respectively, V_1), then v_p is also visible from the next clockwise or counterclockwise vertex of v_l on the boundary of F.*

Lemma 6.4.21 *Assume that $v_p \in V_1$ is visible from $v_m \in V_2$ and $v_q \in V_1$ is visible from $v_l \in V_2$ (i.e., $v_p v_m$ and $v_q v_l$ are visible segments). If v_q is a vertex of R_1 between v_p and v_i and if v_m is a vertex of R_2 between v_l and v_{i+1}, then segments $v_p v_l$ and $v_q v_m$ lie inside F (Figure 6.12(a)).*

Let us state a property of bipartite permutation graphs which corresponds to Lemma 6.4.21. Let $V = \{1, 2, \ldots, n\}$ denote the vertex set of a graph H. The graph H is a *permutation graph* if there is a permutation π of V such that for every pair of vertices $u < w$, (u, w) is an edge in H if and only if $\pi(u) > \pi(w)$ [132, 284]. Figure 6.12(b) shows the permutation of vertices of a permutation graph. A graph is a *bipartite graph* if its vertices can be partitioned into two sets such that there is no edge of the graph connecting vertices of the same set. A graph is called a *bipartite permutation graph* if it is both bipartite and a permutation graph [61]. A *strong ordering* of a bipartite graph B with vertex sets V_1 and V_2 is an ordering of V_1 and V_2 such that if there are edges (u, w') and (u', w) in B, where $u, u' \in V_1$, $u < u'$, $w, w' \in V_2$ and $w < w'$, then B has also edges (u, w) and (u', w'). We have the following lemma.

Lemma 6.4.22 *A bipartite graph is a permutation graph if and only if it has a strong ordering [313].*

Let us look at the geometric structures of a tower polygon F in the light of bipartite permutation graphs. For all of the consecutive vertices v_m and v_{m+1} of V_2, let u_m denote the intersection point of R_1 and $\overrightarrow{v_m v_{m+1}}$. It can be seen that for any three consecutive points u_{m-1}, u_m and u_{m+1}, the point u_m lies between u_{m-1}

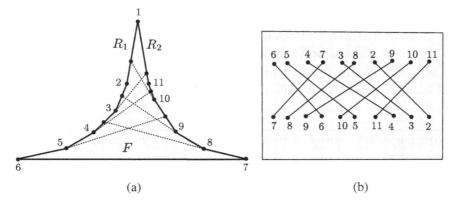

Figure 6.13 (a) A tower polygon F with extension of edges of R_1 and R_2. (b) The geometric representation of the permutation of $V_1 \cup V_2$ of F.

and u_{m+1} on R_1. By extending each edge of R_2, locate the position of u_m on R_1 for every vertex v_m of V_2. Construct the merged order of vertices of $V_1 \cup V_2$ for R_1 by traversing R_1 from v_i to v_j in the clockwise order and by inserting each vertex v_m of V_2 in the merged order according to the position of u_m on R_1. For the tower polygon in Figure 6.13(a), the merged order of vertices for R_1 is 6, 5, 4, 7, 3, 8, 2, 9, 10 and 11. Similarly, by extending the edges of R_1 to R_2, the merged order of vertices of $V_1 \cup V_2$ for R_2 can be constructed by traversing R_2 from v_{i+1} to v_j in counterclockwise order. For the tower polygon in Figure 6.13(a), the merged order of vertices for R_2 is 7, 8, 9, 6, 10, 5, 11, 4, 3 and 2. The geometric representation of these two merged lists for the tower polygon in Figure 6.13(a) is shown in Figure 6.13(b), which corresponds to a permutation of $V_1 \cup V_2$. This structure in a tower polygon is used for characterizing visibility graphs of tower polygons.

Let G be the visibility graph of a tower polygon F. Remove the edges from G that correspond to the edges of R_1 and R_2 in F and remove the vertex from G that corresponds to the apex of F. The remaining graph of G, denoted as G', is called the *cross-visible sub-graph* of G. It can be seen that G' is a bipartite graph and it satisfies Lemma 6.4.22. We have the following necessary and sufficient condition for recognizing visibility graphs of a tower polygon.

Theorem 6.4.23 *A graph G is the visibility graph of a tower polygon if and only if its cross-visible sub-graph G' is a bipartite permutation graph.*

Exercise 6.4.4 *Prove Theorem 6.4.23.*

The above theorem suggests that in order to recognize a given graph G as the visibility graph of a tower polygon, construct G' from G and test whether G' is a bipartite permutation graph. It can be tested in linear time whether G' is a bipartite permutation graph [61, 313]. However, to construct G' from G, it is necessary to identify a Hamiltonian cycle C in G which corresponds to the boundary of a tower polygon. Moreover, three vertices of C have to be identified, which correspond to convex vertices of a tower polygon. So, the problem of recognizing visibility graphs of tower polygons is now reduced to the problem of locating a Hamiltonian cycle C in G and identifying three special vertices in C.

Exercise 6.4.5 *Design a linear time algorithm for recognizing bipartite permutation graphs [61, 313].*

Let w be a vertex of the given graph G such that it is adjacent to exactly two other vertices of G. If no such vertex w exists, then G is not the visibility graph of a tower polygon as the apex of any tower polygon F can see only its two adjacent vertices on the boundary of F. So, we assume that such a vertex w exists in G. If there are two such vertices w in G, then one of them corresponds to the apex of F and the other one corresponds to a vertex of the base of F. If there are three or more such vertices w in G, then G cannot be the visibility graph of any tower polygon. Since there can be at most two such vertices w, considering each vertex w as the vertex corresponding to the apex of F, the recognition algorithm tests whether G is the visibility graph of a tower polygon. If it fails for both vertices, then G is not the visibility graph of a tower polygon.

Without loss of generality, we assume that there is only one such vertex w in G. Treating w as the vertex corresponding to the apex of F, the remaining vertices of G are partitioned into two ordered sets V_1 and V_2 such that the vertices of V_1 and V_2 correspond to the sequence of vertices of R_1 and R_2 of F, respectively. Label w as v_j (see Figure 6.14). Label two neighbors of v_j in G as v_{j+1} and v_{j-1}. Observe that if v_{j+1} and v_{j-1} are not connected by an edge in G, then G is not the visibility graph of any tower polygon. So, we assume that v_{j+1} and v_{j-1} are connected by an edge in G. The vertex v_{j+1} becomes the first vertex in V_1 and similarly, v_{j-1} becomes the first vertex of V_2. The ordered sets V_1 and V_2 are constructed by labeling a pair of vertices of G at each iteration, one belonging to V_1 and the other belonging to V_2, until all vertices of G are labeled. Assume that v_p and v_m are the last vertices added to V_1 and V_2, respectively. We know that v_p and v_m are connected by an edge in G. The vertices $v_m, v_{m+1}, \ldots, v_{p-1}, v_p$ are called *labeled vertices* of G, and the remaining vertices of G are called *unlabeled vertices*. We have the following lemma on the labeling of the next pair of vertices of G.

Lemma 6.4.24 *Let v_p and v_m be the last pair of vertices of G that has been labeled. Let K be a maximal clique such that (i) v_p and v_m are vertices of K, and (ii) the remaining vertices of K are unlabeled vertices of G. If K has five or more vertices, then G is not the visibility graph of a tower polygon.*

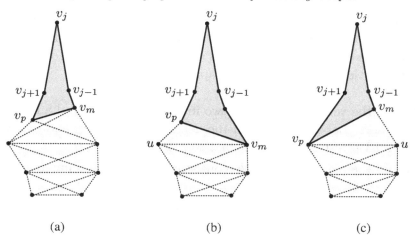

Figure 6.14 (a) The labeled vertices v_{j+1} and v_p belong to V_1, and labeled vertices v_{j-1} and v_m belong to V_2. The other vertices are not yet labeled. (b) The unlabeled vertex u is added to V_1. (c) The unlabeled vertex u is added to V_2.

Corollary 6.4.25 *If G is the visibility graph of a tower polygon, then K is the maximal clique in G having one or two unlabeled vertices.*

Let W be the set of all unlabeled vertices of G that are neighbors of both v_p and v_m in G. If the vertices of W do not form a clique or the size of W is more than two, then G is not the visibility graph of a tower polygon by Lemma 6.4.24. So, we assume that the vertices of $W \cup \{v_p\} \cup \{v_m\}$ is a clique K of size three or four. If K has four vertices (see Figure 6.14(a)), one unlabeled vertex of K is labeled as v_{p+1} and the other unlabeled vertex of K is labeled as v_{m-1}. Then v_{p+1} and v_{m-1} are added to V_1 and V_2, respectively. If K has three vertices, then the unlabeled vertex u of K is added to either V_1 or V_2. For the graph in Figure 6.14(b), u is added to V_1. The vertex u is added to V_1 (or V_2) if (i) there is no unlabeled vertex in G that forms a clique with u and v_p (respectively, v_m), and (ii) there exists a unlabeled vertex that forms a clique with u and v_m (respectively, v_p). For the graph in Figure 6.14(c), u is added to V_2. If u cannot be added to either V_1 or V_2, then G is not the visibility graph of a tower polygon. By repeating this process of labeling of vertices of G, the ordered sets of vertices V_1 and V_2 can be constructed. We have the following lemma.

Lemma 6.4.26 *If the given graph G is the visibility graph of a tower polygon F, then using the method of labeling, the vertices of G can be partitioned into three sets of vertices $\{v_j\}$, $V_1 = \{v_{j+1}, v_{j+2}, \ldots, v_i\}$ and $V_2 = \{v_{j-1}, v_{j-2}, \ldots, v_{i+1}\}$ such that v_j corresponds to the apex of F, and the ordered sets of vertices V_1 and V_2 correspond to the sequence of vertices of R_1 and R_2 of F respectively.*

Once V_1 and V_2 are known, the cross-visible sub-graph G' can be constructed from G. If G' satisfies Theorem 6.4.23, then G is the visibility graph of a tower polygon. In the following, we state the major steps of the algorithm for recognizing the given graph G of n vertices as the visibility graph of a tower polygon.

Step 1. Locate the vertex w of degree two in G which has formed a clique with two of its neighbors. Label w as v_1 and the neighbors of w as v_2 and v_n. Add v_2 and v_n to V_1 and V_2, respectively. Assign 2 to p and n to m.

Step 2. Locate the maximal clique K consisting of v_p, v_m and unlabeled vertices of G.

Step 3. *If* $|K| = 2$ or $|K| > 4$ *then goto* Step 8.

Step 4. *If* $|K| = 4$ *then*

    Step 4a. Increment p by 1, label an unlabeled vertex of K as v_p and add it to V_1.

    Step 4b. Decrement m by 1, label the unlabeled vertex of K as v_m, add it to V_2 and *goto* Step 6.

Step 5. Let u be the unlabeled vertex of K. *If* K is the only clique with u and v_p in the remaining unlabeled graph of G *then* increment p by 1, label u as v_p and add it to V_1 *else* decrement m by 1, label u as v_m and add it to V_2.

Step 6. *If* all vertices of G are not labeled *then goto* Step 2.

Step 7. Construct the cross-visible sub-graph G' of G using V_1 and V_2. *If* G' is a bipartite permutation graph *then* report that G is the visibility graph of a tower polygon and *goto* Step 9.

Step 8. Report that G is not the visibility graph of a tower polygon.

Step 9. Stop.

The correctness of the algorithm follows from Lemma 6.4.26 and Theorem 6.4.23. Let us analyze the time complexity of the algorithm. Step 1 can be performed in $O(n)$ time. Step 2 involves locating the maximal clique K containing v_p and v_m in the unlabeled graph of G. Let W_1 be the unlabeled vertices of G that are adjacent to v_p. Let $W_2 \subset W_1$ be the vertices in G that are adjacent to v_m. So, the vertices of W_2 with v_p and v_m have formed the current maximal clique K. It can be seen that the vertices in $W_1 - W_2$ must belong to V_2 and these vertices can be ordered as they correspond to consecutive reflex vertices of R_2 in a tower polygon. This ordering helps to locate the maximal clique containing a vertex of W_2 for subsequent iterations. It means that the current maximal clique K can be located in time proportional to its size. Therefore, Step 2 can be executed in $O(n)$ time. Similarly, Step 5 can also be executed in $O(n)$ time. Constructing and testing G' in Step 7 can be done in $O(n)$ time [61, 313]. Hence, the overall time complexity of the recognition algorithm is $O(n)$. We summarize the result in the following theorem.

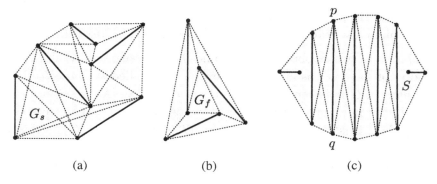

(a)   (b)   (c)

Figure 6.15 (a) The segment visibility graph G_s of a set S of disjoint line segments. (b) The segment visibility graph G_f of these three line segments is 4-connected. (c) There are four empty convex quadrilaterals in this set S of seven line segments.

Theorem 6.4.27 *The visibility graph of a tower polygon of n vertices can be recognized in $O(n)$ time.*

6.5 Characterizing a Sub-Class of Segment Visibility Graphs

In this section, we present the characterization of a special class of segment visibility graphs given by Everett *et al.* [136]. They have characterized those segment visibility graphs that do not have K_5 (a complete graph of five vertices) as a minor. This class of graphs is called K_5-*free* segment visibility graphs. Their characterization gives a straightforward polynomial time algorithm for recognizing this class of graphs.

Let S be a set of n disjoint line segments in the plane. If the line segment uw joining two endpoints u and w of different segments in S does not intersect any segment in S (except at u and w), then uw is called *visible segment* in S. The *segment visibility graph* G_s of S is a graph whose $2n$ vertices represent $2n$ endpoints of line segments in S and whose edges represent visible segments in S (see Figure 6.15(a)). A graph M is called a *minor* of a graph G if M can be obtained from G by a sequence of vertex deletions, edge deletions and edge contractions. It can be seen that K_4 in any segment visibility graph corresponds to an empty convex quadrilateral formed by four endpoints of segments in S assuming no three-segment endpoints of K_4 are collinear. Figure 6.15(c) shows four empty convex quadrilaterals in a set of seven line segments. We have the following lemma.

Lemma 6.5.1 *There are at least $n-3$ empty convex quadrilaterals in S for $|S| \geq 4$.*

Exercise 6.5.1 *Prove Lemma 6.5.1.*

A graph is called *planar* if it can be embedded on the plane such that no two edges intersect. We know that Kuratowski's theorem characterizes planar graphs as those graphs that do not have K_5 or $K_{3,3}$ as a minor [58, 224], where $K_{3,3}$ denotes the complete bipartite graph with three vertices in each vertex set.

The similarity between planar graphs and K_5-*free* segment visibility graphs is that both do not have K_5 as a minor. A graph G is called k-*connected* if there are k disjoint paths in G between any two vertices of G [58]. A *cutset* in a graph G is a set of minimum number of vertices in G whose removal disconnects G. If G is k-*connected*, then k is the size of cutset in G (denoted as $k(G)$). If $k(G) = 1$, the vertex in the cutset is called a *cut vertex*. The characterization of K_5-*free* segment visibility graphs is based on the property that this class of graphs are not 4-*connected* graphs (except for one particular segment visibility graph). The only S whose segment visibility graph (say, G_f) is K_5-*free* and 4-*connected* is shown in Figure 6.15(b). We have the following lemmas.

Lemma 6.5.2 *The graph G_f is the only K_5-free segment visibility graph of S which is 4-connected.*

Proof. We know from Lemma 6.5.1 that there exists at least an empty convex quadrilateral in S. It means that in a K_5-*free* segment visibility graph G_s for $|S| \geq 4$, there exists a sub-graph H of G_s isomorphic to K_4. If G_s is 4-*connected*, it follows from Menger's theorem [58] that for every vertex u of G_s not in H, u is connected to each vertex of H by four disjoint paths in G_s. It means that G_s has K_5 as a minor, which is a contradiction. For $|S| < 4$, the result can be checked by enumeration.   □

Corollary 6.5.3 *The size of a cutset in any K_5-free segment visibility graph except G_f is less than four.*

Lemma 6.5.4 *No K_5-free segment visibility graph of S contains a cut vertex.*

Proof. Since S can always be triangulated and triangulated graphs are 2-*connected*, G_s contains no cut vertex.   □

Lemma 6.5.5 *If a segment visibility graph G_s of a set of n disjoint line segments S does not contain K_5 as a minor, then at least one endpoint of every segment in S is a vertex of the convex hull of S.*

Proof. If S has a segment pq such that neither p nor q is a vertex of the convex hull of S, then by contacting the corresponding edge of pq in G_s, a minor in G_s can be constructed which is K_5, and this is a contradiction.   □

In order to recognize a given graph G as a K_5-*free* segment visibility graph, it can be checked whether G is G_f. If G is isomorphic to G_f, then G is G_s. Otherwise, if $k(G)$ is not 2 or 3, then G is not G_s. We assume from now on that the size of a cutset in G is 2 or 3. We need some more properties of G_s before the edges of G that correspond to segments of S can be identified. We have the following lemma.

Lemma 6.5.6 *There is a path in a K_5-free segment visibility graph G_s consisting of only the vertices of a cutset in G_s.*

Exercise 6.5.2 *Prove Lemma 6.5.6.*

Any path that satisfies Lemma 6.5.6 is called a *separating path* in G_s. We know from Lemma 6.5.5 that one endpoint of every segment in S is a vertex of the convex hull of S. Suppose there is a segment pq in S such that both endpoints p and q are vertices of the convex hull of S. Assume that p and q are not two consecutive vertices on the boundary of the convex hull of S (see Figure 6.15(c)). In such situations, $k(G_s) = 2$. In fact, this is the only situation when G_s can have a cutset of size 2 as stated in the following lemma.

Lemma 6.5.7 *If a cutset consists of two vertices u and v in a K_5-free segment visibility graph G_s of S (Figure 6.15(c)), then u and v correspond to endpoints of the same segment pq in S and p and q are two non-adjacent vertices on the boundary of the convex hull of S.*

Exercise 6.5.3 *Prove Lemma 6.5.7.*

The above lemma suggests that if the given G has a cutset of size 2, the edge in G connecting these two vertices, which is a separating path in G, corresponds to a segment in S. Remove both vertices of the cutset and all edges incident on these vertices from G. This removal decomposes G into two disjoint components as no vertex of one component is connected by an edge in G to any vertex of other component. Again, if any component has a cutset of size 2, decompose this component again into two components. This process is repeated till the size of a cutset in every component is 3 or all those edges of G, that correspond to segments in S, are identified. The remaining problem is to identify those edges of every component which correspond to segments in S. This can be solved by treating each component as the given graph G having a cutset of size 3.

In order to recognize a given graph G, we need a characterization of G_s for $k(G_s) = 3$. Since a cutset in G_s consists of three vertices, by Lemma 6.5.6 there is a separating path in G_s consisting of these three vertices. It can be seen that this separating path must correspond to a geometric path in S that contains a segment of S. We have the following lemmas on separating paths in G_s.

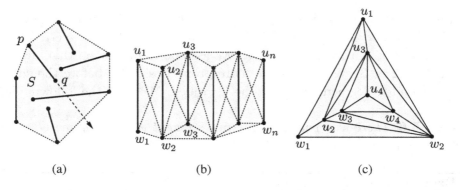

(a)   (b)   (c)

Figure 6.16 (a) The ray drawn from p through q intersects a segment of S. (b) A segment visibility graph of a set of vertical segments which is *3-connected* and K_5-*free*. (c) A planar embedding (up to $u_4 w_4$) of the graph in the previous figure.

Lemma 6.5.8 *If $k(G_s) = 3$, then one of the edges in every separating path in G_s corresponds to a segment in S.*

Proof. Let Q be a separating path consisting of three vertices of a cutset in G_s. Let Q' be the geometric path in S corresponding to Q. Since Q is a separating path in G_s which has connected two non-adjacent vertices on the exterior face of G_s, no two endpoints of a segment in S can see each other across Q'. Therefore, one of the edges in Q' must be a segment of S. Hence, one of the edges of Q corresponds to a segment of S. ☐

Corollary 6.5.9 *The geometric path Q' connects two non-adjacent vertices of the convex hull of S.*

Lemma 6.5.10 *Let pq be a segment in S such that (i) the corresponding edge of pq belongs to a separating path in the segment visibility graph of S which is K_5-free and 3-connected, and (ii) p is a vertex of the convex hull of S. No segment of S is intersected by $\overrightarrow{pq}$.*

Proof. The proof follows from the fact that if $\overrightarrow{pq}$ intersects any segment in S (see Figure 6.16(a)), the segment visibility graph of S contains K_5 as a minor. ☐

Exercise 6.5.4 *Prove Lemma 6.5.10.*

The above lemma suggests that segments in S, whose segment visibility graph is K_5-*free* and 3-*connected*, can be considered to be vertical segments. Let us consider a class of graphs D such that any graph H in this class can be constructed from a set of edges $\{u_1 w_1, \ldots, u_n w_n\}$ as follows (see Figure 6.16(b)). For $1 \leq i \leq n$, u_i and w_i are connected in H to u_{i+1} and w_{i+1} by four edges forming K_4. Moreover, for

$1 \leq i \leq n-1$, if $u_{i-1}u_{i+1}$ is not an edge of H, u_iu_{i+2} can be an edge in H and if $w_{i-1}w_{i+1}$ is not an edge of H, w_iw_{i+2} can be an edge in H. The edges u_1w_1 and u_nw_n are called the *first* and *last links* of H, respectively. The embedding in Figure 6.16(c) shows that the graph H is a maximal planar graph which corresponds to a triangulation of S.

Observe that H is a segment visibility graph, where links in H correspond to vertical segments in S. In fact, every graph in D is a segment visibility graph and its 3-*connected* components can be embedded similar to Figure 6.16(b). Recall that G_s can be 2-*connected* but it may have 3-*connected* components (see Lemma 6.5.7). The embedding of 3-*connected* components of G_s is essentially unique as long as the extension of any segment in S does not intersect any other segment of S, except may be for the first and last links (see Lemma 6.5.10). We have the following characterization.

Theorem 6.5.11 *The class of K_5-free segment visibility graph is exactly the class $D \cup \{G_f\}$.*

Proof. Proof follows from Lemmas 6.5.5, 6.5.7, 6.5.8 and 6.5.10. □

To recognize a given graph G as a segment visibility graph, which is K_5-*free* and 3-*connected*, start from a vertex of G of degree 3 and label link by link using the similar method as stated in the algorithm for recognizing a tower polygon in Section 6.4.2. We have the following theorem.

Theorem 6.5.12 *A K_5-free segment visibility graph of $2n$ vertices can be recognized in polynomial time.*

> **Exercise 6.5.5** *Design an $O(n)$ time algorithm for identifying the links in segment visibility graphs of $2n$ vertices, which are 3-connected and K_5-free [136].*

6.6 A Few Properties of Vertex-Edge Visibility Graphs

In this section, we present a few properties of vertex-edge visibility graphs of simple polygons given by O'Rourke and Streinu [275]. We assume that the vertices of a simple polygon P are labeled $v_1, v_2, \ldots, v_n$ in counterclockwise order, and no three vertices are collinear in P. So, the edges on the boundary of P in counterclockwise order are $v_1v_2, v_2v_3, \ldots, v_nv_1$. Let V_v and V_e denote the ordered set of vertices and edges of P in counterclockwise order. The *vertex-edge visibility graph* G_{ve} of P is a bipartite graph with nodes V_v and V_e, and arcs between $v_i \in V_v$ and $v_jv_{j+1} \in V_e$ if and only if v_i is visible from some internal point z of v_jv_{j+1} in P. Note that z is some point of v_jv_{j+1} other that v_j and v_{j+1}. Figure 6.17(a) shows a simple

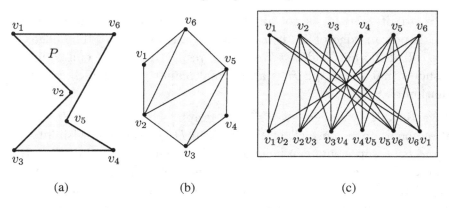

Figure 6.17 (a) A simple polygon P. (b) The visibility graph of P. (c) The vertex-edge visibility graph of P.

polygon P, and its visibility graph G_v is shown in Figure 6.17(b). The vertex-edge visibility graph G_{ve} of P is shown in Figure 6.17(c). Given a simple polygon P, G_{ve} of P can be constructed with a little modification of Hershberger's algorithm [186] for computing the visibility graph G_v of a simple polygon (see Section 5.2). In the sequel, G_v is also referred as a *vertex visibility graph*.

We know that two consecutive vertices v_i and v_{i+1} are mutually visible in P. If v_{i-1} is not visible in P from any internal point of v_iv_{i+1}, then v_i is a reflex vertex in P. Therefore, v_{i-1} is not connected by an arc to v_iv_{i+1} in G_{ve}. Conversely, if v_{i-1} is not connected by an arc to v_iv_{i+1} in G_{ve}, then v_i is a reflex vertex in P. Thus, the reflex vertices of P can be determined uniquely from G_{ve}. On the other hand, it is not a straightforward task to identify reflex vertices of P from G_v as discussed in Section 6.2.1. It appears that vertex-edge visibility graphs capture more geometric structures of polygons than vertex visibility graphs. In the following lemmas, we establish the relationship between G_v and G_{ve} of the same polygon P.

Lemma 6.6.1 *If v_i is connected by arcs to $v_{j-1}v_j$ and v_jv_{j+1} in G_{ve}, then (v_i, v_j) is a visible pair in G_v.*

Lemma 6.6.2 *If (v_i, v_j) is a visible pair in G_v, then v_i is connected by an arc to $v_{j-1}v_j$ or v_jv_{j+1} (or both) in G_{ve}.*

Lemma 6.6.3 *Assume that v_i is connected by arcs to two non-adjacent nodes v_jv_{j+1} and v_kv_{k+1} in G_{ve} and no intermediate node in G_{ve} is connected by an arc to v_i. Then, exactly one of Cases A or B holds.*

Case A: (i) In G_v, (v_i, v_{j+1}) is a visible pair but not (v_i, v_k), and (ii) in G_{ve}, v_{j+1} is connected to v_kv_{k+1} by an arc but there is no arc connecting v_k to v_jv_{j+1} (Figure 6.18(a)).

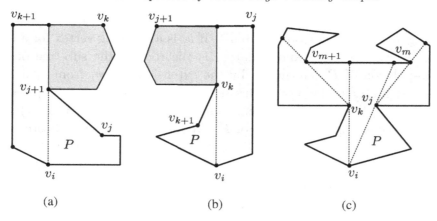

Figure 6.18 (a) The extension of $v_i v_{j+1}$ from v_{j+1} meets $v_k v_{k+1}$. (b) The extension of $v_i v_k$ from v_k meets $v_j v_{j+1}$. (c) The vertices v_j and v_k are blocking vertices of invisible pairs (v_i, v_m) and (v_i, v_{m+1}) respectively.

Case B: (i) In G_v, (v_i, v_k) is a visible pair but not (v_i, v_{j+1}), and (ii) in G_{ve}, v_k is connected to $v_j v_{j+1}$ by an arc but there is no arc connecting v_{j+1} to $v_k v_{k+1}$ (Figure 6.18(a)).

Corollary 6.6.4 *In G_v, v_{j+1} and v_k are the blocking vertices for invisible pairs (v_i, v_k) and (v_i, v_{j+1}) in Case A and Case B, respectively.*

Exercise 6.6.1 *Prove Lemma 6.6.3.*

The above lemmas can be used to construct G_v from G_{ve} as follows. For each node $v_i \in V_v$, consider the nodes N_i in V_e that are connected to v_i by arcs in G_{ve}. Consider two nodes $v_j v_{j+1}$ and $v_k v_{k+1}$ consecutive in N_i. If $j + 1 = k$, then connect v_i to v_{j+1} by an edge in G_v as they are visible in P by Lemma 6.6.1. Otherwise, if Case A (or Case B) of Lemma 6.6.3 is satisfied, then v_i is connected to v_{j+1} (respectively, v_k) by an edge in G_v. We have the following theorem.

Theorem 6.6.5 *The vertex visibility graph G_v can be constructed from the vertex-edge visibility graph G_{ve} in time proportional to the size of G_{ve}.*

Using Corollary 6.6.4, the shortest path tree in P rooted at any vertex (say, $SPT(v_i)$) can be constructed from G_{ve} as follows. For details on shortest path trees, see Section 3.6. From a given G_{ve}, locate all vertices of P that are visible from v_i using G_v and they are connected to v_i as children of v_i in $SPT(v_i)$. Recall that G_v can be computed from G_{ve}. Consider two nodes v_j and v_k of N_i consecutive in the counterclockwise order in N_i. Assume that v_k belongs to the counterclockwise boundary of P from v_j to v_i (see Figure 6.18(c)). If v_j and v_k are two consecutive vertices of P, then v_j and v_k are leaves of $SPT(v_i)$. Otherwise, test whether v_j or v_k are blocking vertices using Corollary 6.6.4. If v_j is a blocking vertex for an invisible pair, say, (v_i, v_m), then we know that v_j is the root of the sub-tree of $SPT(v_i)$ in the sub-polygon of P determined by the extension of $v_i v_j$ from v_j to the edge $v_m v_{m+1}$. Treating v_j as the root in this sub-polygon, compute $SPT(v_j)$ recursively. Analogously, if v_k is a blocking vertex, compute the sub-tree of $SPT(v_i)$ rooted at v_k in the corresponding sub-polygon of P. We have the following theorem.

Theorem 6.6.6 *Given the vertex-edge visibility graph G_{ve} of a simple polygon P, the shortest path tree from a vertex inside P can be constructed from G_{ve} in time proportional to the size of G_{ve}.*

The *edge-edge visibility graph G_e* of P is a graph with nodes V_e, and arcs between nodes $v_i v_{i+1} \in V_e$ and $v_j v_{j+1} \in V_e$ if and only if some internal point of $v_i v_{i+1}$ is visible from an internal point of $v_j v_{j+1}$ in P. Although G_e is a natural extension of G_{ve}, G_e does not seem to capture more geometric structure of P than G_{ve}. In fact G_e can be constructed from G_{ve} using the following lemma.

Lemma 6.6.7 *Nodes $v_i v_{i+1}$ and $v_j v_{j+1}$ are connected by an arc in G_e if and only if the shortest paths $SP(v_i, v_{j+1})$ and $SP(v_{i+1}, v_j)$ in P do not share any vertex.*

The above lemma suggests that G_e can be constructed once the shortest paths between every pair of vertices in P are known. Since they can be computed from G_{ve} using Theorem 6.6.6, G_e can be constructed from G_{ve}. Using the method similar to the method of constructing G_v from G_{ve} stated earlier in this section, G_{ve} can also be constructed from G_e. So, it may be concluded that G_{ve} and G_e are equivalent.

6.7 Computing Maximum Clique in a Visibility Graph

In this section, we present the algorithm of Ghosh *et al.* [167] for computing the maximum clique in the visibility graph G of a simple polygon P in $(n^2 E)$ time, where n and E are the number of vertices and edges of G, respectively. The algorithm assumes that G is given along with the Hamiltonian cycle C, where C corresponds to the boundary of P. The *maximum clique* in G is a complete sub-graph of G with the largest number of vertices. For example, the maximum clique in G shown in Figure 6.19(a) consists of vertices v_1, v_3, v_5, v_6, v_7, v_8, v_9 and v_{10}. There may be two or more maximum cliques in G with the same number of vertices. We are interested in locating any one of them. Observe that the maximum clique in G corresponds to a convex polygon inside P formed by the largest number of vertices (see Figure 6.19(b)).

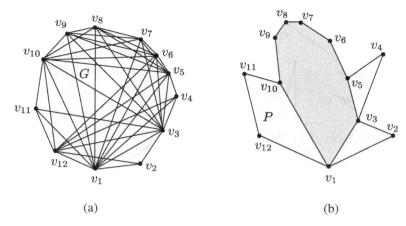

(a)   (b)

Figure 6.19 (a) The maximum clique in G consists of vertices v_1, v_3, v_5, v_6, v_7, v_8, v_9 and v_{10}. (b) The vertices forming the largest convex polygon in P are the vertices of the maximum clique in the visibility graph of P.

Exercise 6.7.1 *Let S be a set of n points in the plane. Design an $O(n^3)$ time algorithm for computing the largest subset S' of S such that points in S' form a convex polygon Q with no point of $S - S'$ lying inside Q [40].*

Assume that the vertices of C are labeled $v_1, v_2, \ldots, v_n$ in counterclockwise order. Let $C(v_j, v_m)$ denote the portion of C from v_j to v_m in counterclockwise order. For each vertex $v_i \in G$, G_i denotes the induced sub-graph of G formed by v_i with its neighboring vertices in G. In Figure 6.19(a), G_3 is the entire visibility graph since all vertices of the graph are neighbors of v_3. The sub-polygon of P formed by the vertices of G_i is called the *fan F_i* with v_i as the *fan vertex*. The fan F_i is referred as *convex fan* if the internal angle at v_i is convex in F_i. It can be seen that the order of vertices on the boundary of F_i follows the order in C.

Observe that if the maximum clique in G contains a vertex v_i, then all vertices of the maximum clique belong to G_i as they are neighbors of v_i in G. Using this observation, the algorithm first computes maximum cliques in $G_1, G_2, \ldots, G_n$ and then takes the clique with the largest size as the maximum clique in G. So, it is enough to present the procedure for computing the maximum clique in G_i.

Without loss of generality, we assume that all vertices of G are neighbors of v_i. This assumption implies that F_i is P and therefore, the angular order of vertices around v_i in F_i is same as the order of vertices in C. For any edge $(v_p, v_q) \in G_i$, if there exists an edge (v_k, v_m) in G_i such that $v_k \in C(v_{p+1}, v_{q-1})$ and $v_m \in C(v_{q+1}, v_{p-1})$, we say that there is a *cross-visibility* across (v_p, v_q) [154, 157]. For any vertex v_j, if there is no *cross-visibility* across (v_i, v_j) (see Figure 6.20(a)), then all vertices of the maximum clique in G_i belong to either $C(v_i, v_j)$ or $C(v_j, v_i)$. So, G_i can be partitioned into two induced sub-graphs formed by vertices of $C(v_i, v_j)$ and

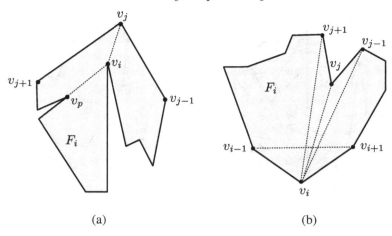

(a)   (b)

Figure 6.20 (a) There is no cross-visibility across (v_i, v_j) as well as across (v_i, v_p). (b) The vertex v_j is the sole blocking vertex for (v_{j-1}, v_{j+1}).

$C(v_j, v_i)$. So, the maximum clique in G_i can be computed by computing maximum cliques in these two sub-graphs. Let v_p be a vertex of $C(v_j, v_i)$. Again, if there is no cross-visibility across (v_i, v_p) (see Figure 6.20(a)), then the induced sub-graph formed by vertices of $C(v_j, v_i)$ can again be partitioned into two sub-graphs as stated earlier. This process of partitioning sub-graphs continues till no further partition is possible. We have the following lemmas.

Lemma 6.7.1 *The graph G_i can be partitioned into sub-graphs using the criteria of cross-visibility such that one of them totally contains the maximum clique in G_i.*

Corollary 6.7.2 *There can be at most one sub-graph of G_i whose corresponding fan is not a convex fan.*

Proof. Since the edges used for partitioning G_i are all incident at v_i, these edges divide the reflex angle at v_i in F_i. After the division, only one of them can be reflex at v_i. Hence, there can be at most one sub-graph of G_i after partition whose corresponding fan is not a convex fan. □

Lemma 6.7.3 *All edges of G_i used for partitioning G_i can be located in $O(E)$ time.*

Exercise 6.7.2 *Prove Lemma 6.7.3.*

Without loss of generality, we assume that there is a cross-visibility across (v_i, v_j) in G_i for every $v_j \in C(v_{i+2}, v_{i-2})$. If (v_{j-1}, v_{j+1}) is an edge in G_i, then v_j is a convex vertex in F_i. If (v_{j-1}, v_{j+1}) is not an edge in G_i (see Figure 6.20(b)), v_j is a blocking vertex for (v_{j-1}, v_{j+1}). For properties of blocking vertices, see Section 6.2.1. The vertex v_i is the only other blocking vertex for (v_{j-1}, v_{j+1}) as (v_i, v_{j-1}) and (v_i, v_{j+1})

are edges in G_i (see Figure 6.20(a)). If v_i is used to block the visibility between v_{j-1} and v_{j+1} in F_i, then there is no cross-visibility across (v_i, v_j) contradicting the assumption that there is a cross-visibility across (v_i, v_j) (see Figure 6.20(a)). Therefore, v_j must be a reflex vertex in F_i (see Figure 6.20(b)). We state this observation in the following lemma.

Lemma 6.7.4 *If (v_{j-1}, v_{j+1}) is not an edge in G_i but cross-visibility exists across (v_i, v_j), then v_j must be a reflex vertex in F_i.*

By traversing C once, all reflex vertices of F_i can be identified using the above lemma. For computing the maximum clique in G_i, the algorithm needs the property that v_i is a convex vertex in F_i. If (v_{i-1}, v_{i+1}) is not an edge in G_i, then v_i is not a convex vertex in F_i and there is no clique in G_i with vertices v_{i-1} and v_{i+1}. So, sub-graphs of G_i are constructed in such way that their corresponding fans are convex fans as follows (see Figure 6.21(a)). Let (v_{i+1}, v_k) be the edge in G_i such that no vertex of $C(v_{k+1}, v_{i-1})$ is a neighbor of v_{i+1}. The vertex v_k is called the *furthest adjacent vertex* of v_{i+1}. It can be seen that the corresponding fan of the induced sub-graph of G_i formed by v_i with vertices of $C(v_{i+1}, v_k)$ is a convex fan. Let v_m be the first vertex of C in counterclockwise order from v_{i+1} such that v_{i-1} is the furthest adjacent vertex of v_m. Using the furthest adjacent vertices of $v_{i+2}, \ldots, v_m$ as stated earlier, the corresponding sub-graphs of G_i are constructed, and they are visibility graphs of convex fans. Since the maximum clique in G_i belongs to one of these sub-graphs, the maximum clique is computed by computing maximum cliques in these sub-graphs of G_i.

From now on, we assume that v_i is a convex vertex in F_i, i.e., (v_{i-1}, v_{i+1}) is an edge in G_i. Let (v_k, v_l) and (v_p, v_k) be two edges of G_i such that $v_p \in C(v_i, v_{k-1})$ and $v_l \in C(v_{k+1}, v_{i-1})$. We know that the three vertices v_l, v_k and v_p belong to a clique in G_i if and only if (v_l, v_p) is an edge in G_i. All pairs of such edges (v_k, v_l) and (v_p, v_k) satisfying this property are called *valid pairs of edges* at v_k. So, every valid pair of edges at any vertex $v_k \in C(v_{i+1}, v_{i-1})$ forms a clique of three vertices in G_i. The edge (v_p, v_k) is called an *incoming edge* of v_k and the other edge (v_k, v_l) is called an *outgoing edge* of v_k. Note that any edge is an incoming edge of one vertex and an outgoing edge of the other vertex. We have the following lemma on valid pairs of edges in G_i.

Lemma 6.7.5 *If an outgoing edge (v_k, v_l) at v_k forms a valid pair with an incoming edge (v_p, v_k) at v_k, then for every incoming edge (v_q, v_k) at v_k, where $v_q \in C(v_i, v_p)$, (v_k, v_l) forms a valid pair with (v_q, v_k) at v_k.*

Proof. Since (v_k, v_l) has formed a valid pair with (v_p, v_k), the internal angle at v_k in F_i (say, α) formed by (v_k, v_l) and (v_p, v_k) is convex. Since any incoming edge (v_q, v_k) divides α in F_i, the internal angle at v_k in F_i formed by (v_k, v_l) and (v_q, v_k)

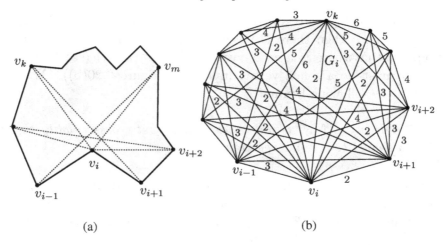

(a)   (b)

Figure 6.21 (a) The vertices v_k and v_{i-1} are the furthest adjacent vertices of v_{i+1} and v_m, respectively. (b) Weights are assigned to the outgoing edges at v_i, $v_{i+1}, \ldots, v_k$.

is also convex. So, (v_l, v_q) must be an edge in G_i as v_l and v_q are visible in F_i. Therefore, (v_k, v_l) forms a valid pair with (v_q, v_k) at v_k. □

Using valid pairs of edges, weights are assigned to edges of G_i for computing the maximum clique in G_i. The weight of 2 is assigned to edges (v_i, v_{i+1}), $(v_i, v_{i+2}), \ldots (v_i, v_{i-2})$. Consider v_{i+1}. Since (v_i, v_{i+1}) is the only incoming edge at v_{i+1} and all vertices of G_i are connected to v_i (see Figure 6.21(b)), (v_i, v_{i+1}) forms a valid pair with every outgoing edge at v_{i+1}. Assign the weight of 3, which is the size of the clique, to every outgoing edge at v_{i+1}. For the next vertex v_{i+2}, (v_i, v_{i+2}) and (v_{i+1}, v_{i+2}) are incoming edges at v_{i+2} and each of them forms a valid pair with every outgoing edge at v_{i+2}. Therefore, assign the weight of 4, which is the size of the clique, to every outgoing edge at v_{i+2}. Note that the weight of 4 is obtained by adding one to the maximum among weights of incoming edges at v_{i+2}.

Consider any vertex v_k (see Figure 6.21(b)). Assume that the weight on every incoming edge at v_k has already been assigned. For every outgoing edge (v_k, v_l) at v_k, find the maximum among weights on those incoming edges at v_k that have formed valid pairs with (v_k, v_l), add one to the maximum weight, and assign the weight to (v_k, v_l). In this method, weights on all outgoing edges at v_k are assigned. By traversing $C(v_{i+1}, v_{i-1})$ in counterclockwise order, weights are assigned to all edges in G_i. We have the following lemma.

Lemma 6.7.6 *The size of the maximum clique in G_i is the same as the largest weight among weights on edges of G_i.*

Exercise 6.7.3 *Prove Lemma 6.7.6.*

Let (v_k, v_l) be an edge in G_i with the maximum weight. Starting from (v_k, v_l), all vertices of the maximum clique in G_i can be located by traversing backward as follows. Without loss of generality, (v_k, v_l) is considered as an outgoing edge at v_k. Let MC denote the ordered set of vertices of the maximum clique in G_i from v_l to v_i. Initialize MC by adding v_l and v_k to MC. Locate an incoming edge at v_k (say, (v_p, v_k)) such that (v_k, v_l) has formed a valid pair with (v_p, v_k) at v_k, and the weight on (v_p, v_k) is one less than that of (v_k, v_l). Add v_p to MC as it is the next vertex of v_k in MC. In the same way, the next vertex of v_p in MC can again be found by locating an appropriate incoming edge at v_p. The process is repeated till v_i is added to MC. Thus all vertices of MC can be located using weights on edges of G_i and valid pairs of edges in G_i. We have the following lemma.

Exercise 6.7.4 *Write the procedure for locating the maximum clique in the visibility graph G_i of a convex fan F_i under the assumption that there exists cross-visibility across every edge connecting a vertex of $C(v_{i+2}, v_{i-2})$ to the fan vertex v_i.*

Lemma 6.7.7 *The vertices of the maximum clique MC in G_i can be located $O(E)$ time.*

Proof. We first show that the time complexity of assigning weights to all outgoing edges at any vertex v_k is proportional to the degree of v_k. Assume that the weight on every incoming edge at v_k has already been assigned. Consider the outgoing edges at v_k in counterclockwise order starting from (v_k, v_{k+1}). Also consider the incoming edges of v_k in counterclockwise order starting from (v_i, v_k). Consider the first outgoing edge (v_k, v_{k+1}). Let (v_p, v_k) be the incoming edge of v_k such that (v_p, v_{k+1}) is an edge in G_i but the next incoming edge of v_k does not form a valid pair with (v_k, v_{k+1}). While considering incoming edges of v_k from (v_i, v_k) to (v_p, v_k), the procedure can compute the maximum among weights on these edges, which gives the weight of (v_k, v_{k+1}). For assigning the weight on the next outgoing edge of (v_k, v_{k+1}), it is enough to consider the incoming edges of v_k from (v_p, v_k) rather than from (v_i, v_k) (see Lemma 6.7.5). In this process, weights on all outgoing edges of v_k can be computed in time proportional to the degree of v_k. Therefore, assigning weights to all outgoing edges at v_k for all k takes $O(E)$ time. Since vertices of MC can also be located in $O(E)$ time by scanning backward starting from an edge of G_i with maximum weight, the maximum clique MC in G_i can be computed in $O(E)$ time. $\qquad \square$

In the following, we state the major steps for locating the vertices of the maximum clique in the given visibility graph G.

Step 1. Construct $G_1, G_2, \ldots, G_n$ from G.

Step 2. Initialize the set S to empty. *For* every graph G_i, partition G_i into sub-graphs using cross-visibility and add them to S.

Step 3. *For* every sub-graph Q in S, *if* Q is not the visibility graph of a convex fan *then* decompose Q into visibility graphs of convex fans and replace Q by these decomposed sub-graphs in S.

Step 4. *For* each sub-graph Q of S, assign weights on edges of Q using valid pairs of edges and locate the vertices of the maximum clique in Q from the weighted sub-graph Q.

Step 5. Choose the largest clique among the maximum cliques in sub-graphs of S and assign the clique as the maximum clique in G.

Step 6. Output the maximum clique in G and Stop.

The correctness of the algorithm follows from Lemmas 6.7.1, 6.7.4, 6.7.5 and 6.7.6. Let us analyze the time complexity of the algorithm. Step 1 takes $O(nE)$ time as each sub-graph can be constructed in $O(E)$ time. By Lemma 6.7.3, G_i can be partitioned in $O(E)$ time and therefore, partitioning $G_1, G_2, \ldots, G_n$ in Step 2 takes $O(nE)$ time. After the decomposition in Step 3, there can be at most $O(n^2)$ sub-graphs in S due to Corollary 6.7.2. So, Step 3 can be executed in $O(n^2E)$ time. By Lemma 6.7.7, the maximum clique in a sub-graph of S can be computed in $O(E)$ time and there are $O(n^2)$ sub-graphs in S. So, Step 4 takes $O(n^2E)$ time. Hence, the overall time complexity of the algorithm is $O(n^2E)$. We summarize the result in the following theorem.

Theorem 6.7.8 *Assume that the visibility graph G of a simple polygon is given along with the Hamiltonian cycle in G corresponding to the boundary of the polygon. The maximum clique in G can be computed in $O(n^2E)$ time, where n and E denote the number of vertices and edges of G.*

6.8 Computing Maximum Hidden Vertex Set in a Visibility Graph

In this section, we present an $O(nE)$ time algorithm given by Ghosh *et al.* [167] for computing the maximum hidden vertex set in the visibility graph G of a convex fan F, where n and E denote the number of vertices and edges of G. A maximum *hidden vertex set* in G is the set of maximum number of vertices in which no two vertices are neighbors in G. Assume that the Hamiltonian cycle C in G corresponding to the boundary of F is given along with G. We also assume that the vertices of C are labeled $v_1, v_2, \ldots, v_n$ in counterclockwise order. Let v_i be a vertex of G such that all vertices G are neighbors of v_i, and (v_{i-1}, v_{i+1}) is an edge in G. We take v_i as the fan vertex of F.

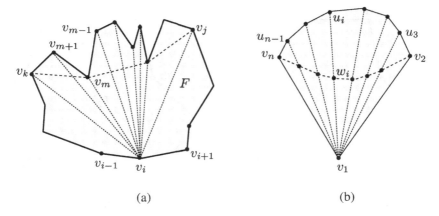

(a) (b)

Figure 6.22 (a) The vertex v_m is the next vertex of v_k in the Euclidean shortest path between v_j and v_k in F. (b) The vertex v_i is placed either at u_i or w_i to construct convex fans with v_1 as the fan vertex.

Recall that for any two vertices v_j and v_k, $C(v_j, v_k)$ denotes the portion of C in counterclockwise order from v_j to v_k. Assume that $v_j \in C(v_i, v_k)$. If $(v_j, v_k) \in G$, then both v_j and v_k cannot be in a hidden vertex set in G. If (v_j, v_k) is not an edge in G, then both v_j and v_k can be in a hidden vertex set in G. Suppose, there exists a vertex $v_m \in C(v_j, v_k)$ such that $(v_k, v_m) \in G$ and no vertex of $C(v_j, v_{m-1})$ is a neighbor of v_k in G. This implies that the the Euclidean shortest path between v_j and v_k in F passes through v_m, and v_m is the next vertex of v_k in the path (see Figure 6.22(a)). Using this property, the maximum hidden vertex set in $C(v_j, v_k)$ (denoted as $H(v_j, v_k)$) can be located by the following lemma of Ghosh *et al.* [163] (after a minor modification). Let $|H(v_j, v_k)|$ denote the number of vertices of $H(v_j, v_k)$.

Lemma 6.8.1 *For any two vertices v_j and v_k of G where $v_k \in C(v_j, v_{i-1})$, $|H(v_j, v_k)| = \max(|H(v_j, v_{m-1})| + |H(v_{m+1}, v_k)|, |H(v_j, v_{k-1})|)$, where $(v_m, v_k) \in G$ and no vertex of $C(v_j, v_{m-1})$ is a neighbor of v_k in G.*

Proof. If v_k does not belong to $H(v_j, v_k)$, then $H(v_j, v_k) = H(v_j, v_{k-1})$. If $v_k \in H(v_j, v_k)$, then $H(v_j, v_k)$ does not contain v_m as $(v_k, v_m) \in G$. Since no vertex of $C(v_j, v_{m-1})$ is a neighbor of any vertex of $C(v_{m+1}, v_k)$ in G, $H(v_j, v_k) = H(v_j, v_{m-1})$ $\cup H(v_{m+1}, v_k)$. So, $|H(v_j, v_k)| = \max(|H(v_j, v_{m-1})| + |H(v_{m+1}, v_k)|, |H(v_j, v_{k-1})|)$. □

Using the above lemma, $|H(v_j, v_k)|$ can be computed for all pairs of v_j and v_k in $C(v_{i+1}, v_{i-1})$. Let $|H(v_p, v_q)|$ be the largest in G for some pair of vertices v_p and v_q. Vertices in $H(v_p, v_q)$ are located by scanning C in clockwise order from v_q to v_p. The overall time complexity of the algorithm is $O(nE)$ as the algorithm takes $O(E)$ time for every vertex v_j. We summarize the result in the following theorem.

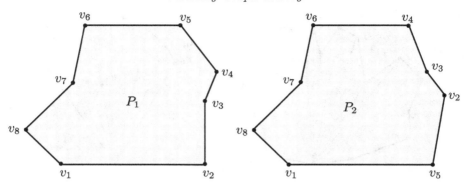

Figure 6.23 Two simple polygons are not similar but their visibility graphs are isomorphic.

Theorem 6.8.2 *Assume that the visibility graph G of a convex fan is given along with the Hamiltonian cycle in G corresponding to the boundary of the fan. The maximum hidden vertex set in G can be computed in $O(nE)$ time, where n and E denote the number of vertices and edges of G.*

> **Exercise 6.8.1** *Design an $O(n^2)$ time algorithm for computing the maximum hidden vertex set in a simple polygon P of n vertices, where P is weakly visible from one of its convex edges [163].*

6.9 Notes and Comments

In Section 6.7, it was shown that the problem of computing the maximum clique in a visibility graph G can be solved in polynomial time. However, the algorithm needs an additional input in the form of a Hamiltonian cycle. Can this problem be solved in polynomial time without any additional information? The algorithm presented in Section 6.8 is for computing the maximum hidden vertex set in the visibility graph of a very special class of polygons. Can this problem be solved for the visibility graph G of other classes of simple polygons in polynomial time if the Hamiltonian cycle in G corresponding to the boundary of the polygon is given along with G?

Two graphs $G_1 = (V_1, E_1)$ and $G_2 = (V_2, E_2)$ are *isomorphic* if and only if there is a bijection f that maps vertices of V_1 to vertices of V_2 such that an edge $(u, w) \in E_1$ if and only if the edge $(f(u), f(w)) \in E_2$. We show that the number of non-isomorphic visibility graphs of simple polygons of n vertices can be exponential. Construct convex fans of n vertices $v_1, v_2 \ldots v_n$ (in counterclockwise order) with v_1 as the fan vertex as follows (see Figure 6.22(b)). Let $u_2, u_3, u_4, \ldots u_n$ be a convex chain of points in counterclockwise order. Mark u_2 and u_n as v_2 and v_n, respectively. Connect v_1 with v_2 by an edge. Similarly, connect v_1 with v_n by an edge. For all i between 3 and $n-1$, take a point w_i on the segment $v_i u_i$ such that $w_3, w_4, \ldots w_{n-1}$ form a chain of reflex points facing v_1. For every vertex v_i of $2 < i < n$, place v_i

either at u_i or w_i and connect v_i to v_{i-1} by an edge. Finally, connect v_n to v_{n-1} by an edge to complete the construction of the fan. So, the number of convex fans that can be constructed in this way by all possible combinations of two positions of $v_3, v_4 \ldots v_{n-1}$ is 2^{n-3}. However, the visibility graph of each fan in this family of 2^{n-3} fans is isomorphic to the visibility graph of one other fan in the family due to symmetry. Therefore, there are 2^{n-4} convex fans in this family that have non-isomorphic visibility graphs. We have the following lemma.

Lemma 6.9.1 *The number of non-isomorphic visibility graphs of simple polygons of n vertices is at least 2^{n-4}.*

Let G_1 and G_2 be the visibility graphs of simple polygons P_1 and P_2, respectively. Let C_1 (or C_2) denote the Hamiltonian cycles in G_1 (respectively, G_2) that corresponds to the boundary of P_1 (respectively, P_2). Polygons P_1 and P_2 are called *similar* if and only if there is a bijection f that maps adjacent vertices on the boundary of P_1 to that of boundary of P_2 such that $f(G_1) = G_2$ [244]. It has been shown by Avis and ElGindy [39] that the similarity of P_1 and P_2 of n vertices can be determined in $O(n^2)$ time. Therefore, given G_1 and G_2 along with C_1 and C_2, the corresponding visibility graphs similarity problem can also be solved in $O(n^2)$ time. It can be seen that the two simple polygons in Figure 6.23 are not similar but their visibility graphs are isomorphic. We have the following observation from Lin and Skiena [244].

Lemma 6.9.2 *Two simple polygons with isomorphic visibility graphs may not be similar polygons.*

Exercise 6.9.1 *Let S be a set of n disjoint line segments in the plane such that one endpoint of every segment of S belongs to the convex hull of S. Design an $O(n \log n)$ time algorithm for computing a simple polygon P (if it exists) such that all segments of S appear as edges of P and the remaining edges of P are visible segments between the endpoints of S [293].*

7

Visibility and Link Paths

7.1 Problems and Results

Assume that a point-robot moves in straight-line paths inside a polygonal region P. Every time it has to change its direction of the path, it stops and rotates until it directs itself to the new direction. In the process, it makes several turns before reaching its destination. If straight line motions are 'cheap' but rotations are 'expensive', minimizing the number of turns reduces the cost of the motion although it may increase the length of the path. This motivates the study of link paths inside a polygonal region P. For more details on applications of such paths, see the review article of Maheshwari *et al.* [253].

A *link path* between two points s and t of a polygon P (with or without holes) is a path inside P that connects s and t by a chain of line segments (called *links*). A *minimum link path* between s and t is a link path connecting s and t that has the minimum number of links (see Figure 7.1). Observe that there may be several link paths between s and t with the minimum number of links. The *link distance* between any two points of P is the number of links in the minimum link path between them.

The problem of computing the minimum link path between any two points inside a simple polygon were first studied by ElGindy [126] and Suri [318]. Using weak visibility, Suri gave an $O(n)$ time algorithm for this problem [318, 319] which we present in Section 7.2.1. Using a different method involving complete visibility, Ghosh [155, 156] later gave an alternative algorithm for this problem which also runs in $O(n)$ time. In Section 7.2.2, we present Ghosh's algorithm. One of the steps of Ghosh's algorithm was simplified by Hershberger and Snoeyink [188] and this is also presented in Section 7.2.2. For this problem in a polygon with holes, Mitchell *et al.* [262] gave an algorithm that runs in $O(E\alpha(n)\log^2 n)$ time and $O(E)$ space, where E is the number of edges in the visibility graph of the polygon and $\alpha(n)$ is the inverse Ackermann function. We present their algorithm in Section 7.3.

Suri [318, 319] showed that minimum link paths from a point s to all vertices of a simple polygon can also be computed in $O(n)$ time. For this problem in a

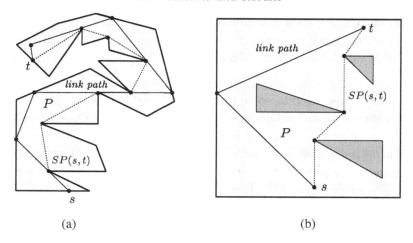

Figure 7.1 A minimum link path and the Euclidean shortest path between two points s and t are shown (a) inside a simple polygon and (b) inside a polygon with holes.

polygon with holes, Mitchell *et al.* [262] presented an algorithm that runs in $O((E + ln)^{2/3}n^{2/3}l^{1/3}\log^{3.11} n + E\log^3 n)$ time and $O(E)$ space, where l is the length of the longest link path from s to any vertex of the polygon.

The *link diameter* of a simple polygon P is the maximum link distance between any two points inside P. The link distance between s and t in Figure 7.1(a) is the link diameter of the polygon. Since there always exists a pair of vertices in P such that their link distance is the diameter of P, the link diameter of P can be computed in $O(n^2)$ time by computing minimum link paths in $O(n)$ time from each vertex to all other vertices of P. Using an involved method, Suri [319] showed that the link diameter of P can be computed in $O(n\log n)$ time. Suri [320] also presented an algorithm for computing an approximate link diameter of P which can be less than the link diameter of P by at most two links.

Consider any point w inside P. Let r_w denote the maximum among link distances between w and any point of P. For every other point u in P, if $r_u \geq r_w$, then r_w is called the *link radius* of P. The set of all such points w in P is called the *link center* of P. Lenhart *et al.* [241] gave an $O(n^2)$ time algorithm for computing the link center and link radius of P. We present their algorithm in Section 7.4. Consider the problem of locating a diagonal v_iv_j in a triangulation of P such that the maximum link distance from v_iv_j to any point of P is minimized. Note that v_iv_j may not always intersect the link center of P. However, it lies very close to the link center of P. Using a central diagonal of P, Djidjev *et al.* [111] showed that the link center and link radius of P can be computed in $O(n\log n)$ time. It is still open whether the link center of P can be computed in $O(n)$ time.

A simple polygon P is said to be *k-visible* if there exists a segment st inside P such that the link distance from each point on st to any point of P is at most k.

The problem of locating such a segment st inside P for the smallest k is called the *k-visibility problem*. With the help of a central diagonal of P and the link center of P, this problem can be solved in $O(n \log n)$ time by the algorithm of Aleksandrov *et al.* [16].

Link paths have been used to solve minimum nested polygon problems. A polygon K is called *nested* between two given simple polygons P and Q, where $Q \subset P$, when it circumscribes Q and is inscribed in P (i.e. $Q \subset K \subset P$). The problem here is to compute a nested polygon K with the minimum number of vertices. If both P and Q are convex, Aggarwal *et al.* [12] gave an $O(n \log k)$ algorithm for computing a minimum nested polygon K, where n is the total number of vertices of P and Q, and k is the number of vertices of K. We present their algorithm in Section 7.5.1. If P or Q is not convex, K can still be a convex polygon. Ghosh [155] presented an $O(n)$ time algorithm to determine whether K is a convex polygon. When K is a convex polygon, Wang [336] and Wang and Chan [337] showed that the algorithm of Aggarwal *et al.* [12] can be used to compute K after pruning some regions of P; they presented an $O(n \log n)$ algorithm for pruning P. Using the notion of complete visibility, Ghosh [155] showed that the pruning of P can be done in $O(n)$ time and therefore, a minimum nested convex polygon K can be computed in $O(n \log k)$ time. If K is not a convex polygon, Ghosh and Maheshwari [159] presented an $O(n)$ time for computing such K. We present their algorithm in Section 7.5.2 along with the algorithm of Ghosh [155] for determining whether K is a non-convex polygon. For special classes of polygons, Dasgupta and Veni Madhavan [104] presented approximation algorithms for computing nested polygons. Bhadury *et al.* [46] studied the problem of computing nested polygons in the context of art gallery problems.

Alsuwaiyel and Lee [17] proved that the problem of computing a minimum link path between a pair of points inside a simple polygon such that the entire polygon is weakly visible from the link path is NP-hard. They gave an $O(n^2)$ time approximation algorithm for this problem and the link path computed by the approximation algorithm is at most thrice the optimal. Alsuwaiyel and Lee [18] also gave approximation algorithms for a minimum link path watchman route in simple polygons. This problem for a polygon with holes has been studied by Arkin *et al.* [22]. A *watchman route* in a polygon is a polygonal path such the every point of the polygon is visible from some point on the path.

Guibas *et al.* [179] studied the problem of simplifying a polygon or polygonal subdivision using the minimum number of links. They showed that approximating subdivisions and approximating with simple chains are NP-hard. They also suggested approximation algorithms for some variation of the problem.

Link paths of a given homotopy class were studied by Hershberger and Snoeyink [188]. Two link paths between the same pair of points are said to be *homotopic* if there is a continuous function that maps one path to the other. The problem of minimizing both the length and the number of links in a path was studied by Arkin *et al.* [23] and Mitchell *et al.* [261]. Kahan and Snoeyink [206] studied the bit complexity of link distance problems for a computational model with finite precision arithmetic.

Link path problems have also been studied for rectilinear polygons. A polygon P is said to be *rectilinear* if the edges of P are aligned with a pair of orthogonal coordinate axes. In other words, P is a rectilinear polygon if the internal angle at every vertex of P is $90°$ or $270°$. Link paths in a rectilinear polygon P are rectilinear paths as the links in the path are parallel to edges of P. De Berg [108] presented an $O(n)$ time algorithm for computing a minimum rectilinear link path between any two points in a rectilinear polygon P without holes. He also showed that the rectilinear link diameter of P can be computed in $O(n \log n)$ time. Later, Nilsson and Schuierer [267] presented an $O(n)$ time algorithm for this problem. Nilsson and Schuierer [268] also presented an $O(n)$ time algorithm for computing the rectilinear link center of P. Das and Narasimhan [102] presented an $O(n \log n)$ time algorithm for computing a minimum rectilinear link path between any two points in a polygon with rectilinear holes. Maheshwari and Sack [252] gave $O(n)$ time algorithms for nested polygon problems in rectilinear polygons. The problem of computing a watchman tour in rectilinear polygons was studied by Kranakis *et al.* [222]. Rectilinear polygons can be viewed as a special case of *c*-oriented polygons, where edges are parallel to a fixed set of *c* orientations. Link paths in *c*-oriented polygons were studied by Hershberger and Snoeyink [188] and Adegeest *et al.* [5].

7.2 Computing Minimum Link Paths in Simple Polygons

7.2.1 Using Weak Visibility: $O(n)$ Algorithm

In this section, we present an $O(n)$ time algorithm of Suri [318] for computing a minimum link path between two given points s and t inside a simple polygon P. We assume that the vertices of P are labeled $v_1, v_2, \ldots, v_n$ in counterclockwise order. Let $MLP(s,t)$ denote a minimum link path between s and t in P.

Exercise 7.2.1 *Let s and t be two points inside a simple polygon P of n vertices. Let u_1 and d_1 be the boundary points of P such that the segment u_1d_1 lies inside P. Cut P into two sub-polygons using u_1d_1. Design an $O(n)$ time algorithm to determine whether s and t belong to the same or different sub-polygons of P.*

Compute the visibility polygon $V(s)$ of P from s by the algorithm of Lee [230] (see Section 2.2.1). It can be seen that $V(s)$ is the set of all points of P that can be reached by one link from s (see Figure 7.2). If $t \in V(s)$, then the segment st is the

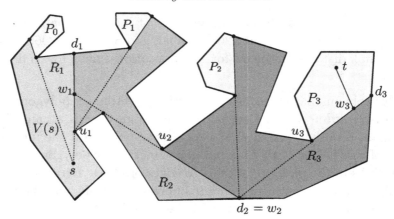

Figure 7.2 Every $MLP(s,t)$ intersects $u_1 d_1$, $u_2 d_2$ and $u_3 d_3$, which are constructed edges of visibility polygons R_1, R_2 and R_3, respectively.

minimum link path from s to t. Let us denote the region $V(s)$ as R_1 and P as P_0. We have the following lemma.

Lemma 7.2.1 *The visibility polygon of P_0 from s is the set R_1 of all points of P_0 that can be reached from s by one link.*

Consider the other situation when t cannot be reached from s by one link. Since $t \in P_0 - R_1$, every $MLP(s,t)$ must intersect a constructed edge of R_1 in order to reach t. In fact, every $MLP(s,t)$ intersects the same constructed edge (say, $u_1 d_1$) of R_1 (see Figure 7.2), as P is a closed and bounded region. However, they intersect at different points of $u_1 d_1$. We have the following lemma.

Lemma 7.2.2 *There exists a $MLP(s,t)$ such that the first turning point of the $MLP(s,t)$ lies on the constructed edge $u_1 d_1$.*

Proof. Consider any $MLP(s,t)$. Let w_1 be the point of intersection of $u_1 d_1$ and $MLP(s,t)$. So, the path of $MLP(s,t)$ between s and w_1 can be replaced by the link sw_1 to construct another $MLP(s,t)$ whose first turning point is w_1. □

Let us identify the constructed edge $u_1 d_1$ among all constructed edges of R_1. Remove R_1 from P_0 and it splits P_0 into sub-polygons. Identify the sub-polygon (say, P_1) containing t. So, the constructed edge of R_1, which is on the boundary of P_1, is $u_1 d_1$.

The problem is now to locate the first turning point w_1 on $u_1 d_1$. Let us compute the set of all points R_2 of P_1 that can be reached from s by two links (see Figure 7.2). In other words, R_2 is the set of all points of P_1 that can be reached by one link from some point of $u_1 d_1$. It can be seen that R_2 is the weak visibility polygon of P_1 from $u_1 d_1$. Compute R_2. If $t \in R_2$, take any point on $u_1 d_1$ as w_1 such that tw_1 is a link lying inside R_2. So, $MLP(s,t)$ consists of sw_1 and $w_1 t$. Otherwise, remove R_2 from P_1. Again, P_1 splits into sub-polygons and one of the sub-polygons of P_1 (say, P_2) contains t. Let $u_2 d_2$ be the constructed edge of R_2 such that it is an edge on the boundary of P_2. This process of locating P_i and computing R_{i+1} from the constructed edge $u_i d_i$ continues until t becomes visible from $u_{m-1} d_{m-1}$, where m is the link distance between s and t. We state the above facts in the following lemmas.

Lemma 7.2.3 *Let $u_i d_i$ be the constructed edge of R_i such that after removing R_i from P_{i-1}, $u_i d_i$ is an edge on the boundary of the sub-polygon P_i containing t. For $1 \le i < m$, every $MLP(s,t)$ intersects $u_i d_i$ and there exists a $MLP(s,t)$ whose i-th turning point lies on $u_i d_i$.*

Lemma 7.2.4 *For $1 \le i < m$, the set of all points R_{i+1} of P_i that can be reached from s by $i+1$ links is the weak visibility polygon of P_i from $u_i d_i$.*

Based on the above lemmas, we present the major steps of the algorithm for computing $MLP(s,t)$ in P_0. The index i is initialized to 1.

Step 1. Compute the visibility polygon R_i of P_{i-1} from s. *If* t is visible from s, *then* report st as $MLP(s,t)$ and *goto* Step 6.

Step 2. Locate the sub-polygon of P_{i-1} containing t and call it P_i. Locate the constructed edge of R_i on the boundary of P_i and call it $u_i d_i$.

Step 3. *If $i > 1$ then* assign the intersection point of $u_{i-1} d_{i-1}$ and $\overrightarrow{d_i u_i}$ to w_{i-1}.

Step 4. Compute the weak visibility polygon R_{i+1} of P_i from $u_i d_i$. *If* t is not visible from $u_i d_i$ *then* $i := i + 1$ and *goto* Step 2.

Step 5. Locate a point $w_i \in V(t)$ on $u_i d_i$ and report $MLP(s,t) = (sw_1, w_1 w_2, \ldots, w_i t)$.

Step 6. Stop.

Correctness of the algorithm follows from Lemmas 7.2.1, 7.2.2, 7.2.3 and 7.2.4. Let us analyze the time complexity of the algorithm. Using the algorithm of Lee [230] (see Section 2.2.1), the visibility polygons from s in Step 1 can be computed in $O(n)$ time. Let us explain how to locate P_i in Step 2. Let ud be any constructed edge of R_i. We know that one of the endpoints of every constructed edge is a vertex of P. Without loss of generality, we assume that u is a vertex v_j of P. Let $v_k v_{k+1}$ be the edge of P such that $d \in v_k v_{k+1}$. Let v_p be a vertex visible from t, i.e., $v_p \in V(t)$. If ud intersects tv_p, the intersection point becomes w_i. Otherwise, by comparing j, k, p, the portion of the boundary of P_{i-1} forming the boundary of P_i can be determined. Once P_i is known, the constructed edge of R_i associated with P_i becomes $u_i d_i$. Therefore, by spending $O(1)$ time for each constructed edge of R_i, $u_i d_i$ can be located. Since there can be only one constructed edge for every reflex vertex of P, Step 2 can be executed in $O(n)$ time. The running time of Step 4 is $O(n)$ as each visibility polygon R_{i+1} from $u_i d_i$ can be computed in time proportional to the number of vertices of R_{i+1} as follows.

Compute the shortest path tree $SPT(s)$ in P_0 rooted at s in $O(n)$ time by the algorithm of Guibas *et al.* [178] (see Section 3.6.1) and then compute the shortest path map $SPM(s)$ in $O(n)$ time by the algorithm of Hershberger [186] (see Section 5.2). It can be seen that vertices of R_1 are children of s in $SPT(s)$ and $u_1 d_1$ is an extension edge of $SPM(s)$. Assume that u_1 is a vertex of P_0 and d_1 is a point on the boundary of P_0. Take the sub-tree $SPT(u_1)$ of $SPT(s)$ rooted at u_1 and compute $SPT(d_1)$ by shifting the root from u_1 to d_1 as in the algorithm of Hershberger [186]. It follows from Lemma 5.2.1 that vertices of R_2 are only those vertices of P_1 whose parents in $SPT(u_1)$ and $SPT(d_1)$ are different. Since $SPT(u_1)$ and $SPT(d_1)$ are the same in $R_3, R_4, \ldots, R_{m-1}$, the time taken for locating vertices of R_2 is proportional to the number of vertices of R_2. Compute $SPM(d_1)$. It follows from Lemma 5.2.2 that constructed edges of R_2 are extension edges of $SPM(u_1)$ and $SPM(d_1)$. Repeating this process of computations for $u_2 d_2, u_3 d_3, \ldots u_{m-1} d_{m-1}$, weak visibility polygons $R_3, R_4, \ldots, R_{m-1}$ can be computed in a total time of $O(n)$. Note that whether or not t belongs to R_{i+1} can be determined in time proportional to the size of R_{i+1}. Hence the overall time complexity of the algorithm is $O(n)$. We summarize the result in the following theorem.

Theorem 7.2.5 *A minimum link path between two given points inside a simple polygon of n vertices can be computed in $O(n)$ time.*

Exercise 7.2.2 *Design an $O(n)$ time algorithm for computing minimum link paths from a given point inside a simple polygon P to all vertices of P [318, 319].*

7.2.2 Using Complete Visibility: $O(n)$ Algorithm

In this section, we present an alternative algorithm given by Ghosh [155, 156] for computing a minimum link path in $O(n)$ time between two given points s and t inside a simple polygon P. While presenting this algorithm, we also present the simplification suggested by Hershberger and Snoeyink [188] for one of the steps of Ghosh's algorithm.

Let $SP(s,t) = (s, u_1, ..., u_k, t)$. We know that $SP(s,t)$ can be computed in $O(n)$ time by the algorithm of Lee and Preparata [235] (see Section 3.6.1), once P is triangulated in $O(n)$ time by the algorithm of Chazelle [71] (see Theorem 1.4.6). From now on, we assume that P is given along with a triangulation of P. An edge $u_j u_{j-1}$ of $SP(s,t)$ is called *eave* if u_{j-2} and u_{j+1} lie on the opposite sides of the

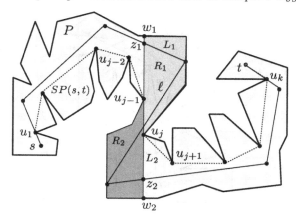

Figure 7.3 The portion of the link path L_1 between z_1 and z_2 can be replaced by the segment $z_1 z_2$.

line passing through u_j and u_{j-1} (see Figure 7.3). If an edge $u_k u_{k+1}$ of $SP(s,t)$ is a sub-segment of a link in a link path, we say that the link path contains $u_k u_{k+1}$. We have the following lemma on eaves of $SP(s,t)$.

Lemma 7.2.6 *There exists a minimum link path between s and t that contains all eaves of $SP(s,t)$.*

Proof. Consider a minimum link path L_1 between s and t such that L_1 does not contain an eave $u_{j-1} u_j$ of $SP(s,t)$. Let w_1 and w_2 be the closest points among the intersection points of $bd(P)$ with $\overrightarrow{u_j u_{j-1}}$ and $\overrightarrow{u_{j-1} u_j}$ respectively (see Figure 7.3). So $w_1 w_2$ partitions P into four disjoint regions and two of these regions (say R_1 and R_2) do not contain s or t. Since P is a closed and bounded region, there exists a link ℓ in L_1 with one endpoint in R_1 and the other endpoint in R_2 as every link path from s must intersect $u_{j-1} u_j$ in order to reach t. Let z_1 and z_2 be the intersection points of L_1 with $u_{j-1} w_1$ and $u_j w_2$, respectively. A new link path L_2 can be constructed from L_1 by removing the portion of L_1 between z_1 and z_2, and adding the segment $z_1 z_2$. This modification has removed ℓ totally and therefore, L_2 is a minimum link path between s and t containing the eave $u_{j-1} u_j$. If there exists another eave $u_{i-1} u_i$ that is not contained in L_2, remove the portion of L_2 as before to construct another minimum link path L_3 between s and t containing both eaves $u_{j-1} u_j$ and $u_{i-1} u_i$. By repeating this process, a minimum link path between s and t can be constructed that contains all eaves of $SP(s,t)$. $\square$

The above lemma suggests a procedure for constructing a minimum link path between s and t in P.

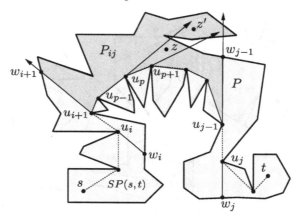

Figure 7.4 The construction of the sub-polygon P_{ij}.

(i) Decompose P into sub-polygons by extending each eave from both ends to $bd(P)$.

(ii) If two consecutive extensions intersect at a point z, then z is a turning point of the minimum link path between s and t.

(iii) Construct minimum link paths connecting the extensions of every pair of consecutive eaves on $SP(s,t)$ to form a minimum link path between s and t.

Let us consider one such sub-polygon between the non-intersecting extensions of two consecutive eaves $u_i u_{i+1}$ and $u_{j-1} u_j$ of $SP(s,t)$ (see Figure 7.4). Let w_{i+1} and w_{j-1} be the extension points on $bd(P)$ of the eaves $u_i u_{i+1}$ and $u_{j-1} u_j$, respectively. Since w_{i+1} and w_{j-1} belong to the counterclockwise boundary of P from u_j to u_i (i.e., $bd(u_j, u_i)$), they can be computed by checking the intersection of $\overrightarrow{u_i u_{i+1}}$ and $\overrightarrow{u_j u_{j-1}}$ with the edges on $bd(u_j, u_i)$. This means that the extension points of all eaves of $SP(s,t)$ can be computed in $O(n)$ time. Let P_{ij} denote the sub-polygon bounded by $bd(w_{j-1}, w_{i+1})$, the segment $w_{i+1} u_{i+1}$, $SP(u_{i+1}, u_{j-1})$ and the segment $u_{j-1} w_{j-1}$. Note that since $SP(u_{i+1}, u_{j-1})$ does not contain any eave, no vertex of $bd(w_{j-1}, w_{i+1})$ belongs to $SP(u_{i+1}, u_{j-1})$, and therefore, P_{ij} is a simple sub-polygon.

Let L_{ij} denote a minimum link path from a point on $u_{i+1} w_{i+1}$ to some point on $u_{j-1} w_{j-1}$. A link path is called *convex* if it makes only left or only right turns at every turning point in the path. It has been observed by Ghosh [155] that L_{ij} is a convex path inside P_{ij} and this has been proved formally by Chandru *et al.* [69]. We prove this observation in the following lemma.

Lemma 7.2.7 *A minimum link path L_{ij} is a convex path inside P_{ij}.*

Proof. Without loss of generality, we assume that $SP(u_{i+1}, u_{j-1})$ makes a right turn at every vertex in the path (see Figure 7.5). Let $L_{ij} = (z_1 z_2, ..., z_{q-1} z_q)$, where

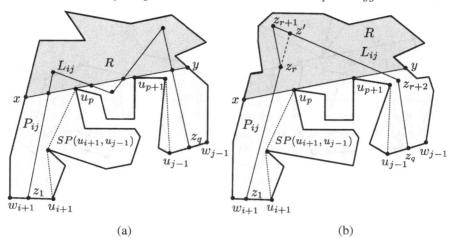

(a) (b)

Figure 7.5 (a) The segment xy intersects L_{ij} at four points. (b) L_{ij} makes a left turn at z_r.

$z_1 \in u_{i+1}w_{i+1}$ and $z_q \in u_{j-1}w_{j-1}$. To prove the lemma, it suffices to show that L_{ij} makes a right turn at turning points z_2, z_3, ..., z_{q-1} while it is traversing from z_1 to z_q.

Consider an edge $u_p u_{p+1}$ of $SP(u_{i+1}, u_{j-1})$ (see Figure 7.5). Let x and y denote the closest points of intersection on $bd(w_{j-1}, w_{i+1})$ with $\overrightarrow{u_{p+1}u_p}$ and $\overrightarrow{u_p u_{p+1}}$ respectively. Let R denote the region of P_{ij} bounded by xy and $bd(y, x)$. If L_{ij} intersects xy at three or more points (Figure 7.5(a)) or R contains three or more turning points of L_{ij}, then the number of links in L_{ij} can be reduced using xy, contradicting its minimality. So, we assume that L_{ij} intersects xy at two points and R contains at most two turning points (say, z_r and z_{r+1}) of L_{ij} (see Figure 7.5(b)). If L_{ij} makes a left turn at z_r, then extend the link $z_{r-1}z_r$ from z_r meeting the link $z_{r+1}z_{r+2}$ at a point z'. It means that there exists another link path $z_1 z_2, \ldots, z_{r-1}z'$, $z'z_{r+2}, \ldots, z_{q-1}z_q$, which has one link less that L_{ij}, and this is a contradiction. So, L_{ij} makes a right turn at z_r. Analogous arguments show that L_{ij} also makes a right turn at z_{r+1}. Since every turning point of L_{ij} lies in one such region of P_{ij} corresponding to an edge of $SP(u_{i+1}, u_{j-1})$, L_{ij} makes a right turn at z_2, z_3, ..., z_{q-1}.

The above arguments also show that L_{ij} does not cross any edge of $SP(u_{i+1}, u_{j-1})$ and therefore, it remains inside P_{ij}. $\square$

In order to compute a convex link path L_{ij}, we need the definitions of left and right tangents from a point $z \in P_{ij}$ to $SP(u_{i+1}, u_{j-1})$. The segment zu_p is called the *left tangent* (or *right tangent*) of z at the vertex $u_p \in SP(u_{i+1}, u_{j-1})$ (see Figure 7.4) if zu_p lies inside P_{ij} and z lies to the right of $\overrightarrow{u_{p-1}u_p}$ (respectively, $\overrightarrow{u_p u_{p-1}}$) and to the left of $\overrightarrow{u_p u_{p+1}}$ (respectively, $\overrightarrow{u_{p+1}u_p}$). Note that for all points $z' \in P_{ij}$ that lie to the right of $\overrightarrow{u_{p-1}u_p}$ and to the left of $\overrightarrow{u_p u_{p+1}}$, $z'u_p$ may not be the left tangent of

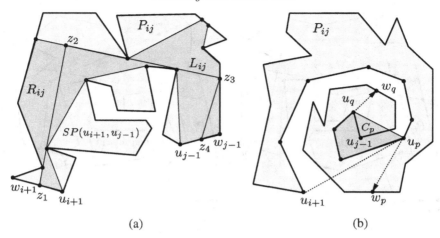

Figure 7.6 (a) The greedy path z_1z_2, z_2z_3, z_3z_4 inside P_{ij} is a minimum link path connecting $u_{i+1}w_{i+1}$ to $u_{j-1}w_{j-1}$. (b) The convex set C_p is the region enclosed by $SP(u_p, u_q)$ and the segment u_pu_q.

z' if the segment $z'u_p$ does not lie inside P_{ij}. So, some points of P_{ij} may not have the left or right tangent to $SP(u_i, u_j)$. We have the following lemma.

Lemma 7.2.8 *If a point $z \in P_{ij}$ is on a convex path between $u_{i+1}w_{i+1}$ and $u_{j-1}w_{j-1}$ inside P_{ij}, then z has both left and right tangents.*

Proof. We prove the lemma only for the left tangent of z. The proof for the right tangent of z is analogous. Let u_p be the vertex of $SP(u_{i+1}, u_{j-1})$ such that z lies to the right of $\overrightarrow{u_{p-1}u_p}$ and to the left of $\overrightarrow{u_pu_{p+1}}$. If the segment zu_p lies inside P_{ij}, then zu_p is the left tangent of z. If zu_p does not lie inside P_{ij}, it means that $bd(w_{j-1}, w_{i+1})$ has intersected zu_p. Since z belongs to a convex path between $u_{i+1}w_{i+1}$ and $u_{j-1}w_{j-1}$ inside P_{ij} by assumption, $bd(w_{j-1}, w_{i+1})$ has intersected zu_p by intersecting the convex path, which is a contradiction. So, zu_p is the left tangent of z. □

Let R_{ij} denote the set of all points of P_{ij} such that every point of R_{ij} has both left and right tangents to $SP(u_i, u_j)$ (see Figure 7.6(a)). We explain later the procedure for computing R_{ij}. Assume that R_{ij} has been computed. L_{ij} can be constructed in R_{ij} as follows (see Figure 7.6(a)). Let $z_1 \in u_{i+1}w_{i+1}$ denote the first turning point of L_{ij}. If w_{i+1} belongs to R_{ij} then $z_1 = w_{i+1}$. Otherwise, z_1 is the furthest point of u_{i+1} on $u_{i+1}w_{i+1}$ that belongs to R_{ij} (i.e., the next clockwise vertex of u_{i+1} in R_{ij}). Draw the right tangent from z_1 to $SP(u_{i+1}, u_{j-1})$ and extend the tangent until it meets the boundary of R_{ij} at some point z_2. Again, draw the right tangent from z_2 to $SP(u_{i+1}, u_{j-1})$ and extend the tangent until it meets the boundary of R_{ij} at some point z_3. Repeat this process of construction until a point z_q is found on $u_{j-1}w_{j-1}$. Thus, the greedy path z_1z_2, z_2z_3,...,$z_{q-1}z_q$ is constructed between $u_{i+1}w_{i+1}$ and $u_{j-1}w_{j-1}$. We have the following lemma.

Lemma 7.2.9 *The greedy path* z_1z_2, z_2z_3, ..., $z_{q-1}z_q$ *is a minimum link path inside* P_{ij}, *where* $z_1 \in u_{i+1}w_{i+1}$ *and* $z_p \in u_{j-1}w_{j-1}$.

Proof. Since no link of any minimum link path connecting $u_{i+1}w_{i+1}$ to $u_{j-1}w_{j-1}$ can intersect more than one of the left tangents from z_1, z_2,...,z_{q-1} to $SP(u_{i+1}, u_{j-1})$, the greedy path z_1z_2, z_2z_3, ..., $z_{q-1}z_q$ is a minimum link path. □

Considering the first and the last edge of $SP(s,t)$ as eaves on $SP(s,t)$, the greedy paths between the extensions of every pair of consecutive eaves on $SP(s,t)$ are computed and then they are connected as stated earlier to form a minimum link path between s and t.

Let us discuss the procedure for computing R_{ij}. For computing R_{ij}, the algorithm of Ghosh [155, 156] partitions P_{ij} into sub-polygons by extending some of the edges of $SP(u_{i+1}, u_{j-1})$ to the boundary of P_{ij} such that (i) no two extensions pass through the same triangle in the triangulation of P, and (ii) the portion of $SP(u_{i+1}, u_{j-1})$ in each sub-polygon (say, $SP(u_p, u_q)$) does not make a total turn of more than 2π (see Figure 7.6(b)). Treating the region enclosed by $SP(u_p, u_q)$ and the segment $u_p u_q$ as a convex set C_p, compute the complete visibility polygon from C_p of the sub-polygon of P_{ij} bounded by $u_q w_q$, $bd(w_q, w_p)$, $w_p u_p$ and $u_p u_q$ (see Figure 7.6(b)). It can be seen that the union of these complete visibility sub-polygons from such convex sets C_p is R_{ij} (see Section 3.8) and the time taken to compute R_{ij} from P_{ij} is proportional to the size of P_{ij}.

The region R_{ij} can also be computed using shortest path trees as shown by Chandru *et al.* [69]. In the following lemma, we present their main idea used in computing R_{ij} (see Figure 7.7(a)).

Lemma 7.2.10 *For any vertex* $v_i \in bd(w_{j-1}, w_{i+1})$, *the left and right tangents of* v_i *lie inside* P_{ij} *if and only if the parents of* v_i *in* $SPT(u_{i+1})$ *and* $SPT(u_{j-1})$ *are vertices of* $SP(u_{i+1}, u_{j-1})$.

Proof. If a vertex $u_p \in SP(u_{i+1}, u_{j-1})$ is the parent of v_i in $SPT(u_{i+1})$, then $v_i u_p$ is the left tangent of v_i by the definition of left tangent. Conversely, if the left tangent of v_i (say, $v_i u_p$) lies inside P_{ij}, then $v_i u_p$ is tangential to $SP(u_{i+1}, u_{j-1})$ at u_p by the definition of left tangent of v_i. Therefore, u_p is the parent of v_i in $SPT(u_{i+1})$. Analogous arguments hold for the right tangent of v_i. □

Using the above lemma, vertices of P_{ij} that belong to R_{ij} can be identified by traversing $SPT(u_{i+1})$ and $SPT(u_{j-1})$. Hence, R_{ij} can be computed in time proportional to the size of P_{ij} (see Section 3.3.2).

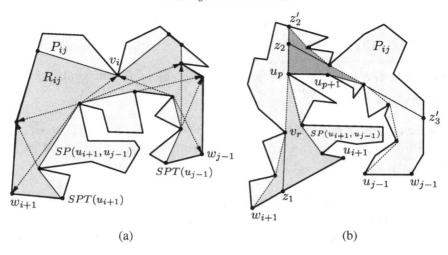

(a)   (b)

Figure 7.7 (a) The parent of each vertex of R_{ij} is a vertex of $SP(u_{i+1}, u_{j-1})$ in both $SPT(u_{i+1})$ and $SPT(u_{j-1})$. (b) The vertex u_p is the last vertex of $SP(u_{i+1}, u_{j-1})$ visible from $u_{i+1}w_{i+1}$.

It has been shown by Hershberger and Snoeyink [188] that there is no need to compute R_{ij} as the greedy path $z_1 z_2, z_2 z_3, ..., z_{q-1} z_q$ connecting $u_{i+1}w_{i+1}$ to $u_{j-1}w_{j-1}$ can be computed directly inside P_{ij} as follows. Let u_p be the vertex of $SP(u_{i+1}, u_{j-1})$ such that the first link $z_1 z_2$ passes through u_p (see Figure 7.7(b)). Let us explain how u_p can be identified. Since $z_1 u_p$ is the right tangent of z_1, each vertex of $SP(u_{i+1}, u_p)$ is visible from some point of $u_{i+1}w_{i+1}$ and no vertex of $SP(u_{p+1}, u_{j-1})$ is visible from any point of $u_{i+1}w_{i+1}$. This means that while traversing $SP(u_{i+1}, u_{j-1})$ from u_{i+1} to u_{j-1}, u_p is the last vertex such that $SP(u_{i+1}, u_p)$ and $SP(w_{i+1}, u_p)$ are disjoint (see Corollary 3.2.8).

Using the triangulation of P_{ij}, compute $SP(w_{i+1}, u_{i+2})$, $SP(w_{i+1}, u_{i+3})$, ... till a vertex u_l is reached such that $SP(u_{i+1}, u_l)$ and $SP(w_{i+1}, u_l)$ are not disjoint. So, u_{l-1} is the vertex u_p. Let $v_r \in bd(w_{j-1}, w_{i+1})$ be the previous vertex of u_p in $SP(w_{i+1}, u_p)$ (see Figure 7.7(b)). Observe that if v_r is same as w_{i+1}, then $z_1 = w_{i+1}$. Otherwise, the intersection point of $\overrightarrow{u_p v_r}$ and $u_{i+1}w_{i+1}$ is the point z_1. Using the triangulation of P_{ij}, extend $z_1 u_p$ from u_p to the boundary of P_{ij} meeting it at a point z_2'. Treating $v_p z_2'$ as $u_{i+1}w_{i+1}$, z_2 can be located on $u_p z_2'$ as before. By repeating this process, the greedy path $z_1 z_2, z_2 z_3, ..., z_{q-1} z_q$ can be computed in P_{ij} without computing R_{ij}.

Observe that vertices of $SP(w_{i+1}, u_p)$ are the vertices of the convex hull of $bd(v_d, w_{i+1})$, where $v_d u_p$ is a diagonal in the triangulation of P_{ij}. It means that all vertices of $SP(w_{i+1}, u_p)$ belong to those triangles that are on the path from w_{i+1} to u_p in the dual of the triangulation of Pij. Therefore, it is enough to consider these triangles to compute $SP(w_{i+1}, u_p)$. Hence, the greedy path inside P_{ij} can be computed in time proportional to the number of vertices of P_{ij}.

In the following, we present the main steps of the algorithm for computing a minimum link path between two given points s and t inside a simple polygon P.

Step 1. Compute $SP(s, t)$ using the algorithm of Lee and Preparata [235].

Step 2. Decompose P into sub-polygons by extending each eave of $SP(s, t)$ from both ends to $bd(P)$. Also extend the first and the last edges of $SP(s, t)$ to $bd(P)$.

Step 3. In each sub-polygon of P, construct the greedy path between the extensions of the eaves.

Step 4. Connect the greedy paths using the extension of the eaves to form a minimum link path between s and t.

The correctness of the algorithm follows from Lemmas 7.2.6, 7.2.7 and 7.2.9. We have already shown that the algorithm runs in $O(n)$ time. We summarize the result in the following theorem.

Theorem 7.2.11 *A minimum link path between two given points inside a simple polygon of n vertices can be computed in $O(n)$ time.*

7.3 Computing Minimum Link Paths in Polygons with Holes

In this section, we present the algorithm of Mitchell *et al.* [262] for computing a minimum link path between two given points s and t inside a polygon P with holes. The algorithm runs in $O(E\alpha(n) \log^2 n)$ time and $O(E)$ space, where E is the number of edges in the visibility graph of P and $\alpha(n)$ is the inverse of Ackermann's function. This algorithm can be viewed as the generalization of that of Suri [318] (see Section 7.2.1). Let $MLP(s, t)$ denote a minimum link path between s and t in P.

Compute the visibility polygon $V(s)$ of P from s. This can be computed by the algorithm of Asano [27] in $O(n \log n)$ time (see Section 2.3). Observe that $V(s)$ is the set of all points of P that can be reached by one link from s (see Figure 7.8(a)). If $t \in V(s)$, then the segment st is the minimum link path from s to t. Let us denote the region $V(s)$ as R_1 and P as P_0. We have the following lemma.

Lemma 7.3.1 *The visibility polygon of P_0 from s is the set R_1 of all points of P_0 that can be reached from s by one link.*

Consider the other situation when t cannot be reached by one link. Observe that since the given polygon P_0 contains holes, removing R_1 from P_0 does not split P_0 into disjoint sub-polygons as in the case of a simple polygon and therefore, all

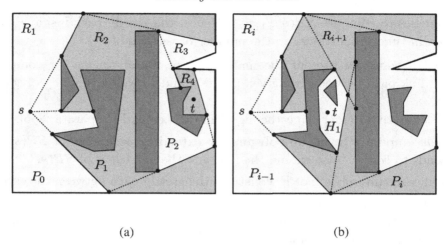

(a)   (b)

Figure 7.8 (a) The target point t can be reached from s in four links as $t \in R_4$. (b) The region H_1 is a cell formed due to the intersection of two constructed edges of R_{i+1}.

constructed edges of R_1 (denoted as E_1) are considered for computing $MLP(s,t)$, as any one of them can be intersected by $MLP(s,t)$. Let P_1 denote the region $P_0 - R_1$.

Let R_2 denote the set of all points of P_1 that can be reached from s by two links (see Figure 7.8(a)). In other words, R_2 is the set of all points of P_1 that can be reached by one link from some point of any constructed edge in E_1. It can be seen that R_2 is the union of weak visibility polygons of P_1 from constructed edges in E_1. Compute R_2. If $t \in R_2$, take any point w_1 on a constructed edge in E_1 such that tw_1 lies inside R_2. So, $MLP(s,t)$ consists of sw_1 and w_1t. Otherwise, compute R_3, which is the union of weak visibility polygons of $P_1 - R_2$ (denoted as P_2) from constructed edges of R_2 (say, E_2). This process of computing R_{i+1} in P_i from constructed edges in E_i continues till t becomes visible from a constructed edge in E_{m-1}, where m is the link distance between s and t. We have the following lemmas.

Lemma 7.3.2 *For $1 \le i < m$, the set of all points R_{i+1} of P_i that can be reached from s by $i+1$ links is the union of weak visibility polygons of P_i from constructed edges in E_i.*

Lemma 7.3.3 *For $1 \le i < m$, there exists a $MLP(s,t)$ in P_0 whose i-th turning point lies on a constructed edge in E_i.*

Once t becomes visible from some constructed edge $ud \in E_{m-1}$, turning points $w_1, w_2, \ldots, w_{m-1}$ of $MLP(s,t)$ can be located using Lemma 7.3.3 as follows. Take a point $w_{m-1} \in ud$ such that $w_{m-1}t$ lies inside R_m. Locate a point w_{m-2} on a constructed edge in E_{m-2} such that w_{m-2}, u and d are collinear and the segment

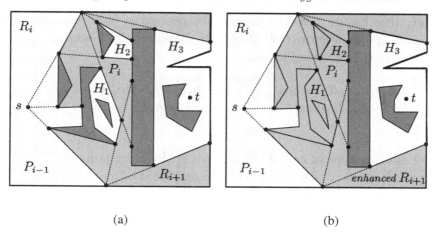

(a)   (b)

Figure 7.9 (a) Cells H_1 and H_2 do not contain t. (b) Cells H_1 and H_2 and the holes enclosed by them are included in the enhanced R_{i+1}.

$w_{m-2}w_{m-1}$ lies inside R_{m-1}. Similarly, other turning points $w_{m-3}, w_{m-4}, \ldots, w_1$ can also be located in this manner. Hence, $MLP(s,t)$ consists of links $sw_1, w_1w_2, \ldots, w_{m-1}t$.

Let us discuss the problem of computing R_{i+1} in P_i for $i \geq 1$. We know that R_{i+1} is the union of weak visibility polygons of P_i computed from every constructed edge in E_i. Suppose E_i has only one constructed edge ud. Using the algorithm of Suri and O'Rourke [321] (see Section 3.4), the weak visibility polygon $V(ud)$ of P_i from ud can be computed in $O(n^4)$ time. It has been shown by Suri and O'Rourke that there can be $O(n^2)$ constructed edges in $V(ud)$ and some of them may be intersecting each other. As a result, there can be $O(n^4)$ boundary edges of $V(ud)$. It means that for computing R_{i+2}, the weak visibility polygon has to be computed from each of the $O(n^4)$ boundary edges of $V(ud)$. The discussion suggests that a large computation time is required to carry out this process. Therefore, the construction of a full boundary representation of R_{i+1} is avoided for $i \geq 1$.

> **Exercise 7.3.1** *Let P be a polygon with holes with a total of n vertices. Draw a diagram showing that the number of constructed edges of the weak visibility polygon of P from a given segment inside P can be $O(n^4)$ [321].*

Observe that due to intersections of constructed edges of R_{i+1} among themselves, there can be several bounded regions (called *cells*) which are not visible from any constructed edge in E_i but every such region is enclosed by the points of R_{i+1}. In Figure 7.8(b), the region H_1 is a cell as it is formed due to the intersection of two constructed edges of R_{i+1}. If a cell H_1 contains t (see Figure 7.8(b)), it is enough to consider H_1 as P_{i+1} as every path from s to t intersects boundary edges of H_1 and therefore non-polygonal boundary edges of H_1 constitute E_{i+1}. If t is not contained in a cell H_1 (see Figure 7.9(a)), H_1 and the regions of holes enclosed by H_1 are included in R_{i+1} (see Figure 7.9(b)), which simplifies the boundary of R_{i+1}. We state this fact in the following lemma.

Lemma 7.3.4 *If a cell, formed in P_i due to constructed edges of R_{i+1}, does not contain t, then the cell along with the regions of holes enclosed by the cell can be added to R_{i+1}.*

Consider another type of cell H_2 that is not enclosed by points of R_{i+1} but all its non-polygonal boundary edges are parts of constructed edges of R_{i+1}. If H_2 does not contain t (see Figure 7.9(a)), it means that no $MLP(s,t)$ passes through any point of H_2 and therefore, H_2 can also be included in the enhanced R_{i+1} as Lemma 7.3.4 holds for H_2 (see Figure 7.9(b)). Since only one cell of either type contains t (see Figure 7.9(b)), all other cells can be included in R_{i+1} and therefore, the enhanced R_{i+1} becomes a simple polygon, which is denoted as Q_i. So, by enhancing R_{i+1}, a simple polygon Q_i is constructed inside P_i.

The cell in P_i containing t can be identified as follows. Construct the single face f containing t in the arrangement of constructed edges of E_{i+1} and all polygonal edges of P_i using the algorithm of Edelsbrunner *et al.* [118]. For computing a single face in an arrangement of N line segments, this algorithm takes $O(N\alpha(N)\log^2 N)$ time. Observe that the same polygonal edge can occur on the boundary of the face containing t at every iteration and therefore, the total cost becomes $O(n^2\alpha(n)\log^2 n)$ in the worst case. However, Mitchell *et al.* showed that the total cost can be reduced to $O(E\alpha(n)\log^2 n)$, where E is the number of edges in the visibility graph of P. Their algorithm first constructs the arrangement consisting of only the constructed edges in E_{i+1} along with those polygonal edges in P_i that contain the endpoints of these constructed edges in E_{i+1}, and then identifying the face in the arrangement, which is a part of f. For more details on identifying f, see the original paper.

Observe that the algorithm for computing arrangements needs only the constructed edges of R_{i+1} to locate the face f in P_i. This means that there is no need to compute the entire R_{i+1}. Later, we explain how constructed edges of R_{i+1} can be computed using the visibility graph of P without computing the region R_{i+1}.

Before the algorithm computes weak visibility polygons from the non-polygonal boundary edges of Q_i, Q_i is further simplified using the paths of minimum length between appropriate boundary points of Q_i as stated in the following lemma.

Lemma 7.3.5 *Let $chain(z_1, z_k)$ denote a portion of the boundary of Q_i such that z_1 and z_k are points on the boundary of P and all edges of $chain(z_1, z_k)$ are constructed edges of Q_i (Figure 7.10(a)). Let $mpath(z_1, z_k)$ denote the path between z_1 and z_k inside P_i of minimum length such that the region enclosed by $mpath(z_1, z_k)$ and $chain(z_1, z_k)$ lies inside P_i. If a point $y \in P_i - Q_i$ is visible from some point on $mpath(z_1, z_k)$, then y is also visible from some point on $chain(z_1, z_k)$.*

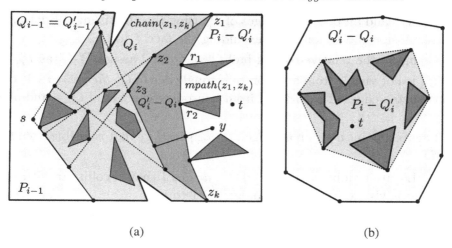

(a) (b)

Figure 7.10 (a) The region bounded by $mpath(z_1, z_k)$ and $chain(z_1, z_k)$ is added to Q_i to form the relative convex hull Q_i'. (b) The boundary of Q_i consists of only one closed chain consisting of sub-segments of constructed edges in E_{i+1}.

Exercise 7.3.2 *Prove Lemma 7.3.5.*

The above lemma suggests that by replacing each portion of non-polygonal boundary of Q_i by its corresponding $mpath$, Q_i can be modified to another simple polygon Q_i'. So, the non-polygonal edges of Q_i' can be used to compute weak visibility polygons for the next stage. The polygon Q_i' is called the *relative convex hull* of Q_i. Let us explain how $mpath(z_1, z_k)$ can be computed (see Figure 7.10(a)). Scan the edges of $chain(z_1, z_k)$ from z_1 till a point m_1 is reached such that the segment $z_1 m_1$ passes through a vertex r_1 of P_i. It can be seen that m_1 is the intersection point of $chain(z_1, z_k)$ with the boundary of the visibility polygon of P_i from z_1. So, r_1 is the next vertex of z_1 in $mpath(z_1, z_k)$. Continue the scan treating r_1 as z_1 till a point m_2 (and the vertex r_2) is located or z_k is reached. Thus, the intermediate vertices $r_1, r_2, \ldots$ of $mpath(z_1, z_k)$ can be located.

It may so happen that Q_i is bounded only by the constructed edges in E_{i+1} (see Figure 7.10(b)). In such a situation, we have only one closed chain and no point of the chain belongs to the polygonal boundary. Therefore, the boundary of Q_i' is the boundary of the convex hull of those holes that are lying inside the closed chain.

In the following, we present the major steps of the algorithm for computing $MLP(s, t)$ in P_0', where $P_0' = P$. The index i is initialized to 0.

Step 1. Compute the visibility polygon R_{i+1} of P_i' from s. If t is visible from s, report st as $MLP(s, t)$ and *goto* Step 7.

Step 2. Add the constructed edges of R_{i+1} to E_{i+1}.

Step 3. Construct the single face f containing t in the arrangement of constructed edges of E_{i+1} and all polygonal edges of P_i' using the algorithm of Edelsbrunner *et al.* [118]. Assign the region of P_i' excluding the face f to Q_i.

Step 4. Compute the relative convex hull Q_i' of Q_i and assign P_i'-Q_i' as P_{i+1}'.

Step 5. *If* t *is not visible from any non-polygonal edge of* Q_i' *then* $i := i+1$, compute all constructed edges of R_{i+1} in P_i' from non-polygon edges of Q_{i-1}' and *goto* Step 2.

Step 6. Locate a point w_{i+1} on an edge $u_{i+1}d_{i+1}$ in E_{i+1} that is visible from t. *While* $i \geq 1$ *do*

  Step 6a. Locate a point w_i on an edge $u_i d_i$ in E_i that is collinear with u_{i+1} and d_{i+1} and is visible from w_{i+1}. Assign $i - 1$ to i.

Step 7. Report $MLP(s, t) = (sw_1, w_1w_2, \ldots, w_{i+1}t)$.

Step 8. Stop.

The correctness of the algorithm follows from Lemmas 7.3.1, 7.3.2, 7.3.3, 7.3.4 and 7.3.5. Before we analyze the time complexity of the algorithm, we state a pre-processing step which allows constructed edges of all weak visibility polygons in P to be computed in $O(E)$ time. Compute the visibility graph of P in $O(n \log n + E)$ time by the algorithm of Ghosh and Mount [165] (see Section 5.3.2). This algorithm first triangulates P using plane-sweep and then constructs funnel sequences for all triangulating edges and polygonal edges in P, giving the visibility graph of P. So, by traversing a funnel sequence using the pointers CCW, CW, CCX, CX and REV, the vertices of P that are weakly visible from the base of the funnel can be located.

Let ud be a constructed edge of R_i, where d is a point on a polygonal edge $v_j v_{j+1}$ (see Figure 7.11(a)). In order to compute the constructed edges of the weak visibility polygon from ud, it is necessary to locate vertices of P visible from ud, and this can be done by traversing the funnel sequence for the base ud. On the other hand, there is no funnel sequence in the visibility graph P with ud as the base because d is not a vertex of P. So, the algorithm incorporates d as a vertex in the visibility graph of P by adding all edges dd' to the visibility graph of P, where d' is a vertex visible from d. It can be seen that all vertices of P visible from d are also weakly visible from the edge $v_j v_{j+1}$. Therefore visible vertices of d belong to the funnel sequence for $v_j v_{j+1}$, which can be located by traversing the funnel sequence for $v_j v_{j+1}$.

Observe that there can be several constructed edges that are incident on $v_j v_{j+1}$. If the non-vertex endpoint of every constructed edge incident on $v_j v_{j+1}$ is incorporated as a vertex of the visibility graph of P, it may involve repeated traversal of the same vertices of the funnel sequence for $v_j v_{j+1}$. On the other hand, we need the visibility polygons only from those non-vertex endpoints on $v_j v_{j+1}$ that are on the boundary of the relative convex hulls. Since there can be at most two such non-vertex endpoints on $v_j v_{j+1}$ that can belong to the relative convex hulls, the funnel sequence for $v_j v_{j+1}$ can be traversed at most twice. Hence the total time required to

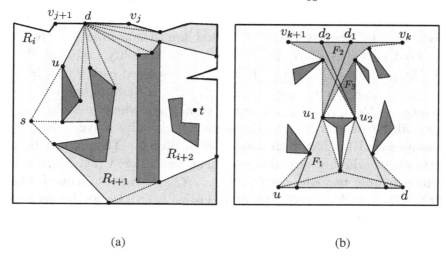

(a)   (b)

Figure 7.11 (a) The vertices of R_{i+1} visible from non-vertex endpoint d belong to the funnel sequence for $v_j v_{j+1}$. (b) The funnels F_2 and F_3 share edges of the visibility graph of P.

compute the visibility polygons from two non-vertex endpoints on every polygonal edge is $O(E)$.

Assume that the algorithm has incorporated the non-vertex endpoint d of a constructed edge ud as a vertex in the visibility graph of P (see Figure 7.11(b)). Consider a constructed edge $u_1 d_1$ of the weak visibility polygon from ud, where u_1 is a vertex of P and d_1 is a point on some polygonal edge $v_k v_{k+1}$. Observe that $u_1 d_1$ is an extension of an edge on the side of a funnel F_1 (with ud as a base) from the apex u_1 to $v_k v_{k+1}$. In fact, u_1 is also the apex of another funnel F_2 with base $v_k v_{k+1}$. This polygonal edge $v_k v_{k+1}$ can be located by traversing the visibility graph of P from the apex u_1 using pointers CCX or CX at each vertex of P in the path, (which is a side of F_2) until $v_k v_{k+1}$ is reached. Once $v_k v_{k+1}$ is located, $u_1 d_1$ can be constructed.

It may happen that another constructed edge $u_2 d_2$ of the weak visibility polygon from ud is also incident on $v_k v_{k+1}$ (see Figure 7.11(b)). Let F_3 be the funnel with the apex u_2 and the base $v_k v_{k+1}$. It can be seen that the sides of F_2 and F_3 may have the same edges up to a vertex before they bifurcate to u_1 and u_2. Keeping the history of the earlier traversal of the side of F_2, repeated traversal of the common edges of F_2 and F_3 can be avoided. This means that the entire funnel sequence for $v_k v_{k+1}$ can be traversed only once for computing all constructed edges in P incident on $v_k v_{k+1}$. Therefore, the total time required for computing all constructed edges in P is $O(E)$.

Let us analyze the time complexity of the algorithm after the visibility graph of P has been computed in $O(n \log n + E)$ time by the algorithm of Ghosh and Mount [165]. Consider Step 1. Locate the triangle in the plane-sweep triangulation of P containing s. Considering each side of this triangle as a base, traverse their funnel sequences to locate vertices of P that are visible from s. Then compute all constructed edges E_1 of R_1 by traversing the visibility graph of P as stated above. So, Step 1 takes $O(n)$ time. It has been discussed earlier that Step 3 takes $O(E\alpha(n)\log^2 n)$ time. Step 4 takes $O(E\alpha(n))$ time as the total number of edges on the boundaries of $Q_0, Q_1, \ldots, Q_{m-2}$ can be $O(E\alpha(n))$, where m is the link distance between s and t. Consider Step 5. Compute the visibility polygon $V(t)$ of P from t in the same way $V(s)$ has been computed in Step 1. Then it can be tested in $O(\log|V(t)|)$ time whether any given segment lies inside $V(t)$. Since a vertex of P can belong to only two edges of $Q'_0, Q'_1, \ldots, Q'_{m-2}$, the total time for testing all edges of $Q'_0, Q'_1, \ldots, Q'_{m-2}$ until t becomes visible is $O(n\log n)$. It has been shown earlier that all constructed edges of $R_1, R_2, \ldots, R_{m-1}$ can be computed in $O(E)$ time. Hence, the overall time complexity of the algorithm is $O(E\alpha(n)\log^2 n)$. We summarize the result in the following theorem.

Theorem 7.3.6 *A minimum link path between two given points inside a polygon P with holes with a total of n vertices can be computed in $O(E\alpha(n)\log^2 n)$ time, where E is the number of edges in the visibility graph of P and $\alpha(n)$ is the inverse of Ackermann's function.*

7.4 Computing Link Center and Radius of Simple Polygons

In this section, we present an $O(n^2)$ time algorithm of Lenhart *et al.* [241] for computing the link center, link radius and link diameter of a simple polygon P. We assume that the vertices of P are labeled $v_1, v_2, \ldots, v_n$ in counterclockwise order. As defined earlier, the link center of P is the set of all points $w \in P$ at which the maximum link distance from w to any point of P is minimized (see Figure 7.12(a)). Recall that the maximum link distance of w is called the link radius of P. In Figure 7.12(a), the link radius of P is 2.

We know that the link distance between any two points u and u' of P can be computed by computing a minimum link path from u to u'. Suppose, P is partitioned into regions $Q_1, Q_2, \ldots, Q_m$ such that for $1 \leq i \leq m$, all points of Q_i is reachable by i links from u (see Figure 7.12(b)). This means that Q_1 is the visibility polygon of P from u, Q_2 is the union of weak visibility polygons of $P - Q_1$ from constructed edges of Q_1, Q_3 is the union of weak visibility polygons of $P - Q_1 - Q_2$ from constructed edges of Q_2 and so on. This partition helps in computing the link distance from u to any other point u' in P by locating the region Q_i containing u'. The partition of P into regions $Q_1, Q_2, \ldots, Q_m$ has been introduced by Suri [318, 319] and is called the *window partition* of P for u. We refer to the union of regions $Q_1, Q_2, \ldots, Q_k$ as k-visibility regions of u, where $1 \leq k \leq m$.

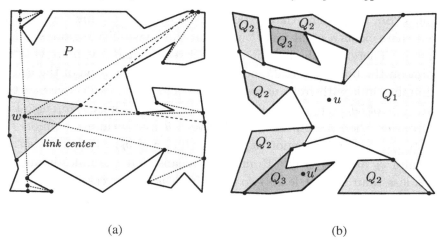

Figure 7.12 (a) Shaded region is the link center of P and all points of P can be reaches by two links from any point w of the link center. (b) The window partitioning of P for u.

Consider first the problem of computing the link radius r of P. If a point w in the link center of P is known, then compute the window partition $Q_1, Q_2,..., Q_m$ of P for w. So, r is same as m. If no point of the link center is known, then r can be computed once the link diameter d of P is known. As defined earlier, the link diameter of P is the maximum link distance between any two points inside P. In Figure 7.12(a), the link diameter of P is 4. We have the following lemmas on the link diameter of P.

Lemma 7.4.1 *Let r and d be the link radius and link diameter of P. Then $\lceil d/2 \rceil \leq r \leq \lceil (d/2) \rceil + 1$.*

Lemma 7.4.2 *The maximum of link distances among all pairs of vertices of P is the link diameter of P.*

Exercise 7.4.1 *Prove Lemmas 7.4.1 and 7.4.2.*

Compute the window partition of P for each vertex of P and choose a pair of vertices which have the maximum link distance (say d'). By Lemma 7.4.2, d' is same as d. Once d is known, r can be computed from d using Lemma 7.4.1. Once r is known, the link center of P can be computed using the following lemma.

Lemma 7.4.3 *The link center of P is the intersection of all r-visibility regions of P for every convex vertex in P.*

Proof. Let w be a point in the common intersection region of all r-visibility regions of P for every convex vertex in P. If w belongs to the link center of P, then the lemma holds. So, we assume that w does not belong to the link center of P. This means that there exists a point $u \in P$ such that the r-visibility region of P for u does not include w. Therefore, the link distance between w and u is more that r. Let u' be the point on the boundary of P such that uu' is the extension of the last link $w'u$ in the minimum link path from w to u. Let v_j and v_k be two convex vertices such that all vertices of $bd(v_j, v_k)$ are reflex vertices and u' belongs $bd(v_j, v_k)$. If v_j or v_k is visible from w', then the link distance between w and u cannot be more than r as w belongs to the r-visibility region of P for both v_j and v_k, which is a contradiction. If both v_j and v_k are not visible from w', it means that the link distance between w and u is less than r as at least two links from w' are necessary to reach v_j and v_k in minimum link paths from w to v_j and v_k, which is a contradiction. Hence, w belongs to the link center of P. $\square$

Exercise 7.4.2 *Prove that the link center of a simple polygon is a convex region [241].*

In the following, we present the major steps of the algorithm for computing the link radius r, link diameter d and link center lc of P. Initialize i, d and r by 1.

Step 1. Compute the window partition of P for v_i and assign the number of regions in the partition to d'.

Step 2. *If $d' > d$ then $d := d'$.*

Step 3. *If $i \neq n$ then $i := i + 1$ and goto Step 1.*

Step 4. Assign $\lceil d/2 \rceil$ to r.

Step 5. Initialize lc by P. Initialize i by 1.

Step 6. *If v_i is a convex vertex then*

   Step 6a. Compute r-visibility region of P for v_i and take its intersection with lc.

   Step 6b. Assign the common intersection region to lc.

Step 7. *If lc is empty then $r := r + 1$ and goto Step 5.*

Step 8. *If $i \neq n$ then $i := i + 1$ and goto Step 6.*

Step 9. Report lc as the link center of P. Report r and d as the link radius and link diameter of P, respectively.

The correctness of the algorithm follows from Lemmas 7.4.1, 7.4.2 and 7.4.3. Note that Step 5 can be executed at most twice as the link radius r of P can be $\lceil d/2 \rceil$ or $\lceil (d/2) \rceil + 1$.

Let us analyze the time complexity of the algorithm. The window partition of P for a vertex v_i in Step 1 can be computed in $O(n)$ as follows. Compute the shortest path tree $SPT(v_i)$ in P rooted at v_i in $O(n)$ time by the algorithm of Guibas *et al.* [178] (see Section 3.6.1). It can be seen that vertices of Q_1 are children of v_i in

$SPT(v_i)$. Let V_1 denote these vertices. Compute the shortest path map $SPM(v_i)$ in $O(n)$ time by the algorithm of Hershberger [186] (see Section 5.2). Observe that all non-polygonal edges on the boundary of Q_1 are those extension edges of $SPM(v_i)$ whose one endpoint is a vertex of V_1. Thus, the boundary of Q_1 can be identified in time proportional to the size of Q_1 after $SPT(v_i)$ and $SPM(v_i)$ have been computed in $O(n)$ time.

Let $v_j u$ be an extension edge of $SPM(v_i)$ on the boundary of Q_1. We know that v_j belongs to V_1 and u is a point on the boundary of P. Take the sub-tree $SPT(v_j)$ of $SPT(v_i)$ and compute $SPT(u)$ by shifting the root from v_j to u as in the algorithm of Hershberger [186]. It follows from Lemma 5.2.1 that vertices of $SPT(v_j)$ belonging to Q_2 are only those vertices of $SPT(v_j)$ whose parents in $SPT(u)$ are different. Therefore, vertices of $SPT(v_j)$ that are weakly visible from $v_j u$ can be identified in a time that is proportional to the number of such vertices. Note that although $SPM(v_j)$ is available from $SPM(v_i)$, $SPM(u)$ needs to be computed in order to identify the extension edges of $SPM(u)$ that are on the boundary of Q_2. This can also be done in a time that is proportional to the number of vertices that are weakly visible from $v_j u$. Repeat this process for all extension edges of $SPM(v_i)$ on the boundary of Q_1. Thus, entire Q_2 can be constructed in a time that is proportional to its size as the shifting of roots along extension edges involve disjoint sub-trees of $SPT(v_i)$. Analogously, $Q_3, Q_4, \ldots, Q_m$ can also be computed in a time that is proportional to their respective sizes. Hence, the window partitioning of P in Step 1 for each vertex can be done in $O(n)$ time. Since Step 1 is executed for each vertex of P, Step 1 takes $O(n^2)$ time.

Let us discuss the time complexity of Step 6a. Since the window partitioning of P for v_i has already been computed in Step 1, the r-visibility region of P for v_i (say, VR_i) is known. To compute $VR_i \cap lc$, the procedure traverses the boundary of lc in counterclockwise order and checks whether the current vertex v_p is an endpoint of a non-polygonal edge (say $v_p u$) of VR_i. If so, it computes the intersection point u' of $v_p u$ with the boundary of lc by traversing lc from v_p in the clockwise or counterclockwise direction depending upon the position of u. So, $v_p u'$ divides lc into two parts and one part is removed from lc. It may so happen that there is no intersection point u' as the entire $v_p u$ (except the vertex v_p) lies outside lc, which can be tested in constant time. In that case, either lc remains unchanged or lc becomes empty. Once the intersection of lc and all non-polygonal edges of VR_i with common vertices have been computed, the remaining portion of lc is considered as the current lc. The procedure then traverses the boundary of VR_i and checks whether the current vertex v_q is an endpoint of a non-polygonal edge (say, $v_q u$) of VR_i and v_q is not a vertex of lc. If so, compute the intersection of lc with $v_q u$ using a method that is similar to the procedure for computing the kernel of a simple polygon (see Section 2.4). Thus, $VR_i \cap lc$ can be computed in $O(n)$ time. Since Step 6a is executed for each convex vertex of P, Step 6a can take $O(n^2)$ time in

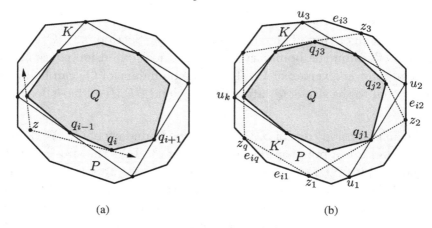

(a)   (b)

Figure 7.13 (a) The polygon K is a minimum nested polygon between two convex polygons P and Q. (b) The nested polygon K' has one more vertex than a minimum nested polygon K.

the worst case. Hence, the overall time complexity of the algorithm is $O(n^2)$. We summarize the result in the following theorem.

Theorem 7.4.4 *The link center, link radius and link diameter of a simple polygon P of n vertices can be computed in $O(n^2)$ time.*

7.5 Computing Minimum Nested Polygons

7.5.1 Between Convex Polygons: $O(n \log k)$ Algorithm

In this section, we present an $O(n \log k)$ algorithm of Aggarwal *et al.* [12] for computing a minimum nested polygon K between two given convex polygons P and Q, where $Q \subset P$, n is the total number of vertices of P and Q, and k is the number of vertices of K (see Figure 7.13(a)). A simple polygon K is called *nested* between P and Q, when it circumscribes Q and is inscribed in P (i.e. $Q \subset K \subset P$). The problem here is to compute a nested polygon K with the minimum number of vertices. We assume that the vertices of P and Q are labeled in counterclockwise order p_1, $p_2, \ldots, p_m$ and $q_1, q_2, \ldots, q_l$, respectively, where $m + l = n$.

Let R denote the annular region between P and Q, i.e., $R = P - Q$. Draw the tangent from a point $z \in R$ to Q meeting Q at a vertex q_i such that both vertices q_{i-1} and q_{i+1} lie to the left of $\overrightarrow{zq_i}$ (see Figure 7.13(a)). We call zq_i as the *left tangent* of z. The right tangent from z to Q is defined analogously. It can be seen that both tangents of z lie inside R as P and Q are convex. Let z_1 be a point on the boundary of P (denoted as $bd(P)$). Draw the left tangent from z_1 to Q and extend the tangent until it meets $bd(P)$ at some point z_2 (see Figure 7.13(b)). Again, draw the left tangent from z_2 to Q and extend the tangent until it meets $bd(P)$ at some point z_3. Repeat this process of construction until a point $z_q \in bd(P)$ is found such that the segment $z_q z_1$ lies inside R. This greedy path $z_1 z_2$, $z_2 z_3$, $\ldots$, $z_{q-1} z_q$ along with the link $z_q z_1$ gives a nested polygon K' in R. Note that K' can be computed in $O(n)$ time. For any two turning points z_i and z_j for $i < j$, z_j is called the *forward projection point* of z_i and z_i is called the *backward projection point* of z_j. We have the following observations.

Lemma 7.5.1 *Let* $z_1 z_2$, $z_2 z_3$, $\ldots$, $z_q z_1$ *be the edges of a convex polygon* K' *nested between* P *and* Q *such that vertices* z_1, z_2, $\ldots$, z_q *are on the boundary of* P *and edges* $z_1 z_2$, $z_2 z_3$, $\ldots$, $z_{q-1} z_q$ *are tangential to* Q. *The polygon* K' *has at most one more vertex than a minimum nested polygon* K *between* P *and* Q.

Proof. Since no edge of K can intersect more than one of the left tangents from z_1, z_2, $\ldots$, z_{q-1} (see Figure 7.13(b)), the polygon K' has at most one more vertex than K. □

Corollary 7.5.2 *For* $1 \leq i \leq q - 1$, *the region of* R *bounded by* $z_i z_{i+1}$ *and the counterclockwise boundary of* P *from* z_i *to* z_{i+1} *contains a vertex of* K.

Lemma 7.5.3 *There exists a minimum nested polygon* K *between* P *and* Q *such that all vertices of* K *belong to the boundary of* P.

Exercise 7.5.1 *Prove Lemma 7.5.3.*

Let us explain the procedure for computing K from K'. We know from Corollary 7.5.2 and Lemma 7.5.3 that there is a vertex of K lying on the counterclockwise boundary of P from z_1 to z_2 (denoted as $bd_p(z_1, z_2)$). If the position of a vertex (say, u_1) of K on $bd_p(z_1, z_2)$ is known (see Figure 7.13(b)), the edges $u_1 u_2$, $u_2 u_3$, $\ldots$, $u_k u_1$ of K can be computed by constructing the greedy path starting from u_1. Note that $q - 1 \leq k \leq q$ by Lemma 7.5.1. Therefore, the problem of computing K has been reduced to finding the position of u_1 on $bd_p(z_1, z_2)$.

Suppose a point w is moved along $bd_p(z_1, z_2)$ starting from z_1 and for each position of w, the greedy path from w is computed. It can be seen that when w reaches u_1 (see Figure 7.13(b)), the last link in the greedy path from w 'collapses' to a point, which gives K as it has one edge less than K'. On the other hand, it is not feasible to compute the greedy path from every point w on $bd_p(z_1, u_1)$. So, the algorithm first divides $bd_p(z_1, z_1)$ into intervals and then composes a unique function for every interval which maps any point w in the interval to the last turning point of the greedy path from w. Using these functions, the algorithm locates a point $u_1 \in bd_p(z_1, z_2)$ such that u_1 is same as u_{k+1} and then constructs K by computing the greedy path from u_1 to u_1.

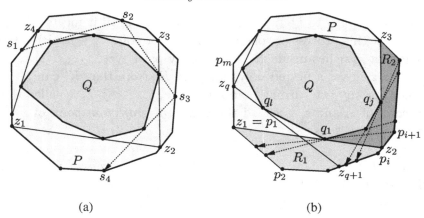

(a)   (b)

Figure 7.14 (a) The reverse greedy path from s_1 is (s_1s_2, s_2s_3, s_3s_4). (b) The intervals on $bd_p(z_1, z_2)$ in $R_1 \cup R_2$ are computed using backward projection points of A_2 on $bd_p(z_1, z_2)$.

Let us first explain the procedure for computing intervals on $bd_p(z_1, z_2)$. Recall that the greedy path z_1z_2, z_2z_3, $\ldots$, $z_{q-1}z_q$ alternatively touches a vertex q_j of Q and meets an edge e_i of P. This alternating sequence $(e_{i1}, q_{j1}, e_{i2}, q_{j2}, .., e_{iq})$ of vertices and edges (see Figure 7.13(b)), where $z_1 \in e_{i1}$ and $z_q \in e_{iq}$, is called the *link sequence* of z_1 [69]. Observe that there is a neighborhood of z_1 on $bd(P)$ such that for any point in the neighborhood, the link sequence is the same. We define an *interval* on $bd(P)$ to be the largest such neighborhood forming a segment, which is an edge or a subset of an edge on $bd(P)$. We have the following observation.

Lemma 7.5.4 *A point w is an endpoint of an interval on $bd_p(z_1, z_2)$ if and only if (i) w is a vertex of P on $bd_p(z_1, z_2)$, or (ii) the greedy path from w turns at some vertex of P or passes through an edge of Q.*

Proof. Proof of the lemma follows from the definition of the link sequence.   □

Using the above lemma, $bd_p(z_1, z_2)$ can be divided into intervals using backward projection points of (i) vertices of P, and (ii) those points that are extensions of edges of Q to $bd(P)$. Backward projection points can be computed as follows. For any point s_1 on $bd(P)$, draw the right tangent from s_1 to Q and extend the tangent meeting $bd(P)$ at some point s_2 (see Figure 7.14(a)). If $s_2 \in bd_p(z_1, z_2)$, then s_2 is the backward projection point of s_1 on $bd_p(z_1, z_2)$. If $s_2 \notin bd_p(z_1, z_2)$, compute s_3 by drawing the right tangent from s_2 and extend the tangent meeting $bd(P)$ at s_3. This process of computing backward projection points continues until a point on $bd_p(z_1, z_2)$ is reached. We call this path s_1s_2, s_2s_3, $\ldots$ the *reverse greedy path* from s_1.

Observe that the intervals on $bd_p(z_1, z_2)$ can be computed in $O(nk)$ time by traversing the boundaries of P and Q once in counterclockwise order and by computing the reverse greedy path (of size at most k) from each vertex or extension point on $bd(P)$. Once the intervals are computed, the greedy paths from every endpoint of all intervals on $bd_p(z_1, z_2)$ can also be computed in $O(nk)$ time.

Let us show that there is a unique function associated with each interval of $bd_p(z_1, z_2)$. We start with the link sequence $(e_{i1}, q_{j1}, e_{i2}, q_{j2}, .., e_{iq})$ of z_1 (see Figure 7.13(b)). We know the coordinates of z_1 and q_{j1}, and the equation of e_{i2}. Therefore, the coordinates of z_2 can be obtained from those of z_1 using the following pair of bilinear functions.

$$x(z_2) = (a_1.x(z_1) + b_1.y(z_1) + c_1)/(d_1.x(z_1) + f_1.y(z_1) + g_1)$$
$$y(z_2) = (a_2.x(z_1) + b_2.y(z_1) + c_2)/(d_1.x(z_1) + f_1.y(z_1) + g_1)$$

where $x()$, $y()$ denote the abscissa and ordinate values of a point. The coefficients a_1, b_1, c_1, d_1, f_1, g_1, a_2, b_2 and c_2 depend on the coordinates of q_{j1} and the equation of e_{i2}. It can be seen that the above pair of bilinear functions map points in the neighborhood of z_1 to points in the neighborhood of z_2. Similarly, we have a pair of bilinear functions that map points in the neighborhood of z_2 to points in the neighborhood of z_3. By composing these two pairs of functions, we obtain a pair of bilinear functions which map points in the neighborhood of z_1 to points in the neighborhood of z_3. By composing k times, a pair of bilinear functions can be obtained which map points in the neighborhood of z_1 to points in the neighborhood of z_q. This pair of functions is called the *projection function* of z_1. Observe that the coefficients of the projection function of z_1 depend on the vertices and edges of the link sequence of z_1. This multiple composition shows that there is a unique function for each interval of $bd_p(z_1, z_2)$ and it takes constant time to evaluate the function.

Exercise 7.5.2 *Prove that given the coefficients of a projection function, its fixed point can be computed in $O(1)$ time [69].*

Once the projection functions for each interval of $bd_p(z_1, z_2)$ are composed, it can be checked whether there is a fixed point u_1 of the projection function of any interval on $bd_p(z_1, z_2)$ (see Figure 7.13(b)). The fixed point of a projection function can be found in $O(1)$ time by finding eigenvalues and their corresponding eigenvectors of the matrix formed by the coefficients of the projection function [69]. We have the following theorem.

Theorem 7.5.5 *Given two convex polygons P and Q with a total of n vertices $(Q \subset P)$, a minimum nested polygon K between P and Q can be computed in $O(nk)$ time, where k is the number of vertices of K.*

It can be seen that the above algorithm runs in $O(nk)$ time because the number of backward projection points in a reverse greedy path can be at most k. We show that it is possible to restrict the number of backward projection points to $\log k$ using projection functions and a divide and conquer strategy. In presenting our divide and conquer algorithm, we adopt the method of merging intervals as suggested by Chandru *et al.* [69].

Let us define regions R_1, R_2, ..., R_q with respect to the greedy path z_1z_2, z_2z_3, ..., z_qz_{q+1}, where z_qz_{q+1} intersects z_1z_2 (see Figure 7.14(b)). Without loss of generality, we assume that z_1 is p_1. We also assume that z_1z_2 and z_qz_{q+1} are tangential to Q at vertices q_1 and q_l respectively. The counterclockwise boundary of Q from a vertex q_r to a vertex q_t is denoted as $bd_q(q_r, q_t)$. Let R_1 denote the region of R bounded by the segment q_1z_1, $bd_p(z_1, z_2)$ and the segment z_2q_1 (see Figure 7.14(b)). So, the initial intervals on $bd_p(z_1, z_2)$ are p_1p_2, p_2p_3, ..., p_iz_2, where z_2 belongs to the edge p_ip_{i+1}. The endpoints of the intervals are stored in the list A_1 in counterclockwise order, where the first and last elements in A_1 are z_1 and z_2. Assume that z_2z_3 is tangential to Q at the vertex q_j. Let R_2 denote the region of R bounded by the segment q_1z_2, $bd_p(z_2, z_3)$, the segment z_3q_j and $bd_q(q_1, q_j)$ (see Figure 7.14(b)). Extend the edges in $bd_q(q_1, q_j)$ to $bd_p(z_2, z_3)$ and insert the extension points on $bd_p(z_2, z_3)$, which divides edges of $bd_p(z_2, z_3)$ into intervals. The endpoints of intervals on $bd_p(z_2, z_3)$ are then stored in the list A_2 in counterclockwise order, where the first and last elements in A_2 are z_2 and z_3. The regions R_3, R_4, ..., R_q and the intervals on their boundaries are defined analogously. Note that R_1, R_2, ..., R_{q-1} are disjoint, whereas R_1 and R_q are overlapping.

Starting from A_1, final intervals on $bd_p(z_1, z_2)$ can be computed by combining R_1, R_2, ..., R_q as follows. Firstly, intervals on $bd_p(z_1, z_2)$ are computed in $R_1 \cup R_2$. It can be seen that backward projection points of A_2 on $bd_p(z_1, z_2)$ and points in A_1 can be merged according to their counterclockwise order to form intervals on $bd_p(z_1, z_2)$ in $R_1 \cup R_2$ (see Figure 7.14(b)). The endpoints of these intervals are again stored in A_1. Moreover, projection functions of all intervals in $R_1 \cup R_2$ are composed and they map points of an interval on $bd_p(z_1, z_2)$ to points in the corresponding interval on $bd_p(z_2, z_3)$. Since the forward projection points of A_1 on $bd_p(z_2, z_3)$ can always be computed using these projection functions, there is no need to store these forward projected points on $bd_p(z_2, z_3)$ in A_2. Similarly, intervals on $bd_p(z_3, z_4)$ in $R_3 \cup R_4$ are computed using A_3 and A_4, and the endpoints of these intervals are again stored in A_3 along with the projection functions of these intervals.

Let us compute intervals on $bd_p(z_1, z_2)$ in $R_1 \cup R_2 \cup R_3 \cup R_4$. The task is to compute backward projection points of A_3 on $bd_p(z_1, z_2)$, which can be done in two steps. The backward projection points of A_3 on $bd_p(z_2, z_3)$ are first computed by drawing right tangents from points of A_3 and extending them to $bd_p(z_2, z_3)$ as in a reverse greedy path. Then, these backward projected points on $bd_p(z_2, z_3)$ are projected backward on $bd_p(z_1, z_2)$ using the inverse of the projection functions associated with A_1 which map points of $bd_p(z_1, z_2)$ to points of $bd_p(z_2, z_3)$. Now, backward projection points of A_3 on $bd_p(z_1, z_2)$ and points in A_1 can be merged according to their counterclockwise order to form intervals on $bd_p(z_1, z_2)$ in $R_1 \cup R_2 \cup R_3 \cup R_4$. The endpoints of these intervals are again stored in A_1. The projection functions of intervals formed by points in A_1 to intervals on $bd_p(z_4, z_5)$ can be composed using the projection functions (i) from $bd_p(z_1, z_2)$ to $bd_p(z_2, z_3)$ (composed in $R_1 \cup R_2$), (ii) from $bd_p(z_2, z_3)$ to $bd_p(z_3, z_4)$ (composed after drawing right tangents in this iteration), and (iii) from $bd_p(z_3, z_4)$ to $bd_p(z_4, z_5)$ (composed in $R_3 \cup R_4$).

Observe that the first set of backward projection points of A_3 (on $bd_p(z_2, z_3)$) have been computed by drawing right tangents and only then the last set of backward projection points (on $bd_p(z_1, z_2)$) are computed using the inverse of the projection functions. During the merging step in general, the first and the last backward projection points in any reverse greedy path are computed and computation of all intermediate backward projection points in the path are skipped using the inverse of the projection functions. Therefore, at most $\log k$ backward projection points (or turning points) are computed in the reverse greedy path from a point on $bd(P)$ to $bd_p(z_1, z_2)$, which helps in computing K in $O(n \log k)$ time.

The above process of computation can be repeated until the intervals on $bd_p(z_1, z_2)$ are computed in $R_1 \cup R_2 \cup \ldots \cup R_{q-1} \cup R_q$. In the following, we present the major steps of the algorithm for computing a minimum nested polygon K under the assumption that q is a power of 2.

Step 1. Construct the greedy path $z_1 z_2$, $z_2 z_3$, $\ldots$, $z_{q-1} z_q$, $z_q z_{q+1}$, where $z_1 \in bd(P)$ and $z_q z_{q+1}$ intersects $z_1 z_2$. Introduce points z_1, z_2, $\ldots$, z_q as vertices of P.

Step 2. Construct the regions R_1, R_2, $\ldots$, R_q with respect to the greedy path from z_1. Initialize the ordered lists A_1, A_2, $\ldots$, A_q by the vertices of P and extension points of edges of Q to $bd(P)$. Assign q to j.

Step 3. *For $i = 1$ to $j/2$ do*

Step 3a. Compute the intervals on $bd_p(z_{2i-1}, z_{2i})$ in $R_{2i-1} \cup R_{2i}$ by merging points in A_{2i-1} and the backward projection points of A_{2i} on $bd_p(z_{2i-1}, z_{2i})$ in counterclockwise order and store their endpoints in A_{2i-1}.

Step 3b. Compose the projection functions in $R_{2i-1} \cup R_{2i}$ of intervals on $bd_p(z_{2i-1}, z_{2i})$ formed by the points in A_{2i-1}.

Step 3c. $R_i := R_{2i-1} \cup R_{2i}$ and $A_i := A_{2i-1}$.

Step 4. *If $j \neq 1$ then $j := j/2$ and goto* Step 3.

Step 5. Locate a fixed point u_1 in an interval of $bd_p(z_1, z_2)$.

Step 6. Construct a minimum nested polygon K by computing the greedy path from u_1 and Stop.

It can be seen that the above algorithm runs in $O(n \log k)$ time as Step 3 takes $O(n)$ time and it is repeated $\log k$ times. We summarize the result in the following theorem.

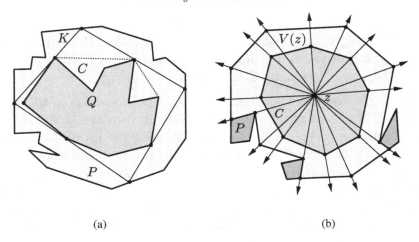

(a)   (b)

Figure 7.15 (a) Although P and Q are non-convex polygons, K is a convex polygon which contains the convex hull C of Q. (b) Rays are drawn from z through every vertex of C and $V(z)$ to form wedges.

Theorem 7.5.6 *Given two convex polygons P and Q with a total of n vertices $(Q \subset P)$, a minimum nested polygon K between P and Q can be computed in $O(n \log k)$ time, where k is the number of vertices of K.*

7.5.2 Between Non-Convex Polygons: $O(n)$ Algorithm

In this section, we present two algorithms for computing a minimum nested polygon K between two given simple polygons P and Q given by Ghosh [155] and Ghosh and Maheshwari [159], where $Q \subset P$, n is the total number of vertices of P and Q and k is the number of vertices of K. If K is convex, the algorithm of Ghosh [155] computes K in $O(n \log k)$ time. If K is not convex, the algorithm of Ghosh and Maheshwari [159] computes K in $O(n)$ time.

As defined earlier, a simple polygon K is called *nested* between P and Q, when it circumscribes Q and is inscribed in P (i.e. $Q \subset K \subset P$). The problem here is to compute a nested polygon K with the minimum number of vertices. We assume that the vertices of P and Q are labeled in counterclockwise order $p_1, p_2, \ldots, p_m$ and $q_1, q_2, \ldots, q_l$, respectively, where $m + l = n$. The boundaries of P and Q are denoted as $bd(P)$ and $bd(Q)$, respectively.

It has been shown in Section 7.5.1 that if both P and Q are convex, K is also a convex polygon. If P or Q is not a convex polygon, K can still be a convex polygon as shown in Figure 7.15(a). Therefore, we first determine whether K is convex or not. This can be checked in $O(n)$ time by the algorithm of Ghosh [155]. We start our presentation of Ghosh's algorithm with the following lemma.

Lemma 7.5.7 *There exists a nested convex polygon between P and Q if and only if the boundary of P does not intersect the convex hull of Q.*

Proof. If $bd(P)$ does not intersect the convex hull of Q, there exists a point $z \in bd(P)$ such that both tangents from z to Q lie inside P. Since the entire boundary of P (including z) lies outside the convex hull of Q by assumption, the region of P enclosed by the two tangents of z and the convex hull of Q form a nested convex polygon.

Let us prove the converse. If a nested convex polygon K exists, $bd(P)$ must lie in the exterior of K by definition. Since K is a convex polygon containing Q and the convex hull of Q is the smallest convex set containing Q, the convex hull of Q also lies inside K. Therefore, $bd(P)$ does not intersect the convex hull of Q. $\square$

The above lemma suggests that it is necessary to check whether $bd(P)$ intersects the convex hull of Q (denoted as C), which can be done in $O(n)$ time using the algorithm of Ghosh [151] for detecting the intersection between two star-shaped polygons. We state this algorithm in the following steps as presented in Ghosh [155].

Step 1. Compute the convex hull C of Q by the algorithm of Graham and Yao [175].

Step 2. Take a point z of Q and compute the visibility polygon $V(z)$ of P from z by the algorithm of Lee [230] (see Section 2.2.1).

Step 3. Divide the plane into wedges by drawing rays from z through every vertex of C and $V(z)$ (Figure 7.15(b)).

Step 4. Merge the angular order of vertices of C and $V(z)$ around z to form the sorted angular order of wedges.

Step 5. Check the intersection between the pair of edges in each wedge by traversing the wedges in sorted angular order around z.

Step 6. *If* an intersection is detected *then* report that K is not a convex polygon *else* report that K is a convex polygon.

> **Exercise 7.5.3** *Let Q be a star-shaped polygon inside an arbitrary simple polygon P ($Q \subset P$). Prove that the boundary of the visibility polygon of P from a point z in the kernel of Q intersects Q if and only if the boundary of P intersects Q [151].*

The correctness and the time complexity of the above algorithm follow from Graham and Yao [175], Lee [230] and Ghosh [151]. We summarize the result in the following theorem.

Theorem 7.5.8 *Given two simple polygons P and Q with a total of n vertices ($Q \subset P$), it can be determined in $O(n)$ time whether there exists a convex nested polygon between P and Q.*

Let us consider the situation when K is convex. Before K can be computed, P is pruned to another polygon P' such that every nested convex polygon K lies inside P'. We have the following observation.

Lemma 7.5.9 *Let P' be the set of all points of P such that both tangents from any point $z \in P' - C$ to C lie inside P. Every nested convex polygon K' between P and C lies inside P'.*

Proof. Let z be a point inside $K' - C$. Since K' is a convex polygon and lies inside P, two tangents drawn from z to C lie inside K' as well as P. Hence K' lies inside P' by the definition of P'.   □

Corollary 7.5.10 *Every minimum nested convex polygon K lies between P' and C.*

Exercise 7.5.4 *Let C be a convex polygon inside a simple polygon P i.e. $C \subset P$. Let P' be the set of all points of P such that both tangents from any point $z \in P' - C$ to C lie inside P. Design an $O(n)$ time algorithm for computing P', where n is the total number of vertices of P and C [155].*

The polygon P' is called the *complete visibility polygon* of P from C. Since P' can be computed in $O(n)$ time, a minimum nested polygon K between P' and C can be computed in $O(n \log k)$ time by the algorithm of Aggarwal *et al.* [12] (presented in Section 7.5.1). Note that though P' is not a convex polygon, the algorithm of Aggarwal *et al.* [12] can still be used as P' is completely visible from C as shown by Wang [336] and Wang and Chan [337]. In the following, we present the major steps for computing a convex nested polygon K.

Step 1. Compute the convex hull C of Q by the algorithm of Graham and Yao [175].

Step 2. Check the intersection between $bd(P)$ and C by the algorithm of Ghosh [151]. *If* an intersection is detected *then* report that there is no convex nested polygon between P and Q and *goto* Step 5.

Step 3. Compute the complete visibility polygon P' of P from C (see Exercises 3.8.1 and 7.5.3).

Step 4. Construct a minimum nested convex polygon K between P' and C by the algorithm of Aggarwal *et al.* [12] and report K.

Step 5. Stop.

The correctness of the algorithm follows from Lemma 7.5.9, Theorem 7.5.8 and Aggarwal *et al.* [12]. Let us analyze the time complexity of the algorithm. We know that Steps 1, 2 and 3 can be performed in $O(n)$ time. Step 4 takes $O(n \log k)$ time. Hence, the overall time complexity of the algorithm is $O(n \log k)$. We summarize the result in the following theorem.

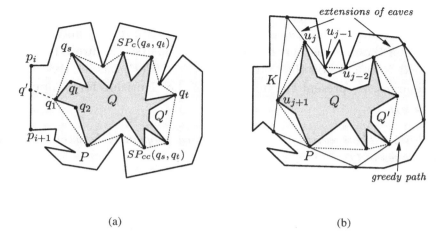

Figure 7.16 (a) The boundary of the relative convex hull Q' of Q is the union of $SP_c(q_s, q_t)$ and $SP_{cc}(q_s, q_t)$. (b) A minimum nested non-convex polygon K is formed by the greedy path and the extensions of the eaves of Q'.

Theorem 7.5.11 *Given two simple polygons P and Q with a total of n vertices $(Q \subset P)$, a minimum nested convex polygon K between P and Q can be computed in $O(n \log k)$ time, where k is the number of vertices of K.*

Let us consider the other situation where K is not convex. This means that $bd(P)$ has intersected the convex hull C of Q. So, a simple polygon $Q' \subset C$ is constructed such that Q' is the smallest perimeter polygon inside P containing Q (see Figure 7.16(a)). This polygon Q' is called the *relative convex hull* of Q with respect to P. Note that all vertices of C belong to Q'. To compute Q', we need a triangulation of the region $P - Q$.

Without loss of generality, we assume that the vertex q_1 of Q is a vertex of C (see Figure 7.16(a)). Extend $q_1 q_2$ from q_1 meeting $bd(P)$ at a point q' on an edge $p_i p_{i+1}$. Cut $P - Q$ along $q' q_1$ to construct a simple polygon $(q_2, q_1, q', p_{i+1}, p_{i+2}, \ldots, p_i, q', q_1, q_l, q_{l-1}, \ldots, q_2)$ and triangulate this polygon in $O(n)$ time using the algorithm of Chazelle [71] (see Theorem 1.4.6). This triangulation can be considered a triangulation of $P - Q$ with an additional vertex q'.

Let q_s and q_t be two vertices of C (see Figure 7.16(a)). It can be seen that there exists two disjoint paths in $P - Q$ from q_s to q_t passing through two disjoint set of triangles T_c and T_{cc} in the triangulation of $P - Q$. Compute the Euclidean shortest path from q_s to q_t in T_c using the algorithm of Lee and Preparata [235] and call it $SP_c(q_s, q_t)$. Similarly, compute the Euclidean shortest path from q_s to q_t in T_{cc} and call it $SP_{cc}(q_s, q_t)$. It can be seen that the union of $SP_c(q_s, q_t)$ and $SP_{cc}(q_s, q_t)$ is the boundary of Q'.

Let $Q' = (u_1, u_2, \ldots, u_r, u_{r+1}, \ldots, u_1)$, where $u_1 = q_s$ and $u_r = q_t$. As defined in Section 7.2.2, an edge $u_{j-1}u_j$ of Q' is called an *eave* if u_{j-2} and u_{j+1} lie on the opposite side of the line passing through u_{j-1} and u_j (see Figure 7.16(b)). Observe that there exists an eave on the boundary of Q' as $bd(P)$ has intersected C. In the following lemmas, we present the main idea of the algorithm for computing K (see Figure 7.16(b)).

Lemma 7.5.12 *There exists a minimum nested polygon K between P and Q containing all eaves of Q'.*

Proof. Proof follows along the line of the proof of Lemma 7.2.6.   □

Lemma 7.5.13 *The greedy paths inside $P - Q$ connecting the extensions of eaves of Q' form a minimum nested non-convex polygon K between P and Q.*

Exercise 7.5.5 *Prove Lemmas 7.5.13.*

In the following, we present the major steps of the algorithm for computing K under the assumption that $bd(P)$ has intersected C.

Step 1. Construct a triangulation of $P - Q$ using the algorithm of Chazelle [71].

Step 2. Let q_s and q_t be two vertices of both Q and C. Compute $SP_c(q_s, q_t)$ and $SP_{cc}(q_s, q_t)$ inside $P - Q$ by the algorithm of Lee and Preparata [235] and take their union to form the boundary of Q'.

Step 3. Extend each eave of Q' from both ends to the boundary of $P - Q$.

Step 4. Compute the greedy path inside $P - Q$ connecting the extensions of every pair of consecutive eaves of Q' by the algorithm of Ghosh [155] presented in Section 7.2.2.

Step 5. Connect the greedy paths using the extension of eaves to construct a minimum nested polygon K and Stop.

The correctness of the algorithm follows from Lemmas 7.5.12 and 7.5.13, and Theorem 7.5.8. Let us analyze the time complexity of the algorithm. We know that Steps 1 and 2 take $O(n)$ time. Extensions of eaves of Q' to the boundary of $P - Q$ can be computed in Step 3 in $O(n)$ time as shown in Section 7.2.2. Since the extension of eaves partitions $P - Q$ into disjoint regions, the greedy paths in these regions can also be computed in $O(n)$ time. Therefore, Step 4 takes $O(n)$ time. Hence, the overall time complexity of the algorithm is $O(n)$. We summarize the result in the following theorem.

Theorem 7.5.14 *Given two simple polygons P and Q with a total of n vertices ($Q \subset P$), a minimum nested non-convex polygon K between P and Q can be computed in $O(n)$ time.*

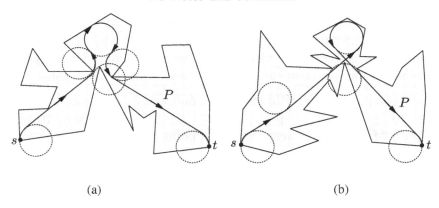

(a)   (b)

Figure 7.17 (a) The path of bounded curvature from s to t is simple but not convex. (b) The path of bounded curvature is self-intersecting.

7.6 Notes and Comments

Link paths going around a convex chain, like convex nested polygons, can be used to define isomorphism between points of two polygons. Note that in Section 6.9, isomorphism between two polygons is defined with respect to vertices of the polygons. Here, two simple polygons are called *isomorphic* if there is one-to-one mapping between their internal points (including vertices) that preserves visibility. Using link paths structure, MacDonald and Shermer [251] established necessary and sufficient conditions for isomorphism between two spiral polygons and gave an $O(n^2)$ time algorithm for detecting such isomorphism.

Consider the following problem on path planning of a point robot, whose path is of *bounded curvature*. Given two points s and t inside a polygon P with or without holes and two directions of travel at s and t, the bounded curvature problem is to compute a path inside P from s to t consisting of straight-line segments (or links) and circular arcs such that (i) the radius of each circular arc is at least 1, (ii) each link on the path is the tangent between the two consecutive circular arcs on the path, (iii) the given initial direction at s is tangent to the path at s, and (iv) the given final direction at t is tangent to the path at t. Figure 7.17(a) shows that there exists a simple but non-convex path of bounded curvature from s to t. A path of bounded curvature is called *convex* if it makes only right turns or only left turns. Note that there is no convex and simple path of bounded curvature between s and t in the polygon of Figure 7.17(a). On the other hand, a path of bounded curvature may not always be simple as shown in Figure 7.17(b).

For this problem, Agarwal *et al.* [10] proposed an $O(n^2 \log n)$ time algorithm for computing a shortest path of bounded curvature in a convex polygon P without holes. If P is a simple polygon and there exists a convex and simple path of bounded curvature from s to t inside P, the path can be computed in $O(n^4)$ time by the algorithm of Boissonnat *et al.* [57]. Their algorithm computes the path exploiting the relationship between Euclidean shortest paths, link paths, paths of bounded curvature and complete visibility. These are the only two polynomial time algorithms known for this problem in a polygon with or without holes.

Let us mention parallel algorithms for the minimum link path and nested polygon problems considered in this chapter. Consider the problem of computing the minimum link path $MLP(s,t)$ between two given points s and t inside a simple polygon P. Chandru *et al.* [69] gave an algorithm for computing $MLP(s,t)$ following the sequential algorithm of Ghosh [155, 156] (presented in Section 7.2.2), combining a divide and conquer strategy with projection functions in computing the greedy path. Their algorithm runs in $O(\log n \log \log n)$ time using $O(n)$ processors in the CREW-PRAM model of computations. Using this algorithm, Chandru *et al.* [69] gave another algorithm for computing the minimum nested polygon between two simple polygons, which also runs in $O(\log n \log \log n)$ time using $O(n)$ processors in the CREW-PRAM model of computations.

Using the above algorithm of Chandru *et al.* [69], Ghosh and Maheshwari [161] showed that minimum link paths from a point in a simple polygon P to all vertices of P can be computed in $O(\log^2 n \log \log n)$ time using $O(n)$ processors in the CREW-PRAM model of computations. They also gave an algorithm for computing the link center of a simple polygon P in $O(\log^2 n \log \log n)$ time using $O(n^2)$ processors in the CREW-PRAM model of computations. Lingas *et al.* [245] gave parallel algorithms for rectilinear link paths in rectilinear polygons.

Exercise 7.6.1 *Design an $O(n \log n)$ time algorithm for locating a diagonal uw in a simple polygon P of n vertices such that the difference between the maximum link distances from uw to opposite sides of uw in P is at most one [111].*

8

Visibility and Path Queries

8.1 Problems and Results

Let $q_1, q_2, \ldots, q_m$ be a set of internal points of a polygon P with holes with a total of n vertices. Consider the problem of computing visibility polygons of points $q_1, q_2, \ldots, q_m$ in the polygon P. Since the visibility polygon of P from each point q_i can be computed in $O(n \log n)$ time by the algorithm of Asano [27] (see Section 2.3), the problem can be solved in $O(mn \log n)$ time. Suppose m is quite large compared to n. In that case, it may be a good idea to construct data structures by processing P once so that the visibility polygon from each query point q_i can be computed in less than $O(n \log n)$ time with the help of these data structures. In fact, it has been shown by Asano *et al.* [28] that after spending $O(n^2)$ time in preprocessing of P, the visibility polygon from each query point q_i can be computed in $O(n)$ time. Thus the overall time complexity for solving this problem is reduced from $O(mn \log n)$ to $O(mn)$. Such problems, that require a large number of computations of similar type on the same polygonal domain, are known as *query problems* in computational geometry [291]. Efficiency of a query algorithm is judged on the basis of the query time of the algorithm, the space occupied by the data structure of the algorithm, and the time required during the preprocessing of the algorithm. Here, we consider query problems on visibility, shortest paths and link paths.

> **Exercise 8.1.1** *Design a query algorithm for determining whether a query point lies inside a convex polygon C of m vertices in $O(\log m)$ query time taking $O(m)$ preprocessing time and space [291].*

Let us start with the ray-shooting problem. Let q be a point inside a simple polygon P. Let $\overrightarrow{q}$ denote the ray from q in the given direction. Let q' be the closest point of q among all the intersection points of $\overrightarrow{q}$ with the boundary of P. So, the segment qq' lies inside P and q' is visible from q. For a given query $\overrightarrow{q}$ in P, the problem of ray shooting is to answer the query by locating q'. We know that the visibility polygon $V(q)$ of P from q can be computed in $O(n)$ time by the algorithm of Lee [230] (see Section 2.2.1). So, by traversing the boundary of $V(q)$, q' can be located in $O(n)$ time.

Chazelle and Guibas [76] first showed that q' can be computed in optimal $O(\log n)$ query time. Using the geometric transformation of point-line duality, they developed data structures for answering each ray-shooting query in optimal query time. To build the data structures, their algorithm requires preprocessing of P which takes $O(n \log n)$ time and $O(n)$ space. Using hourglass structures, Guibas *et al.* [178] showed that the preprocessing time of P can be improved to $O(n)$ keeping the query time and the space requirement unchanged.

Using a different method, Chazelle *et al.* [73] later developed another query algorithm for the same problem which also answers each ray-shooting query in optimal $O(\log n)$ query time. Their algorithm requires $O(n)$ preprocessing time and space. In a preprocessing step, P is decomposed into geodesic triangles. A region of P bounded by the shortest paths between three vertices of P is called a *geodesic triangle*. It has been shown by Chazelle *et al.* [73] that the path of $\vec{q}$ in P can be traced in $O(\log^2 n)$ query time using this geodesic triangulation. The query time is then improved to $O(\log n)$ using a weight-balanced binary search tree [256] and a data structuring technique called *fractional cascading* [74, 75]. Soon after, Hershberger and Suri [190] showed an alternative method for answering a query in $O(\log n)$ query time using weight assignments in place of fractional cascading. Their query algorithm also requires $O(n)$ preprocessing time and space. We present the query algorithms of Chazelle *et al.* [73] in Sections 8.2.

Consider the ray-shooting problem in a polygon P with h holes. For a given query $\vec{q}$ in P, q' can be located in $O(n)$ time by traversing the boundary of the visibility polygon $V(q)$ of P. Since computing $V(q)$ takes $O(n \log h)$ time [27] (see Section 2.3), each query can be answered in $O(n \log h)$ time. It has been shown both by Chazelle *et al.* [73] and Hershberger and Suri [190] that each ray-shooting query can be answered in $O(\sqrt{h} \log n)$ query time, where n is the total number of vertices of P. The preprocessing of P takes $O(n\sqrt{h} + h^{3/2} \log h + n \log n)$ time. The query time of their algorithms is an improvement by a factor of $O(\log n)$ over that of an earlier algorithm proposed by Agarwal [6].

Let q be a query point inside a simple polygon P. Consider the problem of reporting the visibility polygon $V(q)$ of P from q (see Figure 2.1(a)). We know that $V(q)$ can be computed in $O(n)$ time without any preprocessing of P by the algorithm of Lee [230] (see Section 2.2.1). Recall that this algorithm always requires $O(n)$ time even though the number of vertices of $V(q)$ (say, k) is less than n, i.e., the algorithm is not output sensitive. Guibas *et al.* [181] showed that it is possible to report $V(q)$ in $O(\log n + k)$ query time. During the preprocessing of P, their query algorithm decomposes P into visibility cells in $O(n^3)$ time and then these cells are stored using $O(n^3)$ space. Using a similar method of decomposing P into visibility cells, Bose *et al.* [60] developed another query algorithm which also reports $V(q)$

in $O(\log n + k)$ query time. The algorithm takes $O(n^3 \log n)$ preprocessing time and $O(n^3)$ space. If the query point q lies outside P, the algorithm can also report the external visibility polygon of P from q in the same query time. Representing P as an union of disjoint canonical pieces, Aronov et al. [26] showed that the preprocessing time and space requirement can be reduced to $O(n^2 \log n)$ and $O(n^2)$, respectively. However, the query time of their algorithm increases to $O(\log^2 n + k)$. We present the query algorithm of Bose et al. [60] in Section 8.3.1.

Consider the corresponding problem of reporting $V(q)$ in a polygon P with h holes (see Figure 2.1(b)). We know that $V(q)$ can be computed in $O(n \log h)$ time by the algorithm of Asano [27] (see Section 2.3). Asano et al. [28] first showed that $V(q)$ can be reported in $O(n)$ query time after preprocessing steps taking $O(n^2)$ time and $O(n^2)$ space. Their query algorithm uses point-line duality to find the angular sorted order of vertices of P around q, and then uses triangulation and set-union operations to compute portions of edges of P that are visible from q. It may be noted that the query time of this algorithm is always $O(n)$ even though the number of vertices of $V(q)$ (of size k) may be less than n. Vegter [335] showed that the query time can be a function of the output size k. His query algorithm reports $V(q)$ in $O(k \log(n/k))$ query time after preprocessing steps taking $O(n^2 \log n)$ time and $O(n^2)$ space. Recently, Zarei and Ghodsi [346] showed that $V(q)$ can be reported in $O((1 + \min(h, k)) \log n + k)$ query time after preprocessing steps taking $O(n^3 \log n)$ time and $O(n^3)$ space. If P is a convex polygon containing only convex holes, Pocchiola and Vegter [287] presented a query algorithm that reports $V(q)$ in $O(k \log n)$ query time. During the preprocessing of P, their algorithm decomposes P into a visibility complex taking $O(n \log n + E)$ time and $O(E)$ space, where E is the number of edges in the visibility graph of P. We present the query algorithm of Asano et al. [28] in Section 8.3.2.

Let pq be a query segment inside a simple polygon P. Consider the problem of reporting the weak visibility polygon $V(pq)$ of P from pq (see Figure 3.3(b)). We know that without preprocessing of P, $V(pq)$ can be computed in $O(n)$ time by the algorithm of Guibas et al. [178] (see Section 3.3.2). Aronov et al. [26] showed that $V(pq)$ of size k can be reported in $O(k \log^2 n)$ query time after preprocessing steps taking $O(n^2 \log n)$ time and $O(n^2)$ space. Recently, Bose et al. [60] showed that the query time can be reduced to $O(k \log n)$. However, their algorithm takes $O(n^3 \log n)$ preprocessing time and $O(n^3)$ space. Consider a related problem for a fixed segment pq inside P. Let $u \in P$ be a query point. Let $p'q' \subseteq pq$ be the segment visible from u. The problem is to report $p'q'$ for each query point u. Guibas et al. [178] showed that $p'q'$ can be reported in $O(\log n)$ query time after P is processed taking $O(n)$ time and $O(n)$ space.

Consider the query problem of reporting the Euclidean shortest path $SP(s,t)$ between two points s and t inside a simple polygon P (see Figure 7.1(a)). If s is fixed and t is a query point, $SP(s,t)$ can be reported in $O(\log n + k)$ query time by the query algorithm of Guibas *et al.* [178], where k is the number of edges in $SP(s,t)$. The preprocessing step takes $O(n)$ time and $O(n)$ space as it involves computing the shortest path tree from s to all the vertices of P. If both s and t are query points, $SP(s,t)$ can still be answered in $O(\log n + k)$ query time with $O(n)$ preprocessing time and $O(n)$ space as shown by Guibas and Hershberger [177]. The algorithm decomposes P into sub-polygons in a balanced fashion by diagonals in a triangulation of P and uses these sub-polygons to construct $O(n)$ funnels and hourglasses in P. The funnels and hourglasses, that are lying in the path between s and t in P, are then combined to compute $SP(s,t)$. This problem in a polygon with holes has been studied by Chen *et al.* [85] and Chiang and Mitchell [86]. We present the query algorithm of Guibas and Hershberger [177] for reporting $SP(s,t)$ in Section 8.4.1.

Consider the query problem of reporting the minimum link path $MLP(s,t)$ between two points s and t inside a simple polygon P (see Figure 7.1(a)). If s is fixed and t is a query point, $MLP(s,t)$ can be reported in $O(\log n + k)$ query time by the query algorithm of Suri [320], where k is the number of links in $MLP(s,t)$. In the preprocessing step, the algorithm computes a window tree from s in P taking $O(n)$ time and $O(n)$ space and, using this tree, the query algorithm reports $MLP(s,t)$ in $O(\log n + k)$ query time. If the query problem is to report just the link distance k between s and t and not the path, k can be reported in $O(\log n)$ query time by this algorithm of Suri. In fact, the problem of reporting k was considered earlier by ElGindy [126] and Reif and Storer [297]. Their query algorithms report k in $O(\log n)$ query time although the preprocessing time is $O(n \log n)$. If both s and t are query points, Arkin *et al.* [23] showed that k and $MLP(s,t)$ can be reported in $O(\log n)$ query time and $O(\log n + k)$ query time, respectively. Preprocessing steps take $O(n^3)$ time and space. Reducing the preprocessing cost to $O(n^2)$, they showed that k can be reported in $O(\log n)$ query time with an error of at most 1. Related query problems on link paths between two simple polygons were studied by Arkin *et al.* [23] and Chiang and Tamassia [87].

Let us state the method used by the query algorithm of Arkin *et al.* [23] for computing $MLP(s,t)$ in P. The algorithm computes window partitioning of P during preprocessing (i) from every vertex of P, and (ii) from every extension point on $bd(P)$ of edges of the visibility graph of P. It can be seen that endpoints of these windows divide edges of P into intervals and these intervals satisfy the property that the link sequence of the greedy link path in P from any point of an interval to a point of some other interval is the same. For every such pair of intervals, projection functions are composed which are used during queries for computing $MLP(s,t)$. Adopting this method for computing $MLP(s,t)$, we design a simpler query algorithm for this problem, which is presented in Section 8.4.2. Although the query time of our algorithm for computing $MLP(s,t)$ remains $O(\log n + k)$, preprocessing steps take $O(n^3 \log n)$ time and space, which is a factor of $O(\log n)$ more than the cost in preprocessing of the query algorithm of Arkin *et al.* [23].

Query problems on shortest paths and minimum link paths in L_1 metric are studied for rectilinear polygons. As defined earlier, P is a rectilinear polygon if the internal angle at every vertex of P is 90° or 270°. Consider the query problem of reporting the rectilinear shortest path $RSP(s, t)$ between two points s and t inside a simple rectilinear polygon P. $RSP(s, t)$ can be reported in $O(\log n + k)$ query time by the query algorithm of de Berg [108], where k is the number of edges in $RSP(s, t)$. Preprocessing steps take $O(n \log n)$ time and $O(n \log n)$ space. Later, Lingas *et al.* [245] and Schuierer [303] reduced the preprocessing cost to $O(n)$ keeping the same query time. If both s and t are vertices of P, the query time of their algorithms becomes $O(1 + k)$. Their method computes the rectilinear path which is optimal in both L_1 and the rectilinear link metric (known as the smallest path [254]). For the corresponding query problems on rectilinear link paths, the same query time and preprocessing cost can be achieved using the query algorithms of de Berg [108], Lingas *et al.* [245] and Schuierer [303]. The shortest path query problem in P with rectilinear holes was studied by Atallah and Chen [33, 34], Chen *et al.* [80] and ElGindy and Mitra [130]. The corresponding query problem on rectilinear link paths was studied by Das and Narasimhan [102] and de Rezende *et al.* [109].

8.2 Ray-Shooting Queries in Simple Polygons

In this section, we present the query algorithm of Chazelle *et al.* [73] for answering ray-shooting queries inside a simple polygon P. The ray-shooting problem is to locate the intersection point q' of a given query $\vec{q}$ with $bd(P)$ such that q' is visible from q. The algorithm of Chazelle *et al.* answers each ray-shooting query $\vec{q}$ in optimal $O(\log n)$ query time by locating q'. The algorithm partitions P into geodesic triangles and using this triangulation, a query can be answered in $O(\log^2 n)$ query time. The query time is then improved to $O(\log n)$ using a weight-balanced binary tree [256] and fractional cascading [74, 75]. Preprocessing steps require $O(n)$ time and $O(n)$ space. The algorithm of Chazelle *et al.* [73] used the query algorithm of Guibas and Hershberger [177] (presented in Section 8.4.1) for decomposing P into geodesic triangles in $O(n)$ time. Here we use a different method for this decomposition. We assume that the vertices of P are labeled $v_1, v_2, \ldots, v_n$ in counterclockwise order.

The algorithm starts by partitioning P into a *balanced geodesic triangulation*. Compute shortest paths (i.e., geodesic paths) $SP(v_1, v_{\lfloor n/3 \rfloor})$, $SP(v_{\lfloor n/3 \rfloor}, v_{\lfloor 2n/3 \rfloor})$ and $SP(v_{\lfloor 2n/3 \rfloor}, v_1)$ (see Figure 8.1). Taking the middle vertex $v_{\lfloor n/6 \rfloor}$ of $bd(v_1, v_{\lfloor n/3 \rfloor})$, compute $SP(v_1, v_{\lfloor n/6 \rfloor})$ and $SP(v_{\lfloor n/6 \rfloor}, v_{\lfloor n/3 \rfloor})$. Analogously, taking middle vertices $v_{\lfloor n/2 \rfloor}$ and $v_{\lfloor 5n/6 \rfloor}$ of $bd(v_{\lfloor n/3 \rfloor}, v_{\lfloor 2n/3 \rfloor})$ and $bd(v_{\lfloor 2n/3 \rfloor}, v_1)$, respectively, compute (i) $SP(v_{\lfloor n/3 \rfloor}, v_{\lfloor n/2 \rfloor})$ and $SP(v_{\lfloor n/2 \rfloor}, v_{\lfloor 2n/3 \rfloor})$, (ii) $SP(v_{\lfloor 2n/3 \rfloor}, v_{\lfloor 5n/6 \rfloor})$ and

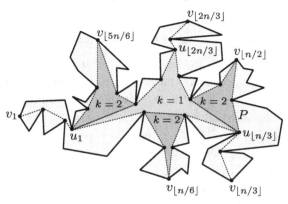

Figure 8.1 The polygon P is partitioned into geodesic triangles up to the stage $k = 2$.

$SP(v_{\lfloor 5n/6 \rfloor}, v_1)$. Repeat this process of computing shortest paths taking middle vertices till the shortest paths connect pairs of vertices, one vertex apart. So, these shortest paths partition P into disjoint regions called *geodesic triangles* of P. Observe that since the boundary of a geodesic triangle is formed by three shortest paths, each shortest path contributes a reflex chain of vertices on the boundary of the triangle. It can be seen that the total number of shortest path edges used for partitioning P into geodesic triangles cannot not exceed $n - 3$.

Exercise 8.2.1 *Let R be the region of P bounded by $bd(v_1, v_{\lfloor n/3 \rfloor})$ and $SP(v_1, v_{\lfloor n/3 \rfloor})$. Prove that $SP(v_1, v_{\lfloor n/6 \rfloor})$ and $SP(v_{\lfloor n/3 \rfloor}, v_{\lfloor n/6 \rfloor})$ lie totally inside R.*

Exercise 8.2.2 *Design an algorithm to partition P into geodesic triangles in $O(n \log n)$ time.*

Let u_1, $u_{\lfloor n/3 \rfloor}$ and $u_{\lfloor 2n/3 \rfloor}$ be three vertices of P (see Figure 8.1) such that (i) $SP(v_{\lfloor n/3 \rfloor}, v_1)$ and $SP(v_{\lfloor 2n/3 \rfloor}, v_1)$ meet at u_1, (ii) $SP(v_1, v_{\lfloor n/3 \rfloor})$ and $SP(v_{\lfloor 2n/3 \rfloor}, v_{\lfloor n/3 \rfloor})$ meet at $u_{\lfloor n/3 \rfloor}$, and (iii) $SP(v_1, v_{\lfloor 2n/3 \rfloor})$ and $SP(v_{\lfloor n/3 \rfloor}, v_{\lfloor 2n/3 \rfloor})$ meet at $u_{\lfloor 2n/3 \rfloor}$. If u_1 is same as v_1, this means that $SP(v_{\lfloor n/3 \rfloor}, v_1)$ and $SP(v_{\lfloor 2n/3 \rfloor}, v_1)$ are disjoint. Similarly, it is possible to have $u_{\lfloor n/3 \rfloor} = v_{\lfloor n/3 \rfloor}$ or $u_{\lfloor 2n/3 \rfloor} = v_{\lfloor 2n/3 \rfloor}$. It can be seen that the region of P enclosed by $SP(u_1, u_{\lfloor n/3 \rfloor})$, $SP(u_{\lfloor n/3 \rfloor}, u_{\lfloor 2n/3 \rfloor})$ and $SP(u_{\lfloor 2n/3 \rfloor}, u_1)$ is a geodesic triangle. We refer $SP(v_1, u_1)$, $SP(v_{\lfloor n/3 \rfloor}, u_{\lfloor n/3 \rfloor})$ and $SP(v_{\lfloor 2n/3 \rfloor}, u_{\lfloor 2n/3 \rfloor})$ as *tails* of this geodesic triangle. A geodesic triangle along with its three tails is called a *kite*. A kite may have an empty geodesic triangle if the shortest path between two end vertices of the kite passes though the third end vertex of the kite.

It can be seen that each kite appears at a unique stage k while partitioning P into geodesic triangles. For example, the kite with end vertices v_1, $v_{\lfloor n/3 \rfloor}$ and $v_{\lfloor 2n/3 \rfloor}$

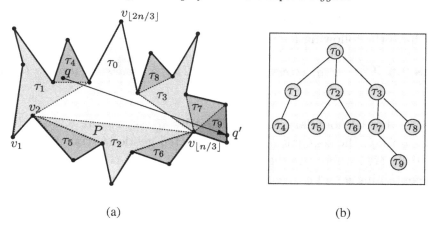

(a)   (b)

Figure 8.2 (a) The polygon P is decomposed into kites τ_0, τ_1, τ_2, τ_3, τ_4, τ_5, τ_6, τ_7, τ_8, τ_9. (b) Kites of the polygon P are represented in the geodesic tree.

appear when $k = 1$ (see Figure 8.1). Observe that for $k > 1$, one of the sides of a kite at stage k shares an edge with a kite at stage $k - 1$ and the other two sides share edges with two kites at stage $k + 1$ (if they exist). At the kth stage, there are at most 3.2^{k-1} shortest paths and some of these shortest paths share edges with shortest paths computed at earlier stages. We have the following observation.

Lemma 8.2.1 *The number of kites constructed at the k-th stage during the partition of P is 1 for $k = 1$ and at most 3.2^{k-2} for $k > 1$.*

Let us represent the kites of P computed by the above method by a free tree of degree 3 called the *geodesic tree*, which is denoted as GT (see Figure 8.2). The kite computed in the first stage is represented as the root of GT and the three kites at stage $k = 2$ are represented as children of the root of GT as each of them share an edge with the kite at stage $k = 1$. Similarly, the kites at stage k are represented as nodes of GT at depth $k - 1$ with their parents at depth $k - 2$. We have the following lemma.

Lemma 8.2.2 *The height and diameter of GT are at most $\log n$ and $2 \log n$, respectively.*

Observe that after P is partitioned into geodesic triangles, a non-polygonal edge in the partition is shared by two geodesic triangles but the same edge can be present in the tails of several kites. For example, the edge $v_1 v_2$ in Figure 8.2(a) is shared by kites τ_0, τ_1, τ_2 and τ_5. Therefore, if a node α of GT corresponds to a kite τ, then only the geodesic triangle of τ is stored at α and not the tails of τ. This method helps in keeping the space complexity linear as each non-polygonal edge of the partition is stored twice. So, GT can also be viewed as a representation of geodesic triangles of P. We have the following lemma.

Lemma 8.2.3 *A query $\overrightarrow{q}$ intersects at most $2 \log n$ geodesic triangles (or kites) in P.*

Proof. Let q' be the boundary point of P hit by $\overrightarrow{q}$ (see Figure 8.2(a)). In order to reach from q to q', the segment qq' has intersected geodesic triangles of P that are on the path in GT, where the the first and last nodes of GT represent the geodesic triangles containing q and q', respectively. Since the number of such triangles intersected by qq' is at most the diameter of GT (see Figure 8.2(b)), qq' can intersected at most $2 \log n$ geodesic triangles of P by Lemma 8.2.2.   □

The above proof suggests a method for locating q' as follows. Locate the geodesic triangle α_1 containing q. Using binary search on each concave side of α_1, locate the edge of α_1 intersected by $\overrightarrow{q}$. Let w be the point of intersection. If the edge containing w is a polygonal edge, w is q'. Otherwise, w is the entry point to the next geodesic triangle α_2 in the path from q to q'. Let $\overrightarrow{w}$ be the ray starting from the point w in the same direction as $\overrightarrow{q}$. Using binary searches again on the concave sides of α_2, locate the intersection point of $\overrightarrow{w}$ with the boundary of α_2. This process is repeated until q' is found.

Let us analyze the time complexity of the above method. It has been shown by Edelsbrunner *et al.* [119] and Kirkpatrick [216] that by preprocessing a planar subdivision of triangles of having n edges in $O(n)$ time, data structures can be built so that a query point can be located in the planar subdivision in $O(\log n)$ time. Note that the geodesic triangles in P can be partitioned into triangles in $O(n)$ time. Using this method, the geodesic triangle α_1 containing q can be located in $O(\log n)$ time. We know that the binary search for checking the intersection of $\overrightarrow{q}$ with a side of a geodesic triangle can be performed in $O(\log n)$ time. We also know from Lemma 8.2.3 that $\overrightarrow{q}$ intersects at most $2 \log n$ geodesic triangles of P. Therefore, q' can be located in $O(\log^2 n)$ time. We have the following theorem.

Theorem 8.2.4 *A given simple polygon P of n vertices can be preprocessed in $O(n \log n)$ time and $O(n)$ space so that each ray-shooting query $\overrightarrow{q}$ in P can be answered in $O(\log^2 n)$ query time.*

Let us explain how the query time can be improved to $O(\log n)$. Let $\alpha_1, \alpha_2, \ldots, \alpha_m$ be the geodesic triangles intersected by qq' in the order from q to q', where $q \in \alpha_1$, $q' \in \alpha_m$ and $m \leq 2 \log n$. For any geodesic triangle α_i for $1 \leq i \leq m$, the concave chain of α_i intersected by $\overrightarrow{q}$ is called the *front chain* of α_i (see Figure 8.3(a)). Note that if $\overrightarrow{q}$ intersects two concave chains of α_i, the closer one is the front chain of α_i. Consider the other two chains of α_i. If there exists a parallel line of $\overrightarrow{q}$ which is tangential to one of the chains of α_i, the chain is called the *side chain* of α_i (see

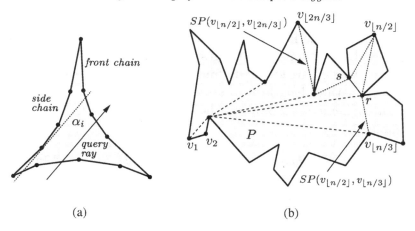

(a)   (b)

Figure 8.3 (a) The front and side chains of a geodesic triangle α_i are shown with respect to a query ray. (b) The segment rs lies inside P.

Figure 8.3(a)). The problem is now to identify front chains of $\alpha_1, \alpha_2, \ldots, \alpha_m$ and then locate intersection points of $\overrightarrow{q}$ with these chains. Moreover, the entire task has to be carried out in $O(\log n)$ time.

The intersection point of $\overrightarrow{q}$ with the front chain of α_i on some edge $v_l v_r$ can be located using a binary search. It can be seen that the total number of binary searches required to locate subsequent intersection points depends on the size of the pocket of $v_l v_r$, where the pocket of $v_l v_r$ is $bd(v_l, v_r)$ (or $bd(v_r, v_l)$) if $q' \in bd(v_l, v_r)$ (respectively, $q' \in bd(v_r, v_l)$). So, we use a weight-balanced binary tree, with each leaf, representing an edge of the front chain and being weighted by the number of vertices in the pocket of the corresponding edge of the chain. In this tree, the cost of locating $v_l v_r$ is $O(1 + \log(W/w))$, where w is the size of the pocket of $v_l v_r$ and W is the total size of all pockets of the front chain of α_i. Let $n_1, n_2, \ldots, n_m$ be the size of the successive pockets into which $\overrightarrow{q}$ enters. Then, the cost of locating q' is bounded by

$$\log n + \sum_j \log \frac{n_j}{n_{j+1}}$$

which is $O(\log n)$.

The above analysis is based on the assumption that every time $\overrightarrow{q}$ enters into a geodesic triangle, it can be determined in $O(1)$ time which is the front chain of the geodesic triangle before the intersection point is computed on the chain by binary search. So, it is necessary to calculate the cost of identifying side chains of $\alpha_1, \alpha_2, \ldots, \alpha_m$. For each geodesic triangle α of P, create a fictitious node and link it to the three roots of weight balanced binary trees representing the three concave sides of α. It can be seen that each non-polygonal edge of a geodesic triangle is a leaf in two such trees. All such pairs of leaves are also connected by edges giving a big free tree whose every node has degree at most three. For each geodesic triangle α, an array representing the slopes of all edges of α is assigned to the node representing α in the big free tree. This gives the fractional cascading structure which allows searching along a path of length m in $O(m + \log n)$ time [74, 75]. Since m can be at most $2 \log n$ by Lemma 8.2.3, q' can be located in $O(\log n)$ time. We have the following lemma.

Lemma 8.2.5 *Each ray-shooting query $\vec{q}$ in P can be answered in $O(\log n)$ time using fractional cascading.*

In the following we present the major steps of the query algorithm for locating q'.

Step 1. Partition P into geodesic triangles and construct the geodesic tree GT.

Step 2. Construct the data structure by the algorithm of Kirkpatrick [216] for locating a query point in the geodesic triangle.

Step 3. Represent each side of every geodesic triangle α by a weight balanced binary tree and connect them to form a big free tree.

Step 4. *For* each geodesic triangle α, construct the array representing the slopes of all edges of α and then assign it to the node representing α in the big free tree.

Step 5. *For* each query $\vec{q}$ *do*

Step 5a. Locate the geodesic triangle of P containing the point q.

Step 5b. Using fractional cascading, locate the point q'.

Step 5c. Report q'.

Step 6. Stop.

The correctness of the algorithm follows from Theorem 8.2.4 and Lemma 8.2.5. Let us analyze the time complexity of the algorithm. It has already been established in Lemma 8.2.5 that q and q' can be located in Step 5 in $O(\log n)$ time. We know that the data structures in Steps 2, 3 and 4 can be constructed in $O(n)$ time. Partitioning P into geodesic triangles in Step 1 can also be done in $O(n)$ time as follows.

Compute $SPT(v_1)$ by the algorithm of Guibas *et al.* [178] in $O(n)$ time (see Section 3.6.1). So, $SP(v_1, v_{\lfloor n/3 \rfloor})$ and $SP(v_1, v_{\lfloor 2n/3 \rfloor})$ have been computed. To complete the computation of the geodesic triangle at the first stage, $SP(v_{\lfloor n/3 \rfloor}, v_{\lfloor 2n/3 \rfloor})$ has to be computed. We take a different approach in computing $SP(v_{\lfloor n/3 \rfloor}, v_{\lfloor 2n/3 \rfloor})$.

We know that $v_{\lfloor n/2 \rfloor}$ is the middle vertex of $bd(v_{\lfloor n/3 \rfloor}, v_{\lfloor 2n/3 \rfloor})$ (see Figure 8.3(b)). Suppose $SP(v_{\lfloor n/2 \rfloor}, v_{\lfloor 2n/3 \rfloor})$ and $SP(v_{\lfloor n/2 \rfloor}, v_{\lfloor n/3 \rfloor})$ are known. Then, $SP(v_{\lfloor n/3 \rfloor}, v_{\lfloor 2n/3 \rfloor})$ can be computed by drawing the tangent between $SP(v_{\lfloor n/2 \rfloor}, v_{\lfloor 2n/3 \rfloor})$ and $SP(v_{\lfloor n/2 \rfloor}, v_{\lfloor n/3 \rfloor})$ provided the tangent (say, rs) lies inside P. Initialize r and s by the next vertex of $v_{\lfloor n/2 \rfloor}$ on $SP(v_{\lfloor n/2 \rfloor}, v_{\lfloor n/3 \rfloor})$ and $SP(v_{\lfloor n/2 \rfloor}, v_{\lfloor 2n/3 \rfloor})$ respectively. Note that if $SP(v_{\lfloor n/2 \rfloor}, v_{\lfloor n/3 \rfloor})$ and

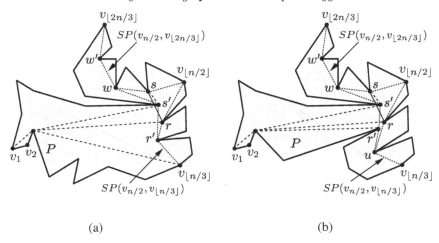

Figure 8.4 (a) The segment $r's'$ is the cross-tangent between $SP(v_1, w)$ and $SP(v_{\lfloor n/3\rfloor}, r)$. (b) The cross-tangent between $SP(v_1, w)$ and $SP(v_{\lfloor n/3\rfloor}, r)$, does not lie inside P.

$SP(v_{\lfloor n/2\rfloor}, v_{\lfloor 2n/3\rfloor})$ meet at some vertex v_j other than $v_{\lfloor n/2\rfloor}$, then $SP(v_j, v_{\lfloor n/2\rfloor})$ is common to both the paths. In that case, r and s are assigned to the next vertices of v_j. Without loss of generality, we assume that v_j is $v_{\lfloor n/2\rfloor}$. We have the following four cases.

Case 1. The parent of s in $SPT(v_1)$ lies to the left of $\overrightarrow{rs}$ and the parent of r in $SPT(v_1)$ lies to the right of $\overrightarrow{sr}$ (Figure 8.3(b)).

Case 2. The parent of s in $SPT(v_1)$ lies to the right of $\overrightarrow{rs}$ and the parent of r in $SPT(v_1)$ lies to the right of $\overrightarrow{sr}$ (Figure 8.4).

Case 3. The parent of s in $SPT(v_1)$ lies to the left of $\overrightarrow{rs}$ and the parent of r in $SPT(v_1)$ lies to the left of $\overrightarrow{sr}$ (Figure 8.5(a)).

Case 4. The parent of s in $SPT(v_1)$ lies to the right of $\overrightarrow{rs}$ and the parent of r in $SPT(v_1)$ lies to the left of $\overrightarrow{sr}$ (Figure 8.5(b)).

Consider Case 1. It can be seen that the current rs lies inside P (see Figure 8.3(b)). If rs is the tangent between $SP(v_{\lfloor n/2\rfloor}, v_{\lfloor n/3\rfloor})$ and $SP(v_{\lfloor n/2\rfloor}, v_{\lfloor 2n/3\rfloor})$, then $SP(v_{\lfloor n/3\rfloor}, v_{\lfloor 2n/3\rfloor})$ is the concatenation of $SP(v_{\lfloor n/3\rfloor}, r)$, rs and $SP(s, v_{\lfloor 2n/3\rfloor})$. Otherwise, if rs is not a tangent to $SP(v_{\lfloor n/2\rfloor}, v_{\lfloor 2n/3\rfloor})$ at s, then assign s to the next vertex of s on $SP(v_{\lfloor n/2\rfloor}, v_{\lfloor 2n/3\rfloor})$. Otherwise, assign r to the next vertex of r on $SP(v_{\lfloor n/2\rfloor}, v_{\lfloor n/3\rfloor})$. Test the above four cases for the new rs.

Consider Case 2. It can be seen that the current rs does not lie inside P (see Figure 8.4). This means that $SP(v_1, v_{\lfloor 2n/3\rfloor})$ has intersected rs. Let ww' be the first edge on $SP(v_{\lfloor n/2\rfloor}, v_{\lfloor 2n/3\rfloor})$ while moving from s to $v_{\lfloor 2n/3\rfloor}$ such that $w' \in SP(w, v_{\lfloor 2n/3\rfloor})$ and w it is the parent of w' in $SPT(v_1)$ (see Figure 8.4(a)). Observe that w and its parent in $SPT(v_1)$ have formed an eave on $SP(v_{\lfloor n/3\rfloor}, v_{\lfloor 2n/3\rfloor})$, and w is the

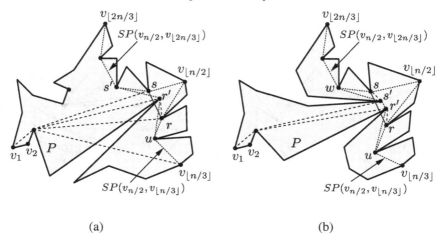

Figure 8.5 (a) The segment $r's'$ is the cross-tangent between $SP(v_1, u)$ and $SP(v_{\lfloor 2n/3 \rfloor}, s)$. (b) The segment $r's'$ is the tangent between $SP(v_1, u)$ and $SP(v_1, w)$.

vertex where $SP(r, v_{\lfloor 2n/3 \rfloor})$ and $SP(v_1, v_{\lfloor 2n/3 \rfloor})$ meet. Locate the cross-tangent $r's'$ between $SP(v_1, w)$ and $SP(v_{\lfloor n/3 \rfloor}, r)$, where $s' \in SP(v_1, w)$ and $r' \in SP(v_{\lfloor n/3 \rfloor}, r)$. So, $SP(v_{\lfloor n/3 \rfloor}, v_{\lfloor 2n/3 \rfloor})$ is the concatenation of $SP(v_{\lfloor n/3 \rfloor}, r')$, $r's'$, $SP(s', w)$ and $SP(w, v_{\lfloor 2n/3 \rfloor})$.

Observe that there may not always be a cross-tangent between $SP(v_1, w)$ and $SP(v_{\lfloor n/3 \rfloor}, r)$ that lies inside P (see Figure 8.4(b)). In that case, a similar approach as above is taken by locating r' on $SP(v_1, SP(v_{\lfloor n/3 \rfloor}))$ instead of $SP(v_{\lfloor n/3 \rfloor}, r)$. Therefore, $r's'$ becomes the tangent (and not the cross-tangent) between $SP(v_1, SP(v_{\lfloor n/3 \rfloor}))$ and $SP(v_1, SP(v_{\lfloor 2n/3 \rfloor}))$. The remaining task is to construct $SP(v_{\lfloor n/3 \rfloor}, r')$. Let u be the vertex where $SP(r, v_{\lfloor n/3 \rfloor})$ and $SP(r', SP(v_{\lfloor n/3 \rfloor}))$ meet. So, $SP(v_{\lfloor n/3 \rfloor}, v_{\lfloor 2n/3 \rfloor})$ is the concatenation of $SP(v_{\lfloor n/3 \rfloor}, u)$, $SP(u, r')$, $r's'$, $SP(s', w)$ and $SP(w, v_{\lfloor 2n/3 \rfloor})$.

It can be seen that Case 3 is analogous to Case 2 (see Figure 8.5(a)). In Case 4, the tangent $r's'$ is drawn between $SP(v_1, SP(v_{\lfloor n/3 \rfloor}))$ and $SP(v_1, SP(v_{\lfloor 2n/3 \rfloor}))$ (see Figure 8.5(b)), and the remaining portions of $SP(v_{\lfloor n/3 \rfloor}, v_{\lfloor 2n/3 \rfloor})$ are constructed as before by locating vertices w and u on $SP(s, v_{\lfloor 2n/3 \rfloor})$ and $SP(r, v_{\lfloor n/3 \rfloor})$, respectively.

The above method shows that with the help of $SPT(v_1)$, $SP(v_{\lfloor n/3 \rfloor}, v_{\lfloor 2n/3 \rfloor})$ can be computed correctly from $SP(v_{\lfloor n/2 \rfloor}, v_{\lfloor 2n/3 \rfloor})$ and $SP(v_{\lfloor n/2 \rfloor}, v_{\lfloor n/3 \rfloor})$. It can be seen that the time for computing $SP(v_{\lfloor n/3 \rfloor}, v_{\lfloor 2n/3 \rfloor})$ is proportional to the sum of (i) the number of vertices of $SPT(v_1)$ included in $SP(v_{\lfloor n/3 \rfloor}, v_{\lfloor 2n/3 \rfloor})$, and (ii) the number of vertices of $SP(v_{\lfloor n/2 \rfloor}, v_{\lfloor 2n/3 \rfloor})$ and $SP(v_{\lfloor n/2 \rfloor}, v_{\lfloor n/3 \rfloor})$ not included in $SP(v_{\lfloor n/3 \rfloor}, v_{\lfloor 2n/3 \rfloor})$.

The above method suggests that once the shortest paths between the vertices at the leaves of GT are computed, the entire geodesic partitioning of P can be computing by drawing tangents and cross-tangents with the help of $SPT(v_1)$. Since there can be at most one intermediate vertex between the pair of vertices at the leaf level of GT, all shortest paths at the leaf level of GT can be computed in $O(n)$ time. Applying the above method at each intermediate node of GT, P can be partitioned into geodesic triangles in $O(n)$ time. We have the following lemma.

Exercise 8.2.3 *Let v_j be a vertex in the shortest path between a pair of vertices at some stage $k > 1$. Prove that if v_j is not in the shortest path of any pair of vertices at the stage $k - 1$, then no shortest path at stages $k' < k$ passes through v_j.*

Lemma 8.2.6 *A geodesic triangulation of P can be constructed in $O(n)$ time.*

We summarize the result in the following theorem.

Theorem 8.2.7 *A given simple polygon P of n vertices can be preprocessed in $O(n)$ time and $O(n)$ space so that each ray-shooting query $\overrightarrow{q}$ in P can be answered in $O(\log n)$ query time.*

8.3 Visibility Polygon Queries for Points in Polygons

8.3.1 *Without Holes:* $O(\log n + k)$ *Query Algorithm*

In this section, we present the query algorithm of Bose *et al.* [60] for reporting the visibility polygon $V(q)$ of a query point q inside a simple polygon P in $O(\log n + k)$ query time, where k is the number of vertices of $V(q)$. The algorithm takes $O(n^3 \log n)$ preprocessing time and $O(n^3)$ space. In a preprocessing step, the algorithm decomposes P into a set of disjoint regions and stores their adjacency relationship. To answer a query, the algorithm locates the region (say, c_i) containing the query point in $O(\log n)$ time, and then traverses a subset of regions starting from c_i using the adjacency relationship to extract $V(q)$, taking $O(k)$ time. We assume that the vertices of P are labeled $v_1, v_2, \ldots, v_n$ in counterclockwise order.

Consider the visibility polygon $V(v_j)$ from a vertex v_j. We know that each constructed edge $v_l u$ of $V(v_j)$ defines a region or pocket of P that is not visible from v_j (see Figure 8.6(b)). If the pocket is bounded by $v_l u$ and $bd(v_l, u)$, then the pocket and $v_l u$ are called a *right pocket* and a *right constructed edge* of $V(v_j)$, respectively. Otherwise, the pocket and $v_l u$ are called a *left pocket* and a *left constructed edge* of $V(v_j)$, respectively.

The algorithm starts by decomposing P into disjoint regions called *visibility cells*. Compute visibility polygons $V(v_1), V(v_2), \ldots, V(v_n)$. Let W_j denote the set of all constructed edges of $V(v_j)$. For all j, add W_j to P. These constructed edges decompose P into a planar subdivision $C = (c_1, c_2, \ldots, c_m)$, where each face c_i of

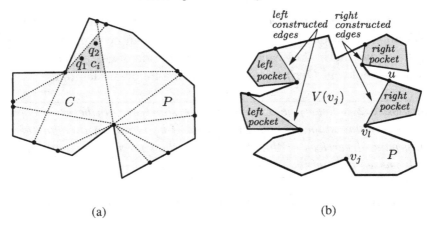

       (a)   (b)

Figure 8.6 (a) Since q_1 and q_2 are two points in the same visibility cell c_i, vertices in $V(q_1)$ and $V(q_2)$ are the same. (b) The disjoint regions of $P - V(v_j)$ are pockets of $V(v_j)$.

the subdivision C is called a *visibility cell* (see Figure 8.6(a)). We have the following observations.

Lemma 8.3.1 *For any two points q_1 and q_2 in any visibility cell c_i of C, the vertices of P in $V(q_1)$ and $V(q_2)$ are the same.*

Proof. Assume on the contrary that there exists a vertex v_p in P such that $v_p \in V(q_1)$ but $v_p \notin V(q_2)$. This means that q_1 lies inside $V(v_p)$ and q_2 lies inside a pocket of $V(v_p)$. Therefore, a constructed edge in $V(v_p)$ has intersected c_i with one part of c_i containing q_1 and the other part containing q_2. Hence, c_i is not a visibility cell, which is a contradiction. $\square$

Lemma 8.3.2 *The number of visibility cells in the planar subdivision C is $O(n^3)$.*

Proof. We know that the number of constructed edges in the visibility polygon of a vertex in P is $O(n)$. So, the total number of constructed edges in $V(v_1)$, $V(v_2), \ldots, V(v_n)$ is $O(n^2)$. Let $v_l u$ be a constructed edge in the visibility polygon of a vertex v_j. It can be seen that at most two constructed edges of $V(v_i)$ for $i \neq j$ can intersect $v_l u$. So, there are $O(n)$ intersection points on $v_l u$. Therefore, there are $O(n^3)$ intersection points on all constructed edges in $V(v_1)$, $V(v_2), \ldots, V(v_n)$ giving the bound on the number of vertices and edges of C. Since C is a planar subdivision, the number of faces of C is $O(n^3)$. Hence, the number of visibility cells in the planar subdivision C is $O(n^3)$. $\square$

Exercise 8.3.1 *Draw a simple polygon P such that the number of visibility cells in the planar subdivision C of P is $\Omega(n^3)$.*

For every visibility cell c_i, take a point $q_i \in c_i$ and compute $V(q_i)$ in $O(n)$ time by the algorithm of Lee [230] (see Section 2.2.1). By Lemma 8.3.1, the vertices of $V(q_i)$ are the vertices of the visibility polygon of any query point q lying in c_i. However, the boundaries of $V(q_i)$ and $V(q)$ are not identical as constructed edges on the two boundaries are different. Let $v_l u$ be a constructed edge of $V(q_i)$. Let $v_s v_{s+1}$ be the edge of P containing the point u. It can be seen that $\overrightarrow{q v_l}$ intersects $v_s v_{s+1}$ at some point (say, u') and $v_l u'$ is a constructed edge of $V(q)$. Thus, for every constructed edge in $V(q_i)$, the corresponding constructed edge of $V(q)$ can be computed. Hence, $V(q)$ can be obtained from $V(q_i)$ in time proportional to the size of $V(q)$.

Let us discuss the procedure for locating the visibility cell in C containing a query point q. The planar subdivision C can be constructed from constructed edges in $O(n^3 \log n)$ time using sweep-line methods given in Edelsbrunner [117]. If constructed edges are in *general position*, C can be computed in $O(n^3)$ time by the algorithm of Chazelle and Edelsbrunner [72]. Since constructed edges may not be in general position, the cost of computing C is considered $O(n^3 \log n)$ time. After this construction, C is preprocessed for planar point location in $O(n^3 \log n)$ time by the algorithm of Kirkpatrick [216]. After this preprocessing, the visibility cell in C containing a query point q can be located in $O(\log n)$ time. In the following, we present the major steps of the query algorithm for computing $V(q)$ in P.

Step 1. Compute visibility polygons $V(v_1), V(v_2), \ldots, V(v_n)$ by the algorithm of Lee [230] and form the set W containing all constructed edges of these visibility polygons.

Step 2. Compute the planar subdivision C using constructed edges in W by the algorithm given in Edelsbrunner [117].

Step 3. Construct the data structure for locating a query point in C by the algorithm of Kirkpatrick [216].

Step 4. *For* every visibility cell c_i of C, take a point $q_i \in c_i$ and compute $V(q_i)$ by the algorithm of Lee [230].

Step 5. *For* each query point q *do*

  Step 5a. Locate the visibility cell c_i of C containing the point q.

  Step 5b. Compute $V(q)$ from $V(q_i)$.

  Step 5c. Report $V(q)$.

Step 6. Stop.

Theorem 8.3.3 *A given simple polygon P of n vertices can be preprocessed in $O(n^4)$ time and $O(n^4)$ space so that the visibility polygon $V(q)$ of each query point q in P can be computed in $O(\log n + k)$ query time, where k is the number of vertices of $V(q)$.*

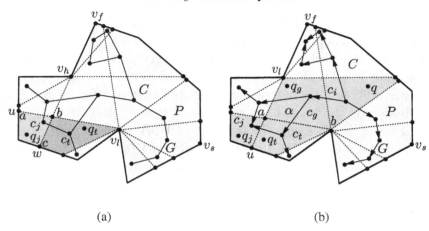

(a)   (b)

Figure 8.7 (a) The dual graph G of C. (b) Each edge of G is assigned a direction to indicate the loss of a visible vertex.

It can be seen that the preprocessing cost of the above algorithm is dominated by the cost of computing visibility polygons from $O(n^3)$ points $q_1, q_2, \ldots, q_m$ in Step 4. In order to reduce the cost, we modify the algorithm showing that it is enough to compute visibility polygons from one representative point of $O(n^2)$ visibility cells having special properties. Let c_j be a visibility cell in C (see Figure 8.7(a)) such that for every adjacent visibility cell c_t of c_j, q_t sees all vertices of $V(q_j)$, where q_t and q_j are points of c_t and c_j, respectively, and in addition, q_t sees one more vertex of P (say, v_f). Intuitively, if the segment separating c_j and c_t is crossed from c_j to c_t, one more vertex becomes visible. Observe that the segment separating c_j and c_t is a part of a constructed edge of $V(v_f)$ and c_j lies inside the pocket of that constructed edge. All visibility cells of C satisfying the property of c_j are referred to as *minimal visibility cells*. We have the following observation.

Lemma 8.3.4 *The number of minimal visibility cells in C is $O(n^2)$.*

Proof. Let $v_l u$ be a constructed edge of $V(v_s)$ (see Figure 8.7(a)). Let ab be a boundary segment of a minimal visibility cell c_j such that ab is a part of $v_l u$. Without loss of generality, we assume that $v_l u$ is a left constructed edge of $V(v_s)$. Let bc be the next clockwise segment of ab on the boundary of c_j and it is a part of a constructed edge $v_h w$ of $V(v_f)$. Since c_j is a minimal visibility cell, c_j lies in the pocket of $V(v_s)$ as well as in the pocket of $V(v_f)$. Observe that since $v_h w$ has intersected $v_l u$, $v_h w$ does not intersect any other left constructed edge of $V(v_s)$ as pockets in a visibility polygon are disjoint. This observation suggests that although there can be $O(n^2)$ intersection points on all left constructed edges of $V(v_s)$, only $O(n)$ intersection points can be on the boundary of minimal visibility cells that are also points on left constructed edges of $V(v_s)$. The same bound holds for right constructed edges of $V(v_s)$. Since there are n visibility polygons, there are $O(n^2)$ minimal visibility cells in C.   □

Exercise 8.3.2 *Draw a simple polygon P such that the number of minimum visibility cells in the planar subdivision C of P is $\Omega(n^2)$.*

Let us identify minimal visibility cells from the dual graph G of C. Represent every visibility cell of C as a node in G and connect two nodes by an edge in G if and only if their corresponding visibility cells are adjacent in C (see Figure 8.7(a)). Let ab be a segment on the boundary of two adjacent visibility cells c_t and c_g (see Figure 8.7(b)), where ab is a part of a constructed edge of the visibility polygon of some vertex v_s. We know that v_s is visible from every point of one of c_t and c_g (say, c_g) and is not visible from any point of other visibility cell c_t. Assign a direction from c_g to c_t in the corresponding edge in G. Intuitively, a directed edge in G represents the loss of a visible vertex in the direction from one visibility cell to its adjacent visibility cell. We have the following observation.

Lemma 8.3.5 *If there is no outward edge from a node in G, the corresponding visibility cell of the node is a minimal visibility cell in C (Figure 8.7(b)).*

For every minimal visibility cell c_j, take a point $q_j \in c_j$ and compute $V(q_j)$ in $O(n)$ time by the algorithm of Lee [230] (see Section 2.2.1). Note that $O(n^2)$ visibility polygons can be computed in $O(n^3)$ time. Let c_i be the visibility cell containing the query point q. If c_i is a minimal visibility cell c_i, $V(q)$ can be computed from $V(q_i)$ as stated earlier. Consider the other situation when c_i is not a minimal visibility cell (see Figure 8.7(b)). Consider any directed path α in G from the node representing c_i to a node representing a minimal visibility cell (say, c_j). Let c_t be the next visibility cell of c_j on α. Let v_f be the vertex of P such that the boundary segment separating c_j and c_t is a part of a constructed edge $v_l u$ of $V(v_f)$. We know that v_l belongs to $V(q_j)$. If $v_l u$ is a right (or, left) constructed edge, insert v_f in $V(q_j)$ as the next clockwise (or counterclockwise) vertex of v_l to obtain $V(q_t)$, where $q_t \in c_t$. If $v_l v_f$ is not a polygonal edge, add the appropriate constructed edge at v_l to $V(q_t)$. Take the next visibility cell c_g of c_t on α and compute $V(q_g)$ from $V(q_t)$. Repeat this process till $V(q)$ is computed. It can be seen that the length of α is less than k and therefore, $V(q)$ can be computed from $V(q_j)$ in $O(k)$ time. We have the following lemma.

Lemma 8.3.6 *The visibility polygon $V(q)$ can be computed from the visibility polygon from a point in a minimal visibility cell using the dual graph G of C in $O(k)$ time.*

In the following, we present the major steps of the modified query algorithm for computing $V(q)$ in P.

Step 1. Compute visibility polygons $V(v_1)$, $V(v_2), \ldots, V(v_n)$ by the algorithm of Lee [230] and form the set W containing all constructed edges of these visibility polygons.

Step 2. Compute the planar subdivision C using constructed edges in W by the algorithm given in Edelsbrunner [117].

Step 3. Construct the data structure for locating a query point in C by the algorithm of Kirkpatrick [216].

Step 4. Compute the dual graph G of C and assign a direction to each edge of G. Identify all minimal visibility cells in C using depth-first search on G.

Step 5. *For* every minimal visibility cell c_j of C, take a point $q_j \in c_j$ and compute $V(q_j)$ by the algorithm of Lee [230].

Step 6. *For* each query point q *do*

> **Step 6a.** Locate the visibility cell c_i of C containing the point q.
>
> **Step 6b.** Take a directed path α in G from the node representing c_i to a node representing a minimal visibility cell c_j.
>
> **Step 6c.** Traverse α in the opposite direction and obtain $V(q)$ by inserting the remaining visible vertices of q in $V(q_j)$.
>
> **Step 6d.** Report $V(q)$.

Step 7. Stop.

The correctness and the time complexity of the algorithm follow from Lemmas 8.3.2, 8.3.4 and 8.3.6. We summarize the result in the following theorem.

Theorem 8.3.7 *A given simple polygon P of n vertices can be preprocessed in $O(n^3 \log n)$ time and $O(n^3)$ space so that the visibility polygon $V(q)$ of each query point q in P can be computed in $O(\log n + k)$ query time, where k is the number of vertices of $V(q)$.*

8.3.2 With Holes: $O(n)$ Query Algorithm

In this section, we present the query algorithm of Asano *et al.* [28] for computing the visibility polygon $V(q)$ of a query point q in a polygon P with holes (see Figure 8.8(a)). The algorithm reports $V(q)$ in $O(n)$ query time after preprocessing steps taking $O(n^2)$ time and $O(n^2)$ space. The algorithm uses point-line duality to find the sorted angular order of vertices of P around q, and then uses triangulation and set-union operations to compute portions of edges of P that are visible from q. It may be noted that the query time of this algorithm is always $O(n)$ even though the number of vertices of $V(q)$ may be less than n.

As in the algorithm of Asano [27] for computing $V(q)$ once for one point q (see Section 2.3), we need to sort the vertices of P in angular order around q. On the

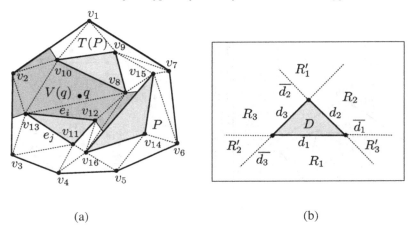

(a)   (b)

Figure 8.8 (a) The visibility polygon $V(q)$ of a query point q in a polygon P with holes. (b) Six regions are formed by lines $\overline{d_1}$, $\overline{d_2}$ and $\overline{d_3}$ drawn through the sides of a triangle D.

other hand, the vertices of P cannot be sorted directly for every query point q as it costs $O(n \log n)$ time for each query point. Using the duality transform between points and lines, the sorted angular order of vertices of P with respect to any query point q can be obtained in $O(n)$ query time.

In the first preprocessing step of the algorithm, the vertices of P are transformed into lines in the dual plane forming an arrangement of lines. For more details of this transformation, see the proof of Lemma 5.3.2. The planar subdivision formed by this arrangement can be constructed in $O(n^2)$ time and space by the algorithm of Chazelle *et al.* [77] or Edelsbrunner *et al.* [120]. For any point $u \in P$, let $L(u)$ denote the line in the the dual plane. Given a query point q, the line $L(q)$ is inserted in the arrangement taking $O(n)$ time. Observe that the line connecting q and a vertex v_i of P in the original plane corresponds to the intersection point of $L(q)$ and $L(v_i)$ in the dual plane. By properties of the duality transformation, the ordering by slope of the lines passing through q and every vertex v_i corresponds to the ordering by x-coordinates of intersection points of $L(q)$ with every line $L(v_i)$ in the dual plane. Using this property, the ordering of vertices of P in increasing order of angle at q can be obtained from their ordering of slopes in $O(n)$ time. We have the following lemma.

Lemma 8.3.8 *The sorted angular order of vertices of P around a query point q can be computed in $O(n)$ query time using $O(n^2)$ space and $O(n^2)$ preprocessing time.*

Once the sorted angular order of vertices of P around q is known, $V(q)$ can be computed by angular sweep following the algorithm of Asano [27] (see Section 2.3). However, this method takes $O(n \log n)$ time. The query algorithm adopts a different method for computing $V(q)$ and takes $O(n)$ time.

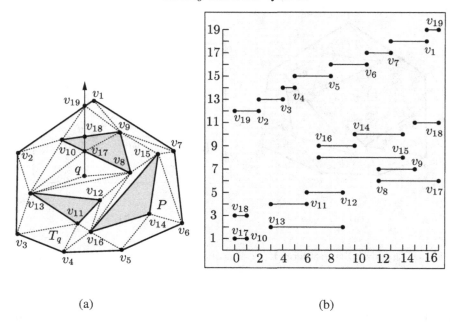

(a)   (b)

Figure 8.9 (a) Vertices v_{17}, v_{18} and v_{19} are introduced in P on the vertical ray drawn from q. (b) Each edge of S_q is represented on orthogonal axes as a horizontal segment.

The algorithm uses another preprocessing step for assigning ranks to edges of P with respect to q. Let e_i and e_j be two edges of P such that e_i is closer to q than e_j (see Figure 8.8(a)). Then the rank assigned to e_j is greater than that of e_i, i.e., $rank(e_i) < rank(e_j)$. Let S denote the set of edges $e_1, e_2, \ldots, e_n$ of P. To assign ranks to all edges in S, we need a relation $\prec_q$ on S. For every pair of edges e_i and e_j in S, $e_i \prec_q e_j$ if a ray from q intersects both e_i and e_j and the intersection point with e_i is closer to q than the intersection point with e_j. Observe that the directed graph of the $\prec_q$ can have cycles, and therefore, $\prec_q$ may not be a partial order. To convert it to a partial order, each edge in S, intersecting the upward vertical ray from q, is split into two parts at the point of intersection (see Figure 8.9(a)). Let S_q denote the set of all edges of S including split edges of S. It can be seen that the relation $\prec_q$ is now a partial order on the edges of S_q. We have the following observation.

Lemma 8.3.9 *The rank of an edge in S_q is its rank in a total order compatible with the relation $\prec_q$.*

Triangulate P by the algorithm of Ghosh and Mount [165] in $O(n \log n)$ time and $O(n)$ space (see Section 5.3.2). Using the triangles, construct the data structure by the algorithm of Kirkpatrick [216] so that a query point q can be located in the triangle containing q in $O(\log n)$ query time. Also triangulate the internal region of every hole of P by the algorithm of Ghosh and Mount. Let $T(P)$ denote the resulting triangulation of P and its holes (see Figure 8.8(a)). Note that the computation of $T(P)$ and the construction of the data structure for planar point location are done in preprocessing steps of the algorithm.

Let us return to the discussion of assigning ranks to edges of S_q. The algorithm first computes a total order on the edges of $T(P)$ in which $\prec_q$ on S_q is embedded. Then, a total order on S_q is computed from the total order on the edges of $T(P)$. From the total order on S_q, ranks of edges in S_q are computed as suggested in Lemma 8.3.9.

Connect q by diagonals to three vertices of the triangle containing q. Locate the triangles of $T(P)$ intersected by the vertical ray from q (see Figure 8.9(a)). Cut these triangles into two parts using this vertical ray and triangulate each non-triangular face by adding a diagonal. The resulting triangulation is denoted as T_q. It can be seen that the above method computes T_q from $T(P)$ in $O(n)$ time and each edge of S_q is an edge of T_q.

Let us construct a directed graph $G(T_q)$ on the edges of T_q. Consider a triangle D formed by triangulating edges d_1, d_2, and d_3 of T_q (see Figure 8.8(b)). Let $\overline{d_1}$, $\overline{d_2}$ and $\overline{d_3}$ denote the lines containing edges d_1, d_2, and d_3, respectively. Let $h(\overline{d_1})$, $h(\overline{d_2})$ and $h(\overline{d_3})$ denote the half-planes of $\overline{d_1}$, $\overline{d_2}$ and $\overline{d_3}$, respectively such that they do not contain D. Let $R_1 = h(\overline{d_1}) - (h(\overline{d_2}) \cup h(\overline{d_3}))$. Similarly, let $R_2 = h(\overline{d_2}) - (h(\overline{d_1}) \cup h(\overline{d_3}))$ and $R_3 = h(\overline{d_3}) - (h(\overline{d_1}) \cup h(\overline{d_2}))$. Let $R_1' = h(\overline{d_2}) \cap h(\overline{d_3})$. Similarly, let $R_2' = h(\overline{d_1}) \cap h(\overline{d_3})$ and $R_3' = h(\overline{d_1}) \cap h(\overline{d_2})$. It can be seen that $R_1, R_2,$ R_3, R_1', R_2', R_3' and D are faces of the arrangement of lines $\overline{d_1}, \overline{d_2}$ and $\overline{d_3}$. Directed edges in $G(T_q)$ are introduced between $d_1, d_2,$ and d_3 depending upon the location of q in the arrangement of $\overline{d_1}, \overline{d_2}$ and $\overline{d_3}$ as follows (see Figure 8.8(b)).

Case 1. If q is an internal point of R_1, add edges from d_2 to d_1 and from d_3 to d_1 in $G(T_q)$ as rays from q intersect d_1 before intersecting either d_2 or d_3. The cases where q is an internal point of R_2 or R_3 are analogous.

Case 2. If q is an internal point of R_1', add edges from d_1 to d_2 and from d_1 to d_3 in $G(T_q)$ as rays from q intersect either d_2 or d_3 before intersecting d_1. The cases where q is an internal point of R_2' or R_3' are analogous.

Case 3. If q is a boundary point of both R_2 and R_3', add an edge from d_3 to d_2 in $G(T_q)$ as rays from q intersect d_2 before intersecting d_3. The cases where q is a boundary point of other faces (excluding D) are analogous.

Case 4. If $q \in D$, add no edges to $G(T_q)$ as rays from q do not cross any pair of edges of D.

Using the above four cases, all directed edges are introduced between edges in T_q which gives $G(T_q)$. We have the following observation on $G(T_q)$.

Lemma 8.3.10 *The directed graph $G(T_q)$ is acyclic. Moreover, for every pair of edges e_i and e_j in S_q such that $e_i \prec_q e_j$, there is a directed path from e_j to e_i in $G(T_q)$.*

Exercise 8.3.3 *Prove Lemma 8.3.10.*

It can be seen that a topological order of $G(T_q)$ is a total order on T_q in which $\prec_q$ is embedded. Therefore, a total order on S_q can be obtained, which gives the ranking of edges in S_q by Lemma 8.3.9. Since the number of vertices and edges of $G(T_q)$ is $O(n)$, the topological sort [221] as well as the ranking of edges in S_q can be done in $O(n)$ time. We have the following lemma.

Lemma 8.3.11 *For a query point q, the ranking of edges in S_q can be done in $O(n)$ query time using $O(n)$ space and $O(n \log n)$ preprocessing time.*

Let us label the edges $e_1, e_2, \ldots, e_m$ of S_q according to their ranks, where $m < 2n$. After relabeling, e_i in S_q represents the edge with rank i, i.e., $rank(e_i) = i$. We also define ranks for two endpoints of e_i according to their positions in the sorted angular order around q. For every edge e_i of S_q, a_i and b_i denote the ranks of two endpoints of e_i in the sorted angular order around q in the counterclockwise direction, where $a_i < b_i$.

Let us identify the edges in S_q that are partially or totally visible from q. It can be seen that e_1 is totally visible from q. Consider the next edge e_2. If no ray from q intersects both e_1 and e_2, then e_2 is also totally visible from q. In other words, if $b_2 < a_1$ or $b_1 < a_2$, then e_2 is also entirely visible from q. If every ray from q that intersects e_1 also intersects e_2, then no point of e_2 is visible from q. Otherwise, a part of e_2 is visible from q. Consider the next edge e_3. Again, comparing with e_1 and the visible portion of e_2, the portion of e_3 visible from q can be determined. In this process, the visible portions of edges in S_q can be determined in $O(n^2)$ time.

We show that the above method of considering edges in the increasing order of ranks can be implemented in $O(n)$ time. Let us represent each edge e_i of S_q on orthogonal axes as a horizontal segment s_i connecting two points with co-ordinates (a_i, i) and (b_i, i) (see Figure 8.8(b)). Consider the vertical line L_i with a_i as x-coordinate in the orthogonal representation of S_q. Let s_j be the segment with the smallest y-coordinate (i.e., the lowest segment) intersected by L_i. It can be seen that e_j is partially or totally visible from q in P because e_j is the edge with the smallest rank intersected by the ray drawn from q through the endpoint of e_i which corresponds to a_i. Therefore, the problem of computing $V(q)$ now becomes the problem of computing the lowest segment at each x-coordinate in the orthogonal representation of S_q.

This problem is solved using the set-union algorithm of Gabow and Tarjan [146]. The set-union algorithm starts with disjoints sets, and allows two operations $find(k)$

and $link(k)$ on these sets. The operation $find(k)$ returns the maximum element of the set containing k, and $link(k)$ unites the set containing k with the set containing $k + 1$. The algorithm of Gabow and Tarjan can perform a sequence of $find(k)$ and $link(k)$ operations, on-line, in time proportional to the number of operations.

In the context of identifying lowest segments, the set-union algorithm starts with $N_x + 2$ disjoint sets $\{0\}, \{1\}, \ldots, \{N_x\}, \{N_x + 1\}$, where N_x is the maximum x-coordinate in the orthogonal representation of S_q. For any segment s_i, the operation $find(k)$ takes a_i as the value of k and locates the x-coordinate c such that (i) the lowest segments intersected by the vertical lines with x-coordinates from a_i to c have already been computed, and (ii) the lowest segment intersected by the vertical line with $c + 1$ as the x-coordinate is yet to be computed. In other words, $find(a_i)$ gives the leftmost x-coordinate that is at least a_i and immediately to the right of which the lowest segment is not known. The set-union algorithm for determining lowest segments in the orthogonal representation of S_q is given below. The index i is initialized to 0.

Step 1. Increment i by 1 and $c := find(a_i)$.

Step 2. *While $c < b_i$ do begin visible$(c) := s_i$; link(c); $c := find(c)$ end.*

Step 3. *If $i < |S_q|$ then goto* Step 1.

Step 4. Report the visible segments of S_q by scanning the array $visible[0..N_x]$ and Stop.

The above algorithm performs $link(k)$ operation at most once for each x-coordinate. Observe that once $link(c)$ is performed, the value c is never returned again by any $find$ operation. Therefore, $find$ and $link$ operations are performed at most $O(n)$ times. Hence, the above algorithm runs in $O(n)$ time. We have the following lemma.

Lemma 8.3.12 *The lowest segments in the orthogonal representation of S_q can be determined in $O(n)$ time.*

Once lowest segments and their order in the orthogonal representation of S_q are known, $V(q)$ can be constructed easily from their corresponding edges in P. In the following, we present the major steps of the query algorithm for computing $V(q)$ in P.

Step 1. Transform every vertex of P into a line in the dual plane and compute the planar subdivision A formed by the arrangement of these lines using the algorithm of Chazelle *et al.* [77].

Step 2. Triangulate P and its holes by the algorithm of Ghosh and Mount [165].

Step 3. Construct the data structure by the algorithm of Kirkpatrick [216] for locating a query point q in the triangle of the triangulation of P.

Step 4. *For each query point q do*

Step 4a. Transform q into a line $L(q)$ in the dual plane and compute the intersection points of $L(q)$ with edges in A. From the intersection points, obtain the sorted angular order of vertices P around q.

Step 4b. Let $T(P)$ denote a copy of the triangulation of P and its holes. Locate the triangle of $T(P)$ containing q and add three diagonals connecting q to the vertices of the triangle. Cut the triangles of $T(P)$ that are intersected by the vertical ray from q, and triangulate each non-triangular face by adding a diagonal to obtain a new triangulation T_q.

Step 4c. Form a directed graph $G(T_p)$ by assigning direction between edges of T_p using Cases 1 to 4.

Step 4d. Take the polygonal edges of $T(P)$ to form the set S_q. Assign the ranks to edges in S_q from the total order in $G(T_p)$.

Step 4e. Construct the orthogonal representation of S_q and find the lowest segments using the set-union operations $find(k)$ and $link(k)$.

Step 4f. Compute $V(q)$ using the lowest segments and their order.

Step 4g. Report $V(q)$.

Step 5. Stop.

The correctness and the time complexity of the query algorithm follow from Lemmas 8.3.8, 8.3.11 and 8.3.12. We summarize the result in the following theorem.

Theorem 8.3.13 *A polygon P with holes with a total of n vertices can be preprocessed in $O(n^2)$ time and space so that the visibility polygon $V(q)$ of each query point q in P can be computed in $O(n)$ query time.*

8.4 Path Queries Between Points in Simple Polygons

8.4.1 Shortest Paths: $O(\log n + k)$ Query Algorithm

In this section, we present the query algorithm of Guibas and Hershberger [177] for computing the Euclidean shortest path $SP(s,t)$ between two query points s and t inside a simple polygon P. The algorithm computes $SP(s,t)$ in $O(\log n + k)$ query time, where k is the number of edges in $SP(s,t)$. Preprocessing steps take $O(n)$ time and space. The algorithm decomposes P into sub-polygons in a balanced fashion by diagonals in a triangulation of P and uses these sub-polygons to construct $O(n)$ funnels and hourglasses in P. The funnels and hourglasses lying in the path between s and t in P are then combined to compute $SP(s,t)$. We assume that the vertices of P are labeled $v_1, v_2, \ldots, v_n$ in counterclockwise order.

The algorithm starts by decomposing P into sub-polygons. In order to compute $SP(s,t)$ in $O(\log n + k)$ query time, P is decomposed in such a way that $SP(s,t)$ passes through only a logarithmic number of sub-polygons. For decomposing P, the

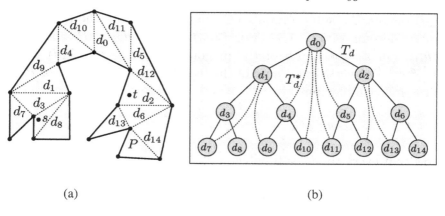

(a)   (b)

Figure 8.10 (a) The polygon P is decomposed into triangles in a balanced fashion by diagonals $d_0, d_1, \ldots, d_{14}$. (b) Additional edges are added to the decomposition tree T_d to form the factor graph T_d^*.

polygon cutting theorem of Chazelle [70] is used recursively. The theorem states that any simple polygon P of n vertices for $n \geq 4$ has a diagonal that divides P into two sub-polygons with at least $((n/3) + 1)$ vertices and at most $(2(n/3) + 1)$ vertices. Applying the theorem recursively on each sub-polygon, P can be decomposed into triangles (see Figure 8.10(a)) and the decomposition is called a *balanced decomposition* of P.

Exercise 8.4.1 *Assume that the given polygon P has been triangulated. Design an algorithm for a balanced decomposition of P of n vertices in $O(n \log n)$ time [70].*

We know that P can be triangulated in $O(n)$ by the algorithm of Chazelle [71] (see Theorem 1.4.6). From the triangulation of P, a balanced decomposition of P can be computed in $O(n)$ time by the algorithm of Guibas *et al.* [178]. We have the following lemma.

Lemma 8.4.1 *A balanced decomposition of P can be constructed by diagonals in a triangulation of P in $O(n)$ preprocessing time.*

Let us construct a binary tree T_d whose nodes represent diagonals used in the balanced decomposition of P (see Figure 8.10(b)). Let d_0 be the diagonal used to cut P into two sub-polygons P_1 and P_2. So, d_0 is at the root of T_d. Let d_1 and d_2 be the diagonals used to cut P_1 and P_2, respectively. So, d_1 and d_2 are the children of d_0 in T_d. The children of d_1 in T_d are those diagonals that are used to cut two sub-polygons of P_1. Similarly, the children of d_2 in T_d are those diagonals that are used to cut two sub-polygons of P_2. In this fashion, the decomposition tree T_d is constructed from the diagonals used in the balanced decomposition of P.

Let $P(d)$ denote the sub-polygon which has been cut by the diagonal d during the balanced decomposition of P. So, $P(d_0)$ is P, $P(d_1)$ is P_1 and $P(d_2)$ is P_2. Let $depth(d)$ denote the depth of the diagonal d in T_d. So, $P(d)$ has no more than $O((\frac{2}{3})^{depth(d)}n)$ vertices because of the balanced decomposition of P. This fact suggests the following lemma.

Lemma 8.4.2 *The height of T_d is $O(\log n)$.*

We know that every time a sub-polygon $P(d)$ is cut by a diagonal d into two sub-polygons (say, $P'(d)$ and $P''(d)$), d becomes an edge on the boundary of both $P'(d)$ and $P''(d)$. This implies that all the diagonals that are on the boundary of $P(d)$ are ancestors of d in T_d and therefore, there can be at most $depth(d)$ diagonals on the boundary of $P(d)$, which is $O(\log n)$. We state this fact in the following lemma.

Lemma 8.4.3 *The number of diagonals on the boundary of $P(d)$ is at most $depth(d)$.*

Let the diagonal d' be the parent of d in T_d. We know that d' is a diagonal on the boundary of $P(d)$, $depth(d) > depth(d')$, and $depth(d')$ is the largest among the depths of other diagonals on the boundary of $P(d)$. Connect d by edges to all diagonals (including d') on the boundary of $P(d)$. Once such edges are added in T_d for all $d \in T_d$, the resulting graph is called the *factor graph* of T_d and is denoted as T_d^* (see Figure 8.10(b)). We have the following lemmas on T_d^*.

Lemma 8.4.4 *The degree of a node in T_d^* is $O(\log n)$.*

Proof. For any diagonal d as a node in T_d^*, there are at most $depth(d)$ edges in T_d^* connecting d to diagonals of lesser depth in T_d^* due to Lemma 8.4.3. Moreover, d has edges in T_d^* to diagonals of higher depth. Observe that once $P(d)$ is cut by d, d is an edge on the boundary at most two sub-polygons at every level of subsequent decompositions and therefore, d has edges to at most two diagonals at each depth greater than $depth(d)$ in T_d^*. Hence, the degree of d in T_d^* is $O(\log n)$. $\square$

Lemma 8.4.5 *The number of edges in T_d^* is $O(n)$.*

Proof. Let d and d' be two diagonals in T_d^* such that d' is a leaf in the sub-tree of T_d^* rooted at d. Let $height(d)$ denote the height of d in T_d^*. So, $height(d) = depth(d') - depth(d)$. If $height(d)$ is h, it can be proved by induction that $P(d)$ contains at least $\lfloor (\frac{3}{2})^{h-1} + 1 \rfloor$ triangles of a triangulation of $P(d)$. As the sub-polygons corresponding to diagonals with the same height h are disjoint, there can be $O((\frac{2}{3})^h n)$ diagonals in T_d^* with height h. We know that T_d^* has $n-3$ diagonals as nodes in T_d^* and from each diagonal d, there are $2 \times height(d)$ edges to descendants in T_d^* as there are at most two edges from d to nodes at each depth in T_d^*. So, the number of edges in T_d^* is

$$\sum_{d \in T_d^*} 2 \times height(d) = O(\sum_{k \leq 1 + \log_{3/2} n} h \left(\frac{2}{3}\right)^h n) = O(n).$$

□

Let us define separating diagonals in the triangulation of P. Consider any diagonal d in T_d. We know that d partitions P into two sub-polygons. If query points s and t lie on different sub-polygons of d, then $SP(s,t)$ must intersect d in order to reach t from s. Such diagonals d are called *separating diagonals*. In Figure 8.10(a), separating diagonals in the order from s to t are $d_3, d_1, d_9, d_4, d_{10}, d_0, d_{11}, d_5, d_{12}$. Note that separating diagonals may be different for different pairs of query points s and t. We have the following lemma.

Lemma 8.4.6 *There can be $O(n)$ separating diagonals in T_d for a pair of query points.*

Let d_s (or d_t) denote the first (respectively, last) separating diagonal that is intersected by $SP(s,t)$ while traversing from s to t. Let d_{min} denote the separating diagonal having minimum depth in T_d. It can be seen that d_{min} is the least common ancestor of d_s and d_t in T_d. In Figure 8.10, d_3, d_0 and d_{12} are d_s, d_{min} and d_t respectively. All separating diagonals in the path in T_d from d_s to d_{min} and from d_{min} to d_t (including d_s, d_t and d_{min}) are called *principal separating diagonals*. The set of all principal separating diagonals in the order from d_s to d_t is denoted as D_{st}. In Figure 8.10(b), $d_s = d_3$, $d_{min} = d_0$ and $d_t = d_{12}$ and $D_{st} = (d_3, d_1, d_0, d_5, d_{12})$. Note that d_2 is not a principal separating diagonal although it is in the path from d_{12} to d_0 in T_d. On the other hand, although d_9 is a separating diagonal, d_9 is not a principal separating diagonal because d_9 is not in the path from d_3 to d_0 in T_d. We have the following lemmas.

Lemma 8.4.7 *There are at most $O(\log n)$ principal separating diagonals in D_{st}.*

Proof. Since the diagonals in D_{st} in the order from d_s (and d_t) to d_{min} are of strictly decreasing depth, there are $O(\log n)$ principal separating diagonals in D_{st} due to Lemma 8.4.2.

□

Lemma 8.4.8 *Any two consecutive principal separating diagonals in D_{st} are connected by an edge in T_d^*.*

Proof. Let d and d' denote two consecutive diagonals in D_{st}. We know that either d' is an edge on the boundary of $P(d)$ or d is an edge on the boundary of $P(d')$. So, d and d' are connected by an edge in T_d^*.

□

Let us state the procedure for locating diagonals in D_{st}. Construct the data structure in $O(n)$ preprocessing time by the algorithm of Kirkpatrick [216] for planar point location. Using this data structure, the triangles containing s and t in the triangulation of P are located in $O(\log n)$ query time. Let v_i, v_j and v_k be the vertices of the triangle containing s. Assume that v_k belongs to $bd(v_i, v_j)$. If $v_i v_j$ is d_s, then all three vertices of the triangle containing t belong to $bd(v_j, v_i)$, which can be tested in $O(1)$ time by comparing the numbering of these vertices. Otherwise, similar tests are carried out for $v_j v_k$ and $v_k v_i$ to identify d_s. Using the analogous method, d_t can also be located in $O(1)$ time. For every diagonal d from d_s to d_t in T_d, check whether d is a separating diagonal. Thus, all principal separating diagonals in D_{st} are located in $O(\log n)$ query time. We state this fact in the following lemma.

Lemma 8.4.9 *All principal separating diagonals in D_{st} can be identified in $O(\log n)$ query time using $O(n)$ preprocessing time and space.*

Once the diagonals in D_{st} are known, $SP(s, t)$ is computed in $O(\log n)$ query time by 'combining' hourglasses formed by adjacent diagonals in D_{st}. Hourglasses for all pairs of diagonals connected by edges in T_d^* are computed during preprocessing so that the hourglasses formed by adjacent diagonals in D_{st} are readily available for computing $SP(s, t)$. Before we explain how adjacent hourglasses can be combined in order to compute $SP(s, t)$, we state a preprocessing step for computing hourglasses corresponding to edges of T_d^*.

Let $v_a v_b$ and $v_c v_d$ be two non-intersecting diagonals in P such that v_a, v_b, v_d and v_c are in counterclockwise order on the boundary of P. Let $H(ab, cd)$ be the region of P bounded by $v_a v_b$, $v_c v_d$, $SP(v_a, v_c)$ and $SP(v_b, v_d)$ (see Figure 8.11(a)). The region $H(ab, cd)$ is called a *hourglass* in P for diagonals $v_a v_b$ and $v_c v_d$. We refer $SP(v_a, v_c)$ and $SP(v_b, v_d)$ as the *upper* and *lower chains* of $H(ab, cd)$, respectively. If $SP(v_a, v_c)$ and $SP(v_b, v_d)$ are disjoint, $H(ab, cd)$ is called an *open hourglass* (see Exercise 5.3.4). Otherwise, $H(ab, cd)$ is called a *closed hourglass* as no point of $v_a v_b$ is visible from any point of $v_c v_d$ (see Figure 8.11(b)). This implies that $H(ab, cd)$ is the union of two funnels with bases $v_a v_b$ and $v_c v_d$, and the shortest path connecting apexes of these two funnels. We know that $SP(v_a, v_c)$ and $SP(v_b, v_d)$ can be computed by the algorithm of Lee and Preparata [235] in time proportional to the number of vertices of $H(ab, cd)$ (see Section 3.6.1). For every edge of T_d^* connecting diagonals d and d', the hourglass for d and d' is constructed during preprocessing. Computing all these hourglasses takes $O(n^2)$ preprocessing time and space as there are $O(n)$ edges in T_d^* by Lemma 8.4.5.

Consider the problem of combining hourglasses for adjacent pairs of diagonals in D_{st}. Let $v_a v_b$, $v_c v_d$ and $v_e v_f$ three consecutive diagonals in D_{st} in the order from s to t (see Figure 8.11(a)). As before, we assume that v_f, v_c, v_a, v_b, v_d and v_f, are in counterclockwise order on the boundary of P. Consider the case where both $H(ab, cd)$ and $H(cd, ef)$ are open hourglasses (see Figure 8.11(a)). The problem is

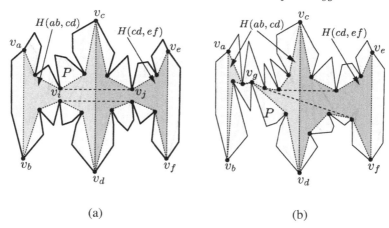

Figure 8.11 (a) Both $H(ab, cd)$ and $H(cd, ef)$ are open hourglasses. (b) $H(ab, cd)$ is a closed hourglass whereas $H(cd, ef)$ is an open hourglass.

to compute $SP(v_a, v_e)$ and $SP(v_b, v_f)$. Draw the tangent between $SP(v_a, v_c)$ and $SP(v_c, v_e)$. Let $v_i v_j$ be the tangent where $v_i \in SP(v_a, v_c)$ and $v_j \in SP(v_c, v_e)$. If $v_i v_j$ lies inside P, then $SP(v_a, v_e)$ is the concatenation of $SP(v_a, v_i)$, $v_i v_j$ and $SP(v_j, v_e)$. If the tangent between $SP(v_b, v_d)$ and $SP(v_d, v_f)$ also lies inside P (see Figure 8.11(a)), $SP(v_b, v_f)$ can be computed analogously.

Consider the other situation where $v_i v_j$ does not lie inside P. So, $v_i v_j$ is intersected by $SP(v_b, v_d)$ or $SP(v_d, v_f)$ (see Figure 8.12). If the cross-tangent between $SP(v_b, v_d)$ and $SP(v_c, v_e)$ is incident on a vertex $v_h \in SP(v_c, v_j)$ (see Figure 8.12(a)), then $SP(v_b, v_d)$ has intersected $v_i v_j$. Similarly, if the cross-tangent between $SP(v_a, v_c)$ and $SP(v_d, v_f)$ is incident on a vertex $v_h \in SP(v_i, v_c)$ (see Figure 8.12(b)), then $SP(v_d, v_f)$ has intersected $v_i v_j$. In such a situation, $SP(v_a, v_e)$ is the concatenation of $SP(v_a, v_i)$, $SP(v_i, v_j)$ and $SP(v_j, v_e)$. Note that $H(ab, ef)$ is a closed hourglass. If $v_i v_j$ has been intersected by $SP(v_b, v_d)$ or $SP(v_d, v_f)$, $SP(v_i, v_j)$ can be computed using appropriate cross-tangents between lower and upper chains of $H(ab, cd)$ and $H(cd, ef)$.

Exercise 8.4.2 *Let $H(ab, cd)$ and $H(cd, ef)$ be two open hourglasses such that the tangent between upper chains is intersected by both lower chains. Draw $H(ab, cd)$ and $H(cd, ef)$ and mark all edges (including tangents) of $SP(v_a, v_e)$.*

Consider the case where $H(ab, cd)$ is a closed hourglass and $H(cd, ef)$ is an open hourglass (see Figure 8.11(b)). We know that $H(ab, cd)$ consists two funnels and the shortest path connecting the apexes of these two funnels. Let $v_g \in SP(v_a, v_c)$ be the apex of the funnel with base $v_c v_d$. Treating v_g as both v_a and v_b, draw the tangents and cross-tangents as stated in the previous case. Using these tangents, compute

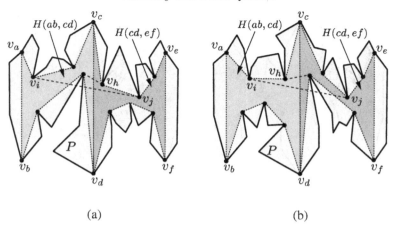

(a)   (b)

Figure 8.12 The tangent v_iv_j between upper chains of $H(ab,cd)$ and $H(cd,ef)$ is intersected by the lower chain of (a) $H(ab,cd)$ or (b) $H(cd,ef)$.

$SP(v_g,v_e)$ and $SP(v_g,v_f)$. So, $SP(v_a,v_e)$ is the concatenation of $SP(v_a,v_g)$, and $SP(v_g,v_e)$. Similarly, $SP(v_b,v_f)$ is the concatenation of $SP(v_b,v_g)$ and $SP(v_g,v_f)$. If $H(ab,cd)$ is an open hourglass and $H(cd,ef)$ is a closed hourglass, they can be combined to form $H(ab,ef)$ using the method analogous to the previous case. If both $H(ab,cd)$ and $H(cd,ef)$ are closed hourglasses, tangents are drawn between those two funnels having v_cv_d as the common base.

> **Exercise 8.4.3** *Let $H(ab,cd)$ and $H(cd,ef)$ be two closed hourglasses. Draw $H(ab,cd)$ and $H(cd,ef)$ and mark all edges (including tangents) of $SP(v_a,v_e)$ and $SP(v_b,v_f)$.*

In the procedure for combining $H(ab,cd)$ and $H(cd,ef)$, the query algorithm uses binary search for computing the tangent or a cross-tangent between the convex parts of two chains following the method of Overmars and Leeuwen [277] for computing tangents between two convex chains of points for dynamic maintenance of the convex hull. Using their method, all tangents and cross-tangents for any pair of adjacent hourglasses (of total m vertices) during the process of combining can be located in $O(\log m)$ time. We have the following lemma.

Lemma 8.4.10 *Two adjacent hourglasses of total m vertices can be combined in $O(\log m)$ time.*

Using the above procedure, combine the adjacent pair of hourglasses formed by diagonals in D_{st}. Combine the resulting hourglasses again in the pairwise manner by the above procedure. Repeat this process till the hourglass (say, H_{st}) for diagonals d_s and d_t is formed. Take the triangle formed by s with d_s, and treating this triangle as a funnel with s as the apex and d_s as the base, combine the funnel with H_{st} (see

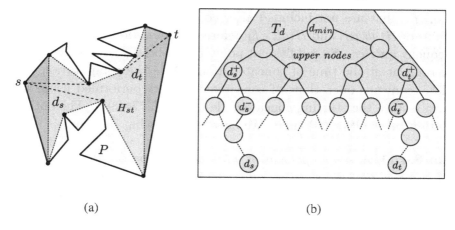

(a)   (b)

Figure 8.13 (a) Two funnels with apexes s and t are combined with H_{st} to compute $SP(s,t)$. (b) Hourglasses for diagonals (i) d_s and d_s^-, (ii) d_s^- and d_s^+, (iii) d_s^+ and d_t^+, (iv) d_t^+ and d_t^-, and (v) d_t^- and d_t are combined to form H_{st}.

Figure 8.13(a)). The resulting hourglass, consisting of a path (which can be empty) and a funnel with base d_t, is again combined with the funnel whose apex is t and base is d_t. It can be seen that the final hourglass has degenerated into a path which is $SP(s,t)$.

Exercise 8.4.4 *Let q be a query point lying outside the given convex polygon C of m vertices. Design a query algorithm for computing both tangents from q to C in $O(\log m)$ query time and $O(m)$ preprocessing time [291].*

Let us calculate the query time required for computing $SP(s,t)$. The lower (and upper) chain of every hourglass computed during preprocessing is stored as a concatenable queue which can be realized by a height-balanced tree. Concatenable queues support binary search, split and merge operations [14]. Since adjacent hourglasses are combined in a pairwise manner, which takes $O(\log n)$ time by Lemma 8.4.10, and there are $O(\log n)$ diagonals in D_{st} by Lemma 8.4.7, the entire process of combining adjacent hourglasses can be done in $O(\log^2 n)$ query time.

Consider the problem of concatenating two chains of $H(ab,cd)$ and $H(ab,ef)$ to form a chain of $H(ab,ef)$. Since chains of $H(ab,cd)$ and $H(ab,ef)$ are stored as concatenable queues, two portions of the chains, connected by the tangent, can be concatenated in $O(1)$ time without any extra space. In Figure 8.11(a), the upper chain of $H(ab,cd)$ is split at v_i to form two convex chains. Similarly, the upper chain of $H(cd,ef)$ is split at v_j to form two convex chains. Now, the convex chain formed by $SP(v_a,v_i)$ is concatenated with the convex chain formed by $SP(v_j,v_e)$ giving the upper chain of $H(ab,ef)$. Observe that the portions of chains of $H(ab,cd)$

and $H(ab, ef)$, that are not included after concatenation, should be preserved because chains of $H(ab, cd)$ and $H(ab, ef)$ before concatenation may again be required for subsequent queries. So, additional pointers to these portions are stored along with the tangent at the time of concatenation. Once the computation of $SP(s, t)$ is complete, converse operations of concatenations are performed using the stored pointers to restore the starting concatenable queues [277, 291]. The entire process of restoration takes $O(\log^2 n)$ time. We have the following theorem.

Theorem 8.4.11 *A simple polygon P of n vertices can be preprocessed in $O(n^2)$ time and space so that the shortest path between two query points s and t in P can be computed in $O(\log^2 n + k)$ query time, where k is the number of edges in the shortest path.*

Exercise 8.4.5 *Design a query algorithm for computing the shortest path between two query points s and t in a simple polygon P of n vertices taking $O(\log n + k)$ query time and $O(n^3)$ preprocessing time and space, where k is the number of edges in the shortest path.*

During preprocessing, hourglasses for pairs of diagonals corresponding to edges in T_d^* are constructed directly by the algorithm of Lee and Preparata [235]. Using the procedure for combining two adjacent hourglasses explained above, the preprocessing time and space for constructing hourglasses corresponding to edges in T_d^* can be reduced to $O(n)$ as follows.

Let $P(d)$ be a sub-polygon of m vertices. Let $P'(d)$ and $P''(d)$ be two sub-polygons that can be obtained by cutting $P(d)$ using the diagonal d. Assume that for every diagonal d' on the boundary of $P'(d)$, the hourglass for d and d' has been computed. Similarly, we assume that for every diagonal d'' on the boundary of $P''(d)$, the hourglass for d and d'' has been computed. Using the procedure for combining two adjacent hourglasses, all hourglasses across d can be computed. Observe that the diagonals of each combined hourglass are connected by an edge in T_d^*.

We know that the time required for computing each such hourglass is $O(\log m)$, which is proportional to $height(d)$. Using involved analysis, Guibas and Hershberger have shown that the additional space required to store each combined hourglass is also $O(height(d))$. This procedure of combining two hourglasses across their common diagonal d can be used in the bottom-up fashion starting with the diagonals represented in the leaves of T_d. It can be seen that all hourglasses computed in this fashion are the hourglasses represented by edges in T_d^*.

We know that the cost of combining two hourglasses across their common diagonal d is proportional to $height(d)$, which in turn is less than $height(w)$, where w and w' are the diagonals of the combined hourglass with $height(w) > height(w')$. Since there are $O(height(w))$ edges in T_d^* connecting w with the diagonals of lower height, the hourglasses corresponding to these edges can be constructed in $O((height(w))^2)$

time and space. So, the construction of all hourglasses takes time and space proportional to

$$\sum_{w \in T_d^*} (height(w))^2 = O\left(\sum_{h \leq 1 + \log_{3/2} n} h^2 \left(\frac{2}{3}\right)^h n \right) = O(n).$$

Let us explain how the query time for computing $SP(s, t)$ can be improved to $O(\log n + k)$ without increasing the preprocessing time and space as suggested by Exercise 8.4.5. Observe that if many shortest path queries are answered, hourglasses for diagonals with low depths in T are used many times. In order to avoid combining these hourglasses over and over again, additional hourglasses are constructed during preprocessing to provide the necessary bypass structure for cutting a logarithmic factor off the query time for computing H_{st}.

Consider T_d. Since T_d represents a balanced decomposition of P, there can be at most $O(n/\log^2 n)$ nodes in T_d with at least $\alpha \log^2 n$ descendents, where α is a parameter which can be used to trade off between preprocessing time and query time. Let U denote the set of nodes of T_d with at least $\alpha \log^2 n$ descendants (see Figure 8.13(b)). Since nodes in U have low depths in T_d, they are referred to as *upper nodes* in T_d. Note that all ancestors of every upper node are also upper nodes in T_d. For every upper node d, add edges in T_d^* between d and all its ancestors. Since d has $O(\log n)$ ancestors, the number of edges added to T_d^* is $O(n/\log n)$.

Let us calculate the preprocessing time and space required for constructing hourglasses corresponding to additional edges in T_d^*. For every upper node d, (i) hourglasses are constructed for diagonals along the path from d to the root of T_d, (ii) at most $O(\log n)$ hourglasses are combined during this construction, and (iii) the time required to compute each intermediate hourglass is $O(\log n)$. Since there are $O(n/\log^2 n)$ upper nodes, the construction of hourglasses corresponding to additional edges in T_d^* takes $O(n)$ time and space. We have the following lemma.

Lemma 8.4.12 *Hourglasses in P corresponding to edges of T_d^* can be computed in $O(n)$ time and space.*

With these additional hourglasses, computing H_{st} becomes faster. Consider the diagonals in D_{st}. If d_{min} does not belong to U, then there are $O(\log^2 n)$ edges in $P(d_{min})$ by the definition of U, and d_s and d_t are diagonals on the boundary of $P(d_{min})$. So, the number of hourglasses combined in order to produce H_{st} is $O(\log(\log^2 n)) = O(\log \log n)$ and the time required for combining a pair of hourglasses is $O(\log(\log n)) = O(\log \log n)$. So, H_{st} can be computed in $O(\log \log n)^2$ time.

Consider the other situation where d_{min} belongs to U (see Figure 8.13(b)). Let d_s^- and d_s^+ be two ancestors of d_s in T_d such that d_s^- is a child of d_s^+, d_s^- does not belong to U, and d_s^+ belongs to U. In other words, $d_s^- \notin U$ is an ancestor of d_s having minimum depth in T_d and $d_s^+ \in U$ is an ancestor of d_s having maximum depth in T_d. Two such nodes d_t^- and d_t^+ for d_t are defined analogously. The hourglass for diagonals d_s^- and d_s^+, the hourglass for diagonals d_s^+ and d_t^+ and the hourglass for diagonals d_t^+ and d_t^- are already computed during preprocessing. We know from the analysis mentioned earlier that the hourglass for diagonals d_s and d_s^- and the hourglass for diagonals d_t^- and d_t can be computed in $O(\log \log n)^2$ time. By combining these five hourglasses, H_{st} can be computed in $O(\log \log n)^2 + O(\log n) = O(\log n)$ time. We have the following lemma.

Lemma 8.4.13 *The hourglass H_{st} can be computed in $O(\log n)$ query time.*

Corollary 8.4.14 *The next vertex of s and the previous vertex of t on $SP(s,t)$ can be identified in $O(\log n)$ query time.*

Once H_{st} is computed in $O(\log n)$ time, computing $SP(s,t)$ takes $O(\log n + k)$ query time as all other steps of the query algorithm take $O(\log n)$ time. In the following, we present the major steps of the query algorithm for computing $SP(s,t)$ in P for a pair of query points s and t.

Step 1. Triangulate P by the algorithm of Chazelle [71].

Step 2. Decompose P in a balanced fashion by the algorithm of Guibas *et al.* [178] and construct the corresponding decomposition tree T_d.

Step 3. *For* each pair of diagonals d and d' on the boundary of every sub-polygon formed during the decomposition of P, add an edge between d and d' in T_d to form the factor graph T_d^*.

Step 4. Identify upper nodes of T_d and connect them to all their ancestors by edges in T_d^*.

Step 5. Compute hourglasses corresponding to edges in T_d^* by combining hourglasses pairwise across their common diagonals in the button up fashion starting with the diagonals represented in the leaves of T_d.

Step 6. Construct the data structure by the algorithm of Kirkpatrick [216] for locating a query point in the triangle of the triangulation of P.

Step 7. *For* each pair of query points s and t in P *do*

Step 7a. Locate s and t in the triangles of the triangulation of P and identify diagonals d_s and d_t.

Step 7b. Form the set D_{st} by locating principal separating diagonals between d_s and d_t. Identify the diagonal d_{min} in D_{st}.

Step 7c. *If* d_{min} is not an upper node in T_d *then* construct the hourglass H_{st} by combining hourglasses across the diagonals between d_s and d_t in D_{st} and *goto* Step 7e.

Step 7d. Identify nodes d_s^-, d_s^+, d_t^- and d_t^+ in T_d. Construct the hourglass H_{st} by combining hourglasses across a subset of diagonals between d_s and d_t in D_{st}.

Step 7e. Draw tangents from s and t to H_{st} and identify vertices of $SP(s,t)$.

Step 7f. Report $SP(s,t)$.

Step 8. Stop.

The correctness and the time complexity of the query algorithm follow from Lemmas 8.4.1, 8.4.9, 8.4.10, 8.4.12 and 8.4.13. We summarize the result in the following theorem.

Theorem 8.4.15 *A simple polygon P of n vertices can be preprocessed in $O(n)$ time and space so that the shortest path between two query points s and t in P can be computed in $O(\log n + k)$ query time, where k is the number of edges in the shortest path.*

8.4.2 Link Paths: $O(\log n + k)$ Query Algorithm

In this section, we present a query algorithm for computing the minimum link path $MLP(s,t)$ between two query points s and t inside a simple polygon P in $O(\log n + k)$ query time (see Figure 7.1(a)), where k is the number of links in $MLP(s,t)$. Preprocessing steps of the algorithm take $O(n^3 \log n)$ time and space. We assume that the vertices of P are labeled $v_1, v_2, \dots, v_n$ in counterclockwise order.

During preprocessing, the algorithm considers all pairs of vertices of P, and for each pair of vertices v_i and v_j, a sub-polygon $R_{ij} \subset P$ is computed by the algorithm of Ghosh [155] (see Section 7.2.2) such that turning points of $MLP(v_i, v_j)$ lie on the boundary of R_{ij} and links of $MLP(v_i, v_j)$ pass through vertices of $SP(v_i, v_j)$ (see Figure 8.14(a)). Then, using the algorithm of Aggarwal *et al.* [12] (see Section 7.5.1), the edges on the boundary of R_{ij} are divided into intervals such that the link sequence of the greedy path in R_{ij} from any point of an interval is same. From link sequences, projection functions of intervals in R_{ij} are composed and stored along with the intervals. For a pair of query points s and t, the algorithm locates the sub-polygon containing all turning points of $MLP(s,t)$ on its boundary and then locates these turning points using projection functions of intervals on the boundary of the sub-polygon.

Let us explain the preprocessing step of the algorithm for computing R_{ij} using the algorithm of Ghosh [155] presented in Section 7.2.2. Compute $SP(v_i, v_j)$ (see Figure 8.14(a)). Let u_i and u_j be adjacent vertices of v_i and v_j on $SP(v_i, v_j)$, respectively. Extend $v_i u_i$ from u_i to $bd(P)$ meeting it at a point z. Take a point w_i arbitrary close to z on $bd(P)$ such that $v_i w_i$ meets $SP(v_i, v_j)$ only at v_i and $v_i w_i$ lies inside P. Analogously, extend $v_j u_j$ from u_j to $bd(P)$ meeting it at a point z'. Take a point

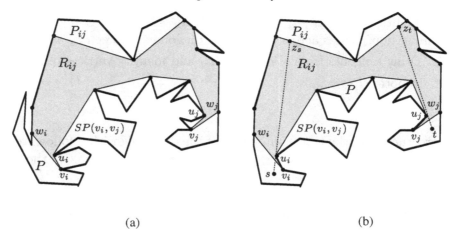

(a)   (b)

Figure 8.14 (a) The sub-polygon P_{ij} is obtained by cutting P by v_iw_i, v_jw_j and those edges of $SP(v_i, v_j)$ that are not eaves of $SP(v_i, v_j)$. (b) The vertices v_i, u_i, v_j and u_j are identified for a pair of points s and t.

w_j arbitrary close to z' on $bd(P)$ such that v_jw_j meets $SP(v_i, v_j)$ only at v_j and v_jw_j lies inside P. Cut P by v_iw_i, v_jw_j and those edges of $SP(v_i, v_j)$ that are not eaves of $SP(v_i, v_j)$. So, P is split into several parts and the part containing both v_i and v_j is denoted as P_{ij}. If $SP(v_i, v_j)$ does not contain an eave, compute the sub-polygon $R_{ij} \subseteq P_{ij}$ such that both tangents from any point $z \in R_{ij}$ to $SP(v_i, v_j)$ lie inside R_{ij}. If $SP(v_i, v_j)$ contains eaves, P_{ij} is partitioned by extending eaves and from these parts of P_{ij}, the sub-polygon R_{ij} is computed.

Consider a pair of points s and t in P such the adjacent vertices of s and t on $SP(s, t)$ are u_i and u_j respectively, and su_i and tw_j intersect v_iw_i and v_ju_j, respectively (see Figure 8.14(b)). Extend su_i from u_i to the boundary of R_{ij} meeting it at z_s. Similarly, extend tu_j from u_j to the boundary of R_{ij} meeting it at z_t. Construct the greedy path from z_s to a point of u_jz_j in R_{ij} by the algorithm of Ghosh [155], which gives $MLP(s, t)$. Let us use this method to compute $MLP(s, t)$ for any pair of query points s and t in P. Using the query algorithm of Guibas and Hershberger [177] (see Section 8.4.1), locate the adjacent vertices of s and t on $SP(s, t)$ and call them u_i and u_j, respectively (see Figure 8.14(b)). Take the adjacent vertex of u_i on $bd(P)$ as v_i, where su_i intersects v_iw_i. Similarly, take the adjacent vertex of u_j on $bd(P)$ as v_j, where tu_j intersects v_jw_j. Since R_{ij} has been computed for all pairs of vertices v_i and v_j of P during preprocessing, $MLP(s, t)$ can be computed in R_{ij} by the above method.

We know from Corollary 8.4.14 that for a pair of query points s and t, locating u_i and u_j takes $O(\log n)$ query time. However, computing $MLP(s, t)$ in R_{ij} by the algorithm of Ghosh [155] takes time proportional to the size of R_{ij}. We show that $MLP(s, t)$ can be computed in R_{ij} in $O(\log n + k)$ query time. After the computation of R_{ij} for all pairs of vertices v_i and v_j of P during preprocessing, each R_{ij} is considered again. By the algorithm of Aggarwal *et al.* [12] presented in Section 7.5.1, the edges on the boundary of R_{ij} are divided into intervals. From link sequences of these intervals, projection functions of intervals in R_{ij} are composed and stored along with intervals. Once z_s is located by binary search on an interval I of R_{ij} during query, the forward projection point of z_s on $u_j z_t$ (say, z_p) can be located using the projection function (say, f) of I. Therefore, the link distance between s and t can be computed in $O(\log n)$ query time.

To compute turning points of $MLP(s,t)$, we follow the method suggested by Chandru *et al.* [69]. Assume that f has been composed of projection functions $f_1, f_2, \ldots, f_g$, where f_1 is composed with f_2, $(f_1 * f_2)$ is composed with f_3 and so on. This means that (f_1) gives the first turning point of z_s, $(f_1 * f_2)$ gives the second turning point of z_s, $(f_1 * f_2 * f_3)$ gives the fourth turning point of z_s, and so on. We know that f_3 is composed of two projection functions (say, f_3' and f_3''). So, the third turning point of z_s can be computed by the projection function $(f_1 * f_2 * f_3')$. Therefore, turning points of $MLP(s,t)$ between z_s and z_p can be computed using these intermediate projection functions in time proportional to the number of turning points. Thus all turning points of $MLP(s,t)$ can be computed in $O(\log n + k)$ query time.

In the following, we present the major steps of the query algorithm for computing $MLP(s,t)$ in P for a pair of query points s and t.

Step 1. Triangulate P by the algorithm of Chazelle [71].

Step 2. Construct the data structure by the algorithm of Kirkpatrick [216] for locating a query point in the triangle of the triangulation of P.

Step 3. For every pair of vertices v_i and v_j of P do

Step 3a. Compute $SP(v_i, v_j)$ by the algorithm of Lee and Preparata [235].

Step 3b. Let u_i and u_j be adjacent vertices of v_i and v_j on $SP(v_i, v_j)$, respectively. Extend $v_i u_i$ from u_i to $bd(P)$ and take a point $w_i \in bd(P)$ close to the intersection point. Extend $v_j u_j$ from u_j to $bd(P)$ and take a point $w_j \in bd(P)$ close to the intersection point.

Step 3c. Cut P by $v_i w_i$, $v_j w_j$ and the edges of $SP(v_i, v_j)$ that are not eaves of $SP(v_i, v_j)$ and identify the sub-polygon P_{ij} containing both vertices v_i and v_j.

Step 3d. Compute the sub-polygon R_{ij} from P_{ij} by the algorithm of Ghosh [155].

Step 3e. By the algorithm of Aggarwal *et al.* [12], compute intervals on the boundary of R_{ij}, compose projection functions of these intervals and store them along with intervals.

Step 4. *For each pair of query points s and t in P do*

Step 4a. Locate s and t in the triangles of the triangulation of P.

Step 4b. Locate adjacent vertices of s and t on $SP(s,t)$ by the algorithm of Guibas and Hershberger [177] and label them as u_i and u_j, respectively.

Step 4c. Choose the appropriate adjacent vertices of u_i and u_j on $bd(P)$ as v_i and v_j, respectively.

Step 4d. Extend su_i from u_i to the boundary of R_{ij} meeting it at a point z_s. Extend tu_j from u_j to the boundary of R_{ij} meeting it at a point z_t.

Step 4e. Locate the interval containing z_s on the boundary of R_{ij} by binary search. Using the projection function of the interval, compute the forward projection point z_p of z_s on $u_j z_t$.

Step 4f. Compute turning points of $MLP(s,t)$ between z_p to z_s by intermediate projection functions associate with intervals of R_{ij}.

Step 4g. Report $MLP(s,t)$.

Step 5. Stop.

The correctness of the algorithm follows from the algorithms of Ghosh [155], Aggarwal *et al.* [12], Guibas and Hershberger [177] and Chandru *et al.* [69]. Let us analyze the time complexity of the algorithm. We know that Steps 1 and 2 take $O(n)$ time. Since Steps 3a and 3d take $O(n)$ time and Step 3e takes $O(n \log n)$ time and space, Step 3 can be executed in $O(n^3 \log n)$ time and space. So, the preprocessing of P can be done in $O(n^3 \log n)$ time and space. It has already been shown that the query time for Step 4 is $O(\log n + k)$. We summarize the result in the following theorem.

Theorem 8.4.16 *A simple polygon P of n vertices can be preprocessed in $O(n^3 \log n)$ time and space so that the minimum link path between two query points s and t in P can be computed in $O(\log n + k)$ query time, where k is the number of links in the path.*

8.5 Notes and Comments

The algorithm of Kirkpatrick [216] has been used for locating positions of query points in a given triangulated polygon P in query algorithms presented in this chapter. Kirkpatrick's algorithm builds subdivision hierarchies of P using triangulation in $O(n)$ time and space. These hierarchies are represented as a layered, directed graph, where the degree of each node of the graph is constant and the total depth of the graph is $O(\log n)$. Using this graph, the query point is located in a triangle inside P in $O(\log n)$ query time.

There are other query algorithms for locating query points in a given planar subdivision P. The first algorithm for this problem was given by Dobkin and Lipton [112]. Their algorithm partitions P into slabs by drawing vertical lines through vertices of P taking $O(n^2 \log n)$ preprocessing time and $O(n^2)$ space. During a query, the slab containing a query point is located by binary search and then another binary search is performed to locate the position of the query point in the region of the slab bounded by two edges of P. Thus, the algorithm answers a query in $O(\log n)$ query time. Preparata [290] showed that by partitioning P into trapezoids in place of slabs, preprocessing time and space can be reduced to $O(n \log n)$ keeping the query time the same.

Lee and Preparata [233] introduced an alternative method and their method partitions P into monotone chains taking $O(n \log n)$ preprocessing time and $O(n)$ space. During a query, discrimination of a query point with monotone chains is performed by binary search to locate the region of P containing the point. However, the query time of the algorithm is $O(\log^2 n)$. Using fractional cascading, the query time of this chain method was improved to $O(\log n)$ by Edelsbrunner *et al.* [119] keeping the preprocessing time and space requirements the same. Sarnak and Tarjan [302] gave another algorithm for point location in $O(\log n)$ query time taking $O(n \log n)$ preprocessing time and $O(n)$ space. Their method combined techniques of slab method, plane sweep and persistence to build a data structure for answering queries. A similar method was also suggested by Cole [94].

Let us mention parallel algorithms for query problems considered in this chapter. Consider the problem of ray shooting in a simple polygon P. For this problem, Goodrich *et al.* [173, 174] gave an algorithm following the sequential algorithm of Chazelle and Guibas [76]. They also gave an algorithm for computing the shortest path between query points in a simple polygon P following the sequential algorithm of Guibas and Hershberger [177]. Both these algorithms run in $O(\log n)$ time using $O(n)$ processors in the CREW-PRAM model of computations. If the triangulation of P is given, Hershberger [187] showed that both these problems can be solved in $O(\log n)$ time using $O(n/\log n)$ processors in the CREW-PRAM model of computations. A parallel algorithm for the problem of computing the minimum link path between two query points in a simple polygon P can be designed by parallelizing each step of the sequential algorithm presented in Section 8.4.2.

Bibliography

[1] J. Abello, O. Egecioglu, and K. Kumar. Visibility graphs of staircase polygons and the weak Bruhat order, I: from visibility graphs to maximal chains. *Discrete & Computational Geometry*, 14:331–358, 1995.

[2] J. Abello and K. Kumar. Visibility graphs and oriented matroids. In *Proceedings of Graph Drawing*, Lecture Notes in Computer Science, volume 894, pages 147–158. Springer-Verlag, Berlin, Germany, 1995.

[3] J. Abello and K. Kumar. Visibility graphs and oriented matroids. *Discrete & Computational Geometry*, 28:449–465, 2002.

[4] J. Abello, H. Lin, and S. Pisupati. On visibility graphs of simple polygons. *Congressus Numerantium*, 90:119–128, 1992.

[5] J. Adegeest, M. H. Overmars, and J. Snoeyink. Minimum-link c-oriented path: Single-source queries. *International Journal of Computational Geometry and Applications*, 4:39–51, 1994.

[6] P. K. Agarwal. Ray shooting and other applications of spanning trees with low stabbing number. *SIAM Journal on Computing*, 21:540–570, 1992.

[7] P. K. Agarwal, N. Alon, B. Aronov, and S. Suri. Can visibility graphs be represented compactly? *Discrete & Computational Geometry*, 12:347–365, 1994.

[8] P. K. Agarwal and M. Sharir. Circle shooting in a simple polygon. *Journal of Algorithms*, 14:69–87, 1993.

[9] P. K. Agarwal and M. Sharir. Circular visibility from a point in a simple polygon. *International Journal of Computational Geometry and Applications*, 3:1–25, 1993.

[10] P.K. Agarwal, T. Biedl, S. Lazard, S. Robbins, S. Suri, and S. Whitesides. Curvature-constrained shortest paths in a convex polygon. *SIAM Journal on Computing*, 31:1814–1851, 2002.

[11] A. Aggarwal. *The art gallery theorem: its variations, applications, and algorithmic aspects.* Ph.D. Thesis, Johns Hopkins University, Baltimore, MD, USA, 1984.

[12] A. Aggarwal, H. Booth, J. O'Rourke, S. Suri, and C. K. Yap. Finding minimal convex nested polygons. *Information and Computing*, 83:98–110, 1989.

[13] A. Aggarwal, S. Moran, P. Shor, and S. Suri. Computing the minimum visible vertex distance between two polygons. In *Proceedings of the 1st Workshop on Algorithms and Data Structures*, Lecture Notes in Computer Science, volume 382, pages 115–134. Springer-Verlag, Berlin, Germany, 1989.

[14] A. Aho, J. H. Hopcroft, and J. D. Ullman. *The Design and Analysis of Algorithms.* Addison-Wesley, Reading, MA, USA, 1974.

[15] A. Aho, J. H. Hopcroft, and J. D. Ullman. *Data Structures and Algorithms.* Addison-Wesley, Reading, MA, USA, 1983.

[16] L. Aleksandrov, H. Djidjev, and J. Sack. An $O(n \log n)$ algorithm for finding a shortest central link segment. *International Journal of Computational Geometry and Applica-*

tions, 10:157–188, 2000.

[17] M. H. Alsuwaiyel and D. T. Lee. Minimal link visibility paths inside a simple polygon. *Computational Geometry: Theory and Applications*, 3:1–25, 1993.

[18] M. H. Alsuwaiyel and D. T. Lee. Finding an approximate minimum-link visibility path inside a simple polygon. *Information Processing Letters*, 55:75–79, 1995.

[19] N. M. Amato. Finding a closest visible vertex pair between two polygons. *Algorithmica*, 14:183–201, 1995.

[20] T. Andreae. Some results on visibility graphs. *Discrete Applied Mathematics*, 40:5–18, 1992.

[21] E. Arkin, M. Held, J. S. B. Mitchell, and S. Skiena. Hamiltonian triangulations for fast rendering. *Visual Computers*, 12:429–444, 1996.

[22] E. Arkin, J. S. B. Mitchell, and C. Piatko. Minimum-link watchman tours. *Information Processing Letters*, 86:203–207, 2003.

[23] E. Arkin, J. S. B. Mitchell, and S. Suri. Logarithmic-time link path queries in a simple polygon. *International Journal of Computational Geometry and Applications*, 5:369–395, 1995.

[24] B. Aronov, A. Davis, T. Dey, S. P. Pal, and D. Prasad. Visibility with multiple reflections. *Discrete & Computational Geometry*, 20:61–78, 1998.

[25] B. Aronov, A. Davis, T. Dey, S. P. Pal, and D. Prasad. Visibility with one reflection. *Discrete & Computational Geometry*, 19:553–574, 1998.

[26] B. Aronov, L. J. Guibas, M. Teichmann, and L. Zhang. Visibility and maintenance in simple polygons. *Discrete & Computational Geometry*, 27:461–483, 2002.

[27] T. Asano. Efficient algorithms for finding the visibility polygons for a polygonal region with holes. *Transactions of IECE of Japan*, E68:557–559, 1985.

[28] T. Asano, T. Asano, L. J. Guibas, J. Hershberger, and H. Imai. Visibility of disjoint polygons. *Algorithmica*, 1:49–63, 1986.

[29] T. Asano, T. Asano, and R. Pinter. Polygon triangulation: Efficiency and minimality. *Journal of Algorithms*, 7:221–231, 1986.

[30] T. Asano, S. K. Ghosh, and T. Shermer. Visibility in the plane. In J.-R. Sack and J. Urrutia, editors, *Handbook of Computational Geometry*, pages 829–876. North-Holland, Amsterdam, The Netherlands, 2000.

[31] T. Asano and G. Toussaint. Computing the geodesic center of a simple polygon. In D. S. Johnson, editor, *Discrete Algorithms and Complexity, Perspectives in Computing*, pages 65–79. Academic Press, New York, 1987.

[32] M. Atallah and D. Z. Chen. Optimal parallel algorithm for visibility of a simple polygon from a point. In *Proceedings of the 5th Annual ACM Symposium on Computational Geometry*, pages 114–123. ACM Press, New York, USA, 1989.

[33] M. Atallah and D. Z. Chen. Parallel rectilinear shortest paths with rectangular obstacles. *Computational Geometry: Theory and Applications*, 1:79–113, 1991.

[34] M. Atallah and D. Z. Chen. On parallel rectilinear obstacle-avoiding paths. *Computational Geometry: Theory and Applications*, 3:307–313, 1993.

[35] M. Atallah and D. Z. Chen. Deterministic parallel computational geometry. In J.-R. Sack and J. Urrutia, editors, *Handbook of Computational Geometry*, pages 155–200. North-Holland, Amsterdam, The Netherlands, 2000.

[36] M. Atallah, D. Z. Chen, and H. Wagener. Optimal parallel algorithm for visibility of a simple polygon from a point. *Journal of the ACM*, 38:516–553, 1991.

[37] M. Atallah, R. Cole, and M. T. Goodrich. Cascading divide-and-conquer: A technique for designing parallel algorithms. *SIAM Journal on Computing*, 18:499–532, 1989.

[38] M. Atallah and M. T. Goodrich. Efficient plane sweeping in parallel. In *Proceedings of the 2nd Annual ACM Symposium on Computational Geometry*, pages 216–225. ACM Press, New York, USA, 1986.

[39] D. Avis and H. ElGindy. A combinatorial approach to polygon similarity. *IEEE Transactions on Information Theory*, IT-2:148–150, 1983.

[40] D. Avis and D. Rappaport. Computing the largest empty convex subset of a set of points. In *Proceedings of the 1st ACM Symposium on Computational Geometry*, pages 161–167. ACM Press, New York, USA, 1985.

[41] D. Avis and G. T. Toussaint. An efficient algorithm for decomposing a polygon into star-shaped polygons. *Pattern Recognition*, 13:395–398, 1981.

[42] D. Avis and G. T. Toussaint. An optimal algorithm for determining the visibility of a polygon from an edge. *IEEE Transactions on Computers*, C-30:910–1014, 1981.

[43] R. Bar-Yehuda and B. Chazelle. Triangulating disjoint Jordan chains. *International Journal of Computational Geometry and Applications*, 4:475–481, 1994.

[44] B. Ben-Moshe, O. Hall-Holt, M. J. Katz, and J. S. B. Mitchell. Computing the visibility graph of points within a polygon. In *Proceedings of the 20th Annual ACM Symposium on Computational Geometry*, pages 27–35. ACM Press, New York, USA, 2004.

[45] P. Bertolazzi, S. Salza, and C. Guerra. A parallel algorithm for the visibility problem from a point. *Journal of Parallel and Distributed Computing*, 9:11–14, 1990.

[46] J. Bhadury, V. Chandru, A. Maheshwari, and R. Chandrasekran. Art gallery problems for convex nested polygons. *INFORMS Journal on Computing*, 9:100–110, 1997.

[47] B. K. Bhattacharya, G. Das, A. Mukhopadhyay, and G. Narasimhan. Optimally computing a shortest weakly visible line segment inside a simple polygon. *Computational Geometry: Theory and Applications*, 23:1–29, 1997.

[48] B. K. Bhattacharya and S. K. Ghosh. Characterizing LR-visibility polygons and related problems. *Computational Geometry: Theory and Applications*, 18:19–36, 2001.

[49] B. K. Bhattacharya, S. K. Ghosh, and T. Shermer. A linear time algorithm to remove winding of a simple polygon. *Computational Geometry: Theory and Applications*, 33:165–173, 2006.

[50] B. K. Bhattacharya and A. Mukhopadhyay. Computing in linear time a chord from which a simple polygon is weakly internally visible. In *Proceedings of the 6th International Symposium on Algorithms and Computation*, Lecture Notes in Computer Science, volume 1004, pages 22–31. Springer-Verlag, Berlin, Germany, 1995.

[51] B. K. Bhattacharya, A. Mukhopadhyay, and G. Narasimhan. Optimal algorithms for two-guard walkability of simple polygons. In *Proceedings of the 12th Workshop on Algorithms and Data Structures*, Lecture Notes in Computer Science, volume 2125, pages 438–449. Springer-Verlag, Berlin, Germany, 2001.

[52] B. K. Bhattacharya, A. Mukhopadhyay, and G. T. Toussaint. A linear time algorithm for computing the shortest line segment from which a polygon is weakly externally visible. In *Proceedings of the 2nd Workshop on Algorithms and Data Structures*, Lecture Notes in Computer Science, volume 519, pages 412–424. Springer-Verlag, Berlin, Germany, 1991.

[53] B. K. Bhattacharya, A. Mukhopadhyay, and G. T. Toussaint. Computing a shortest weakly externally visible line segment for a simple polygon. *International Journal of Computational Geometry and Applications*, 9:81–96, 1999.

[54] B. K. Bhattacharya and G. T. Toussaint. Computing shortest transversals. *Computing*, 46:93–119, 1991.

[55] I. Bjorling-Sachs. Edge guards in rectilinear polygons. *Computational Geometry: Theory and Applications*, 11:111–123, 1998.

[56] I. Bjorling-Sachs and D. L. Souvaine. An efficient algorithm for guard placement in polygons with holes. *Discrete & Computational Geometry*, 13:77–109, 1995.

[57] J.-D. Boissonnat, S. K. Ghosh, T. Kavitha, and S. Lazard. An algorithm for computing a convex path of bounded curvature in a simple polygon. *Algorithmica*, 34:109–156, 2002.

[58] J. A. Bondy and U. S. R. Murty. *Graph Theory with Applications*. North Holland, New York, USA, 1985.

[59] K. S. Booth and G. S. Lueker. Testing for consecutive ones property, interval graphs and graph planarity using pq-tree algorithms. *Journal of Computer and Systems Sciences*,

13:335–379, 1976.

[60] P. Bose, A. Lubiw, and J. Munro. Efficient visibility queries in simple polygons. *Computational Geometry: Theory and Applications*, 23:313–335, 2002.

[61] A. Brandstadt, J. Spinrad, and L. Stewart. Bipartite permutation graphs are bipartite tolerance graphs. *Congressus Numerantium*, 58:165–174, 1987.

[62] M. Breen. Clear visibility and the dimension of kernels of starshaped sets. *Proceedings of the American Mathematical Society*, 85:414–418, 1982.

[63] M. Breen. Clear visibility and unions of two starshaped sets in the plane. *Pacific Journal of Mathematics*, 115:267–275, 1984.

[64] D. Bremner. *Point Visibility Graphs and Restricted-Orientation Polygon Covering*. M.Sc. Thesis, School of Computing Science, Simon Fraser University, Burnaby, BC, Canada, 1993.

[65] D. Bremner and T. Shermer. Point visibility graphs and o-convex cover. *International Journal of Computational Geometry and Applications*, 10:55–71, 2000.

[66] A. Briggs and B. Donald. Visibility-based planning of sensor control strategies. *Algorithmica*, 26:364–388, 2000.

[67] H. Brunn. Uber kerneigebiete. *Mathematische Annalen*, 73:436–440, 1913.

[68] M. Buckinghan. *Circle graphs*. Ph.D. Dissertation, Courant Institute of Mathematical Sciences, New York, USA, 1980.

[69] V. Chandru, S. K. Ghosh, A. Maheshwari, V. T. Rajan, and S. Saluja. NC-algorithms for minimum link path and related problems. *Journal of Algorithms*, 19:173–203, 1995.

[70] B. Chazelle. A theorem on polygon cutting with applications. In *Proceedings of the 23rd IEEE Symposium on the Foundations of Computer Science*, pages 339–349. IEEE Computer Society Press, Los Alamitos, CA, USA, 1982.

[71] B. Chazelle. Triangulating a simple polygon in linear time. *Discrete & Computational Geometry*, 6:485–524, 1991.

[72] B. Chazelle and H. Edelsbrunner. An optimal algorithm for intersecting line segments in the plane. *Journal of the ACM*, 39:1–54, 1992.

[73] B. Chazelle, H. Edelsbrunner, M. Grigni, L. J. Guibas, J. Hershberger, M. Sharir, and J. Snoeyink. Ray shooting in polygons using geodesic triangulations. *Algorithmica*, 12:54–68, 1994.

[74] B. Chazelle and L. J. Guibas. Fractional cascading: I. A data structuring technique. *Algorithmica*, 1:133–162, 1986.

[75] B. Chazelle and L. J. Guibas. Fractional cascading: II. Applications. *Algorithmica*, 1:163–191, 1986.

[76] B. Chazelle and L. J. Guibas. Visibility and intersection problems in plane geometry. *Discrete & Computational Geometry*, 4:551–581, 1989.

[77] B. Chazelle, L. J. Guibas, and D.T. Lee. The power of geometric duality. *BIT*, 25:76–90, 1985.

[78] B. Chazelle and J. Incerpi. Triangulation and shape-complexity. *ACM Transactions of Graphics*, 3:135–152, 1984.

[79] O. Chein and L. Steinberg. Routing past unions of disjoint barriers. *Networks*, 13:389–398, 1983.

[80] D. Chen, K. Klenk, and H.-Y. Tu. Shortest path queries among weighted obstacles in the rectilinear plane. *SIAM Journal on Computing*, 29:1223–1246, 2000.

[81] D. Z. Chen. Efficient geometric algorithms on EREW-PRAM. *IEEE Transactions on Parallel and Distributed Systems*, 6:41–47, 1995.

[82] D. Z. Chen. An optimal parallel algorithm for detecting weak visibility of a simple polygon. *International Journal of Computational Geometry and Applications*, 5:93–124, 1995.

[83] D. Z. Chen. Optimally computing the shortest weakly visible subedge of a simple polygon. *Journal of Algorithms*, 20:459–478, 1996.

[84] D. Z. Chen. Determining weak visibility of a polygon from an edge in parallel. *Interna-*

tional Journal of Computational Geometry and Applications, 8:277–304, 1998.

[85] D. Z. Chen, O. Daescu, and K. Klenk. On geometric path query problems. *International Journal of Computational Geometry and Applications*, 11:617–645, 2001.

[86] Y.-J. Chiang and J. S. B. Mitchell. Two-point Euclidean shortest path queries in the plane. In *Proceedings of the 10th Annual ACM-SIAM Symposium on Discrete Algorithms*, pages 215–224. ACM and SIAM, USA, 1999.

[87] Y.-J. Chiang and R. Tamassia. Optimal shortest path and minimum-link path queries between two convex polygons inside a simple polygonal obstacle. *International Journal of Computational Geometry and Applications*, 7:85–121, 1997.

[88] F. Chin, J. Sampson, and C. A. Wang. A unifying approach for a class of problems in the computational geometry of polygons. *The Visual Computer*, 1:124–132, 1985.

[89] S.-H. Choi, S. Y. Shin, and K.-Y. Chwa. Characterizing and recognizing the visibility graph of a funnel-shaped polygon. *Algorithmica*, 14:27–51, 1995.

[90] S.-Y. Chou and R. C. Woo. A linear-time algorithm for constructing a circular visibility diagram. *Algorithmica*, 14:203–228, 1995.

[91] V. Chvátal. A combinatorial theorem in plane geometry. *Journal of Combinatorial Theory, Series B*, 18:39–41, 1975.

[92] K. L. Clarkson, S. Kapoor, and P. Vaidya. Rectilinear shortest paths through polygonal obstacles in $O(n \log^2 n)$ time. In *Proceedings of the 3rd Annual ACM Symposium on Computational Geometry*, pages 251–257. ACM Press, New York, USA, 1987.

[93] M. Cohen and J. Wallace. *Radiosity and Realistic Image Synthesis*. Academic Press Professional, Boston, MA, USA, 1993.

[94] R. Cole. Searching and storing similar lists. *Journal of Algorithms*, 7:202–220, 1986.

[95] P. Colley, A. Lubiw, and J. Spinrad. Visibility graphs of towers. *Computational Geometry: Theory and Applications*, 7:161–172, 1997.

[96] T. H. Cormen, C. E. Leiserson, R. L. Rivest, and C. Stein. *Introduction to Algorithms*. MIT Press, Cambridge, MA, USA, 2001.

[97] C. Coullard and A. Lubiw. Distance visibility graphs. *International Journal of Computational Geometry and Applications*, 2:349–362, 1992.

[98] D. Crass, I. Suzuki, and M. Yamashita. Search for a mobile intruder in a corridor-the open edge variant of the polygon search propblem. *International Journal of Computational Geometry and Applications*, 5:397–412, 1995.

[99] J. Culberson and R. Reckhow. Orthogonally convex coverings of orthogonal polygons without holes. *Journal of Computer and Systems Science*, 39:166–204, 1989.

[100] G. Das, P. Heffernan, and G. Narasimhan. Finding all weakly-visible chords of a polygon in linear time. *Nordic Journal of Computing*, 1:433–456, 1994.

[101] G. Das, P. Heffernan, and G. Narasimhan. LR-visibility in polygons. *Computational Geometry: Theory and Applications*, 7:37–57, 1997.

[102] G. Das and G. Narasimhan. Geometric searching and link distance. In *Proceedings of the 2nd Workshop on Algorithms and Data Structures*, Lecture Notes in Computer Science, volume 519, pages 262–272. Springer-Verlag, Berlin, Germany, 1991.

[103] G. Das and G. Narasimhan. Optimal linear-time algorithm for the shortest illuminating line segment in a polygon. In *Proceedings of the 10th Annual ACM Symposium on Computational Geometry*, pages 259–266. ACM Press, New York, USA, 1994.

[104] D. Dasgupta and C.E. Veni Madhavan. An approximate algorithm for the minimum vertex nested polygon problem. *Information Processing Letters*, 33:35–44, 1989.

[105] P. Dasgupta, P. Chakrabarti, and S. De Sarkar. A new competitive algorithm for agent searching in unknown streets. In *Proceeding of the 16th Symposium on Foundation of Software Technology and Theoretical Computer Science*, Lecture Notes in Computer Science, volume 1180, pages 32–41. Springer-Verlag, Berlin, Germany, 1995.

[106] A. Datta and C. Icking. Competitive searching in a generalized street. *Computational Geometry: Theory and Applications*, 13:109–120, 1997.

[107] L. Davis and M. Benedikt. Computational models of space: Isovists and isovist fields.

Computer Graphics and Image Processing, 11:49–72, 1979.

[108] M. de Berg. On rectilinear link distance. *Computational Geometry: Theory and Applications*, 1:13–34, 1991.

[109] P. de Rezende, D. T. Lee, and Y. F. Wu. Rectilinear shortest paths with rectangular barriers. *Discrete & Computational Geometry*, 4:41–53, 1989.

[110] J. Dean, A. Lingas, and J.-R. Sack. Recognizing polygons, or how to spy. *The Visual Computer*, 3:344–355, 1988.

[111] H. N. Djidjev, A. Lingas, and J. Sack. An $O(n \log n)$ algorithm for computing the link center of a simple polygon. *Discrete & Computational Geometry*, 8:131–152, 1992.

[112] D. Dobkin and R. Lipton. Multidimensional searching problems. *SIAM Journal on Computing*, 5:181–186, 1975.

[113] D. Dobkin and S. Teller. Computer graphics. In J. Goodman and J. O'Rourke, editors, *Handbook of Discrete and Computational Geometry*, pages 779–814. CRC Press, New York, USA, 1997.

[114] J.-I. Doh and K.-Y. Chwa. An algorithm for determining visibility of a simple polygon from an internal line segment. *Journal of Algorithms*, 14:139–168, 1993.

[115] S. E. Dorward. A survey of object-space hidden surface removal. *International Journal of Computational Geometry and Applications*, 4:325–362, 1994.

[116] H. Edelsbrunner. Finding extreme distance between convex polygons. *Journal of Algorithms*, 6:213–224, 1985.

[117] H. Edelsbrunner. *Algorithms in Combinatorial Geometry*. Springer-Verlag, Berlin, Germany, 1987.

[118] H. Edelsbrunner, L. J. Guibas, and M. Sharir. The complexity and construction of many faces in arrangements of lines and segments. *Discrete & Computational Geometry*, 5:161–196, 1990.

[119] H. Edelsbrunner, L. J. Guibas, and J. Stolfi. Optimal point location in a monotone subdivision. *SIAM Journal on Computing*, 15:317–340, 1986.

[120] H. Edelsbrunner, J. O'Rourke, and R. Seidel. Constructing arrangements of lines and hyperplanes with applications. *SIAM Journal on Computing*, 15:341–363, 1986.

[121] H. Edelsbrunner, J. O'Rourke, and E. Welzl. Stationing guards in rectilinear art galleries. *Computer Vision, Graphics, Image Processing*, 27:167–176, 1984.

[122] A. Efrat and S. Har-Peled. Guarding galleries and terrains. In *Proceedings of the 2nd IFIP International Conference on Theoretical Computer Science*, pages 181–192. Kluwer Academic Publishers, Norwell, MA, USA, 2002.

[123] S. Eidenbenz. Inapproximability results for guarding polygons without holes. In *Proceedings of International Symposium on Algorithms and Computations*, Lecture Notes in Computer Science, volume 1533, pages 427–436. Springer-Verlag, Berlin, Germany, 1998.

[124] S. Eidenbenz. *In-approximability of visibility problems on polygons and terrains*. Ph.D. Thesis, Institute for Theoretical Computer Science, ETH, Zurich, Switzerland, 2000.

[125] S. Eidenbenz. In-approximability of finding maximum hidden sets on polygons and terrains. *Computational Geometry: Theory and Applications*, 21:139–153, 2002.

[126] H. ElGindy. *Hierarchical decomposition of polygons with applications*. Ph.D. Thesis, McGill University, Montreal, Quebec, Canada, 1985.

[127] H. ElGindy. Efficient algorithms for computing the weak visibility polygon from an edge. Technical Report MS-CIS-86-04, University of Pennsylvania, Philadelphia, USA, 1986.

[128] H. ElGindy and D. Avis. A linear algorithm for computing the visibility polygon from a point. *Journal of Algorithms*, 2:186–197, 1981.

[129] H. ElGindy and M. Goodrich. Parallel algorithms for shortest path problems in polygons. *Visual Computer*, 3:371–378, 1988.

[130] H. ElGindy and P. Mitra. Orthogonal shortest route queries among axis parallel rectangular obstacles. *International Journal of Computational Geometry and Applications*,

4:3–24, 1994.

[131] H. ElGindy and G. T. Toussaint. On geodesic properties of polygons relevant to linear time triangulation. *The Visual Computer*, 5:68–74, 1989.

[132] S. Even, A. Pnueli, and A. Lempel. Permutation graphs and transitive graphs. *Journal of the ACM*, 19:400–410, 1972.

[133] H. Everett. *Visibility graph recognition*. Ph.D. Thesis, University of Toronto, Toronto, Canada, 1990.

[134] H. Everett and D. G. Corneil. Recognizing visibility graphs of spiral polygons. *Journal of Algorithms*, 11:1–26, 1990.

[135] H. Everett and D. G. Corneil. Negative results on characterizing visibility graphs. *Computational Geometry: Theory and Applications*, 5:51–63, 1995.

[136] H. Everett, C. T. Hoang, K. Kilakos, and M. Noy. Planar segment visibility graphs. *Computational Geometry: Theory and Applications*, 16:235–243, 2000.

[137] H. Everett, F. Hurtado, and M. Noy. Stabbing information of a simple polygon. *Discrete Applied Mathematics*, 91:67–92, 1999.

[138] H. Everett, A. Lubiw, and J. O'Rourke. Recovery of convex hulls from external visibility graphs. In *Proceedings of the 5th Canadian Conference on Computational Geometry*, pages 309–314, 1993.

[139] O. Faugeras. *Three Dimensional Computer Vision*. MIT Press, Cambridge, MA, USA, 1993.

[140] E. Fink and D. Wood. Planar strong visibility. *International Journal of Computational Geometry and Applications*, 13:173–187, 2003.

[141] S. Fisk. A short proof of Chvatal's watchman theorem. *Journal of Combinatorial Theory, Series B*, 24:374, 1978.

[142] A. Fournier and D. Y. Montuno. Triangulating simple polygons and equivalent problems. *ACM Transactions of Graphics*, 3:153–174, 1984.

[143] M. L. Fredman and R. E. Tarjan. Fibonacci heaps and their uses in improved network optimization algorithms. *Journal of the ACM*, 34:596–615, 1987.

[144] D. R. Fulkerson and O. A. Gross. Incident matrics and interval graphs. *Pacific Journal of Mathematics*, 15:835–855, 1965.

[145] C. P. Gabor, W. Hsu, and K. J. Supowit. Recognizing circle graphs in polynomial time. *Journal of the ACM*, 36:435–473, 1989.

[146] H. N. Gabow and R. E. Tarjan. A linear-time algorithm for a special case of disjoint set union. *Journal of Computer Systems and Science*, 30:209–221, 1985.

[147] J. Garcia-Lopez and P. Ramos-Alonso. Circular visibility and separability. In *Proceedings of the 5th Canadian Conference on Computational Geometry*, pages 18–23, 1993.

[148] M. R. Garey, D. S. Johnson, F. P. Preparata, and R. E. Tarjan. Triangulating a simple polygon. *Information Processing Letters*, 7:175–179, 1978.

[149] L. Gewali. *Efficient algorithms for path planning and visibility problems*. Ph.D. Thesis, University of Texas, Dallas, Texas, USA, 1989.

[150] L. Gewali, M. Keil, and S. Ntafos. On covering orthogonal polygons with star-shaped polygons. *Information Sciences*, 65:45–63, 1992.

[151] S. K. Ghosh. A linear time algorithm for determining the intersection type of two star polygons. In *Proceedings of the 4th Symposium on Foundation of Software Technology and Theoretical Computer Science*, Lecture Notes in Computer Science, volume 181, pages 317–330. Springer Verlag, Berlin, Germany, 1984.

[152] S. K. Ghosh. Approximation algorithms for art gallery problems. In *Proceedings of the Canadian Information Processing Society Congress*, pages 429–434, 1987.

[153] S. K. Ghosh. Computing a viewpoint of a set of points inside a polygon. In *Proceedings of the 8th Symposium on Foundation of Software Technology and Theoretical Computer Science*, Lecture Notes in Computer Science, volume 338, pages 18–29. Springer Verlag, Berlin, Germany, 1988.

[154] S. K. Ghosh. On recognizing and characterizing visibility graphs of simple polygons. In *Proceedings of Scandinavian Workshop on Algorithm Theory*, Lecture Notes in Computer Science, volume 318, pages 96–104. Springer-Verlag, Berlin, Germany, 1988. (Also In Report JHU/EECS-86/14, The Johns Hopkins University, Baltimore, MD, USA, 1986).

[155] S. K. Ghosh. Computing visibility polygon from a convex set and related problems. *Journal of Algorithms*, 12:75–95, 1991.

[156] S. K. Ghosh. A note on computing the visibility polygon from a convex chain. *Journal of Algorithms*, 21:657–662, 1996.

[157] S. K. Ghosh. On recognizing and characterizing visibility graphs of simple polygons. *Discrete & Computational Geometry*, 17:143–162, 1997.

[158] S. K. Ghosh. Approximation algorithms for art gallery problems in polygons. Manuscript, Tata Institute of Fundamental Research, Mumbai, India, January 2006.

[159] S. K. Ghosh and A. Maheshwari. An optimal algorithm for computing a minimum nested nonconvex polygon. *Information Processing Letters*, 36:277–280, 1990.

[160] S. K. Ghosh and A. Maheshwari. An optimal parallel algorithm for determining the intersection type of two star-shaped polygons. In *Proceedings of the 3rd Canadian Conference on Computational Geometry*, pages 2–6, 1991.

[161] S. K. Ghosh and A. Maheshwari. Parallel algorithms for all minimum link paths and link center problems. In *Proceedings of the 3rd Scandinavian Workshop on Algorithm Theory*, Lecture Notes in Computer Science, volume 621, pages 106– 117. Springer-Verlag, Berlin, Germany, 1992.

[162] S. K. Ghosh, A. Maheshwari, S. P. Pal, S. Saluja, and C. E. Veni Madhavan. Computing the shortest path tree in a weak visibility polygon. In *Proceedings of the 11th Symposium on Foundation of Software Technology and Theoretical Computer Science*, Lecture Notes in Computer Science, volume 560, pages 369–389. Springer-Verlag, Berlin, Germany, 1991.

[163] S. K. Ghosh, A. Maheshwari, S. P. Pal, S. Saluja, and C. E. Veni Madhavan. Characterizing and recognizing weak visibility polygons. *Computational Geometry: Theory and Applications*, 3:213–233, 1993.

[164] S. K. Ghosh, A. Maheshwari, S. P. Pal, and C. E. Veni Madhavan. An algorithm for recognizing palm polygons. *The Visual Computer*, 10:443–451, 1994.

[165] S. K. Ghosh and D. M. Mount. An output-sensitive algorithm for computing visibility graphs. *SIAM Journal on Computing*, 20:888–910, 1991.

[166] S. K. Ghosh and S. Saluja. Optimal on-line algorithms for walking with minimum number of turns in unknown streets. *Computational Geometry: Theory and Applications*, 8:241–266, 1997.

[167] S. K. Ghosh, T. Shermer, B. K. Bhattacharya, and P. Goswami. Computing the maximum clique in the visibility graph of a simple polygon. *Journal of Discrete Algorithms*, to appear, 2007.

[168] Z. Gigus, J. Canny, and R. Seidel. Efficiently computing and representing aspect graphs of polyhedral objects. *IEEE Transactions on Pattern Analysis and Machine Intelligence*, 13:542–551, 1991.

[169] P. C. Gilmore and A. J. Hoffman. A characterization of comparability graphs and of interval graphs. *Canadian Journal of Mathematics*, 16:539–548, 1964.

[170] M.C. Golumbic. *Algorithmic Graph Theory and Perfect Graphs*. Academic Press, New York, USA, 1980.

[171] M. T. Goodrich. Triangulating a polygon in parallel. *Journal of Algorithms*, 10:327–351, 1989.

[172] M. T. Goodrich. Parallel algorithms in geometry. In J. Goodman and J. O'Rourke, editors, *Handbook of Discrete and Computational Geometry*, pages 953–967. CRC Press, New York, USA, 1997.

[173] M. T. Goodrich, S. Shauck, and S. Guha. Parallel methods for visibility and shortest

path problems in simple polygons. *Algorithmica*, 8:461–486, 1992.

[174] M. T. Goodrich, S. Shauck, and S. Guha. Addendum to 'parallel methods for visibility and shortest path problems in simple polygons'. *Algorithmica*, 9:515–516, 1993.

[175] R. L. Graham and F. F. Yao. Finding the convex hull of a simple polygon. *Journal of Algorithms*, 4:324–331, 1983.

[176] P. M. Gruber and J. M. Wills, editors. *Handbook of Convex Geometry*. North-Holland, Amsterdam, The Netherlands, 1993.

[177] L. J. Guibas and J. Hershberger. Optimal shortest path queries in a simple polygon. *Journal of Computer and System Science*, 39:126–152, 1989.

[178] L. J. Guibas, J. Hershberger, D. Leven, M. Sharir, and R. E. Tarjan. Linear-time algorithms for visibility and shortest path problems inside triangulated simple polygons. *Algorithmica*, 2:209–233, 1987.

[179] L. J. Guibas, J. Hershberger, J. S. B. Mitchell, and J. Snoeyink. Approximating polygons and subdivisions with minimum-link paths. *International Journal of Computational Geometry and Applications*, 3:383–415, 1993.

[180] L. J. Guibas, J. C. Latombe, S. M. LaValle, D. Lin, and R. Motwani. Visibility-based pursuit-evasion in a polygonal environment. *International Journal of Computational Geometry and Applications*, 9:471–494, 1999.

[181] L. J. Guibas, R. Motwani, and P. Raghavan. The robot localization problem. *SIAM Journal on Computing*, 26:1120–1138, 1997.

[182] E. Györi, F. Hoffmann, K. Kriegel, and T. Shermer. Generalized guarding and partitioning for rectilinear polygons. *Computational Geometry: Theory and Applications*, 6:21–44, 1996.

[183] P. J. Heffernan. Linear-time algorithms for weakly-monotone polygons. *Computational Geometry: Theory and Applications*, 3:121–137, 1993.

[184] P. J. Heffernan. An optimal algorithm for the two-guard problems. *International Journal of Computational Geometry and Applications*, 6:15–44, 1996.

[185] P. J. Heffernan and J. S. B. Mitchell. An optimal algorithm for computing visibility in the plane. *SIAM Journal on Computing*, 24:184–201, 1995.

[186] J. Hershberger. Finding the visibility graph of a polygon in time proportional to its size. *Algorithmica*, 4:141–155, 1989.

[187] J. Hershberger. Optimal parallel algorithms for triangulated simple polygons. *International Journal of Computational Geometry and Applications*, 5:145–170, 1995.

[188] J. Hershberger and J. Snoeyink. Computing minimum link paths of a given homotopy class. *Computational Geometry: Theory and Applications*, 4:63–97, 1994.

[189] J. Hershberger and S. Suri. Efficient computation of Euclidean shortest paths in the plane. In *Proceedings of the 34th IEEE Symposium on the Foundations of Computer Science*, pages 508–517. IEEE Computer Society Press, Los Alamitos, CA, USA, 1993.

[190] J. Hershberger and S. Suri. A pedestrain approach to ray shooting: shoot a ray, take a walk. *Journal of Algorithms*, 18:403–413, 1995.

[191] J. Hershberger and S. Suri. Matrix searching with the shortest path metric. *SIAM Journal on Computing*, 26:1612–1634, 1997.

[192] J. Hershberger and S. Suri. An optimal-time algorithm for Euclidean shortest paths in the plane. *SIAM Journal on Computing*, 28:2215–2256, 1999.

[193] S. Hertel and K. Mehlhorn. Fast triangulation of the plane with respect to simple polygons. *Information and Control*, 64:52–76, 1985.

[194] F. Hoffmann, M. Kaufmann, and K. Kriegel. The art gallery theorem for polygons with holes. In *Proceedings of the 32nd IEEE Symposium on the Foundation of Computer Science*, pages 39–48. IEEE Computer Society Press, Los Alamitos, CA, USA, 1991.

[195] K. Hoffmann, K. Mehlhorn, P. Rosenstiehl, and R. E. Tarjan. Sorting Jordan sequences in linear time using level-linked search trees. *Information and Control*, 68:170–184, 1986.

[196] M. Hoffmann and C. Toth. Alternating paths through disjoint line segments. *Information Processing Letters*, 87:287–294, 2003.

[197] M. Hoffmann and C. Toth. Segment endpoint visibility graphs are hamiltonian. *Computational Geometry: Theory and Applications*, 26:47–68, 2003.

[198] R. Honsberger. *Mathematical Gems II.* Mathematical Associations for America, New York, USA, 1979.

[199] F. R. Hsu, R. C. Chang, and R. C. T. Lee. Parallel algorithms for computing the closest visible vertex pair between two polygons. *International Journal of Computational Geometry and Applications*, 2:135–162, 1992.

[200] C. Icking and R. Klein. The two guards problem. *International Journal of Computational Geometry and Applications*, 2:257–285, 1992.

[201] C. Icking and R. Klein. Searching for the kernel of a polygon: A competitive strategy. In *Proceedings of the 11th Annual ACM Symposium on Computational Geometry*, pages 258–266. ACM Press, New York, USA, 1995.

[202] C. Icking, R. Klein, E. Langetepe, S. Schuierer, and I. Semrau. An optimal competitive strategy for walking in streets. *SIAM Journal on Computing*, 33:462–486, 2004.

[203] L. Jackson and S. K. Wismath. Orthogonal polygon reconstruction from stabbing information. *Computational Geometry: Theory and Applications*, 23:69–83, 2002.

[204] B. Joe. On the correctness of a linear-time visibility polygon algorithm. *International Journal of Computer Mathematics*, 32:155–172, 1990.

[205] B. Joe and R. B. Simpson. Corrections to Lee's visibility polygon algorithm. *BIT*, 27:458–473, 1987.

[206] S. Kahan and J. Snoeyink. On the bit complexity of minimum link paths: superquadratic algorithms for problems solvable in linear time. In *Proceedings of the 12th Annual ACM Symposium on Computational Geometry*, pages 151–158. ACM Press, New York, USA, 1996.

[207] J. Kahn, M. Klawe, and D. Kleitman. Traditional galleries require fewer watchmen. *SIAM Journal of Algebraic and Discrete Methods*, 4:194–206, 1983.

[208] G. Kant. A more compact visibility representation. *International Journal of Computational Geometry and Applications*, 7:197–210, 1997.

[209] S. Kapoor and S. N. Maheshwari. Efficiently constructing the visibility graph of a simple polygon with obstacles. *SIAM Journal on Computing*, 30:847–871, 2000.

[210] S. Kapoor, S. N. Maheshwari, and J. S. B. Mitchell. An efficient algorithm for Euclidian shortest paths among polygonal obstacles in the plane. *Discrete & Computational Geometry*, 18:377–383, 1997.

[211] R. M. Karp and V. Ramachandran. Parallel algorithms for shared-memory machines. In J. Van Leeuwen, editor, *Handbook of Theoretical Computer Science*, volume 1, pages 869–941. Elsevier/The MIT Press, Cambridge, MA, USA, 1990.

[212] Y. Ke. An efficient algorithm for link distance problems inside a simple polygon. Technical Report Report JHU-87/28, Department of Computer Science, The Johns Hopkins University, Baltimore, MD, USA, 1988.

[213] M. Keil. Finding a hamiltonian circits in interval graphs. *Information Processing Letters*, 20:201–206, 1985.

[214] M. Keil. Minimally covering a horizontally convex polygon. In *Proceedings of the 2nd Annual ACM Symposium on Computational Geometry*, pages 43–51. ACM Press, New York, USA, 1986.

[215] S.-H. Kim, S. Y. Shin, and K.-Y. Chwa. Efficient algorithms for solving diagonal visibility problems in a simple polygon. *International Journal of Computational Geometry and Applications*, 5:433–458, 1995.

[216] D. Kirkpatrick. Optimal search in planar subdivision. *SIAM Journal on Computing*, 12:28–35, 1983.

[217] D. Kirkpatrick, M. Klawe, and R. E. Tarjan. Polygon triangulation in $O(n \log \log n)$ time with simple data structures. *Discrete & Computational Geometry*, 7:329–346, 1992.

[218] D. Kirkpatrick and S. Wismath. Determining bar-representability for ordered weighted

graphs. *Computational Geometry: Theory and Applications*, 6:99–122, 1996.

[219] R. Klein. Walking an unknown street with bounded detour. *Computational Geometry: Theory and Applications*, 1:325–351, 1992.

[220] J. Kleinberg. On-line search in a simple polygon. In *Proceedings of the 5th ACM-SIAM Symposium on Discrete Algorithms*, pages 8–15. ACM and SIAM, USA, 1994.

[221] D. Kozen. *The Design and Analysis of Algorithms*. Springer-Verlag, New York, USA, 1992.

[222] E. Kranakis, D. Krizanc, and L. Meertens. Link length of rectilinear Hamiltonian tours in grids. *Ars Combinatoria*, 38:177–192, 1994.

[223] M. A. Krasnosel'skii. Sur un critere pour qu'un domaine soit etoile. *Matematicheskij Sbornik*, 19:309–310, 1946.

[224] C. Kuratowski. Sur le probléme des courbes gauches en topologie. *Fundamental Mathematics*, 15:271–283, 1930.

[225] R. Larson and V. Li. Finding minimum rectilinear distance paths in the presence of barriers. *Networks*, 11:285–304, 1981.

[226] J. C. Latombe. *Robot Motion Planning*. Kluwer Academic Publishers, Boston, MA, USA, 1991.

[227] S. M. LaValle. *Planning Algorithms*. Cambridge University Press, New York, USA, 2006.

[228] S. M. LaValle, B. Simov, and G. Slutzki. An algorithm for searching a polygonal region with a flashlight. *International Journal of Computational Geometry and Applications*, 12:87–113, 2002.

[229] D. T. Lee. *Proximity and reachability in the plane*. Ph.D. Thesis, Coordinated Science Laboratory, University of Illinois, Urbana-Champaign, IL, USA, 1978.

[230] D. T. Lee. Visibility of a simple polygon. *Computer Vision, Graphics, and Image Processing*, 22:207–221, 1983.

[231] D. T. Lee and A. K. Lin. Computational complexity of art gallery problems. *IEEE Transactions on Information Theory*, IT–32:276–282, 1986.

[232] D. T. Lee and A. K. Lin. Computing the visibility polygon from an edge. *Computer Vision, Graphics, and Image Processing*, 34:1–19, 1986.

[233] D. T. Lee and F. P. Preparata. Location of a point in a planar subdivision and its applications. *SIAM Journal on Computing*, 6:594–606, 1977.

[234] D. T. Lee and F. P. Preparata. An optimal algorithm for finding the kernel of a polygon. *Journal of the ACM*, 26:415–421, 1979.

[235] D. T. Lee and F. P. Preparata. Euclidean shortest paths in the presence of rectilinear barriers. *Networks*, 14:393–415, 1984.

[236] J. Lee, S. Park, and K. Chwa. Searching a polygonal room with one door by a 1-searcher. *International Journal of Computational Geometry and Applications*, 10:201–220, 2000.

[237] J. Lee, S. Park, and K. Chwa. Simple algorithms for searching a polygon with flashlights. *Information Processing Letters*, 81:265–270, 2002.

[238] J. Lee, C. Shin, J. Kim, S. Shin, and K. Chwa. New competitive strategies for searching in unknown star-shaped polygons. In *Proceedings of the 13th Annual ACM Symposium on Computational Geometry*, pages 427–429. ACM Press, New York, USA, 1997.

[239] S. H. Lee and K.-Y. Chwa. A new triangulation-linear class of simple polygons. *International Journal of Computer Mathematics*, 22:135–147, 1987.

[240] C. G. Lekkerkerker and J. Ch. Representation of a finite graphs by a set of intervals on the real line. *Fundamental Mathematics*, 51:45–64, 1962.

[241] W. Lenhart, R. Pollack, J.-R. Sack, R. Seidel, M. Sharir, S. Suri, G. T. Toussaint, S. Whitesides, and C. K. Yap. Computing the link center of a simple polygon. *Discrete & Computational Geometry*, 3:281–293, 1988.

[242] N. J. Lennes. Theorems on the simple finite polygon and polyhedron. *American Journal of Mathematics*, 33:37–62, 1911.

[243] S. Y. Lin and C. Y. Chen. Planar visibility graphs. In *Proceedings of the 6th Canadian*

Conference on Computational Geometry, pages 30–35, 1994.

[244] S. Y. Lin and S. Skiena. Complexity aspects of visibility graphs. *International Journal of Computational Geometry and Applications*, 5:289–312, 1995.

[245] A. Lingas, A. Maheshwari, and J.-R. Sack. Optimal parallel algorithms for rectilinear link-distance problems. *Algorithmica*, 14:261–289, 1995.

[246] A. Lopez-Ortiz. *On-line target searching in bounded and unbounded domains*. Ph.D. Thesis, University of Waterloo, Waterloo, Ont., Canada, 1996.

[247] A. Lopez-Ortiz and S. Schuierer. Lower bounds for streets and generalized streets. *International Journal of Computational Geometry and Applications*, 11:401–421, 2001.

[248] A. Lopez-Ortiz and S. Schuierer. Searching and on-line recognition of star-shaped polygons. *Information and Computation*, 185:66–88, 2003.

[249] T. Lozano-Perez and M. A. Wesley. An algorithm for planning collision-free paths among polyhedral obstacles. *Communications of ACM*, 22:560–570, 1979.

[250] A. Lubiw. Decomposing polygons into convex quadrilaterals. In *Proceedings of the 1st ACM Symposium on Computational Geometry*, pages 97–106. ACM Press, New York, USA, 1985.

[251] G. MacDonald and T. Shermer. Isomorphism of spiral polygons. *Discrete & Computational Geometry*, 16:277–304, 1996.

[252] A. Maheshwari and J.-R. Sack. Simple optimal algorithms for rectilinear link path and polygon separation problems. *Parallel Processing Letters*, 9:31–42, 1999.

[253] A. Maheshwari, J.-R. Sack, and H. Djidjev. Link distance problems. In J.-R. Sack and J. Urrutia, editors, *Handbook of Computational Geometry*, pages 519–558. North-Holland, Amsterdam, The Netherlands, 2000.

[254] K. McDonald and J. Peters. Smallest paths in simple rectilinear polygons. *IEEE Transactions on Computer Aided Design*, 11:264–273, 1992.

[255] M. McKenna and G. T. Toussaint. Finding the minimum vertex distance between two disjoint convex polygons in linear time. *Computers and Mathematics with Applications*, 11:1227–1242, 1985.

[256] K. Mehlhorn. *Data Structures and Algorithms, Volume 1: Sorting and searching*. Springer-Verlag, Berlin, Germany, 1984.

[257] K. Mehlhorn. *Data Structures and Algorithms, Volume 3: Multi-Dimensional Searching and Computational Geometry*. Springer-Verlag, Berlin, Germany, 1984.

[258] J. S. B. Mitchell. L_1 shortest paths among obstacles in the plane. *Algorithmica*, 8:55–88, 1992.

[259] J. S. B. Mitchell. Shortest paths among obstacles in the plane. *International Journal of Computational Geometry and Applications*, 6:309–332, 1996.

[260] J. S. B. Mitchell. Geometric shortest paths and network optimization. In J.-R. Sack and J. Urrutia, editors, *Handbook of Computational Geometry*, pages 633–701. North-Holland, Amsterdam, The Netherlands, 2000.

[261] J. S. B. Mitchell, C. Piatko, and E. Arkin. Computing a shortest k-link path in a polygon. In *Proceedings of the 33rd IEEE Symposium on the Foundations of Computer Science*, pages 573–582. IEEE Computer Society Press, Los Alamitos, CA, USA, 1992.

[262] J. S. B. Mitchell, G. Rote, and G. Woeginger. Minimum-link paths among obstacles in the plane. *Algorithmica*, 8:431–459, 1992.

[263] R. Motwani, A. Raghunathan, and H. Saran. Perfect graphs and orthogonally convex covers. *SIAM Journal on Discrete Mathematics*, 2:431–459, 1989.

[264] R. Motwani, A. Raghunathan, and H. Saran. Covering orthogonal polygons with star polygons: the perfect graph approach. *Journal of Computer and Systems Science*, 40:19–48, 1990.

[265] J. I. Munro, M. H. Overmars, and D. Wood. Variations on visibility. In *Proceedings of the 3rd Annual ACM Symposium on Computational Geometry*, pages 291–299. ACM Press, New York, USA, 1987.

[266] G. Narasimhan. On hamiltonian triangulations of simple polygons. *International Jour-*

nal of Computational Geometry and Applications, 9:261–275, 1999.

[267] B. J. Nilsson and S. Schuierer. Computing the rectilinear link diameter of a polygon. In *Proceedings of International Workshop on Computational Geometry 1991, Computational Geometry-Methods, Algorithms and Applications*, Lecture Notes in Computer Science, volume 553, pages 203–215. Springer-Verlag, Berlin, Germany, 1991.

[268] B. J. Nilsson and S. Schuierer. An optimal algorithm for the rectilinear link center of a rectilinear polygon. *Computational Geometry: Theory and Applications*, 6:169–194, 1996.

[269] J. O'Rourke. An alternative proof of the rectilinear art gallery theorem. *Journal of Geometry*, 211:118–130, 1983.

[270] J. O'Rourke. Galleries need fewer mobile guards: A variation on Chvatal's theorem. *Geometricae Dedicata*, 4:273–283, 1983.

[271] J. O'Rourke. *Art Gallery Theorems and Algorithms*. Oxford University Press, New York, USA, 1987.

[272] J. O'Rourke. *Computational Geometry in C*. Cambridge University Press, New York, USA, 1998.

[273] J. O'Rourke and J. Rippel. Two segment classes with Hamiltonian visibility graphs. *Computational Geometry: Theory and Applications*, 4:209–218, 1994.

[274] J. O'Rourke and I. Streinu. Vertex-edge pseudo-visibility graphs: characterization and recognition. In *Proceedings of the 13th Annual ACM Symposium on Computational Geometry*, pages 119–128. ACM Press, New York, USA, 1997.

[275] J. O'Rourke and I. Streinu. The vertex edge visibility graph of a polygon. *Computational Geometry: Theory and Applications*, 10:105–120, 1998.

[276] J. O'Rourke and K. Supowit. Some NP-hard polygon decomposition problems. *IEEE Transactions on Information Theory,*, IT-29:181–190, 1983.

[277] M. H. Overmars and J. V. Leeuwen. Maintenance of configurations in the plane. *Journal of Computer and Systems Sciences*, 23:166–204, 1981.

[278] M. H. Overmars and E. Welzl. New methods for computing visibility graphs. In *Proceedings of the 4th Annual ACM Symposium on Computational Geometry*, pages 164–171. ACM Press, New York, USA, 1988.

[279] M. H. Overmars and D. Wood. On rectangular visibility. *Journal of Algorithms*, 9:372–390, 1988.

[280] S. P. Pal. *Weak visibility and related problems on simple polygons*. Ph.D. Thesis, Indian Institute of Science, Bangalore, India, September 1990.

[281] S. P. Pal, S. Brahma, and D. Sarkar. A linear worst-case lower bound on the number of holes in regions visible due to multiple diffuse reflections. *Journal of Geometry*, 81:5–14, 2004.

[282] S. Park, J. Lee, and K. Chwa. Searching a room by two guards. *International Journal of Computational Geometry and Applications*, 12:339–352, 2002.

[283] M. A. Peshkin and A. C. Sanderson. Reachable grasps on a polygon: the convex rope algorithm. *IEEE Journal on Robotics and Automation*, RA-2:53–58, 1986.

[284] A. Pnueli, A. Lempel, and S. Even. Transitive orientation of graphs and identification of permutation graphs. *Canadian Journal of Mathematics*, 23:160–175, 1971.

[285] M. Pocchiola and G. Vegter. Minimal tangent visibility graphs. *Computational Geometry: Theory and Applications*, 6:303–314, 1996.

[286] M. Pocchiola and G. Vegter. Topologically sweeping visibility complexes via pseudo-triangulations. *Discrete & Computational Geometry*, 16:419–453, 1996.

[287] M. Pocchiola and G. Vegter. The visibility complex. *International Journal of Computational Geometry and Applications*, 6:279–308, 1996.

[288] R. Pollack, M. Sharir, and G. Vegter. Computing of the geodesic center of a simple polygon. *Discrete & Computational Geometry*, 4:611–626, 1989.

[289] D. Prasad, S. P. Pal, and T. Dey. Visibility with multiple diffuse reflections. *Computational Geometry: Theory and Applications*, 10:187–196, 1998.

[290] F. P. Preparata. A new approach to planar point location. *SIAM Journal on Computing*, 10:473–482, 1981.

[291] F. P. Preparata and M. I. Shamos. *Computational Geometry: An Introduction.* Springer-Verlag, New York, USA, 1990.

[292] D. Rappaport. Computing simple circuits from a set of line segments is NP-complete. *SIAM Journal on Computing*, 18:1128–1139, 1989.

[293] D. Rappaport, H. Imai, and G. T. Toussaint. Computing simple circuits from a set of line segments. *Discrete & Computational Geometry*, 5:289–304, 1990.

[294] G. Rawlins. *Explorations in Restricted-Orientation Geometry.* Ph.D. Thesis, Universtiy of Waterloo, Waterloo, Ont., Canada, 1987.

[295] G. Rawlins and D. Wood. Computational geometry with restricted orientations. In *Proceedings of the 13th IFIP Conference on System Modelling and Optimization*, Lecture Notes in Control and Information Science, volume 113, pages 375–384. Springer-Verlag, Berlin, Germany, 1988.

[296] R. Reckhow and J. Culberson. Covering a simple orthogonal polygon with a minimum number of orthogonally convex polygons. In *Proceedings of the 3rd Annual ACM Symposium on Computational Geometry*, pages 268–277. ACM Press, New York, USA, 1987.

[297] J. H. Reif and J. A. Storer. Minimizing turns for discrete movement in the interior of a polygon. *IEEE Journal on Robotics and Automation*, RA-3:194–206, 1987.

[298] H. Rohnert. Shortest paths in the plane with convex polygonal obstacles. *Information Processing Letters*, 23:71–76, 1986.

[299] J.-R. Sack. An O(nlogn) algorithm for decomposing simple rectilinear polygons into quadrilaterals. In *Proceedings of the 20th Allerton Conference*, pages 64–75. Chicago, USA, 1982.

[300] J.-R. Sack and S. Suri. An optimal algorithm for detecting weak visibility of a polygon. *IEEE Transactions on Computers*, 39:1213–1219, 1990.

[301] J.-R. Sack and G. T. Toussaint. Guard placement in rectilinear polygons. In G. T. Toussaint, editor, *Computational Morphology*, pages 153–175. North-Holland, Amsterdam, The Netherlands, 1988.

[302] N. Sarnak and R. E. Tarjan. Planar point location using persistent search trees. *Communications of ACM*, 29:669–679, 1986.

[303] S. Schuierer. An optimal data structure for shortest rectilinear path queries in a simple rectilinear polygon. *International Journal of Computational Geometry and Applications*, 6:205–226, 1996.

[304] S. Schuierer, G. Rawlins, and D. Wood. A generalization of staircase visibility. In *Computational Geometry — Methods, Algorithms and Applications: Proc. Internat. Workshop Comput. Geom. CG '91*, Lecture Notes in Computer Science, volume 553, pages 277–287. Springer-Verlag, Berlin, Germany, 1991.

[305] S. Schuierer and D. Wood. Staircase visibility and computation of kernels. *Algorithmica*, 14:1–26, 1995.

[306] L.G. Shapiro and R.M. Haralick. Decomposition of two-dimensional shape by graph-theoretic clustering. *IEEE Transactions on Pattern Analysis and Machine Intelligence*, PAMI-1:10–19, 1979.

[307] M. Sharir and A. Schorr. On shortest paths in polyhedral spaces. *SIAM Journal on Computing*, 15:193–215, 1986.

[308] X. Shen and H. Edelsbrunner. A tight lower bound on the size of visibility graphs. *Information Processing Letters*, 26:61–64, 1987.

[309] T. Shermer. Hiding people in polygons. *Computing*, 42:109–131, 1989.

[310] T. Shermer. Recent results in art galleries. *Proceedings of the IEEE*, 80:1384–1399, 1992.

[311] S. Y. Shin and T. C. Woo. An optimal algorithm for finding all visible edges in a simple polygon. *IEEE Journal on Robotics and Automation*, RA-5:202–207, 1989.

[312] D. Sleator and R. E. Tarjan. Amortized efficiency of list update and paging rules. *Communications of ACM*, 28:202–208, 1985.

[313] J. Spinrad, A. Brandstadt, and L. Stewart. Bipartite permutation graphs. *Discrete Applied Mathematics*, 18:279–292, 1987.

[314] G. Srinivasaraghavan and A. Mukhopadhyay. A new necessary condition for the vertex visibility graphs of simple polygons. *Discrete & Computational Geometry*, 12:65–82, 1994.

[315] G. Srinivasaraghavan and A. Mukhopadhyay. Orthogonal edge visibility graphs of polygons with holes. *International Journal of Computational Geometry and Applications*, 10:79–102, 2000.

[316] I. Streinu. Non-stretchable pseudo-visibility graphs. In *Proceedings of the 11th Canadian Conference on Computational Geometry*, pages 22–25, 1999.

[317] I. Streinu. Non-stretchable pseudo-visibility graphs. *Computational Geometry: Theory and Applications*, 31:195–206, 2005.

[318] S. Suri. A linear time algorithm for minimum link paths inside a simple polygon. *Computer Graphics, Vision, and Image Processing*, 35:99–110, 1986.

[319] S. Suri. *Minimum link paths in polygons and related problems*. Ph.D. Thesis, Department of Computer Science, Johns Hopkins University, Baltimore, MD, USA, 1987.

[320] S. Suri. On some link distance problems in a simple polygon. *IEEE Journal on Robotics and Automation*, 6:108–113, 1990.

[321] S. Suri and J. O'Rourke. Worst-case optimal algorithms for constructing visibility polygons with holes. In *Proceedings of the 2nd Annual ACM Symposium on Computational Geometry*, pages 14–23. ACM Press, New York, USA, 1986.

[322] I. Suzuki, Y. Tazoe, M. Yamashita, and T. Kameda. Searching a polygonal region from the boundary. *International Journal of Computational Geometry and Applications*, 11:529–553, 2001.

[323] I. Suzuki and M. Yamashita. Search for a mobile intruder in a polygonal region. *SIAM Journal on Computing*, 21:863–888, 1992.

[324] I. Suzuki, M. Yamashita, H. Umemoto, and T. Kameda. Bushiness and a tight worst-case upper bound on the search number of a simple polygon. *Information Processing Letters*, 66:49–52, 1998.

[325] R. Tamassia and I. Tollis. A unified approach to visibility representations of planar graphs. *Discrete & Computational Geometry*, 1:321–341, 1986.

[326] R. E. Tarjan and C. J. Van Wyk. An $O(n \log \log n)$-time algorithm for triangulating a simple polygon. *SIAM Journal on Computing*, 17:143–178, 1988. Erratum in 17 (1988), 106.

[327] H. Tietze. Uber konvexheit im kleinen und im grossen und uber gewisse den punkten einer menge zugeordnete dimensionszahlen. *Math. Z.*, 28:679–707, 1929.

[328] G. T. Tokarsky. Polygonal rooms not illuminable from every point. *American Mathematical Monthly*, 102:867–879, 1995.

[329] G. T. Toussaint. An optimal algorithm for computing the minimum vertex distance between two crossing convex polygons. *Computing*, 32:357–364, 1984.

[330] G. T. Toussaint. Shortest path solves edge-to-edge visibility in a polygon. *Pattern Recognition Letters*, 4:165–170, 1986.

[331] G. T. Toussaint and D. Avis. On a convex hull algorithm for polygons and its application to triangulation problems. *Pattern Recognition*, 15:23–29, 1982.

[332] L. H. Tseng, P. J. Heffernan, and D. T. Lee. Two-guard walkability of simple polygons. *International Journal of Computational Geometry and Applications*, 8:85–116, 1998.

[333] J. Urrutia. Art gallery and illumination problems. In J.-R. Sack and J. Urrutia, editors, *Handbook of Computational Geometry*, pages 973–1023. North-Holland, Amsterdam, The Netherlands, 2000.

[334] F. A. Valentine. *Convex Sets*. McGraw-Hill, New York, USA, 1964.

[335] G. Vegter. The visibility diagram: a data structure for visibility problems and motion

planning. In *Proceedings of the 2nd Scandinavian Workshop on Algorithm Theory*, Lecture Notes in Computer Science, volume 447, pages 97–110. Springer-Verlag, Berlin, Germany, 1990.

[336] C. A. Wang. Finding minimal nested polygons. *BIT*, 31:230–236, 1991.

[337] C. A. Wang and E. P. F. Chan. Finding the minimum visible vertex distance between two nonintersecting simple polygons. In *Proceedings of the 2nd Annual ACM Symposium on Computational Geometry*, pages 34–42. ACM Press, New York, USA, 1986.

[338] R. Wein, P. den Berg, and D. Halperin. The visibility-Voronoi complex and its applications. In *Proceedings of the 21th Annual ACM Symposium on Computational Geometry*, pages 63–72. ACM Press, New York, USA, 2005.

[339] E. Welzl. Constructing the visibility graph for n line segments in $O(n^2)$ time. *Information Processing Letters*, 20:167–171, 1985.

[340] S. K. Wismath. Characterizing bar line-of-sight graphs. In *Proceedings of the 1st ACM Symposium on Computational Geometry*, pages 147–152. ACM Press, New York, USA, 1985.

[341] S. K. Wismath. Point and line segment reconstruction from visibility information. *International Journal of Computational Geometry and Applications*, 10:189–200, 2000.

[342] T. C. Woo and S. Y. Shin. A linear time algorithm for triangulating a point-visible polygon. *ACM Transactions of Graphics*, 4:60–69, 1985.

[343] D. Wood and P. Yamamoto. Dent and staircase visibility. In *Proceedings of the 5th Canadian Conference on Computational Geometry*, pages 297–302, 1993.

[344] M. Yamashita, H. Umemoto, I. Suzuki, and T. Kameda. Searching for mobile intruders in a polygonal region by a group of mobile searchers. *Algorithmica*, 31:208–236, 2001.

[345] C.-K. Yap. Parallel triangulation of a polygon in two calls to the trapezoidal map. *Algorithmica*, 3:279–288, 1988.

[346] A. Zarei and M. Ghodsi. Efficient computation of query point visibility in polygons with holes. In *Proceedings of the 21th Annual ACM Symposium on Computational Geometry*, pages 314–320. ACM Press, New York, USA, 2005.

[347] Z. Zhang. *Applications of visibility space in polygon search problems*. Ph.D. Thesis, School of Computing Science, Simon Fraser University, Burnaby, BC, Canada, 2005.

Index

Printed in the United States
by Baker & Taylor Publisher Services